James Gillespie Birney:

Slaveholder to Abolitionist

James Gillespie Birney, 1792–1857

James Gillespie Birney:

Slaveholder to Abolitionist

BETTY FLADELAND

GREENWOOD PRESS, PUBLISHERS
NEW YORK

Preface

"WHO is James G. Birney?" asked a newspaper editor in the midst of the presidential campaign of 1844; and then he proceeded to answer his own question: "Should he die this day, he has achieved more for the liberty and welfare of his country than all the presidents or other candidates for the presidency, that have lived since Washington died."

James Gillespie Birney was a Southern aristocrat and slaveholder who, from firsthand experience, became convinced of the evils of slavery, gave up a lucrative law practice, a position of influence and respect in his community, his home, and his inheritance, to dedicate his life to the cause of freeing the slaves. He died shortly before the struggle over slavery terminated in civil war. The story of his life is an integral part of the great humanitarian movement of the early nineteenth century to rid the country of the curse of human bondage.

Driven from point to point, refused positions because of his views, threatened and mobbed, Birney stood firmly for what he believed and for the right to speak and print those views. His fight for civil liberty helped to maintain freedom of speech and press in a time when censorship and gag laws were threatening the North as well as the South.

He was an agent for the American Colonization Society, an antislavery editor and lecturer, and an executive of the American Anti-Slavery Society. When the antislavery movement entered its political phase, he was one of the leaders in organizing the Liberty party. In 1840 and 1844 he was its candidate for the presidency.

Three books dealing with the life of Birney have been published previously. In 1844 Beriah Green, an antislavery colleague, published *Sketches of the Life and Writings of James Gillespie Birney,* a campaign document composed largely of excerpts from Birney's own writings. In 1884 William Birney published a short sketch of his father's life which was expanded into a biography, *James G. Birney and His Times: The Genesis of the Republican Party with Some Account of Abolition Movements in the South before 1828.* William Birney's book is remarkably accurate as compared with similar filial tributes, but some of his conclusions were unavoidably colored by his own bias, and there are many factual errors. Some of these inaccuracies may be attributed to the fact that, although William Birney himself took an active part in the political period of the antislavery movement, he did not have all of his father's letters and papers which are now available to a biographer.

When James G. Birney moved from Michigan to New Jersey in 1854, his papers were evidently left behind in the care of his only daughter, Florence, who was married to Charles Jennison of Lower Saginaw (now Bay City). Unknown to historians, they remained in the possession of the Jennison family until their discovery by Professor Dwight L. Dumond in 1936. Most of them subsequently were placed in the William L. Clements Library at the University of Michigan. Those dealing with Birney's part in the antislavery movement were edited by Professor Dumond and were published by the American Historical Association in 1938.

As a human being, Birney had his faults of pride, ambition, and obstinacy. These I have tried to indicate; yet he remains a man whose pride was in service, whose ambition never degenerated into a selfish seeking for success, and whose obstinacy was a determination that the cause of human freedom must not fail. There were some emotional fanatics among the abolitionists; but there were countless more sincere, moderate men whose antislavery efforts were based on intellectual convictions and on deep-seated humanitarianism. By and large, it has been the first group which has received the most attention, and which too often has been accepted as representative of the abolitionists as a whole. Birney's place was in the second group. His native ability and training made him one of its leaders.

The complete history of the antislavery movement remains to be written. When it is, James G. Birney must be given his place among those who gave their "last full measure of devotion" to preserve a Union "conceived in liberty, and dedicated to the proposition that all men are created equal."

ACKNOWLEDGMENTS

I should like to express my appreciation to the staff members of the William L. Clements Library; the Michigan Historical Collections; the Manuscripts Division of the Library of Congress; the Department of History and Archives at Montgomery, Alabama; Centre College; and the libraries of the following universities: Alabama, Kentucky, Princeton, Johns Hopkins, Cornell, and Michigan. In addition I should like to thank Allen H. Wattles of Geneseo, New York, and Dion Birney of Washington, D.C., for information furnished in response to my inquiries. It is impossible to list the many citizens of Danville, Kentucky, and Huntsville, Alabama, who gave of their time to answer my questions, helped me locate materials, and made the work of research so pleasant. I am grateful to Sue Green and Merton L. Dillon for reading the manuscript and making suggestions on style; and to Georgia Cortright for proofreading. Above all I am indebted to Professor Dwight L. Dumond for his guidance and direction through every phase of my research and writing.

BETTY FLADELAND

Aurora, New York
June, 1955

Contents

James Gillespie Birney:

Slaveholder to Abolitionist

Chapter I

The Young Aristocrat

THE year 1792 was a significant one in the history of the new, struggling United States of America. Kentucky was the first state west of the Appalachian Mountains admitted to the Union, setting in motion a tide of expansion which was to continue for over a century and which would not be contained even by the broad expanses of the Pacific Ocean. Precedents of unpredictable significance were established in the admission of this first western state, the most important of which was the failure to seize this opportunity to eradicate an evil which was to threaten the destruction of that Union—Negro slavery.

It was coincidental that the year which witnessed the fastening of slavery on Kentucky, thereby perpetuating it as an institution throughout all of the new southern states, also witnessed the birth of a Kentuckian who was to stand in the foremost ranks of the battle against slavery, James Gillespie Birney, born in Danville on February 4, 1792.

Young James G. Birney had every advantage of birth and circumstance, his home being that of the typical aristocratic family of Kentucky. The Birneys called themselves Irish, although the family line could be traced back to the De Birneys who originally emigrated from France to England in the latter part of the fifteenth century, settling

1

near Norfolk. One of them was created a baronet in 1620. Three brothers of the family accompanied Cromwell to Ireland and were seated at Walsingham, where they became a family of note. Their family motto, *Nil timere, neque timore,* seems to have been no less appropriate for the Kentucky Birneys than for their forebears.[1]

It was from the family homestead at Cootehill, County Cavan, that James's father, James Birney, Sr., had run away at the age of seventeen or eighteen to come to America in 1784.[2] Possessed of nothing but an enterprising nature, he worked in a Philadelphia dry goods store long enough to save a little money, then headed westward. In the autumn of 1788, with a stock of goods bought on credit, he opened a store in Danville, the leading town of Kentucky at the time. The venture was successful. He subsequently established a bagging factory and ropewalk, from which he accumulated a small fortune.

In 1790 James Birney married Martha Reed, daughter of John and Lettice Wilcox Reed. John Reed had himself come from Ireland about a decade previously, as a result of some intrigue against the British, but he had already become a man of social prominence in Danville by the time James Birney arrived. Unimpressed by the newcomer, he refused to give his consent to the marriage; but the young couple, unwilling to accept this verdict, eloped. John Reed's opposition was short-lived, and the family relationship afterward was close. His son-in-law's Irish background and the fact that he proved to be a gentleman as well as a good businessman were reconciling influences.

Martha Reed died within five years of her marriage, leaving a boy of three, James Gillespie, and an infant daughter, Anna Maria. Left alone with two small children, the father wrote to his widowed sister in Ireland, asking her to come to America to take charge of his household. Mrs. Doyle came and with her two other sisters, Mrs. Gillespie and Mrs. Whelan, with their husbands and children. "Aunt Doyle" soon became as dear as a mother to young James and Nancy, as Anna

---

[1] "Nothing to fear, nor to be feared." James Bernie to James G. Birney, June 3, 1843, and Feb. 12, 1844, Birney Papers. The three main collections of Birney MSS are the Birney Papers, in the William L. Clements Library, University of Michigan; the Birney Collection in the Manuscript Division, Library of Congress; and the Birney Manuscripts, in the Boston Public Library.

[2] Unless otherwise specifically stated, the information about the Birney family is taken from William Birney, *James G. Birney and His Times, The Genesis of the Republican Party with Some Account of Abolition Movements in the South before 1828* (New York, 1890).

Maria was called. It was she who presided over the new residence, Woodlawn, which her brother built about a half-mile out of Danville —a large, white house in the Georgian style, set nobly at the top of a sloping lawn at the end of a long lane of trees. Here Birney spent his childhood, playing with his numerous Gillespie, Whelan, and Reed cousins or roaming the woods and pastures with Michael, the colored boy whom Grandfather Reed had given him when he was only six.

When James was eleven, he was sent to Transylvania University at Lexington,[3] having furnished evidence of good moral character as well as the ability to "read English with some degree of facility, and write legibly in small hand." There were probably about one hundred students in 1803, when he entered. The school itself was a plain, two-story, brick building in which there was to be no "hallowing, loud talking, whistling or jumping, or other boisterous noise." Its atmosphere was typical of the schools of the time. Upon entering, James took the required solemn pledge to obey the laws of the university, which prohibited lying, profanity, "playing at unlawful games," or going to a tavern without permission. Monitors were appointed to report breaches of the laws.

Although the rules were strict, there was probably the average amount of boyish pranks and good fun. When recitations were over at five o'clock, there were games of football, wrestling, jumping, "bandy," or "fives." [4]

The school day began with prayers at nine, followed by two orations assigned to the students in rotation and classes until five o'clock. The curriculum included the customary Greek and Latin classics, geography, logic, mathematics, natural philosophy, chemistry, astronomy, history, moral philosophy, English grammar, and belles lettres. Besides daily prayers, students were expected to attend public worship on Sundays, for the trustees had pledged that although the teachings of no one religious sect would be presented, they would "guard against the baneful influence of Sceptical Principles."

The acting president of Transylvania during Birney's stay was the

---

[3] Records of the Proceedings in the Board of Trustees of the Transylvania University, 1799–1810, p. 247.

[4] William Leavy, "Memoir of Lexington and Its Vicinity with Some Notice of Many Prominent Citizens and Its Institutions of Education and Religion," *Register of the Kentucky State Historical Society*, XLI (1943), 44–62; Robert Peter, *Transylvania University, Its Origin, Rise, Decline and Fall* (Louisville, 1896), p. 71.

Rev. James Blythe, somewhat dictatorial in manner but respected as a teacher. Years later, when Birney was about to leave Kentucky because of the unpopularity of his antislavery views, Blythe, then president of Hanover College, met him in Lexington and warned him solemnly not to go to South Hanover "to disturb his college with abolitionism." [5] The other teachers were the Rev. Andrew Steele, James Hamilton, Ebenezer Sharpe, and Robert Hamilton Bishop.

Robert Hamilton Bishop is of special interest as Birney's teacher because he was outstanding as an opponent of slavery and as a friend of the colored people. He published an article called *An Enquiry Concerning the Duty of Christian Heads of Families towards Their Black Servants* and was active in establishing Sabbath schools for colored people in Lexington as well as in preaching to them. Bishop's reaction to Birney's later antislavery activities was in sharp contrast to that of his old colleague, Blythe. When Birney began publishing the *Philanthropist* in Cincinnati in 1836, Bishop wrote him a letter of encouragement and enclosed a ten-dollar contribution toward its support.[6]

When James was at home for the Christmas holidays in 1805, it was decided that he would not return to Transylvania but should go east to finish his education at Princeton, then known as the College of New Jersey, or Nassau Hall. First, however, it would be necessary to study intensely with Dr. James Priestly in Danville in order to meet the admissions requirements. With this prospect in mind, James willingly settled down to a stiff schedule of study for a boy of fourteen: geometry, trigonometry, algebra, grammar, logic, Roman antiquities, moral philosophy, natural theology, and Blackstone's *Commentaries.* He was a good student and won high praise from Dr. Priestly.[7]

It was in these two years at home that James began to be interested in the social life and the political discussions that went on at Woodlawn. He was old enough then to be aware of the place that his father and his grandfather held in the community of Danville, of their consciousness of civic responsibility, of their leadership, and of *noblesse oblige* toward those less fortunate in birth and circumstances. Grandfather Reed, a tall, handsome, by this time white-haired old gentleman, spoke

[5] *Philanthropist* (Cincinnati), April 1, 1836.
[6] R. H. Bishop to Birney, Feb. 4, 1836, Birney Papers.
[7] James Priestly to James Birney, Sr., quoted in William Birney, *James G. Birney and His Times,* pp. 12–14.

in a courtly and cultivated manner; James's father, shorter, darker, strong from the work he did even yet alongside his hired workers and skilled slaves, was impetuous in speech and stubborn in argument. Aunt Doyle, with her shawl over her shoulders, with spectacles and knitting, usually listened to them quietly. Guests from town were entertained liberally; and not infrequently there was a special guest, the up-and-coming young lawyer and politician from Lexington, Henry Clay. Whether there were guests or whether the discussion was a quiet, family one, more and more James was conscious of the recurrence of one topic, Negro slavery.

The question of slavery in Kentucky was as old as the question of statehood itself, and no issue was more controversial. At the very time of James's birth his father and grandfather had been in the midst of the big fight to make Kentucky a free state, to prevent the tragedy of allowing her to enter the Union with the curse of slavery perpetuated within her borders. The constitutional convention had been held in Danville, and for months prior to the convention the town had been stirred by the appeals against slavery of "Father" David Rice, pastor of the Presbyterian Church and one of Kentucky's most learned men. Backed by several other ministers and by many of the neighborhood planters including Mr. Reed and Mr. Birney, Father Rice had been chosen as a delegate to the convention to obtain a provision for the gradual abolition of slavery; but the antislavery delegates had failed by a vote of twenty-six to sixteen. In spite of this, Father Rice had not given up. His speech to the convention was printed in pamphlet form for everyone to read. It was a powerful plea, still quoted:

As creatures of God we are, with respect to liberty, all equal. If one has a right to live among his fellow creatures, and enjoy his freedom, so has another; if one has a right to enjoy that property he acquires by an honest industry, so has another. If I, by force, take that from another, which he has a just right to, according to the law of nature, (which is a divine law) which he has never forfeited, and to which he has never relinquished his claim, I am certainly guilty of injustice and robbery; and when the thing taken is the man's liberty, when it is himself, it is the greatest injustice. . . . As a separate state we are just now come to birth, [was his challenging conclusion] and it depends upon our free choice whether we shall be born in this sin or innocent of it.[8]

[8] David Rice, *Slavery Inconsistent with Justice and Good Policy Proved by a Speech, Delivered in the Convention, Held at Danville, Kentucky* (New York, 1812),

Father Rice left Danville when James was very young, but long after this Aunt Doyle spoke of the stirring antislavery sermons she had heard him preach and of the times when he had been a frequent guest in the Birney home. Perhaps it was no coincidence that James was one day to carry on the great work which Rice had begun as Kentucky's most earnest advocate of abolition. The impressionable child of Rice's day became the zealous crusader in manhood.

Although the first constitution recognized slavery and forbade the legislature to emancipate without consent of the owners and without compensation, the effects of the stand against slavery were also evident.[9] The legislature could prevent slaves from being brought into the state in the commercial slave trade, but it could not prohibit their importation by immigrants; it could legislate for the humane treatment and adequate support of slaves, but only to the extent that slaves not treated with humanity or neglected were to be sold for the benefit of their errant owners. Kentucky, as Rice had warned, had made a "free choice" of whether it wanted to be "born in this sin, or innocent of it." Men then living were to see the day of national calamity to which their action would lead. James Gillespie Birney was to live only until 1857, but by then no one saw more clearly than he the tragedy that was upon the nation.

Again, in 1799, when James was seven, his father and grandfather backed delegates to the new constitutional convention who were pledged to vote for an emancipation clause. Young Henry Clay argued strongly for legislative power to initiate gradual emancipation at any time. But the opponents of slavery, although a strong force in the state, were only a minority. They were again defeated in their main purpose, but the new constitution which went into effect on June 1, 1800, amended the old slavery clause. In the prosecution of slaves for felony, although inquest by a grand jury was not necessary, the legislature could not deny the accused an impartial trial by a petit jury. The fact that the new constitution was difficult to amend, however, effectively prevented further attempts to liberalize the slavery clause.[10]

---

pp. 1, 13. This speech was published in 1792 under the pseudonym "Philanthropos," as _Slavery Inconsistent with Justice and Good Policy._ In 1838 the American Anti-Slavery Society republished it, with notes by Birney, for distribution in Kentucky.

[9] _Journal of the First Constitutional Convention of Kentucky_ . . . , _April 2 to 19, 1792_ (Lexington, 1942), pp. 10, 18.

[10] Thomas D. Clark, _A History of Kentucky_ (New York, 1937), p. 162; _Journal of_

In the years when James was beginning to mature intellectually as he studied with Dr. Priestly, another strong antislavery impulse was evident, originating in the Baptist church under the leadership of the Rev. David Barrow, a native of Virginia. While fighting for the liberty of the American colonies, Barrow had become convinced that holding one's fellow men in bondage was contrary to the principles of the Declaration of Independence, and he had already freed his slaves before moving to Kentucky in 1798. James Birney had gone with his father and Aunt Doyle to hear Barrow preach. The Birneys found his preaching moderate and prudent; but conservative leaders of the Baptist church thought him "radical" and secured his expulsion from the North District Association. Immediately protests arose, with the community divided into two camps. Several of his supporters were ready to go to the length of separating from the regular Baptist church, and they formed the "Baptist Licking-Locust Association, Friends of Humanity." About September, 1807, Barrow published a strong indictment of slavery entitled *Involuntary, Unmerited, Perpetual, Absolute, Hereditary Slavery, Examined, on the Principles of Nature, Reason, Justice, Policy, and Scripture.*[11]

Slavery was confusing to James Birney, but he accepted it. His slave Michael and he had grown up as playmates; but because he was white, he was free, while Michael, who was black, was a slave and had to do his bidding. James's father held that emancipation by the state legislature on an over-all basis was the only solution to the problem and that until that day came one had to be kind to slaves and to protect them. Aunt Doyle, on the other hand, refused to own a slave herself and would not accept the personal services of her brother's slaves at Woodlawn without paying them.

The slavery issue was important in New Jersey when James went there in 1808, the year in which Congress exercised its constitutional authority to prohibit the importation of more slaves. It was one of the burning topics of the day in both the free and the slave states. As recently as 1804 New Jersey had passed its gradual emancipation law,

the Convention Begun and Held at the Capitol in the Town of Frankfort [July 22, 1799] (Frankfort, 1799), pp. 31–32.

[11] John H. Spencer, *A History of Kentucky Baptists from 1769 to 1885, Including More than 800 Biographical Sketches* (Cincinnati, 1886), I, 192–197; Daniel Benedict, *A General History of the Baptist Denomination in America, and Other Parts of the World* (Boston, 1813), II, 248.

and its abolition society was still flourishing. The problem of slavery came up in several ways at Princeton. The president of the college, the Rev. Samuel Stanhope Smith, had published, as early as 1787, *An Essay on the Causes of the Variety of Complexion and Figure in the Human Species,* in which he advanced the theory of the unity of the human race and its descent from a common ancestor, arguing that the difference in the development of the Negro was attributable to geographic and climatic influences as well as conditioning by the state of society in which he had lived. These differences, he suggested, tended to be diminished, and perhaps might be entirely obliterated, as the Negro was exposed to American civilization. This was certainly in direct opposition to the doctrine of biological inequality which formed the basis for the Southern justification of slavery. In his class lectures on moral philosophy, too, Smith considered man as susceptible to improvement. He was no abolitionist, however. While calling emancipation an event to be desired, he hastened to add that public safety necessarily prevented its speedy accomplishment.[12]

Professor John Maclean, a sturdy Scotsman like Bishop at Transylvania, was outspoken against slavery; and Philip Lindsley, the tutor whom James came to know quite well personally, certainly had his doubts about slavery.[13] It was a problem many of the boys were concerned about to the extent that its discussion was carried over into their literary and debating societies. James himself proposed as the topic of one meeting: "Does slavery tend to retard the progress of the arts and sciences?"[14]

James arrived at Nassau Hall in Princeton in the spring of 1808. He formally met President Smith to present his letter of entrance; and gradually he became acquainted with approximately one hundred boys, boys from the deep South, from New England, and from the middle seaboard states, as well as a few fellow Westerners. He was glad for Joseph Cabell Breckinridge, a fellow Kentuckian, as a roommate. Together they could face the Easterners without self-consciousness about

[12] Lectures on Moral Philosophy by Samuel S. Smith, D.D., President of Princeton College, Lecture No. 5, Manuscript Division, Firestone Library, Princeton.

[13] William Birney, *op. cit.,* 27–28; Philip Lindsly [sic], *A Sermon Delivered in the Chapel of the College of New Jersey, August 15, 1824* (Princeton, 1824). Lindsley's complete *Works* were published in three volumes by L. J. Halsey in 1866.

[14] American Whig Society, Minutes, entry for Sept. 4, 1810, Firestone Library, Princeton.

the differences in their speech and clothing. The two of them made a trip to town to buy furnishings for their room, and they paid fees for tuition, board, books, wood, light, library use, servant's wages, and washerwoman's bills, a total for the year of about $180 each. Neither of them had a great deal of money left over—their parents had been urged to be frugal in giving any amount above these necessary expenditures to their sons, as too much spending money was "pernicious to the morals and the studious habits of the youth." [15] But despite these checks, they felt the excitement of their first venture so far from home and the heady confidence which accompanied their first taste of real independence.

Birney was admitted to the sophomore class on condition that he make up English grammar and Kennet's work on Roman antiquities. To enter the sophomore class it was necessary to have read the Greek Testament; Latin through Virgil's *Aeneid,* Sallust, Cicero's orations, Lucien's *Dialogues;* and to understand common arithmetic. Besides Greek and Latin, the first two classes studied mathematics, geography, and Roman antiquities. Birney acquired great proficiency in Latin; he continued to read it throughout his life, and he taught it to his sons when they had no other teacher in the Michigan backwoods. His writings contain frequent allusions to his classical reading. His progress in studies was rapid, and after examination in September, 1808, he was promoted to the junior class.

Morning and evening prayers set a religious tone to the student life. On Sundays the junior class attended lectures on theology, and the senior class, on evidences of natural and revealed religion. The social and intellectual life of the students centered in the two literary societies, the American Whig Society and the Cliosophic Society. Admission to one of them was a sign that one "had arrived." Birney made friends quickly and by June, 1808, was admitted to the Whig Society,[16] which had been founded in 1769 for the promotion of "literature, friendship, and morality." James Madison, Philip Freneau, Aaron Burr, and

---

[15] Information on student life at Princeton is taken from Varnum L. Collins, *Princeton* (New York, 1914); John MacLean, *History of the College of New Jersey* (Philadelphia, 1877); and Thomas J. Wertenbaker, *Princeton, 1746–1896* (Princeton, 1946).

[16] All the information on the American Whig Society activities is taken from the Minutes, 1792–1906; Constitution, 1807; and Ashbel Green's unpublished "History of the American Whig Society"; Firestone Library, Princeton.

Henry Lee had been among its charter members. James was an active member and worked hard for the society, serving at various times in the capacity of moderator, treasurer, censor, and historian. The roll of the club was divided into thirds, each third being responsible in rotation for preparing compositions, debating, or reading and spelling exercises. He made his debut with a composition entitled "A Panegyric on Columbus" and followed that by many more, usually on topics dealing with government or history, his favorite subjects of reading.

Society debates considered a great variety of topics, from "Is the reading of novels beneficial to the female sex?" and "Whether is polygamy consistent with the laws of nature" (both decided in the affirmative) to "Should freedom of press be restrained in a free country?" or "Is one form of religion preferable to another for the welfare of a government?" Among those proposed by Birney were: "Is the sacrifice of one innocent man more injurious to society than the escape of ten guilty?" "Ought war to be waged with privateers?" and "Whether is the merchant or the lawyer more beneficial to his country."

There were no organized athletics at that time, but on the monthly holiday the students sleighed, skated, or perhaps visited the neighboring town. Sometimes these trips to town in search of adventure included visiting a local tavern. One such trip ended disastrously for Birney and his comrade, Edward Mayo. Mayo was charged with having been repeatedly at neighboring towns and taverns, and Birney had been seen at a tavern on Sunday drinking "spirituous liquors." Both were accused of making noise and disturbances in the college. Their cases came before the faculty meeting of March 7, 1809, and both were suspended with orders to leave college immediately.[17]

The incident stirred up a hornet's nest of resentment among the students, to the point that it was rumored that President Smith feared for his life. Apparently the rumor was justified, for when Mayo went back to his room to get his clothes before leaving, President Smith accompanied him to see that he got off. As the two were about to descend the stairs, a group of students armed with tongs and other miscellaneous weapons appeared at the top of the stairs. President Smith probably saved his own life by keeping Mayo between the students and himself as a shield until they got down the stairs, where he could make a dash

[17] Resolves and Minutes of the Faculty, entry for March 7, 1809, Firestone Library, Princeton.

for Mr. Lindsley's room. Just as he dashed the tongs came hurtling down the stairs, barely missing their target.

We can only imagine with what shamefacedness James returned home to face his father, not to mention Dr. Priestly, who had had enough faith in him to recommend that at college he live with a private family to save him the "intrusions" of a college lodging house, as he did not need "the discipline of academic rules to keep him to proper hours and from bad company." James Birney, Sr., though in some respects indulgent, was not long on patience. The fact that James was readmitted before a month had passed indicates parental firmness in requiring him to furnish the requisite "proof of reformation." For a year he kept out of trouble, but in February, 1810, he confessed to the charge of appearing in the classroom intoxicated. By this time he had made a good reputation as a student, and the faculty action was taken with reluctance. As it was a repetition of offense, however, a milder punishment could not be inflicted, and he was again suspended.[18] But again he was reinstated, and he was graduated September 26, 1810, with Intermediate Honors, a few points below the highest honors obtainable.[19]

His education was not completed, however. His father intended to train him for public life, and as law was the steppingstone to politics, he was to study law. James returned to Danville to begin reading Blackstone, but his father soon decided that this would not be sufficient training and that his son should have as mentor a man prominent in politics as well as in jurisprudence. Accordingly it was arranged that Birney read law with Alexander J. Dallas, of Philadelphia. So, without time to become reacclimated to being a Kentuckian again, Birney was on his way back east by the end of 1810.

Philadelphia, still the cultural and intellectual center of the middle eastern states, was a great contrast from the frontier atmosphere of Danville or the small-town seclusion of Princeton. Birney was fortunate in having both the means to indulge his tastes in art and music and the proper background for entree into the best social circles of the city. A pair of his father's thoroughbreds and a smart carriage as well as a handsome allowance from home enabled him to live the life of a man about town.

[18] *Ibid.*, entry for Feb. 22, 1810.
[19] American Whig Society, Status of Members, Firestone Library, Princeton.

Despite his life in the smart set, he made several serious friends too. One of them was James Forten, a colored sailmaker who had worked so industriously he had made a fortune for himself and had earned the respect of his fellow citizens, white and colored alike. Forten was active in antislavery work; he had been born a free Negro and had been partially educated at the school of the Quaker abolitionist Anthony Benezet. Another of Birney's friends was Abraham L. Pennock, an antislavery Quaker merchant who was one of the founders of Haverford College and was later editor of *The Non-Slaveholder*. With these men Birney could continue the discussions in which he had become interested at home and which he had continued to ponder while at Princeton. Certainly this contact with antislavery men must have borne fruit twenty years later.

The most imposing of all the people in James's new life was Alexander J. Dallas himself.[20] He was just short of six feet in height, an erect, dignified man, with carefully curled and powdered silver hair, who was always immaculately dressed from his white cravat to his white-topped boots with their gold knee buckles. The house in which the Dallas family lived, as well as in which Mr. Dallas had his office, was a mansion valued at ten thousand dollars. Next door was the home of the eminent Dr. Benjamin Rush.

Dallas was as active in politics as in law, and to work with him was to know a friend of the great and the near great. Jefferson, Madison, and Monroe sought his advice; Aaron Burr had come to his house for refuge after the fatal duel with Alexander Hamilton; he was a lifelong friend of Albert Gallatin and a friend as well as unofficial partner in law of Jared Ingersoll. In Dallas, Birney saw a man who was not only a great practicing lawyer, but a student of the law, a man imbued with the idea of public service, and a man of literary and social interests as well.

Dallas was himself too busy with public life to give much attention to his individual students, but Birney's years in Dallas' law office were the exciting years of the second war with Great Britain. Cases arising out of violations of the Embargo Act and cases respecting the rights of neutrals punctuated the more routine cases of usury, debts, and land

[20] George Mifflin Dallas, *Life and Writings of Alexander James Dallas* (Philadelphia, 1871), p. 144; Raymond Walters, *Alexander James Dallas; Lawyer—Politician —Financier* (Philadelphia, 1943), p. 112.

titles on which he and his fellow students worked. In 1814, just before Dallas was about to go to Washington to accept his appointment as Secretary of the Treasury, Birney took his bar examination and passed successfully.

At twenty-two he was a full-fledged lawyer ready to return home to begin his career and make a name for himself. And what man of his talents, his training, and his opportunities could not make a name for himself in the rapidly developing West of the early nineteenth century?

Chapter II

Planter and Politician

THE handsome young lawyer cut quite a figure as he walked up Danville's main street greeting old acquaintances and renewing friendships interrupted by his years away at school in the East. He was of average height, his bearing aristocratic, his manner easy, his dress of the latest mode, and his brown hair neatly cut with fashionable sideburns. Although his fastidious dress and sophisticated manners may have given him something of the air of a dandy, the high forehead, the direct look of his blue eyes, and the firm line of his mouth revealed an earnestness of purpose as well as jaunty confidence.

It was easy for young James G. Birney to take his place in the community; the way had already been paved for him even before he hung out his lawyer's shingle in the office downtown. He knew there would be business for him as the new attorney for the bank which had been established in 1806 by three of the town's wealthiest citizens: his father, Robert Craddock, and Joshua Barbee.[1] It seemed only natural, too, that given his training, he should be elected to the town council almost immediately. Much to his father's delight, he also decided to join the Masonic order. Within a year he was a trustee of the Franklin

[1] Calvin M. Fackler, *Early Days in Danville* (Louisville, 1941), p. 236.

14

Lodge in Danville, and within three years he was to rise to the position of Grand Senior Warden of the Grand Lodge of Kentucky.[2]

Politics was an area that Birney entered with zest. In 1815 his hero, Henry Clay, was up for re-election to Congress; but as Clay was off in Europe as a delegate to the peace conference at Ghent, the responsibility for his campaign fell on other shoulders. Perhaps most Kentuckians needed no arousing to return their favorite son to Washington; but James Birney volunteered to do his part to make sure of Clay's success. He was aware that more than Clay's campaign was at stake. The impression he himself made would determine his own future political ambitions. The summer of 1815 was, consequently, a busy one for him, stumping the neighboring counties.

Birney had other things than law and politics on his mind, however. The time had come, he felt, to think seriously of marriage and a family. He was not shy and was certainly one of the town's most eligible bachelors: he was handsome, wealthy, personable and had prospects of a successful future. It was in the role of a Beau Brummel that he frequented the parties and balls of the Danville younger set; but it was with care that he chose as his bride pretty, vivacious Agatha McDowell.

The McDowells were one of the leading families of Kentucky. Agatha's grandfather, Samuel McDowell, had been a member of the Virginia House of Burgesses, a member of the convention which sent delegates to the Continental Congress with instructions to vote for independence, and a colonel in the Revolutionary War. In 1784 he had moved to Mercer County, Kentucky, where he presided over the conventions to consider separation from Virginia and served as president of Kentucky's constitutional convention in 1792. Agatha's father, William McDowell, was United States district judge for Kentucky; her mother was a cousin of James Madison. Her uncle, Ephraim McDowell, became famous as the first surgeon to perform an ovariotomy.

Both families were well pleased with the marriage. James Birney, Sr., a loyal Episcopalian, even forgot his dislike of stanch Presbyterians in his satisfaction at such a fine match for his son. The wedding took place on February 1, 1816, three days before James's twenty-fourth

---

[2] *By-Laws, Rules of Order, Historical Sketch, 1815–1937, and Past Masters of Franklin Lodge No. 28 F.&A.M. Danville, Kentucky* (Danville, [n.d.]), p. 13; *Kentucky Gazette* (Lexington), Sept. 13, 1817. Unless otherwise indicated, the information in this chapter about the Birney family is taken from William Birney, *James G. Birney and His Times.*

birthday. Agatha was only seventeen. James had already bought property from his father and the couple could move into their own home. Among their wedding gifts were several household slaves given by both of their families.

Everything went well for the young newlyweds. Agatha's pride in her home and her husband was complete when the voters of Mercer County gave evidence of the esteem in which they held him by electing him to the state legislature in August.[3] By the time he took his seat in December, she was carrying their first son, James, Jr., who was born on June 7, 1817.[4]

The capital town of Frankfort, when Birney arrived there to serve in the legislature, was still a small, frontier town. Just then its streets were crowded with the carriages and horses of the legislators, and its taverns overflowed with the influx of temporary residents. Almost everywhere one looked one saw small groups of men in earnest conversation over the work before them. State making was important business west of the Alleghenies in the first decades of the nineteenth century. Men who served in the legislatures were conscious of the foundations they were laying for the future. There were towns to be incorporated; roads to be built; lands to be disposed of; courts, prisons, schools to be established; and laws to be passed governing them all.

When the Assembly met, John J. Crittenden was quickly chosen speaker, and business got under way. Birney was elected to several committees: the committee of privileges and elections, a joint committee to examine the state banks, a committee to prepare a bill to prohibit the readings of the reports of sister states in the Kentucky courts, a select committee to make decisions for repairing and enlarging the penitentiary, a committee to prepare a bill to establish an election precinct in Fleming County, a committee to incorporate the Frankfort Lock Navigation Company, and others to deal with petitions to incorporate towns and to authorize the sale of public lands. Towns and businesses were multiplying so rapidly the legislature could hardly keep up with them. Birney was especially concerned with the bill to obtain a charter for a college in Danville, to be named Centre College, and another to

[3] *Journal of the House of Representatives . . . Kentucky, . . . 1816* (Frankfort, 1816), p. 4.

[4] The dates of the children's births are taken from the family Bible, in private possession.

establish a new bank in Danville. He was ready to stand up and be counted as a dissenter, too. At this session a resolution was passed requesting the states of Ohio and Indiana to pass laws imposing penalties on any of their citizens who aided fugitive slaves. "Shall the State of Kentucky," Birney objected, "do what no gentleman would do—turn slavecatcher?" [5]

Between sessions and committee meetings there was a good chance, while dining in the taverns and sitting around in the evenings, for Birney to get to know the other men in Kentucky politics and to test his own political opinions against those of the seasoned veterans. The name of Andrew Jackson, who had just won a victory at New Orleans against the British, was on everyone's tongue. Swept along in the Jackson enthusiasm, Birney concurred in a formal resolution commemorating the victory at New Orleans as a triumph of the "proud votaries of civil liberty over the disciplined vassals of an ambitious monarch." [6]

Among Birney's fellow members in the legislature was William Love, who throughout the session spoke of the visit he intended to make as soon as the session adjourned, to the Territory of Alabama, a real frontier area only then being settled. A young man would have a free field there, either in planting or in politics, by getting in on the ground floor. Love repeatedly urged that Birney accompany him to see for himself, and before the session was over his enthusiasm had won out. Together they set out for Alabama in the spring of 1817.

In 1817 the trip from Danville, Kentucky, to Huntsville, Alabama, was an arduous one either by wagon or on horseback. There were no roads, only rough passageways through the woods which had been made by chopping down trees. Wagons piled high with furniture and other household goods had worn deep ruts where the ground was soft. In other places the travelers bumped over stumps and roots. Where spring rains had made the low places too soft to be crossed without becoming mired, "corduroy" roads were made by filling in logs on which to drive. Difficulties of travel were not enough, however, to pre-

[5] William Birney, *op. cit.*, p. 34.

[6] *Journal House Rep., Ky., 1816*, pp. 262–263, 275, 284; *Acts 26th General Assembly, Ky., 1817* (Frankfort, 1818), pp. 375 and 438; *Olive Branch and Western Union* (Danville), May 19, 1820. The charter for Centre College was not approved until after Birney had left Kentucky.

vent long files of emigrant wagons from wending their way southwest-
ward from Kentucky, Tennessee, Virginia, and the Carolinas.[7]

In the decade following the War of 1812, after the defeat of the
British as well as the Indians in the West, land sales in the Tennessee
Valley were booming. It was to this area that Birney and Love were
headed. Huntsville was already a flourishing town with a land office and
a bank.[8] Emigrants, traders, and land speculators jostled in its muddy
or dusty streets. Here was America in the making, here was opportunity
to prosper and to create and to mold. Even Kentucky seemed to Birney
old and crowded by comparison.

Birney chose his future home carefully. Just about fourteen miles
north of Huntsville on a high, wooded bluff overlooking the junction of
Indian Creek with the beautiful Tennessee River, a small town called
Triana had been started. Its natural beauty was appealing; its commercial future was extremely promising. All that was needed was a
canal connecting it with Huntsville for it to become the cotton shipping
port of northern Alabama. Huntsville seemed certain to be the capital.
Settlers already in the area were loud in praise of the region's pro-
ductivity. The soil was so rich, they boasted, that planters could become wealthy in even the poorest times.[9] His mind made up on the spot,
Birney purchased 235 acres of land from the trustees of Triana, paying
$2,416.[10]

He returned home to settle his business affairs and to arrange for
moving. His business as the bank's attorney had to be wound up, his
public duties entrusted to other hands, and reluctant parents persuaded
that Alabama held a brighter future than Kentucky for the young lawyer
and politician. It did seem best, however, that Agatha and the new
baby remain in Kentucky until a home had been prepared for them.
So early in 1818 Birney set out again, this time accompanied by the
family slaves to help him put things in readiness. His aim was to be
both planter and lawyer, as was customary among Southern gentlemen,

[7] William Birney, *op. cit.,* pp. 36–37; Thomas Jones Taylor, "Early History of
Madison County and Incidentally of North Alabama," *Alabama Historical Quarterly,* I (Winter, 1930).

[8] Matthew P. Blue, "History of Counties of Alabama: Madison County," Manuscript Division, Department of History and Archives, Montgomery.

[9] Huntsville *Republican,* March 10, 1818, and Oct. 7, 1817.

[10] Madison County Deed Record, Book N, pp. 286–287, Madison County Courthouse, Huntsville.

but planting would have to come first until they were settled. Law and politics would come later.

Starting a cotton crop, about which he knew little or nothing, was not an easy task, and Birney soon found that his few household slaves, unused to such work, were insufficient. It was necessary to have more and experienced hands. Purchases were accordingly made, and by 1821 he had bought nineteen Negroes valued at $13,495.[11] These, in addition to the one he had received from his Grandfather Reed, two from the McDowells, ten from his father, and eleven born of the family slaves, made him the owner of forty-three slaves. Owning slaves was consistent with his views at the time. Although he had been exposed to anti-slavery views since childhood, he had not yet arrived at the point where he recognized his individual responsibility in the matter. Like so many of the Southern planters, including Washington and Jefferson, he de-plored the evils inherent in the system but continued to practice it while hoping for its gradual extinction. Up to this point Birney's experience had been with the relatively mild form of slavery which existed in Kentucky. There, in a large degree, slavery was a patriarchal institution, and the personal contact between master and slave often fostered mutual affection. At Woodlawn the slaves had always led an easy life, and the slave driver's whip was unknown.

By the autumn of 1818 Agatha and young James, Jr., were able to join him in their new home, which was tastefully furnished without regard for expense. Agatha shared his enthusiasm for the new area. Friends were quickly made among neighboring planters of a similar social and cultural background to their own, and the young couple was caught up in the social life of lavish entertaining and being en-tertained. Away from the sobering influence and restraining hand of more pious parents and relatives, it was easy to fall into the fast-moving, gay life of the Southern planting aristocracy.

Settlers pushed into the Alabama Territory in such numbers that by 1819 Alabama was asking for statehood, and a constitutional conven-tion was authorized. Immediately Birney's contacts with such national leaders as Henry Clay and John J. Crittenden were drawn upon, and partly through their influence Huntsville was designated as the place

[11] James G. Birney to Col. Stone, in William Birney, *op. cit.*, Appendix D; Planta-tion Record Book of James G. Birney, in private possession.

where the convention would meet. The citizens immediately prepared
two lists of outstanding men. Those on the first list were elected to
represent Madison County at the constitutional convention; those on
the second were chosen members of the first state legislature. Although
Birney was on the second list, he was not idle while the convention was
meeting.[12]

The summer of 1819 was a demanding one. There was the plantation
to see to, slaves to supervise in raising a crop, and already some fear
of what the market conditions would be by autumn. Family responsibilities were growing, too. In May the Birney's second son was born,
whom they named William for Agatha's father. From July 5 to August
2 Birney had to go to Huntsville every day to consult and be consulted
in informal meetings and conversations about the details of setting up
the new government.

Although he did not go so far as his father had in Kentucky on the
question of emancipation, he did secure the inclusion of a liberal slave
clause which was similar to the one in the Kentucky constitution. The
General Assembly was empowered to prohibit the bringing in of slaves
to be sold as merchandise, and it could pass laws of emancipation provided the owners consented or were compensated. The clause further
stated that slaveholders had to supply necessary food and clothing and
treat their slaves humanely. For any crime more serious than petit
larceny a slave was entitled to a trial by jury. Any person dismembering or killing a slave was to be subject to the same punishment as that
which would be meted out if the crime were committed against a white
man. The only exception was in case of a slave insurrection.[13]

Birney's real political duties began with the meeting of the first
General Assembly in Huntsville in 1819. He had thought the Kentucky
legislature a busy place; now he realized how much more was involved
in starting a state government from the beginning. His excellent education and his training in law were distinct assets when he faced the necessity of drawing up bills in clear, compact form. He was appointed to
the rules committee, which would lay the groundwork for legislative

[12] Delegates from Madison County were C. C. Clay, John Leigh Townes, Henry
Chambers, Samuel Mead, Henry Minor, Gabriel Moore, John W. Walker, and John
M. Taylor. See Albert J. Pickett, *History of Alabama, and Incidentally of Georgia
and Mississippi, from the Earliest Period* (Charleston, 1851), p. 635.

[13] Thomas M. Owen, *History of Alabama and Dictionary of Alabama Biography*
(Chicago, 1921), III, 152–155; *Constitution of the State of Alabama, December 6,
1819*, Art. VI, Sec. 1.

procedure, to the important ways and means committee, and to the committee to draw up a bill for administering the governor's oath of office. As a member of the committee to revise the territorial laws and organize the judiciary, he was largely responsible for formulating the procedure for the courts of law and equity in the state. In addition to these major committees, he served on many smaller ones, and he worked on the bills he intended to sponsor personally which were of importance to his own community. He presented Triana's petition for incorporation and a bill to incorporate a library company in Huntsville, and he worked for passage of acts to extend the corporation of the town of Huntsville and to increase the number of its commissioners.[14]

Birney had every right to be proud of the major role he was playing in the state government. Certainly it was an auspicious beginning for a young planter not yet thirty years of age. There seemed to be no reason why he should not go far in public life; his star seemed to be rising. What he had not sufficiently reckoned with, however, was that Andrew Jackson's star had already risen, and unless one hitched one's wagon to Jackson's star in the Alabama of the 1820's, there was little hope of a political future. It is hard to exaggerate the Jackson sentiment of the frontier, and Alabama was in the vanguard of the pro-Jackson tide. The fact that he had cleared the West of the menace of the Indians was more important to the frontiersman than it was to a Philadelphian or a New Yorker. To be the hero of New Orleans was to be more than a mythical hero to the people of Alabama. He had saved their soil and their homes from the British invader.

Birney's lesson in the strength of popular opinion came all too quickly. While the first legislature was sitting, Jackson himself came to Huntsville to attend the races, and the whole town turned out in celebration to honor him. Not to be outdone by the spontaneous gesture of their constituents, the legislators decided it would be fitting for them to commend the general officially. Colonel Howell Rose, one of Jackson's ardent admirers from Autauga County, proposed two resolutions. The first praised Jackson's valor in the War of 1812, particularly at New Orleans; and the second expressed disapproval of the late attempt by some members of Congress to censure Jackson's invasion of Florida in the recent Creek and Seminole wars. Birney was willing to vote for the first resolution, as indeed he had already done in substance in the

[14] *Journal of the House of Representatives of . . . Alabama . . . 1819* (Cahawba, 1820).

Kentucky legislature; but he could not go along with the second resolution.[15] Jackson's high-handed, authoritarian action in the executions
of Arbuthnot and Ambrister was more than he could stomach. Besides,
as Birney was well aware, here was the greatest political threat to Henry
Clay's capturing the presidency, and Birney was still strong for Clay.
As a result of Birney's dissent, he was not re-elected to the state legislature for another term. More than that, he was never again to hold an
elective office in Alabama above the local level. Far from being swayed
by the popular sentiments, Birney continued to work actively against
Jackson's election to the presidency and strenuously opposed most of
his policies while Jackson was in office.[16]

It was not easy for Birney to give up his hopes for a political career.
Ever since boyhood this had been the goal toward which his education
had been directed, and his father's heart had been set on it. In 1821 an
open letter to him, signed only "X," appeared in the *Alabama Republican*, assuring him of the people's confidence in his experience and
abilities and asking him to become a candidate for the national House
of Representatives. Birney knew the attempt would be futile as he
would have to get the votes of too large a section of the state; but he did
consent to having his name placed in nomination to represent Madison
County in the state Senate. Even in his own county sufficient votes could
not be mustered. Undissuaded, a group of loyal backers immediately
presented his name as a candidate for the state Assembly. Again he
was defeated. Their last attempt was made the following year, 1822,
when his name was entered in the senatorial race against David Moore,
but once more victory went to his opponent.[17]

Unfortunately, Birney's prospects as a planter fared no better than
his political aspirations, partly as a result of current hard times and
partly because of personal extravagance. He and Agatha, used to plenty

[15] *Ibid.*, pp. 45, 50; Pickett, *op. cit.*, pp. 661–662.

[16] Many years later Birney used the term "slave driver" in referring to Jackson,
and the charge was rashly printed in Theodore D. Weld's *American Slavery as It Is*
(American Anti-Slavery Society, *Anti-Slavery Examiner*, No. 10; New York, 1839).
Theodore Parker reprinted the accusation in 1848 and, upon being challenged for
proof, asked Birney for an explanation. Birney wrote a rather evasive reply. It seemed
the only "proof" was that Jackson had once ridden along the Choctaw Trace with a
large number of slaves that he was taking to his Alabama plantation. See Weld to
Birney, July 4, 1848; Birney to Theodore Parker, July 5, 1848; and Birney to George
W. Jonson, Jan. 15, 1849, Birney Papers.

[17] *Alabama Republican* (Huntsville), Jan. 19, Feb. 2, July 13, Aug. 3, and Aug. 10,
1821; July 19 and Aug. 9, 1822.

in their own families, had given little thought to economizing, either in making their home or in entertaining. He had been easily carried along with the popular enthusiasm for horse racing, and he frequently gambled on the races. Birney's pride, his love of conviviality, perhaps even a desire to insure his political future by the right contacts led him to overindulgence. He drank too much and gambled too frequently.[18]

Betting on the horses was not his only gamble. His land investments were also gambles, and he, along with everyone else who was riding the crest of the wave of speculation, was caught when it broke in 1819. With the contraction of credits he was hit hard by his inability to meet some rather heavy losses in gambling. By the late summer of 1820 his debts to John McKinley amounted to $7,988. In addition he was security for Samuel Chapman, who had defaulted in payment of $2,652 to McKinley, making a total indebtedness of $10,640, a fortune in 1820. The only way out was to give McKinley a mortgage on his five quarter sections of land, his twenty-eight slaves, his livestock, and all his household furniture.[19] Even then he was not out of trouble. In October, 1820, Irby Jones brought suit for $5,000 in damages because he failed to pay another note of $1,539.40 which he had endorsed for Samuel Chapman. This case, however, was carried over in circuit court to 1823, when it was dismissed because of insufficient grounds. Because of an unpaid note, in 1821 John J. Winston began suit for $2,250, plus $1,000 in damages.[20] This case, too, was eventually dismissed, but the circumstances were embarrassing to him and his family.

As if his own recklessness were not enough, even nature and God seemed to be conspiring against him. In 1821 his cotton crop was a failure.[21] The loss in 1822 of his infant daughter, Margaret, while he was "rapidly pursuing the road to Hell," instead of sobering him, hardened his heart and drove him on to increased indulgence in drinking and gambling [22]—for a time—but again reason, pride, and ambition re-exerted themselves.

This time Birney could not count on financial help from his father.

---

[18] William Birney, *op. cit.*, p. 42 and Appendix D.

[19] Madison County Deed Book F, 1819–1820, p. 428.

[20] Circuit Court Record, 1822–1823, No. 15, p. 159, and No. 11, pp. 124–125, Madison County Courthouse, Huntsville.

[21] Plantation Record Book of James G. Birney.

[22] Birney to Gerrit Smith, Sept. 13, 1835, Birney Collection; Autobiography of Benjamin Woods Labaree, quoted in Dwight L. Dumond, ed., *Letters of James Gillespie Birney, 1831–1857* (New York, 1938), I, 242n.

James Birney, Sr., was not a speculator himself, but he had suffered considerable losses by backing some projects of his son-in-law, John J. Marshall, which had gone amiss. Always concerned lest his daughter should not have the comforts to which she was accustomed, he had backed Marshall financially even though doubting his judgment. When after 1819 the pinch of the depression came, he had lent Marshall nearly $20,000. Although he had accepted a deed of trust for all of Marshall's Negroes and household goods and a tract of land, the kindhearted and indulgent father could not bear to see his daughter reduced to such straits and canceled the debt. His letters to his son were full of despondency, with fears that he would be unprovided for in his old age and would have nothing to leave his children. Nonetheless, he had a concrete proposal for his son—that he give up his mortgaged Alabama plantation and return to Danville to take over the bagging and rope business.[23]

Here was the test for Birney. Should he fall back on his father, capitalize on this chance to get another start with help? Or should he stay in Alabama and prove that he could make his own way, that he was not a failure, that his own ability and resourcefulness were adequate to the challenge of his responsibilities? He chose the latter course, and with this choice the tide of his fortune was to turn.

One decision made, the next was easier—to move from the plantation to Huntsville and return to the practice of law. Reluctant to leave the plantation and the slaves under an overseer, Birney decided to sell it and did so within the year. This meant, also, that the slaves had to be provided for. Michael and his family were retained as house servants. Careful arrangements were made to sell the rest to William Love, who Birney felt would be a good master.[24] Birney's attitude toward slavery was still that of his father: until it was prohibited by law, the most one could do was to protect, in so far as possible, the slaves entrusted to one's care.

In 1823 the Birney family, consisting now of three sons, James, Jr., William, and the baby Dion, moved into Huntsville; and Birney once more hung out his law shingle.

[23] James Birney, Sr., to Birney, July 10 and Sept. 1, 1819; March 22 and Sept. 16, 1820; April 10 and July 10, 1821; and Jan. 26, 1823, Birney Papers.

[24] Birney to Col. Stone, in William Birney, *op. cit.*, Appendix D, and pp. 46–47.

Chapter III

Paths of Righteousness

HUNTSVILLE, Alabama, was a prosperous and pretty town of over two thousand people in 1823. Unlike so many frontier settlements, it had been settled by men who gave some thought to beauty as well as to more utilitarian factors. Located on a bluff at the edge of rolling hills, it commanded a view to the east and south of higher hills covered with a thick growth of hardwood trees. A wonderful natural spring furnished the inhabitants with a continuous flow of clear, cold water. Thought had been given to the laying out of the town, too. Just up the hill from the spring a public square was set aside as the center of town.[1] In it stood the courthouse for Madison County, and around it were the shops and business places. Most of the churches were built just beyond the business district, and in the outer periphery were the residences. Shade trees were growing up along the streets, and fruit orchards were beginning to appear behind many of the estates.

The Huntsville bar contained many of Alabama's outstanding lawyers, several of whom went on to distinguish themselves in either state or national politics. Clement Comer Clay had been a member of the Alabama constitutional convention and first chief justice of the

[1] William Birney, *James G. Birney and His Times*, pp. 44–45.

state Supreme Court, and he was later to be elected state legislator, member of Congress, governor, and finally United States senator; John McKinley, who had moved from Kentucky the year after Birney, became a state legislator, United States senator, and associate justice of the Supreme Court of the United States; Harry I. Thornton, also from Kentucky, was appointed United States district attorney by John Quincy Adams, was elected to the state Supreme Court and to the state Senate, and served as vice-president of the Whig national convention in Baltimore in 1844; James W. McClung also served in the state legislature, where he was speaker of the House and later a senator.[2]

These were the men against whom Birney had to measure himself, and it was exactly what he needed, for it meant measuring up to a high standard if he were to succeed. The first evidence of their approval of him came almost immediately. John McKinley and Harry Thornton suggested that they would back him for the position of solicitor of the fifth circuit, which included the counties of Walker, Blount, Morgan, Jackson, and Madison, among the most populous counties of the state. The legislature accepted their recommendation, and in 1823 Birney was elected. He held the office until he resigned it in 1827.[3]

The position of solicitor was a responsible and demanding job. Successful prosecutions were essential to retaining it, yet at the same time it was necessary to keep a scrupulous regard for justice, even in the face of popular agitation. It meant long hours of study to review the legal knowledge Birney had not practiced for over five years, entailed endless research in the court records, and required that he learn to know the people who would be either his clients or his juries. It meant, above all, winning the confidence of the people to the extent that any jury picked from among them would trust his integrity when he asked for a conviction. This, more than eloquent speaking, was to be responsible for his success.

Birney realized the degree to which he had achieved his goal in one of the hardest cases he was called upon to handle. One day a young man from Jackson County, dressed in country clothes and obviously ill at ease in unaccustomed surroundings, appeared at the law office to ask

[2] Thomas M. Owen, *History of Alabama and Dictionary of Alabama Biography,* III, 342; IV, 1094, 1124, and 1669–1670.

[3] *Acts 6th Annual Sess. General Assembly Alabama* [1824] (Cahawba, 1825), p. 116.

Birney to institute a lawsuit. The charge was lynching. There had been an outbreak of counterfeiting in those early years in Alabama, and the boy's father had been a counterfeiter. Instead of letting the authorities handle the situation, several hundred men, among them many of the best families in the area, banded together to organize a vigilante committee to run the counterfeiters out. The boy's father had been lynched, and then the vigilantes planned to lynch the boy, merely on the suspicion that he had helped his father.

Birney found himself in a delicate situation. Many of the lynchers against whom suit would have to be brought were not only wealthy and respected pillars of the community but his personal friends. Yet, having assured himself of the boy's innocence, he determined to do what he could. A particularly difficult element in the case was that the "lynch club" had gained such power through intimidation that they knew as well as he that no jury in Jackson County would dare to convict them. Moreover, Birney himself was warned that he would be lynched if he appeared in Jackson County. Despite the threat, and despite his friends' entreaties, Birney entered the county boldly, registered at his usual tavern, and even spoke to some of the men he was suing. Not a move was made to harm him; but the lynchers were confident that he could not obtain a conviction. Realizing this very practical consideration, Birney quietly arranged that when the case came to trial it should be tried in Madison rather than in Jackson County. This put a different light on the possibilities, and the men being sued hastened to settle out of court. Damages were paid to the defendant, and, even more significant, their lynch club was disbanded.[4] It was a great victory for Birney.

Another case in which Birney demonstrated his sympathy for the underdog and his determination to see justice done, even in the face of public opinion, was the case of James Helton. Helton, while hunting in the woods near Huntsville one day, came upon a Negro who he assumed was a slave, perhaps a fugitive. He ordered him to halt, but the slave kept on running, whereupon Helton shot and killed him. Here was an example of the kind of offense Birney had insisted on having covered in the slavery clause of the Alabama constitution, that a white man killing or dismembering a slave was just as guilty as if the crime

[4] Beriah Green, *Sketches of the Life and Writings of James Gillespie Birney* (Utica, 1844), pp. 7–8.

were committed against another white man. Birney determined to
bring Helton to justice and secured an indictment against him. Helton
moved across the state line into Tennessee to escape, and such was the
apathy of popular opinion over the murder of a slave that Birney's
efforts to have him extradited proved unavailing.[5]

Within a year after he moved to Huntsville, Birney's career was
assured. As early as February, 1824, his uncle, Thomas Reed, later
United States senator from Mississippi, wrote that reports of Birney's
success in law had reached Natchez.[6] At that time he became the
partner of William Adair, fellow Kentuckian who had migrated to
Alabama in 1818. Adair had been in the state legislature, where he had
served as speaker of the House. Later, in 1832, he was elected to the
circuit court bench.[7]

A return of prosperity enabled Birney to pay his debt to McKinley
and to build a new house. It was a large, brick house, built on a corner
lot. Birney took great pride in his lawn, his trees, and his flowers. Working in the garden in the evenings provided him with the relaxation and
exercise he needed after long days in a hot law office or courtroom.
Once again the Birneys were able to entertain, although in a more sober
fashion than in their earlier years. In 1825 their fourth son was born and
named after an old family friend in Danville, David Bell. James Birney,
Sr., who visited them that summer, was pleased with his son's progress
and with Agatha's well-ordered household.[8] The Birneys were quietly
becoming established as one of Huntsville's leading families. Interested
in the community, both Mr. and Mrs. Birney were active in civic affairs,
she in the Presbyterian Church, he in local government and education.
Conscientiousness and sobriety had won for them the social position
they had coveted.

In the summer of 1827 the Birney-Adair law partnership was succeeded by a partnership with Arthur F. Hopkins.[9] Hopkins had been

[5] American Anti-Slavery Society, *Anti-Slavery Examiner, No. 10* [Theodore
Dwight Weld], *American Slavery as It Is,* p. 46.

[6] Thomas Reed to Birney, Feb. 20, 1824, Birney Papers.

[7] Huntsville *Democrat,* March 9, 1824; Owen, *op. cit.,* III, 11.

[8] James Birney, Sr., to Birney, Sept. 29, 1825, Birney Papers.

[9] Owen dates their partnership from 1826, but the Huntsville *Democrat* has
notices of McKinley and Hopkins as partners up to May 18, 1827. The first notice
of Hopkins and Birney appears in the *Southern Advocate,* June 1, 1827.

a member of the state constitutional convention and of the state legislature. He was later elected to the state Supreme Court in 1836 and to
the United States Senate in 1837.[10] Hopkins, like Birney, was a sociable
man with a love of good company and good talk. Their office soon became the center for other lawyers and law students, or even local citizens,
who dropped around to listen or to take part in the discussions and
debates on local and national issues. These could be exciting, for Birney
was still maintaining unmodified anti-Jackson opinions. During the
presidential campaign of 1824 he had been influential in getting a meeting called for the purpose of trying to get the voters to commit themselves to Clay as a second choice if Jackson did not win the popular
election. The opposition was present in large enough numbers, however, to pass a resolution that it was inexpedient and unnecessary to indicate a second choice. Birney's proposal to try the strength of each
candidate by separate votes also failed.[11]

In the campaign of 1828 Birney worked even more vigorously to
defend the administration against the Jackson forces. He became
acutely conscious of, and disturbed by, the increasing appeals to the
regional unity of the South against the tariff and in defense of slavery.
Birney, still a strong believer in Clay's American System of sectional
interdependence, not only favored the tariff, but in his many speeches
warned against the dangers to the South of nullification and sectional-
ism over the extension of slavery. Birney was named an elector on the
Adams-Rush ticket in Alabama; and his zeal was commended by Henry
Clay, who wrote him from Lexington:

The effort making in Alabama for the Adm[inistrati]on, whatever may be its
issue will have good exterior effect. I have been gratified with the zeal and
attachment of my few friends in that State, among whom I have the satisfaction to know that I have been permitted to consider you as one of the most
distinguished.[12]

With the encouragement of his father, who was still eager for
him to "win high honors in his country," Birney, also in 1828, indicated
his interest in the office of district attorney when the United States
court was extended to Alabama. John McKinley, by this time a senator

---

[10] Owen, *op. cit.*, III, 843.   [11] Huntsville *Democrat*, Aug. 17, 1824.
[12] Henry Clay to Birney, July 25, 1828, in private possession.

from Alabama, promised to use what influence he had with the secretary of state; but Birney was not appointed.[13] Another try, a few years later, for the position of circuit judge for the fifth Alabama circuit, was also unsuccessful. Birney attributed this failure not only to his unpopular political opinions, but also, by that time, to his open support of "some of the benevolent operations of our day, against which strong prejudices existed in the minds of a large majority of the people and of their representatives in the legislature." [14] By that date Birney's antislavery opinions were pronounced. The South had begun to defend most vigorously the institution of slavery as a positive good, and neither he nor anyone else could entertain doubts on the subject and have any chance of a career in Southern politics. His new feelings in regard to the "benevolent operations" stemmed from an experience which changed the course of his whole life, that of religious conversion.

Birney had been brought up an Episcopalian, although in his early childhood when there was no Episcopal church in Danville, he had often been taken by Aunt Doyle to the Presbyterian church. During his adolescence and young manhood, however, he had drifted away from a vital religious faith. The McDowells, on the other hand, were devout Presbyterians, and Agatha continued to attend church and to take the children with her even when her husband did not accompany them. No doubt her quiet influence bore fruit. Now that Birney was settling down as a sober, responsible citizen and father, he began to consider seriously the question of religion. Knowing the touchiness of James Birney, Sr., about being consulted on steps of importance, Birney wrote to him on the subject of joining the church. That, answered his father, was a matter for a man's individual conscience; creed should be secondary to a man's life and actions. Before creed should come the responsibility "to acquit ourselves of all our dutys [sic] to mankind in general and especially to those whose protection and support it is our Bounden duty to provide for." [15] Nevertheless, he was disappointed when his son chose the Presbyterian church.

Perhaps one of the big factors in his choice of the Presbyterian church

[13] John McKinley to Birney, Jan. 2, 1828, Birney Papers.

[14] Arthur F. Hopkins to Birney, Jan. 4, 17, and 25, 1832, Birney Papers; Birney to the Editor of the *Emancipator,* quoted in the *African Repository and Colonial Journal,* XI (1835), 27.

[15] James Birney, Sr., to Birney, June 29, 1826, and March 21, 1833, Birney Papers.

was the revival spirit which was sweeping through its congregations. Starting in western New York through the evangelistic preaching of Charles Grandison Finney, it had spread like wildfire, especially in the frontier areas. Tent meetings and open-air meetings brought hundreds of people who would never have entered a regular church to listen to the preaching of "Hell fire and damnation" sermons and to join in the rousing hymn singing. Every church was adding its mourner's bench for those wrestling with the problem of their souls' salvation.

The revival spirit had much more than an emotional appeal for Birney. Finney's theology went hand in hand with the current upsurge of democratic faith which had its roots in the ideals of Jeffersonian philosophy. Finney taught not only the doctrine of salvation by repentance but by good works as well. An individual's own salvation was made more secure by every effort he made to save others. It was the duty of Christians to try to influence their fellow men and so to keep society moving in the right direction. Man was endowed with certain inalienable or "natural" rights and, if free from restraints, was capable of improving his own station in life and of keeping society moving in the direction of human progress.

Birney's conversion was a far deeper experience than a formal joining of the church: "Old things [were] passed away"; "all things [were] become new." He felt that his life henceforth should be measured by more than a successful career and worldly prosperity. Birney wanted to share his religion with his relatives, his friends, and his law associates, who he hoped would also find this new vision of the better life.

Above all, Birney felt that his beliefs should be translated into actions, and he looked about for fields of action. There were many groups already organized to advance the kingdom of God upon earth, and all clamored for support. Despite surface differences, all led to the uplifting of the poor and the oppressed: the movement for free public education, the temperance, Bible, tract, and peace societies, and the groups working to help the oppressed Indians and Negro slaves. Some of the organizations worked through the churches, some through political channels, others simply through unaffiliated societies. Birney was to try many movements and channels before he found the one to which the rest of his life would be dedicated.

Where should he start? He was already involved in the field of edu-

cation and in civic improvement. These interests he could continue.
When Centre College had been chartered in 1823, Birney had been
made one of its original trustees, and every year since then he had
made a trip back to Danville for the annual meeting.[16] During this time
he had seen Centre grow into one of the leading institutions of higher
learning in the West and one of the strongholds of Presbyterianism.
In 1825 Birney was asked to be a trustee of Greene Academy in Huntsville, a school which had been chartered as early as 1812 by the Mississippi legislature. He served in that position until 1827, attending to
administrative duties and also hearing and reporting on final examinations.[17] Both James, Jr., and William were enrolled at Greene. But
Greene and Centre were private schools; not all families could afford
to pay the cost of tuition and books, and many children were getting
no education at all.

Birney's chance in this area came after his election to the position
of alderman of the city of Huntsville in 1828, followed by his election
as mayor in 1829.[18] He had already made himself familiar with the
free public education movement and was ready with suggestions. An
economical plan known as the Lancastrian system had long been in
use by the schools for the poor in the East and had gained wide acceptance since the American Sunday School Union had adopted it in
1824. By this method one teacher trained a small group of the older
children, who, in turn, taught what they had learned to the younger
pupils. It meant, consequently, rote teaching in the basic three R's.[19]
The Huntsville aldermen proceeded cautiously. In March, 1828, they
authorized the assessor, in taking the census, to list any children under
the age of twenty-one who "by poverty are unable to get any education."
It was not until November, 1829, when Birney was mayor, that a committee was actually appointed to confer with the school commissioners
to devise a system for a primary school. Then things moved quickly.

[16] Day Book of Centre College of Kentucky, Centre College Library, Danville;
*The Twelfth Triennial and Thirty-Sixth Annual Catalogue of the Officers and Stu-
dents of Centre College . . . 1860* (Danville, 1860).

[17] Albert B. Moore, *History of Alabama and Her People* (New York, 1927), I,
316. See also the Huntsville *Democrat,* 1825 through 1827.

[18] *Southern Advocate* (Huntsville), Feb. 8, 1828; *Democrat,* July 17, 1829; City of
Huntsville, Minutes, 1828–1834, pp. 1, 67, and 93, Office of the City Clerk, Huntsville. William dates his father's term as mayor in 1824, but there is no evidence
in the newspapers of the time to indicate an earlier term.

[19] Alice Felt Tyler, *Freedom's Ferment* (Minneapolis, 1944), p. 259.

Within a month it was decided that the school should open as early in 1830 as possible. A special property tax of six and one-half cents per hundred dollars, the sixteenth section fund, the Masonic Hall fund, and private subscriptions and donations would finance it. Jesse H. Posey, a local boy, was chosen as teacher, and the Masonic Hall was to be prepared for use as a schoolroom. Funds were voted for the erection of a "necessary" behind the hall.[20]

Later, as a trustee of the University of Alabama, Birney worked on a committee which drew up a plan to admit from the different counties, on the basis of white population, as many students as the funds would allow, free of charge or expense. This plan, "embracing the youth of all classes," was similar to the one Jefferson had proposed for Virginia. Merit was to be decided by competitive examinations. The plan was adopted by the University of Alabama on July 2, 1830.[21]

Birney capitalized on his office as mayor to work for another reform movement, temperance. Over the country in the wake of the Great Revival men were taking the pledge which would reform America by building happy homes and banishing forever the parasites upon society. Like most frontier towns, Huntsville had been wide open. Drinking led to rowdyness and fighting; these, in turn, to increased problems for the city fathers in maintaining law and order. From personal experience Birney was convinced of the evils of alcohol. Once converted to a principle himself, he became impatient with others who could not or would not admit its truth. Consequently, a week after he became mayor, he secured the passage of a city ordinance prohibiting the sale of intoxicating beverages to be drunk on the premises.[22]

Immediately there was opposition. Led by the Huntsville *Democrat*, that portion of the population which objected to this restriction on their private lives prepared to do battle on the issue. Men cannot be coerced by law into doing good, they argued. No law would stop a drunkard, and why should the town deprive itself of the revenue obtained from taxing liquor? Editorials insinuated that bigotry and intolerance were dominating city administration. Birney considered the attacks personal. He stood them for a month and then took an unprecedented step. In

[20] City of Huntsville, Minutes, 1828–1834, pp. 16–17, 97, 105, 107, 114.

[21] Journal of the Proceedings of the Board of Trustees of the University of Alabama at Their First Session . . . 1822, pp. 260–261, Alabama Collections, University of Alabama Library. Hereafter cited as Journal Trustees University of Alabama.

[22] City of Huntsville, Minutes, p. 42.

an open letter to the voters which he sent to be published in the *Democrat*, he announced that a special election would be held on Saturday, September 5, 1829, at which the voters would approve or disapprove his performance in office. If no vote of confidence resulted, he was ready to resign.

This, one must remember, was almost a century before the acceptance of recall as a governmental procedure, yet no one seemed to question its use in this instance or Birney's authority in the matter. The *Democrat* urged the voters to "give him leave to retire"; while the rival Huntsville paper, the *Southern Advocate*, took its stand in support of Birney. The vote was in his favor, and the editor of the *Democrat*, Thomas J. Sumner, tried to save face gracefully by denying that his previous article had been an attack on Birney. "Your character and standing in society are pretty well known," he wrote, "and if others are disposed to accord to you as much as I am, you must be respected as a worthy citizen and a gentleman." [23]

The heated arguments over the sale of liquor evidently stimulated a temperance movement, for within a month a meeting was held to organize the Huntsville Temperance Society. Arthur Hopkins, Birney's law partner, was chosen chairman and permanent president; and a constitution drafted by Birney was adopted. Members pledged themselves not to use intoxicating beverages except for medicinal purposes, nor allow its use in their families, nor provide it in entertaining. Birney was made a member of the Executive Committee, and the following year was elected to the Executive Committee of the Madison County Temperance Society, an outgrowth of the Huntsville society. [24]

There were other reform societies operating in conjunction with the church and going hand in hand with temperance in the pursuit of happiness. Such were the American Bible Society and the American Tract Society. Together they distributed thousands of publications in an effort to convert America. Agents were sent into every community to organize auxiliaries, and each individual joining became a "home missionary." In 1827 Birney was elected corresponding secretary of the Madison County Bible Society, to which position he was re-elected at least three times. Acting on his proposal, the society undertook the

[23] *Democrat,* Sept. 4 and 11, 1829; *Southern Advocate,* Sept. 4 and 11, 1829.
[24] *Southern Advocate,* Oct. 2, 1829, and Sept. 25, 1830.

project of distributing Bibles to all the destitute in Madison County.[25] In 1831 Birney became one of the directors of the state Bible Society.[26] During these same years he was active in the Sunday school movement and in the Tract Society. From April, 1829, to April, 1831, he was vice-president of the Huntsville Sabbath School and served part of the time as one of the directors of the Sunday School Union of North Alabama, Auxiliary to the American Sunday School Union.[27] At the second annual meeting of the Huntsville Auxiliary Tract Society, held in the Presbyterian Church in January, 1829, Birney was elected president and Mrs. Birney one of the solicitors. The main work of this group was the regular distribution of tracts to every family in town.[28]

As president of the Tract Society, Birney again became involved in a controversy stemming out of letters appearing in the *Democrat*. The accusations this time were against the motives and general worthiness of the society, with implications that the Presbyterians were using this means of converting voters to their faith and thereby taking over political control of the United States. Birney, as usual, could not let charges of insincerity go unanswered and took up the gauntlet with readiness and spirit. The duel by letter between Birney and the anonymous "Justin Martyr" which followed ran through several issues, finally degenerating into accusations of a personal nature. "Martyr" referred to Birney as a confused and angry Don Quixote, ready to do combat with any one who differed in opinion from him; while Birney berated "Martyr" for indulging in accusations without taking the responsibility of signing his real name.[29] Birney's sensitiveness to imputations which involved his integrity was to become increasingly apparent in later years when, as the Liberty party candidate for the presidency of the United States, he was thrown into the cauldron of political greed and intrigue.

In 1824 Birney had been approached by representatives of the Cherokee Indians in northern Alabama and Georgia with the request that he consent to be their legal counsel. At the time he turned them

[25] He was elected in 1829, 1830, and 1833. See the *Democrat*, Aug. 21, 1829, Aug. 19, 1830, and Aug. 27, 1833.
[26] *Alabama State Intelligencer*, Jan. 8, 1831.
[27] *Southern Advocate*, April 3, 1829, April 9, 1830, and Sept. 4, 1829.
[28] *Ibid.*, Feb. 5, 1830, Feb. 12, 1831, and Jan. 28, 1832; *Democrat*, Jan. 23, 1829.
[29] *Democrat*, April 9, 16, 23, and 30, and May 7, 1830.

down. After his conversion this bothered him. Could he, in good conscience, refuse to help this long-suffering people? The honest answer was that he could not, and so, in 1826, he accepted. Prejudice against the Indians was violent, and popular opinion was clamoring for the opening of their valuable lands to white settlement and the removal of the Indians to lands west of the Mississippi. Both Georgia and Alabama moved to extend state jurisdiction over the Indian territory, but the Cherokee Nation insisted on its independence. They did not want to move. They were a settled, Christian, agricultural people with rich cotton fields and productive orchards. With the help of missionaries they were establishing schools; and in 1828 they began publishing their own newspaper, the *Cherokee Phoenix*, at New Echota, Georgia. Some of the nation's chiefs were men with college educations.

Once in the arena, Birney fought earnestly for the Indian cause, supporting their refusal "to recognize the assumption of usurped power, unfounded . . . in Justice, either natural or political, and at the same time in open violation of plighted faith and conventional stipulations." The justice being meted out by the Georgia courts, wrote one of the Cherokee chiefs to Birney, did not come up to his idea of justice: "It might for a *Georgian*, but not for an Indian." [30] The question of Georgia's right to extend her jurisdiction over the Cherokee Nation finally reached the United States Supreme Court in 1832 in the case of *Worcester* v. *Georgia*.

Worcester, a white missionary, had been arrested, along with several others, for remaining in Cherokee territory without permission from the state of Georgia. The case was taken to the Supreme Court on a writ of error with the purpose of testing the Georgia law. Chief Justice Marshall handed down the opinion of the Court in favor of the Indians. Georgia's laws, it concluded, had no jurisdiction over the Cherokee Nation. The matter did not end there, however, since the Supreme Court adjourned without taking any action to enforce its decision, and President Jackson, with his frontiersman's philosophy that the only good Indian was a dead Indian, refused to take any.

Birney felt that the trouble between the Cherokees and Georgia and Jackson's refusal to co-operate with the Supreme Court threatened the

[30] Birney to C. C. Clay, April 26, 1832; Richard Fields to Birney, Feb. 18, and Sept. 13, 1832, Birney Papers.

Union. He was practical enough to see that might would make right on the question of Indian removal, but he thought that the desired end could be accomplished by persuasion rather than by force if someone in whom the Cherokees had confidence were appointed to deal with them. Undoubtedly he would have liked the opportunity to handle such a negotiation himself. If this compromise were accomplished, the Indians would get a fairer deal, the arrested missionaries could be released, Georgia would still have what she wanted, and the Supreme Court would not be brought into disrespect by having its mandates disobeyed.[31] But Birney's efforts were unavailing. The tragic story of the removal of the Cherokees and their long, hopeless trek beyond the Mississippi fed the smoldering flames of anger within Birney against a government which permitted such oppression.

Beriah Green, in the sketch of Birney's life which he wrote for the campaign of 1844, expressed the opinion that Birney's concern for the slave was a direct outgrowth of his work for the Indians. "He could hardly fail to see," concluded Green, "when the wrong of the Indians had thoroughly aroused him, that the sufferings of the Negro flowed from the same bitter fountain." [32] His sympathies for the Indian and for the slave were allied, but rather than the one being the outgrowth of the other, both stemmed from the same source, that being also the motivation for his participation in so many of the benevolent enterprises of his day. His reawakened interest in the slaves began as early as his work for the Indians. Concern for the slave was implanted in Birney from childhood; his religious conversion stirred the latent seed to life and new growth. That its roots were deeper in him explains why antislavery became the cause for which he was willing to give up home, relatives, profession, wealth, and, if it had been asked of him, life itself.

Birney had always been aware of the evil inherent in slavery; but it took an experience such as his religious conversion to make him feel

---

[31] Birney to C. C. Clay, April 26, 1832, Birney Papers. For a complete account see Ulrich B. Phillips, "Georgia and States Rights: A Study of the Political History of Georgia from the Revolution to the Civil War, with Particular Regard to Federal Relations," in American Historical Association, *Annual Report*, 1901, II, 1–224; Charles Warren, *The Supreme Court in United States History* (Boston, 1932), I, 753–777.

[32] Beriah Green, *op. cit.*, p. 10.

any personal guilt in not doing something about it. Again he had to ask himself the questions: Where can I begin? What can I, as an individual, do against an evil that is so firmly entrenched both economically and socially?

Slavery was firmly established in Alabama. It had been introduced into the region early in the eighteenth century under the French regime. Lieutenant Governor Bienville insisted from the beginning, in his dispatches to the French government, that agriculture could not flourish without Negro workers. By 1712 there were twenty Negroes in what was called the colony of Louisiana, and by 1719 one thousand Africans had been imported. From then on trade in slaves seems to have been fairly regular; and by the end of the French period the number continued to increase both by trade directly from Africa and by influx of settlers from the Atlantic seaboard colonies who brought along their slaves. There was a decided increase during the Revolutionary War, when many Tory families of Georgia, South Carolina, and Virginia migrated westward. The census showed that in 1816 the Alabama Territory contained 19,513 whites and 8,832 blacks.[33] As the black population increased proportionately faster than the white, by 1832 they were almost equal. In some counties the slave population outnumbered the free.

In the summer of 1826, while Birney was turning over in his mind the question of what he should do for the cause of the slave, he chanced to come across a copy of a periodical called the *African Repository and Colonial Journal*, began to read, and was struck with the thought that in its message lay an answer for him.[34] The *African Repository* was the publication of the American Colonization Society, which had as its aim the colonizing of the free colored people of the United States in the newly established colony of Liberia, West Africa. The society had been organized as a result of a meeting in Washington, D.C., that opened on December 16, 1816. The Rev. Robert Finley of New Jersey was largely responsible for the details of organization, but the society numbered among its members such prominent men as William H. Crawford, Henry Clay, John Taylor of Caroline County, Andrew Jackson,

---

[33] Albert J. Pickett, *History of Alabama*, I, 200, 211, 254; James Benson Sellers, *Slavery in Alabama* (University, 1950), pp. 1–10, 17.

[34] James G. Birney, *Letter on Colonization, Addressed to the Rev. Thornton J. Mills, Corresponding Secretary of the Kentucky Colonization Society* (New York, 1834), p. 4.

Francis Scott Key, and Daniel Webster.[35] It was intended to be national in scope with no restrictions on membership.

To some it was a benevolent and philanthropic enterprise to help free Negroes, who were denied the society of whites and the legal status of free persons but were forbidden to associate with the slaves. To others it seemed a practical means of ridding the country, particularly the South, of an undesirable group of people. Not only were free Negroes frequently idle and charges on the public, but they were also a constant reminder to the slave of his own more lowly status. Their mere presence was likely to incite slave insurrections. Another group envisioned the Colonization Society as the ultimate solution to the whole problem of slavery. If freed slaves could be removed rather than remain as an unstable element in the community, masters would be more amenable to the idea of manumission. As more Negroes were freed and sent to Africa the rate of natural increase here would be cut; eventually, and gradually, there would be no slaves left.

The first of these arguments appealed to Birney. No one really wanted free colored people around. The Huntsville aldermen, considering them "a serious evil to the slave population," had laid a five-dollar tax on each new, free, colored person moving into the town. Every male over twenty-one already there must pay an annual two-dollar tax.[36] In addition, Birney saw in the colonization plan "a germ of effort capable of expansion adequate to our largest necessities in the extermination of slavery." He decided to support the society, and his first contribution was a monetary one sent in the summer of 1826. Not satisfied with his own donation, he solicited an additional amount from several of his friends and then persuaded the Presbyterian Church to inaugurate an annual collection for the cause. Every Fourth of July thereafter it was duly taken.[37]

He decided to move in another direction. In December he was going to be in Tuscaloosa to attend the session of the Supreme Court, which would coincide with the session of the state legislature. What would be more opportune than for him to contact some of the members and see if he could find someone to introduce a bill for him? The bill he had in mind would make effective the clause in the state constitution

[35] Early Lee Fox, *The American Colonization Society, 1817–1840* (Baltimore, 1919), pp. 46–51.
[36] City of Huntsville, Minutes, p. 22.   [37] James G. Birney, *op. cit.*, p. 4.

that had empowered the legislature to prohibit the bringing in of slaves to be sold as merchandise.

When Birney arrived in Tuscaloosa in December, the draft of the bill was in his pocket. Not only did he succeed in having it introduced,[38] but, much to his joy, it was passed on January 13, 1827. It provided a penalty of one hundred dollars for each slave brought into the state in violation of the law. The offender was also subject to indictment, with threat of a five-hundred-dollar fine and three months' imprisonment. Citizens could bring in slaves for their own use but could not hire or resell them for two years.

Birney was not deceived into interpreting the passage of this bill as evidence of general antislavery sentiment. It was rather an expression of the growing fear of the rapidly increasing black population, for at the same session a joint resolution was adopted "disapproving certain resolutions of the legislatures of the states of Delaware, Connecticut, Illinois, and Indiana, concurring with a resolution of the state of Ohio, proposing the emancipation of slaves, and a resolution of the legislature of New Jersey, recommending a system of foreign colonization." The subject, the Alabama resolution went on to say, was one in which the slave states alone possessed an interest, and interference by the nonslaveholding states was not only impolitic but incompatible with states' rights.[39]

Another avenue for action occurred to Birney—the Masonic organization. Although he had not been an active Mason in Alabama, his Kentucky membership was still good. When he went to Danville for a visit in February, 1827, he went armed with a resolution against the slave trade for which he intended to try to get the backing of the Masonic lodge there:

Whereas the Commerce in Slaves, carried on by importation to this State from other slave-holding States, conflicts with those feelings of benevolence and philanthropy, which it is the duty of every Mason to cherish and inculcate; and is also in direct violation of the laws of the state in which we live; which every worthy Mason is bound to respect and obey, *Therefore Resolved,* as the

[38] William Birney, *op. cit.,* p. 56; Stephen B. Weeks, "Anti-Slavery Sentiment in the South; with Unpublished Letters from John Stuart Mill and Mrs. Stowe," in Southern History Association, *Publications,* II (1898), no. 2, pp. 87–130.

[39] *Acts 8th Annual Sess. General Assembly Alabama [1826]* (Tuscaloosa, 1827).

opinion of this Lodge, that said Commerce is inconsistent with the principles of Free and Accepted Ancient York Masonry, and ought to be discountenanced by every member of the Fraternity.

Again success crowned his efforts. The resolution was passed and published with the request that it be viewed by the Grand Lodge of Kentucky. More than that, a petition was addressed to the state legislature asking an end to importation of slaves into the state unless brought by immigrants.[40]

It was on this visit to Kentucky that Birney began to be aware of a coolness in some of his family relationships. There were indications of disapproval of the new role he was assuming and of his open criticism of a cousin by marriage, Governor Ninian Edwards of Illinois, who had failed to take a stand against slavery when it became a major issue in the question of calling a constitutional convention in Illinois in 1824. Birney contrasted Edwards' lack of action with that of former Governor Coles, who had taken a strong antislavery position.

Yet Birney continued to speak out. In October, 1829, he was invited for the second time, as an honorary member of the Greene Academy Cliosophic Society, to give the Exhibition Day address.[41] It was a big occasion for the school and for the town. Trustees, parents, faculty, and students assembled in all their dignity. It was an era of oratory. The speaker was chosen as much on the basis of his reputation for polished phrases and dramatic delivery as for the thoughts he would leave behind him; but this time Birney decided he would insert what he hoped would be a provocative idea into the midst of the usual patriotic platitudes and well-worn advice. So, when asking the students the rhetorical question, "Do you wish for illustrious names to rouse you up to noble action?" instead of pointing to Washington and Jefferson, or even Madison and Clay, as might have been expected, the answer came: "Go to the Gardiners, the Wilberforces, the Clarksons. . . ." Did the boys get the allusion? Was he being a visionary to think it might do any good to name English abolitionists as examples for young Southerners to emulate? Birney was not to have his answer to that

---

[40] *The Genius of Universal Emancipation* (Baltimore), Nov. 24, 1827, and Jan. 12, 1828.

[41] Committee of the Green Cliosophic Society to Birney, June 13 and June 23, 1828, Birney Papers; *Southern Advocate,* Oct. 9, 1829.

question until many years later, when William Allan, one of the boys who listened to his address that morning, left the South and became an effective worker in the crusade against slavery.

Late in 1829 Birney received a letter from his old Princeton tutor, Philip Lindsley. It was an introduction for Josiah F. Polk, an agent of the American Colonization Society, who was traveling through the West for the purpose of organizing auxiliaries.[42] By the time Polk arrived, Birney had already laid the groundwork. Several interested citizens had been consulted, and arrangements had been made for a meeting at the Presbyterian Church on January 2, 1830. Polk delivered his talk explaining the objectives of the society, and Birney gave a supporting address, with the result that the Madison County Colonization Society was formed. It included as members, according to Birney's opinion, "the very best materials the place afforded." Dr. S. M. Watkins was elected president; vice-presidents were William I. Adair, A. G. Vaughan, and Arthur Hopkins; secretary, C. R. Clifton; treasurer, John Martin; and managers, Dr. R. L. Fearn, Dr. D. M. Wharton, Thomas J. Sumner, and James G. Birney.[43] Birney was much encouraged by its auspicious beginning, which he attributed to the "unusual concentration of intelligence" among the citizens of Huntsville, as well as to the fact that it was a territory in which the blacks outnumbered the whites.[44]

Birney threw himself enthusiastically into the promotion of the new society, while within his mind the larger problems of the slave system continued to revolve. The evil to the slave himself was easily apparent, but were not the evil effects on the master race just as bad? While some masters felt their obligations to the slave, others became arrogant and cruel in possession of complete power over other men's bodies. What of its effects on morals, particularly of the young men? The number of mulattoes in the population was silent testimony in answer to that question. Birney had his own sons to think of. James,

[42] Philip Lindsley to Birney, Dec. 25, 1829, Birney Papers. William Birney says Polk had a letter of introduction from Henry Clay. This may have been in addition to the one from Lindsley.

[43] *Democrat,* Jan. 22, 1830. The report to the *African Repository* has some changes in officers. It includes Dr. Thomas Fearn as one of the vice-presidents and Samuel Morgan as one of the managers. *African Repository and Colonial Journal,* VI (August, 1830), p. 179.

[44] James G. Birney, *op. cit.,* p. 5.

Jr., was already thirteen and showing signs of a domineering tempera-ment. William, Dion, David, and the baby, Arthur, would be growing up. Perhaps it was his duty to take them to a free state, to remove them from contamination with this evil.

While turning over such possibilities in his mind, Birney was given an opportunity to visit the northern states on a mission for the Trustees of the University of Alabama. This would give him a chance to talk to some Northerners and perhaps to clarify his own views or answer some of the questions which were tormenting him.

Birney's official mission in the North was to scout for professors for the university. Almost as soon as Alabama became a state, her leading men had considered establishing a state university. An act authorizing its establishment passed the legislature on December 18, 1821, but the decade was nearly over before definite steps were taken to provide a building and a faculty. The trustees, at a meeting early in 1829, ap-pointed a committee, which included Dr. Thomas Fearn of Huntsville, to take steps toward the selection of professors and tutors and to re-port at the next annual meeting. The choices made included Dr. Philip Lindsley, then president of the University of Tennessee, for moral philosophy; Dr. John F. Wallis, natural history and chemistry; Dr. Gurdon Saltonstall, mathematics; and the Rev. William Hooper, ancient languages.[45] Dr. Lindsley and the Rev. Mr. Hooper, however, declined the appointments. Meanwhile, Thomas Fearn resigned his position as trustee from the fifth judicial circuit, and Birney was elected by the state legislature on January 20, 1830, to succeed him.[46]

On June 28 Governor Moore, as president of the Board of Trustees, called a special session to hasten progress and to consider, among other things, the filling of the vacancies left by Lindsley and Hooper. The result was a resolution

that an agent be appointed to collect and lay before the Board at their next meeting all the information which he can procure as to the qualifications of persons who may be willing to accept of professors of Languages, etc. and

[45] *Democrat,* March 13, 1829, and Jan. 1, 1830; Journal Trustees University of Alabama, p. 236.

[46] For some unknown reason Birney's name is not included in the list of trustees in either the *Historical Catalog* of 1870 or in Palmer's *Register* of 1901. See *Southern Advocate,* July 10, 1830, and *Journal of the Senate . . . Alabama . . . 1829* (Tus-caloosa, 1830), p. 210.

President of the faculty of the University of Alabama, and to accomplish such object the agent be authorized to visit any part of the United States, and shall receive an adequate compensation for his services.

The next day Birney was unanimously chosen as the agent. His compensation was nine hundred dollars.[47]

The choice was a good one. Birney's positions as a trustee of Greene Academy and of Centre College had given him experience in the hiring of teachers. Moreover, he had personal acquaintances and contacts in the East who could introduce him to the right people. In addition to hiring faculty members for the university, he was commissioned to find teachers for a new female seminary which was to be established in Huntsville and for which he was also to be a trustee.

It was early August when Birney set out from Huntsville bound for Philadelphia. Despite the serious problems on his mind and his business responsibilities, he anticipated a pleasant and exciting trip. It was over fifteen years since he had left Philadelphia as an unfledged lawyer. Now he was returning a well-known one, prosperous, and on an important professional mission for his state. In his portfolio were letters of introduction from Governor Gabriel Moore and from Henry Clay.

He arrived early in the morning of August 31.[48] The old streets were still familiar despite the new shops and new names he saw as he drove along, and the same landmarks stood out against the sky. But there was little time to reminisce, with four appointments to be met that morning before he was to see his old friend, George Mifflin Dallas, in the afternoon. Dallas had gone to Russia as secretary to Albert Gallatin in 1813 and on his return had become counsel for the United States Bank. Politically their paths had diverged, for Dallas was one of the most vigorous pro-Jackson men in Pennsylvania.

The meeting was cordial, and in the evening Dallas took Birney to the home of Dr. Joseph Ingersoll, who would be able to make recommendations to Birney. There was little time for the two old friends to visit, however, as Birney's three days in Philadelphia were filled with interviews in the mornings, afternoons, and even evenings. The only

[47] Journal Trustees University of Alabama, pp. 246, 259, 266–272; Ordinances and Resolutions of the Board of Trustees of the University of Alabama, p. 92; Papers of Gabriel Moore, Governors' Letters, Alabama Collection, University of Alabama Library.

[48] Diary of James G. Birney, 1830, entries Aug. 31–Oct. 1, Birney Collection.

sight-seeing he could do was incidental to his business calls. On one point, however, he decided to indulge his own interest in scientific advances by going to see a solar microscope and also the new locomotive engine on display.

Birney had arrived in Philadelphia on Tuesday. On Friday morning he was up at dawn to catch the six o'clock steamboat upriver on his way to Princeton. The company of James Brown, recent ambassador to Paris, made the trip pass quickly. They landed three or four miles above Bristol, from where it was but a short trip by stage to Princeton. Immediately after taking his luggage to Joline's Tavern, Birney talked to members of the faculty. Among those he met was Professor John MacLean, son of the John MacLean who had been on the faculty during his own student days.

But again there was little time to dwell on the old days and the old escapades. His one day at Princeton, filled with interviews, went all too quickly. Early on Saturday morning he left for New Brunswick to make inquiries at Rutgers College, with but a bit of time out to call on an old college friend, George Wood, who had become one of the most distinguished lawyers in New Jersey. Believing that Sunday traveling was breaking the Sabbath, Birney remained in New Brunswick over Sunday, spending the day hearing sermons—one in the morning at the Presbyterian Church, one in the afternoon at the college, also Presbyterian, and another in the evening at the Episcopal Church. He had a few appointments on Monday morning, and then he was off to New York City, where he arrived after dark and found lodging at the American Hotel.

There he had another busy three days, making the rounds of book-sellers to inquire on what terms they would supply a library for the university and interviewing people at Columbia College. Instead of using his one free afternoon for sight-seeing, he paid a visit to a New York court. By Friday, September 10, he was on his way to New Haven. The all-day boat trip was his only chance to relax before the next round of interviews and official calls. During the next two days he called on President Jeremiah Day of Yale, visited the Andrews Female School, took tea at Professor Nathaniel Taylor's, and saw his cousins, Isaac and Thomas Reed. This Sunday he heard three more sermons, one of them by the Rev. Leonard Bacon, whom he found "a very superior man."

The next day's interviews in Hartford brought him his first success. At Miss Catherine Beecher's school he found three young ladies who seemed "interesting and well behaved," "plain" and "unpretending," besides being willing to venture to far-off Alabama. Although Dr. Fearn, whom Birney wrote to consult, wondered if they were not very young, he supposed that being from the North they had "attained settled habits and dignity of manner earlier than the Southern ladies." The Misses Brown, Baldwin, and Southmayd were, accordingly, hired to teach at the Huntsville Female Academy.[49]

Birney's trip from Hartford to Boston was made by way of Northampton, where he saw Solomon Stoddard, who declined the position of professor of languages. He stopped at Amherst, also, but failed to find Dr. Heman Humphrey at home. It was Friday, September 17, when he arrived at the Tremont House in Boston. His hopes to persuade Dr. Wisner to move to Alabama were disappointed, but he was given other names by Dr. Wisner, Dr. Evarts, and Dr. George Ticknor, of Harvard. Among them was that of a nephew of Daniel Webster; so Birney called on the latter also, presenting a letter of introduction from Dr. Chapman in Philadelphia. At Harvard Birney delivered a letter from Henry Clay to President Josiah Quincy, who took time out from his duties to conduct Birney personally on a tour of the Harvard library, then containing thirty thousand volumes.

Sunday in Boston was a high light of the trip for Birney, for he had a chance to hear both William Ellery Channing and Lyman Beecher preach. Channing was disappointing. He fell below Birney's expectations "in everything but in the *finish* of his Essay, for it could scarcely be called a sermon." Neither was Beecher all he had anticipated, for his manner was "not good, tho' sometimes impressive." Again he heard a third sermon, this time in a Baptist church, perhaps to counteract the "essays" of the morning.

On Tuesday, September 21, Birney accompanied Dr. Evarts and Dr. Beecher to commencement exercises at Andover, and from there he went back to Hartford via Springfield, trying, but failing, to see Dr. Wilbur Fisk on the way. Birney was now retracing his steps. In New Haven, and again in New York, he tried to convince Theodore Woolsey that Alabama held a promising future for him. Woolsey was to become president of Yale instead. After a side trip to West Point to visit his

[49] Thomas Fearn to Birney, Oct. 19, 1830, Birney Papers; *Democrat*, Dec. 30, 1830.

nephew, Humphrey Marshall,[50] Birney returned to Philadelphia, via Princeton again, having made the complete circuit in exactly a month. Before setting out for the West and home, he had a farewell dinner with George Dallas.

After stopping in Kentucky on his way home,[51] Birney was back in Alabama and ready to give his report at the November meeting of the Board of Trustees. In addition to the men he had interviewed in the Northeast, he had letters from Henry Tutwiler, at the University of Virginia, D. Veuve, at the University of Louisiana, and a rather colorful character, J. Lakanal, a French regicide and member of Napoleon's Department of Education, who was now president of the College of New Orleans.[52] Birney's first choice for the presidency was still Philip Lindsley, but if Lindsley could not be persuaded to accept, Alva Woods, then president of Transylvania, was his second choice. Both men had been highly recommended by the Eastern educators, and Woods was elected. Birney's recommendation for the chair of ancient languages was Theodore Woolsey. On the first two ballots no candidate received a majority, and as the chances of Woolsey's changing his mind were slim, Birney switched his vote to Henry Tutwiler, who was elected.[53]

Tutwiler was an excellent scholar who had studied at the University of Virginia under men brought from England by Jefferson. In fact, Tutwiler had been a friend and frequent guest of Jefferson himself.[54] He was to become a close friend of Birney and agreed wholly with him

[50] Humphrey Marshall was graduated from West Point, raised the first Kentucky cavalry for the Mexican War, in 1849 was elected to Congress as a Whig, in 1852 received an appointment as Commissioner Plenipotentiary to China, and served another term in Congress from 1855 to 1857. In 1861 he tried to preserve peace, but finally joined the Confederate side and became a brigadier general. During the war he had occasion to visit and give aid to his cousin, William Birney, who was a prisoner in Richmond. William Birney to H. B. Adams, May 8, 1891, William Birney Papers, Sidney Lanier Room, Johns Hopkins University.

[51] William Birney says that it was on his way through Kentucky this time that his father organized a gradual emancipation society. I have found no evidence to substantiate any work along this line until 1833.

[52] Henry Tutwiler to Birney, Sept. 27, 1830 and D. Veuve to Birney, Jan. 22, 1831, Birney Papers; J. Lakanal to Birney [n.d.], Trustees Correspondence, University of Alabama Library; John Charles Dawson, *A French Regicide in Alabama 1824–1837* (Tuscaloosa, 1939).

[53] Fearn to Birney, Oct. 19, 1830; Journal Trustees University of Alabama, p. 276.

[54] Thomas C McCorvey, "Henry Tutwiler, and the Influence of the University of Virginia on Education in Alabama," in Alabama Historical Society *Transactions,* V (1904), 83–106.

on the evils of slavery, but he felt that only by remaining in the slave states, rather than removing out of them, could any good be done.

On the long journey home by stage and then on a sluggish river boat down the Ohio, Birney had had time, finally, to assess the results of his trip. He had met and talked to the leading men of America in the fields of education, religion, and politics. He had been impressed. The idea of moving to a free state was attractive to him; but this was not something he could easily do. He would have to think carefully before giving up property, professional practice, and the work he had begun in civic and benevolent enterprises.

Events in the summer of 1831 strengthened Birney's inclination to move from the slave states. On the night of August 21 Nat Turner, a slave preacher at Southampton, Virginia, led a group of fellow slaves in an uprising which resulted in the massacre of fifty-five white people. There was no evidence of a widespread or organized conspiracy, but the uprising aroused fears that such might be the case, and it resulted in a tightening of restraints on both the free colored persons and on slaves and in renewed feeling on the part of many that the blacks, especially those who were free, should be removed from the country as fast as possible.

It was not so much fear of a slave uprising as it was the reaction of the whites that Birney watched with dismay. In Huntsville the papers were full of reports and articles on the insurrection. People talked of little else. A night watch and patrol system was set up, with a ten o'clock curfew for Negroes which was to be strictly enforced. Warnings were issued against any "incendiary" publications, and there were threats of tar and feathers for peddlers who might circulate them. William Lloyd Garrison's *Liberator,* which had been established that year, was especially criticized as a paper designed to incite a rebellion.[55] In December Governor Gayle wrote to the governors of the other Southern states asking co-operation in suppressing incendiary publications and denouncing Arthur Tappan and "the infuriated demons associated with him." [56] News of the insurrection in Jamaica heightened the tension.

---

[55] See especially *Democrat,* Oct. 6, 1831, and *Southern Advocate,* Oct. 15, 1831. William Birney and Weld were wrong in their belief that the *Liberator* was still unknown in Alabama even in the spring of 1832. See William Birney, *op. cit.,* pp. 109–110.

[56] Albert B. Moore, *op. cit.,* I, 248–249.

Birney, along with others, took the opportunity of reintroducing the law of 1827 against importation of slaves which had been repealed in 1829. It passed in January, 1832, but with several amendments. The new bill prohibited the teaching of any colored person, free or slave, to read or write; forbade free Negroes from associating with slaves without the consent of their masters; limited to five the number of male slaves who could assemble at any one place off the plantation where they worked; and provided the death penalty for anyone circulating seditious or incendiary literature.[57]

This reactionary trend drove Birney to despair over the future of the South and crystallized his determination to leave. That autumn he set out to visit Ohio, Indiana, and Illinois with the idea of selecting a place to which to move. Jacksonville, Illinois, was his choice. Besides being attracted by the beauty and fertility of the land, he was pleased with the apparent intelligence of the population and the hopes of a college of which Edward Beecher was to be the president. James, Jr., and William were already enrolled at Centre College, under the care of their grandfather, and were doing very well there; but there were the four younger sons who, he hoped, could be educated in a free state.

Birney's enthusiasm for the new move was only partially dampened by his father's doubts as to its wisdom. The latter's opinion was that the corruption and fraud in both national and state governments had grown so bad that a separation of states was at hand and that blood must flow. In that case, it would make no difference in which state one lived. Birney should finish the year, at least, in Alabama and refrain from public discussions. That year would tell what would happen to the government. Fears of a slave insurrection were rampant in Kentucky, too, and it might be even more dangerous than Alabama, as the slaves were more free to assemble there. Birney made another trip to Illinois the next spring, however, and brought his father around to agreeing that the move might be the best thing he could do for his family to "save all his children from destruction."[58]

Birney returned to Alabama, advertised his property for sale, and began to liquidate his law practice. In the back of his mind was the

[57] William Birney, *op. cit.*, p. 104; *Southern Advocate*, Jan. 28, 1832; *Democrat*, Feb. 9, 1832; *Acts of Alabama, 1827–1832.*

[58] James Birney, Sr., to Birney, Jan. 10, 1832; Agatha Birney to Birney, May 10, 1832; and William Birney to Agatha Birney, July 3, 1832, Birney Papers.

idea that perhaps he should make this more than a physical move; perhaps he should give up the law entirely and give his full time to some work of a more directly religious or benevolent nature. One Sunday morning he heard a sermon by a visiting minister, the Rev. Benjamin Labaree, who was traveling on an assignment from the Committee of Home Missions of the Presbyterian Synod of Ohio for the purpose of recruiting promising young men for the ministry and soliciting financial aid for their education. Birney was much impressed with what he had to say and paused after the service was over to invite Mr. Labaree to call on him the next day.

Mr. Labaree called at his law office. Birney felt that here was someone who would understand his convictions, someone to whom he could confide his hopes, someone who could advise him. He told of his past life, his drinking, his gambling, then of his religious conversion and of how he felt that he wanted to "devote his life to the cause of truth in some moral or religious enterprise." He knew it would mean a pecuniary loss. He showed Labaree his account books. In the last year he had an income of four thousand dollars from his law practice. Of this he had systematically given a tithe to the church; but still he felt a sense of responsibility for doing more. Mr. Labaree was impressed with his sincerity, "well educated, of devoted Christian spirit, of high benevolent purpose, and waiting for work." [59] What form that work should take was not settled in the law office that morning, but it was to be determined by what was to follow in the summer of 1832.

[59] Dwight L. Dumond, ed., *Letters of James Gillespie Birney*, I, 242n.

Chapter IV

"The Cause of

Unhappy Africa"

TO A man of Birney's religious convictions, the events of the summer of 1832 could be interpreted as nothing less than evidence of divine direction in his life. Just when he was pondering the question of giving his full time to some benevolent work, an opportunity suddenly opened before him. In June he received a letter from Ralph R. Gurley, corresponding secretary of the American Colonization Society. The Board of Managers, Gurley wrote, had heard of Birney's "very deep interest in the great objects of their Institution" and hoped that he might consent to accept an agency for the Southwestern district, comprising the states of Alabama, Mississippi, and Louisiana and the Territory of Arkansas. He would receive a salary of one thousand dollars and traveling expenses payable out of the funds raised in the district. This, Gurley recognized, would be a sacrifice for Birney, but, he wrote, "I hope and pray that your duties may allow you, Sir, to engage with all your influence and energy in this great work of humanity and Religion." [1]

Providential as Gurley's offer seemed, the decision Birney faced was not an easy one. Where did his duty lie? To his children? If so, he

[1] Ralph R. Gurley to Birney, June 12, 1832, Birney Papers.

must take them to a free state. But in doing so, would he be running away from the greater responsibility of trying to do something for the slaves? The salary the society offered him was one thousand dollars and traveling expenses, only one-fourth his income from law. Was it right of him to deprive his family of the comforts to which they were accustomed and the opportunities they had been led to expect? Yet, he thought, if this call was of God, not just of man, it was something he must think about, must pray about.

Birney returned home from the session of the circuit court late in June, 1832, to find a message for him from his pastor, the Rev. John Allan. During his absence a young man from Ohio, Theodore Dwight Weld, had come to Huntsville to give lectures on temperance and on manual labor schools. He had come with a letter of introduction to Birney from Benjamin Labaree, by this time a professor in the Manual Labor Academy, Maury County, Tennessee.[2] Not finding Birney at home, Weld had gone to the Allans'. The message was an invitation for Birney to come to dinner at the Allans' to meet Weld.

Weld, who was to become one of the most eloquent orators of the antislavery cause, was at that time only twenty-nine years old, a man of keen intellect as well as oratorical ability, eager to discuss the problem of slavery with men who were slaveholders themselves. Birney was now forty years old, still struggling with the problem of his beliefs and still striving to find a right course for his life. Immediately upon finishing dinner they retired to the parlor to launch into the topic which was on their minds. Weld and the Rev. Mr. Allan had already been talking for a week. Birney requested that they review for him the ground they had covered and the arguments that had been presented up to that time. Weld did so, with Birney inserting questions on different points as he went along. "The manner and spirit in which these questions were put," wrote Weld many years later, "attracted me. They bespoke the utmost candor, a simple, earnest intent in pursuit of truth, a quick conscience, perfect fairness—the traits of a mind that *could not be partisan.*"

Birney went home that evening without committing himself, but he

[2] Professor Leonard Woods Labaree to Betty Fladeland, May 4, 1951. William Birney spells his name Larrabee, quoting from a letter from Weld. This error may have been in the printing, or it may have resulted from the difficulty of reading Weld's handwriting.

asked Weld to dine at his house the next day to continue the discussion. Looking back at those days "through the mists of half a century," Weld wrote to William Birney in 1882: "Your honored father's bearing and spirit in those conversations so strongly moved me that now that I write that aspect of serene right-mindedness is all undimmed."[3] After several days Birney acknowledged his full endorsement of Weld's antislavery position and confided to him that he intended to free his own slaves as soon as provision could be made for them.

Weld, meanwhile, continued to deliver temperance lectures in Huntsville. The *Southern Advocate* commended his "fervid and manly eloquence" and "strong powers of argumentation" which had gained him "the esteem of all." "We doubt not this gentleman will produce great effect upon public sentiment wherever he may have an opportunity of acting upon its intelligence," wrote the editor. "We wish him great success."[4] The *Democrat,* announcing later the receipt of Weld's *Report on Manual Labor in Literary Institutions,* spoke of him as a gentleman "favorably known" in the community, from whose pen Huntsville and Madison County were ready to receive anything with favor and consideration. One wonders, in view of Weld's subsequent antislavery leadership, how often the editors wished to recall the Godspeed they had extended.

Without a doubt, Weld's sincere conviction and earnest enthusiasm were factors influencing Birney's decision to accept the agency of the American Colonization Society; but Birney's mind was not hastily made up. Weld continued to encourage him by letter. In July he wrote from Tennessee: "I can hardly tell you my dear brother how much I am interested in your decision upon the *great question* which you have under consideration. May the Lord direct you to such a result as shall magnify the name and greatly lighten the burden of human woe." By the end of September, Weld was still expressing his concern: "I am ripe in the conviction that if the Colonization Society does not dissipate the horror of darkness which overhangs the southern country, we are undone. Light breaks *in from no other quarter.* I have very little doubt —in fact none at all—about your ultimate determination. May the Lord

[3] William Birney, *James G. Birney and His Times,* pp. 105–110. William Birney to Stuart Weld, April 7, 1884, and William Birney to Theodore Weld, April 7, 1884, in private possession.
[4] *Southern Advocate,* July 14, and Oct. 13, 1832.

guide you into all truth and duty." [5] Henry Tutwiler, at the University of Alabama, added his voice of entreaty, "I hope that you will find sufficient inducements for remaining in Alabama—is there not danger that by removing from the evil we would forget it and thus fail to contribute our influence?" [6]

Birney wrote to Gurley of his dilemma, "The call given by your Society,—to all appearance, *providential,*—added to the earnest resistance of many of my most esteemed religious friends to my project of removing from amongst them, has really staggered me not a little." [7] Before he gave an answer he wanted to study the whole subject, the aims of the society, its operation, and what would be expected of him. If he was to be an agent, he must be possessed of all the facts and have them "so authenticated as to place their genuineness beyond all manner of doubt." He was particularly concerned as to whether the agency would keep him away from his home and family for months at a time. If the district office could be set up in Huntsville, this would be avoided. Gurley agreed and suggested that much of the work could be accomplished by correspondence and through subordinate agents.

Birney's official appointment as an agent was sent at the end of July. Tennessee had been added to his district. The authorization included soliciting and receiving donations, appointing subordinate agents, forming auxiliary societies, and diffusing information on the plans and operations of the society. The authorization was followed by a letter transmitting a resolution of the Board of Managers that "having full confidence in the integrity and intelligence of Mr. Birney," they submitted to his discretion the course he would pursue. [8]

During the summer of 1832 Birney rejected all new professional business so that he could have time to study the subject of colonization and prepare himself for the work ahead. By the time he wrote his official acceptance of the commission on August 23, he was ready with the following plan of operation: (1) The good will of the legislatures should be gained in order to remove the apprehension that the society sought to interfere with property rights. The subject should be fully discussed before these bodies before introducing it among the people

[5] Theodore Weld to Birney, July 24 and Sept. 27, 1832, Birney Papers.

[6] Henry Tutwiler to Birney, Aug. 20, 1832, Birney Papers.

[7] Birney to Gurley, July 12, 1832, American Colonization Society Papers, Manuscript Division, Library of Congress.

[8] Gurley to Birney, July 26, 1832, and Aug. 14, 1832, Birney Papers.

generally. (2) An expedition should be sent to Liberia, in part as an emotional appeal to the people of New Orleans and the planters. "To display before their eyes the solemn act of returning to their sorrowing mother children now rejoicing in hope," it seemed to Birney, would "move hearts of stone and melt them into tears." (3) The state colonization society in Alabama should be revived. Birney proposed to begin operations in Tennessee. He intended to work through the churches and inquired of Gurley where he could find their resolutions on the subject.

As usual, once his decision was made, Birney was both enthusiastic and optimistic. "I cannot but trust, my dear Sir," he wrote to Gurley, "that the Sun of prosperity is about to break out with great warmth and brilliancy upon the cause of unhappy Africa, and that this cause so intimately connected with the progress of Truth and its triumph in the world will be signally blessed." [9] Birney's appointment was publicly endorsed by a letter in the Huntsville *Democrat* signed "Liberia." He had, wrote the author, "a zeal so tempered with frankness, prudence and benevolence of feeling that those most opposed to Colonization will find nothing in his deportment calculated to alarm their fears." [10]

Anderson & Hanna, E. Webb & Co., and T. & J. Kirkman sent Birney passes allowing him to travel free on their boats, the "Mohawk," the "North Alabama," the "Huntsville," and the "Atlantic," as a mark of friendship for him and out of "respect for the motives that induce you to discharge the duties of agent for the Colonization Society." A. H. Gazzam, of Montgomery, extended the same courtesy on his boats; and Caruthers, Hawn & Co., of Tuscaloosa, invited him to travel free on their stage from Montgomery to Tuscaloosa and Huntsville. These offers pleased Birney, especially as he had already expressed the opinion to Gurley that it would be wise for him to travel as befitting a gentleman in good circumstances, otherwise he would be placed in the position of one "rendering thanks for what the community may do, favorable to the Society," rather than one "to receive thanks from the community."

Birney's aim was to give the people information about the Colonization Society and to convince them that in its success lay their safety. He had to disabuse them of the idea that colonization would result in stir-

[9] Birney to Gurley, Aug. 23, 1832, Am. Col. Soc. Papers.
[10] *Democrat*, Oct. 11, 1832.

ring up the slaves to insurrection. He did not write out his addresses, but he jotted down notes containing bits of factual information or points he wanted to raise on little slips of paper which he could conveniently carry in a handy pocket. His own manner of speaking was not the emotional, evangelistic appeal. He presented a logical, rational argument.

By October he was ready to launch out. His first trip was in response to an invitation from George Weller, corresponding secretary of the Tennessee Colonization Society, to attend the group's anniversary meeting in Nashville on October 1. The legislature would be in session at that time, and a memorial could be presented to it. This meeting was followed by invitations to lecture at Winchester, Pulaski, Elkton, and Fayetteville.[11] Birney's optimism ran away with him. He was, therefore, disappointed at seeing no "immediate and visible effect" of his addresses. This must, he concluded, be the result of his own deficiency as a speaker.[12] The truth, although he was not yet aware of it, was that he had already run up against the two major obstacles to the success of the colonization movement in the South: the difficulty of convincing the slaveholders that it was not an abolitionist scheme to deprive them of their property and the objections of the colored people themselves to removing from this country. The Winchester society had promised to raise two hundred dollars if a particular colored family in its community would consent to go to Liberia, but the mother feared it was some trick to reduce them to slavery. Birney hoped the problem could be partially met by printing a report made by two Negroes from Natchez, Gloster Simpson and Archy Moore, who had visited Liberia and planned to emigrate with their families.

One of the practical difficulties Birney faced, as he had in all the reform organizations in which he had a part, was that of raising money. Attempts to get money from the state legislatures met with very limited success, and there was bitter opposition to requests for federal funds. In the last analysis, therefore, it was necessary to depend on voluntary contributions. Gerrit Smith, wealthy philanthropist of western New York, had suggested that each member of the society contribute one hundred dollars annually; but making such a pledge

[11] George Weller to Birney, Sept. 11, 1832; John Goodwin to Birney, Sept. 11, 1832; Dr. Benjamin Carter to Birney, Sept. 17, 1832; and Robert McKinny to Birney, Oct. 25, 1832, Birney Papers; Birney to Gurley, Oct. 13, 1832, Am. Col. Soc. Papers.
[12] Birney to Gurley, Oct. 13, 1832, Am. Col. Soc. Papers.

the basis of membership would drive away most of the society's supporters. It became part of the procedure, consequently, for each agent to take a collection after each lecture or address that he delivered, although such contributions were often so meager they scarcely covered traveling expenses with nothing left over to be used in actually sending emigrants to Liberia.

One of the immediate projects on which Birney began work was the revival of the colonization societies which had stagnated in Alabama. The Madison County society held its anniversary meeting in Huntsville on September 14. It resulted in positive action along the three following lines: a committee was appointed to draft a memorial to the Alabama legislature on the subject of the emancipation laws, a pledge was made to assist any free colored persons who would consent to move to Liberia, and plans were begun to try to obtain contributions on the Gerrit Smith plan. Early in November an auxiliary society was formed in Lauderdale County, with General John Coffee, one of Andrew Jackson's officers, as president.[13]

The state society, organized in 1830, had never been vigorous. The president, A. S. Lipscomb, had resigned, and the managers had never succeeded in getting together.[14] Birney found strong support in T. Nixon Van Dyke and Henry Tutwiler in Tuscaloosa, but the society there never did become very flourishing. Tutwiler gave his full backing to Birney. "I agree with you entirely as to the evils of slavery," he wrote to Birney in August, ". . . it has always been my opinion that almost all of the moral and political evil in our country may be traced to this fruitful source—it exhausts our soil, corrupts our morals and is the chief cause of that diversity of interest which is fast tending to rend asunder our political fabric." By the fall of 1832 Tutwiler admitted that he looked farther than to the colonization of the free blacks but felt the question of emancipation was not yet ripe for agitation. Colonization, for the present, had arguments of both policy and humanity on its side; and Tutwiler hoped to be out of debt within the year and able to contribute one hundred to two hundred dollars annually. He suggested that Birney should work on the people rather than on the legislators, who, being vote conscious, would fall into line once the people were

[13] *Democrat,* Sept. 6 and 13, 1832; J. W. Gillespie to Birney, Nov. 5, 1832, Birney Papers.
[14] T. Nixon Van Dyke to Birney, Nov. 25, 1832, Birney Papers.

aroused. Another need, he felt, was to quiet objections to what many felt
was an expensive agency system. Birney should clear up this misunder-
standing in his lectures, especially since he was such a good example
of one who went into the work at a loss. By January, 1833, however,
Tutwiler despaired that the "office-hunters" of Tuscaloosa would ever
do much and inquired of Birney whether he could become a member of
the Huntsville society. T. Nixon Van Dyke moved to Tennessee that
year, so another of the dependable workers was lost.

The situation in southern Alabama was equally discouraging. After
spending most of November lecturing in the towns of the Tennessee
Valley near Huntsville, Birney went south from Tuscaloosa to Montgomery and Mobile in December.[15] In both places he took special pains
to controvert charges that the society was an organization of Northern
fanatics and that it was producing restlessness among the slaves. After
his first lecture in Mobile, he was encouraged by the signs of success
and approbation of his remarks; but a second and third attempt brought
out such small audiences that he neither took a collection nor attempted
to organize an auxiliary. It was true he had to compete with a celebrated actress who had just arrived in town; but he believed that his
failure was more probably due to a "deadness to all subjects not of a
business character." In addition he felt the cause had been done some
harm by the Rev. Robert Finley, who had been "indiscreet on the subject of slavery."

Birney was convinced by this time that the appeal to Southerners
must be on a selfish basis and that the fact must be stressed that there
was no connection between the objects of the Colonization Society
and abolition. "There must be no bullying, no threatening," he wrote.
"Indeed the opposition of the abolitionists I consider one of the strongest grounds for recommending it to the people of the South." Although
Birney protested he was not despondent, he was discouraged to the
point of questioning whether the agency should be maintained and
whether his contemplated visit to the Louisiana legislature was worth
the effort. His one hope was that the Virginia legislature might take
some action which would stimulate the other states to appropriate

[15] James Gillespie Birney, Memoranda of donations, collections, subscriptions, etc.,
for the American Colonization Society in Tennessee, Alabama, Mississippi, Louisiana
and Arkansas.—Commencing Sep. 15, '32. In private possession. Hereafter referred
to as Account Book.

money to aid expeditions to Liberia. The Tennessee legislature had voted on such a measure just after Birney's visit there in the autumn, but it had failed by one vote.[16]

Birney's hope now lay in the dispatching of an expedition to Liberia as a means of arousing public interest. In all of his travels he had been securing colonists and raising money so that the expedition could be sent out from New Orleans as soon as possible. In November, George C. Light, the agent from Kentucky, was to start the emigrants moving southward from Louisville, and they were to pick up additional recruits at various points on the way to New Orleans. An outbreak of the dreaded cholera resulted in several postponements, but it was finally decided that April 1, 1833, should be the day of a great rendezvous from the West and Southwest.[17] Birney inserted notices in the newspapers and prepared to go to New Orleans to help with the details. Before leaving, he proposed to his own slaves that they join the expedition, but they all refused absolutely to leave.[18]

Although the emigrants were not to meet until April, Birney set out from Huntsville early in February. He knew it would be a slow voyage by river boat, and there were many details for him to settle in New Orleans. It was arranged that a young man from Ohio named Savage was to accompany the group to Liberia as a teacher; but donations of provisions, clothing, spelling books, and Bibles were to be collected, and a vessel had to be secured. Besides arranging for the sailing, Birney had another commission in New Orleans. Judge James Workman, vice-president of the Louisiana Colonization Society, and a William H. Ireland of New Orleans had both recently died, leaving legacies to the Colonization Society. Ireland left $10,000 and freed all his slaves on the condition that they would agree to go to Liberia. Gurley requested that while Birney was in New Orleans he could attempt to make these bequests available for use as soon as possible.[19]

It was late February when Birney arrived. His first move was to call on Judge Alexander Porter, president of the Louisiana State Colonization Society, to whom he had a letter of introduction from Henry Clay.

[16] Birney to Gurley, Dec. 27, 1832, Am. Col. Soc. Papers; Nathan Green to Birney, Nov. 1, 1832, Birney Papers.

[17] George C. Light to Birney, Dec. 10, 1832, Feb. 7 and March 21, 1833, Birney Papers.

[18] William Birney, *op. cit.*, p. 120n.

[19] Gurley to Birney, Feb. 20, 1833, Birney Papers.

It was not a good beginning. Porter was not encouraging about the prospects of the colonization cause in that area and was too timid even to make a public appeal until more friends had been privately won over. The state society had practically disintegrated, and it was with difficulty that Birney found a few men who would consent to try to arrange another meeting of the society to which the public would be invited.

Finally Birney turned to his church connections, and it was arranged that he should speak on a Sunday evening in the First Presbyterian Church, of which the Rev. Theodore Clapp was the pastor. It was the largest church in the city, and Birney was pleased to see a goodly number assembled. But again there was the same letdown as in Mobile. The people listened attentively, seemed to be interested and convinced, but could not be roused into action. They were "most deplorably inert" except on matters of profitable business deals.

Two more attempts were complete failures. Birney was discouraged to the point of distrusting his own capabilities for the work and suggested to Gurley that he should write to some friend in the district to get a confidential opinion on his qualifications for the agency. "If it should turn out," he wrote, "that I am unfit, my pride, I assure you will not be mortified—and as my ruling motive has been to assist in this great enterprize of philanthropy, I would not for a moment stand in the way of its progress." [20]

Having failed to arouse any interest in New Orleans itself and having arrived a month before the emigrants would assemble, Birney found himself with time on his hands. He could not remain idle, so he decided to accept an invitation to attend a meeting of the Mississippi Colonization Society. On March 22 he was in Natchez, and the Board of Directors of the Mississippi society resolved that they would pay over to him all the funds in their treasury, provided that the parent society would agree to transport any free colored people they might wish to send, up to the amount deposited. As a result Birney was given $2,800 on the spot, with a promise of two hundred more from the society and an additional two hundred entered in his account book as a donation "from two ladies." Two speaking engagements had been made for him on Sunday, in the afternoon in the Presbyterian Church and in the evening at the Methodist Church, both of which were well attended.

[20] Birney to Gurley, March 18, 1833, Am. Col. Soc. Papers.

From Natchez Birney rode on horseback to Port Gibson, forty-five miles away, where he delivered an address in the Presbyterian Church. Bad weather prevented much of a turnout, but he received a collection of sixty dollars. His plans included a lecture at Woodville, also, but news that the emigrants were beginning to gather in New Orleans sent him back there. The Woodville society, however, followed the Natchez example and turned over their whole treasury of $160.[21]

Birney got back to find the emigrants beginning to straggle in. They were a pitiful and motley crew, tired already from the long trips they had made from Kentucky, Tennessee, or Missouri. There were young men and women in the prime of their strength; there were old men and old women bowed and worn from years of cotton picking; and half of the group were children under twelve years of age on whom the yoke of slavery had scarcely fallen. Some of them were free colored people, intelligent and experienced in responsibility; others had been freed only on condition that they go to Africa, were unused to taking care of themselves, and needed to be directed in every move. Some came provided with money from their former owners; some were backed by the community they left; others had nothing. Clothes had to be procured for some, medical services provided for others, and all had to be fed while they waited.

They waited—waited through hot, murky days and rainy spring weather, waited with the fear that each day cholera would strike and claim some of them before they sailed. And it did. Two of the women from Tennessee were never to see the promised land. As with the Israelites in the desert, there were murmurings, fears of the unknown, doubts that they were doing right in leaving the old plantation, master and missus, children and friends. Yet, though the days dragged on while they waited for their number to be complete, there was also hope, hope in their new lives as free men in a world they would build for themselves.[22]

[21] John Ker to Birney, March 9, 1833, Birney Papers; Birney, Account Book, entry of April 9, 1833; Edward McGehee to Birney, April 9, 1833, Birney Papers.

[22] The *Democrat*, May 16, 1833, gives the following statistics on the slaves freed to go to Africa. From Kentucky: 32 by the Reverend Richard Bibb, a Baptist minister; 2 by Dr. Blackburn; 3 by Jonathan Beecroft; 6 by Benjamin Johnson of Hillsborough; 4 by the heirs of Dr. Todd of Bourbon Co.; 1 by A. J. Alexander of Franklin County; 3 by James Hood of Henry Co.; 5 by the Reverend J. D. Paxton, Pastor of the Presbyterian Church in Danville; 4 by A. Minor and D. Caldwell of Mercer Co.; 3 by Mr. Powell of Danville; 2 by President Young of Centre College; 7 by Mrs.

Birney, meanwhile, was busy locating a ship that could be chartered. Only two seemed to be available, one of which he dismissed because its owners insisted that space must be reserved for a cargo of tobacco, which Birney feared would be prejudicial to the health of the passengers. The other one was a brig named the *Ajax,* commanded by Captain William H. Taylor, who asked $3,625 to make the trip, provisions excluded. After taking the precaution of having the ship examined by a sea captain who was a colonizationist, Birney hired it. Then began days of purchasing and loading ship stores, medicines, and clothing, besides some of the tools which would be needed once the emigrants landed in Africa. The total expenses, including Birney's own and those of Mr. Savage, amounted to $4,984.54.[23]

At long last all was in readiness for sailing on April 20. It was a stirring scene. There was the last-minute confusion of getting everyone out to the vessel, the stir on board ship to put things in order, the checking to see that everyone was accounted for; and then 150 black faces turned to take their last look at the land of their enslavement, yet, withal, their homeland. Standing on the shore as the boat drifted out of sight down the river, Birney was overcome with emotion, "exalted and soul-stirring emotion," as he wrote to Gurley:

Memory presented to me Africa, "robbed and spoiled"—"weeping for her children—refusing to be comforted"—now I saw her rejoicing at their return;— I thought of the shriek of phrenzy, the stifled groan of death in the slave-ship, —now, I saw the sober joy of the restored and in their countenances the beams of an elevating and glorious hope;—I saw *Avarice* dragging them to our shores, wringing from them cries of despair and tears of blood;—I now saw Benevolence (oh, that it were unmixed) conducting them to their own, their

Robert Wickliffe of Lexington; 12 by William Dudley of Adair Co.; 6 by Cyrus Walker of Adair Co.; and 1 by Jonathan Hobson of Warren Co. From Tennessee: 6 by William Dotson of Athens; 1 by Dr. Schoolfield of Bledsoe Co.; 3 by the Reverend Dr. Hardin, President of the Manual Labor Academy, Maury Co.; 1 by Mr. Toxey of ——, who gave the slave $1,000; 1 by Mr. Goodlow; 10 by George Ewing, Maryville; and 1 by Mr. Eagleton, Murfreesborough. The Lexington *Observer and Reporter,* May 11, 1833, gives in addition: 1 by Dr. B. Roberts and 1 by Cyrus Edwards of Illinois. For other information see Birney to Gurley, April 8 and April 13, 1833, American Colonization Society Papers; Henry S. Geyer to Birney, Nov. 12, 1832, Birney Papers; Birney, Account Book, entry for April 15, 1833; and the Frankfort *Commonwealth,* May 7, 1833.

[23] Birney's Account Book records only $3,588.75 paid to Captain William H. Taylor. Four months' interest was deducted from the whole sum. See entries April 1–15, 1833.

Father's land, drawing from their grateful hearts tears of joy, and thanks and blessings. Sir, Sir, if it be weakness to sympathize with the miserable made happy—to rejoice, even to tears, at the contemplation of this my country's true glory—to feel an overmastering expansion of heart at this practical exhibition of benevolence so like God's, then I am most weak indeed.[24]

It was a bitter disappointment, consequently, to turn back to the apathetic citizens of New Orleans. Birney had hoped that the sailing of the *Ajax* would arouse public sentiment and had gone to great effort to arrange for a public colonization meeting to capitalize on it. Hoping to arouse local responsibility, he had planned to stay in the background while men from the city conducted the meeting, but to get the ball rolling he had formulated resolutions for them to present. The plan failed utterly. The man who was to present the first resolution did not show up, and the others then declined to proceed with theirs.

It was only after the *Ajax* was on her way out to sea that Birney had time to feel the full shock of the news the recent post had brought to him. His five-year-old son, Arthur Hopkins Birney, had been the victim of scarlet fever. Although sick only about one and a half days, he had suffered greatly, Mrs. Birney wrote, but was patient and willing "to die and live with God" if only he could live to see his father first. There had been no funeral and no mourning apparel because Birney disapproved of both; but the Rev. Mr. Allan had come to the house to pray and sing. Agatha was greatly worried, for the epidemic was still raging. She feared she had had a slight attack herself.[25] Fortunately, a boat was going up the river in a few days and Birney could go home to comfort his family.

Alone with his sorrow in a city of strangers and discouraged by the prospects of the colonization cause in that area, Birney's heart was heavy as he waited. Then, just before he was to set off, he received the crushing news that his only daughter, Martha, a lovely child of three and the darling of the family, had been taken by the fever within a month of her brother.[26] Crushed though he was, he sought consolation in his religious faith and was able to find comfort in the philosophy

[24] Birney to Gurley, April 13, 1833, Am. Col. Soc. Papers.
[25] James, Jr., and Agatha Birney to Birney, March 9, 1833. Notice of his death appears in the *Southern Advocate*, March 9, 1833.
[26] Birney to Gerrit Smith, Sept. 13, 1835, Birney Collection; *Southern Advocate*, April 13, 1833.

expressed in Henry Tutwiler's letter of sympathy: "Did the Gospel of Christ contain no other doctrine than that which teaches us that those who are taken from us in early life have made a happy exchange it would be worth all the systems of all the philosophers who ever lived." [27] He felt no bitterness this time as he had at the time of the death of his first daughter.

Birney had need of his religious faith for the homeward trip. River boats were a slow, tedious means of travel at best. This time, while they were sluggishly pushing their way up river, cholera broke out. One after another of the passengers and crew came down with it until the boat was like a hospital ship. The well had to help care for the sick, not knowing when they also would be stricken. Miraculously, Birney escaped without contracting the fever, and in his escape he saw the hand of God. "Yet I was spared," he wrote to Gurley, "and I would trust, for good to my fellow men." [28]

Once Birney was ready to take up the routine of daily life again he put his mind to analyzing what might be the most effective channel for his colonization endeavors. First of all, he had suggestions in regard to sending expeditions to Liberia, and he recommended to Gurley and the parent society a plan that had already been suggested by Judge Joseph Underwood, of Kentucky. It was that the Colonization Society should purchase a tract of land in Hickman County, Kentucky, below the mouth of the Ohio on the Mississippi River, to serve as a permanent gathering place for prospective emigrants. While waiting for expeditions to depart, they could be kept occupied putting up houses, raising some of their supplies for the voyage, and cutting wood which could be sold to pay for their passage. Perhaps even a school might be established to provide some elementary instruction. Regularly scheduled expeditions would facilitate planning, and the morale of the colonists would not be lowered by postponement and indefinite waiting.

Another suggestion was that the Colonization Society stop appealing directly to Congress for aid, because, besides getting no results, they were awakening the fears of the South that Congress might legislate on a problem that the South had determined must remain untouched by national legislation. Instead, the state legislatures should be induced

---

[27] Tutwiler to Birney, May 8, 1833, Birney Papers.
[28] Birney to Gurley, June 29, 1833, Am. Col. Soc. Papers.

to make appropriations, and eventually those bodies might carry the proposition before Congress.[29]

Birney's own next step was to prepare and publish a series of essays which he hoped would explain clearly the objectives of the Colonization Society, allay the Southern fears of abolitionist domination, and influence public opinion to take "intelligent and salutary action." They were printed in the Huntsville *Democrat* with the request that editors throughout the South would reprint them.[30] The editor of the *Democrat*, welcoming the opportunity to "enrich" the paper with original matter from Birney's pen, offered him its columns freely and added his voice to urge other papers to reprint them: "Friends to the colonization or not! do justice; let your readers have the argument." [31]

Birney stressed the fact that colonization, as a means of helping free colored people and slaves manumitted voluntarily, was both patriotic and benevolent in its underlying motives. It would remove from the country a rapidly growing evil; place the free colored people in a situation where no obstacles would debar them from the enjoyment of life, liberty, and the pursuit of happiness; and make these people instrumental in "elevating Africa's millions to the dignity and blessedness of civilization and Christianity." [32] Special care was taken to answer Southern charges and fears that the Colonization Society was dominated by abolitionist ideas. Quite to the contrary, Birney argued, it was organized chiefly by slaveholders for their own benefit. Even if the idea were a Northern one, that was hardly a sufficient basis for its rejection,

[29] Birney to Gurley, April 13 and June 29, 1833, Am. Col. Soc. Papers.

[30] In November, 1832, a letter printed under the heading "The Colonization Society, No. 1," appeared in the *Democrat*. It was signed only "Africanus," but expressed a similar purpose to that of the 1833 essays. A second one under the same pseudonym was published in March, 1833, contrasting the cost of sending white missionaries to Africa with the cheapness of sending colored Christian colonists who would accomplish the same purpose. This, too, was one of Birney's arguments. It is possible that Birney wrote these two early essays, then decided there was need for a more complete treatment of the subject, and wrote the fifteen essays which were published in 1833 under his own name.

[31] Edward C. Betts, in his *Early History of Huntsville, Alabama 1804–1870* (Montgomery, 1916), p. 58, says that Birney began publishing in the *Southern Advocate*, not the *Democrat*, which would hardly have been "the advocate of such heresy." This is an error. The first essay appeared in the *Democrat*, May 16, 1833. They ran first in the *Democrat* until June 6, when the *Advocate* published two at once and so got ahead; but by July 11 again, and from then on, the *Democrat* was first.

[32] *Democrat*, May 16, 1833.

for by the same logic the South would have to give up its cotton gins and its steamboats, both Yankee inventions.

As a matter of fact, Northern abolitionists, rather than continuing to support colonization, were now fiercely attacking it. Birney cited William Lloyd Garrison as as illustration of this point and gave extracts from the speeches of public men of the North who were colonizationists to show that they were also antiabolitionist. Accusations had been made that the Colonization Society was two-faced, saying to the North that it would aid emancipation and to the South that it would make slavery safer by removing an unstable element, the free Negro. There was no intention to disturb property rights or to upset the peace of society, Birney replied, even though many colonizationists might hope for the eventual removal of the evil of slavery.[33]

It is very evident in these essays that Birney was still far from being an abolitionist himself, and in the sixth and seventh numbers he came close to a defense of the Southern position. He attacked the abolitionists' lack of understanding of the Southern fears of the blacks should they be suddenly freed and said that the abolitionists were too far away from the situation to know anything about the true relationship between master and slave and that by their agitation they were riveting the chains of the slave more securely. He accused the abolitionists of talking about abstract rights without considering their practical aspects. The Declaration of Independence, he thought, referred to our rights as a community of individuals, that is, as a society; but a society can, and sometimes must, for its own protection, withhold rights from individuals within it. Birney thought this withholding of rights justifiable if it prevented some greater evil. On this basis, even slavery might continue to exist if its continuance meant less evil to society than its abolition.[34] Birney was still not certain that slavery was a greater evil than sudden emancipation.

In discussing the position of the free colored population in the South, their influence on the slaves, and the dangers of insurrection,[35] Birney

[33] Essays No. III, IV, and V, in the *Democrat*, May 30, June 6, and June 13, 1833; *Southern Advocate*, June 4, June 11, 1833.

[34] Betts was wrong on this point, too. He says, p. 58, that Birney was, in 1833, an "out and out advocate of the total and immediate abolition of slavery." He must never have read Essays VI and VII in the *Democrat*, June 20 and 27, 1833; and in the *Southern Advocate*, June 18 and June 25, 1833.

[35] William Birney is in error on the publication of these essays. He says, p. 128 of

revealed his own disbelief in the doctrine of biological inequality of blacks and whites. The Negro, he asserted, has like desires, emotions, and ambitions to those of a white man. How then, he asked, could the free blacks, with eagerness to improve their lot, support without hatred a government and society which prohibited their improving it by placing on them social and professional restraints? For this reason, in case of insurrection they would side with the slaves rather than with the free whites. A vital factor in the danger of insurrection was the relative increase of blacks over whites in Mississippi and Alabama.

There had been three stages of settlement in the South. First had come the small farmers with their families, then the slaveholders with their slaves. The slaveholder replaced the homestead farmer; and, more than that, the monopoly of the best lands by the large slaveholders was now discouraging other whites with initiative from coming in. It was to be desired that the border states such as Virginia, Maryland, Tennessee, and Kentucky would free themselves of slavery; but if they did so without colonization, there would be a rush to sell the slaves to the lower South, and this would further increase the number of blacks over whites. With the situation so full of potential danger, challenged Birney, "Are you then content, as citizens, or individuals to remain in a condition which is tending uninterruptedly to extremity?"

The essays grew unmistakably stronger in tone. Birney sometimes strategically inserted antislavery arguments; and signs of uneasiness began to be evident in his reading audience. Conscious of this reaction in public opinion, Birney submitted his fifteenth essay to his friends, Arthur Hopkins and Dr. Thomas Fearn. Both advised him not to publish it. It contained what would have been labeled "incendiary matter" had it been written by a Northerner. "Can things be kept stable—can

---

his biography: "The first two or three were copied from the Huntsville 'Democrat' by a great many slave-state papers; but, as the series went on, the number of copying papers fell off; at the seventh number there were none; and the 'Democrat' itself refused the eighth for prudential reasons." All fifteen of them were published by both the *Democrat* and the *Southern Advocate,* and some of the later ones by the *Southern Mercury* (Huntsville). The Lexington *Observer and Reporter* has some of the later ones. See issues of Aug. 3 and Aug. 10, 1833. An editorial in the *Democrat,* July 11, after ten essays had been published, expressed pleasure that so many journals were copying them. Numbers VIII through XV appear in the *Democrat,* July 4, July 11, July 18, July 25, Aug. 1, Aug. 8, and Aug. 15, 1833; in the *Southern Advocate,* July 4, July 9, July 16, July 23, July 30, Aug. 6, Aug. 13, and Aug. 20, 1833; in the *Southern Mercury,* July 10 and Aug. 10, 1833.

the blacks be retained in subjection when an inequality in numbers so great shall be found to exist?" he asked. If the blacks were held in oppressive restraint, as in the West Indies, they revolted; if kindly treated, raised as playmates to the white children, and taught to read, they imbibed ideas of liberty and equality. This developed "the *man* in every nerve and fiber,—with aroused presentiments of better things in reserve, and with the unquenchable hope of *man* of better things to come."

One of the common Southern arguments in defense of slavery was to point to its existence in the great classical civilizations of Greece and Rome. But, argued Birney, the slaves of ancient times were white and could be freed with no public danger and without constituting a separate and degraded class. Even then, "Rome . . . fell at last by the corruption and effeminacy introduced by her system of slavery—and there were in all these republics instances of cruelty in the treatment of them against which humanity revolts—and the whole soul of modern civilization rebels." [36]

Birney accepted the advice of Hopkins and Fearn; he wrote another Number XV for publication. This was prefaced in the *Democrat* of August 15, 1833, by a letter from Birney explaining that he had begun the essays with the determination not to violate public sentiment knowingly. Now he had heard objections, so he would suspend publication until it could be determined whether these objections were representative of public opinion. If so, he would desist. He asked the help of the editors to find out whether the objections represented only the stereotyped opinion "of those whose minds cannot be elevated to feel any interest in matters of large concernment" and who would prefer to see the newspapers full of fairy stories.

Birney discussed the issue in the essay he did publish. He wrote that some had objected to the articles because they might incite the slaves. Birney was convinced that nothing could ever be accomplished for good in a land without free discussion. If the slaves should be temporarily excited, even that would be the lesser of two evils. Postponement would only mean meeting more dreadful consequences later on. He knew of no restlessness of the slaves owing to the discussion of his articles. Instead, they tried to be more obedient in order to increase their own chances of manumission and emigration to Liberia. He

[36] Unpublished manuscript Essay No. XV.

ended on a note of warning: "If there be amongst us a great monster, spread and spreading over the land, whose smallest scale cannot be touched for fear of his ire, then are we in a deplorable situation indeed." [37]

The editor of the *Democrat* expressed regret at Birney's decision to cease publication, stating that he had welcomed discussion in a tolerant, calm manner of a question so vital and that it was not opposition to the discussion of the subject that he feared, but that there would be too much apathy. He believed that Birney, like so many other leaders in matters of public concern, had been forced to do his work without the benefit of the public support he deserved. Now, urged the editor of the *Democrat,* other editors should speedily answer Birney's request for aid in ascertaining public opinion. "Go on faithful servant!" he encouraged, "such has been the first fate of all great enterprises." [38]

While Birney's essays were being published throughout the summer of 1833, he continued to work as an agent. He had intended to work in Tennessee and Kentucky, but the terrible cholera epidemic paralyzed action. People were too afraid of public gatherings to attend meetings or lectures. In Lexington, Kentucky, the death rate rose as high as fifty in one day, and many people fled town. In some places it was impossible for the living to keep up with the dying to the extent of providing individual burial: large trenches had to be dug in which many bodies could be placed at once.[39] News that cholera had followed the *Ajax* to Liberia dampened the enthusiasm of the colored people for another

[37] No. XV, *Democrat,* Aug. 15, 1833; *Southern Advocate,* Aug. 20, 1833.

[38] Once more it is necessary to correct Betts, who, on p. 59, speaks of the "suppression of their continued publication at Huntsville." The editorial discussed above shows clearly that the decision was Birney's, not the publishers'. Betts also assumes that the reason only seven of the essays were published in the *African Repository and Colonial Journal* was because the Society suppressed them. In the *African Repository,* X (1834), 257, is the statement: "Though not concurring in all the views taken by the writer, we were not deterred by that consideration from copying his essays into the *Repository;* and he may feel assured, that the suspension of their publication after the seventh number proceeded only from the casual loss of the subsequent letters. Should he be able to supply them, it will give us great pleasure to complete the series, though, perhaps, at the risk of renewed censure from intelligent friends who had objected to some passages of the republished numbers, as having a PRO-slavery tendency."

[39] Robert Davidson, *History of the Presbyterian Church in the State of Kentucky; With a Preliminary Sketch of the Churches in the Valley of Virginia* (New York, 1841), pp. 334–335; Lexington *Observer and Reporter,* June 22, 1833.

expedition in the fall. Yet Birney did set in motion a plan to have each auxiliary society in Tennessee send a petition to the legislature before its meeting in September, when Birney was scheduled to address that body. Virginia had already taken the step of appropriating money to aid colonization, and he had hopes that Tennessee, Kentucky, and perhaps Alabama would follow suit.[40] Reports from Montgomery, however, indicated that nothing had been done to promote the cause there since Birney left; and the ardor of the people who had then talked of going to Liberia had considerably cooled.[41]

It was a discouraging outlook. On the one hand was this dreadful apathy; on the other hand was the growing sentiment against free discussion of the slavery problem which he had encountered in the publication of his essays. Even in the religious community, those who were not indifferent defended slavery on Biblical grounds. Speaking against slavery as the abolitionists of the North were doing only made the Southerners defend it more. Efforts in the lower South seemed futile. When Birney did get any response, it was by appealing to the slaveholders' selfish motives or by playing on their fears. Perhaps, he thought, it would be a wiser course to concentrate on the border states and save them before they, too, were lost. Besides, if he were to be honest, he could no longer argue publicly from the selfish basis alone. More and more he was becoming convinced that the slave system was not only dangerous but sinful. He confessed to Gurley:

My mind is ill at ease upon the subject of retaining my fellow-creatures in servitude. I cannot, nor do I believe any honest mind can, reconcile the precept "love thy neighbor as thyself" with the purchase of the body of that neighbor and consigning him to a slavery, a perpetual bondage degrading and debasing him in this world and almost excluding him from the happiness of that which is to come.[42]

Throughout the summer of 1833 the idea of concentrating efforts in the border states took root in Birney's mind. His great hope was that Virginia might take the lead in acting on some scheme of emancipation; then the border states of Kentucky and Maryland, at least, would follow. In that case public pressure might become great enough to bring

---

[40] The Virginia Assembly appropriated $18,000 annually for five years. See the *African Repository and Colonial Journal,* IX (1833–1834), 95.

[41] William Sayre to Birney, Aug. 7, 1833, Birney Papers.

[42] Birney to Gurley, Jan. 24, 1833, Am. Col. Soc. Papers.

the whole system "in shivers to the ground." "If Virg'a be not detached from the number of slaveholding states," he wrote in 1833, "the slavery question must inevitably dissolve the Union, and that before very long." [43]

And so, by the autumn of 1833, Birney had once more decided to move. It was a decision on a different basis this time, however. It was true he had to admit the failure of his efforts for colonization in Alabama; but he was not running away from that failure, he was not giving up his work. He was now more than ever determined that it was the work to which he must give his whole effort; but by moving to Kentucky he could make that effort count for more. He would be striking a blow where it would do the most good. It was true that he could work against slavery even if he lived in a free state such as Illinois; but there were several practical factors to favor Kentucky. His father, in ill health since a fall from a horse in 1829, was eager to have his son near him; and Mrs. Birney, whose health had been rather delicate, preferred not "to try so high a latitude." After living so long in the South she was not enthusiastic about adopting "habits and modes of life so different from those to which she had been accustomed." [44]

Again Birney's friends in Alabama tried to dissuade him. Henry Tutwiler tried to promote his candidacy for a professorship in law at the University of Alabama. By then, however, neither political nor professional appointments could tempt Birney. He had set his feet upon the "narrow way" and was determined to follow where it would lead.

In September Mrs. Birney, with the five boys, James, Jr., William, Dion, David, and the year-and-a-half-old baby, George, set out for Danville to return from what Grandfather Birney had always considered "a land of strangers." It was a much different journey from the one Agatha had made as a new bride in 1818. Now the country was settled, woods had given way to farms and towns, there were roads and comfortable inns where the stage stopped for the night. She might have predicted such changes; but she could never have predicted fifteen years ago the changes that had come in her own life. She was leaving behind in Alabama three small graves in the cemetery. She was leaving, also, many dead hopes and ambitions of her early married life. Her

---

[43] Birney to Gurley, Sept. 24, 1833, Am. Col. Soc. Papers.
[44] Birney to Gerrit Smith, Nov. 14, 1834, Birney Collection.

husband had failed as a planter and as a politician; then he had voluntarily given up his prospects in law. Now they were embarked on a course whose end she could not foretell. This time there were no glittering hopes of success and wealth. This time she knew that there would be bitterness, and suffering, and unhappiness.

Birney remained in Huntsville to wind up his business affairs. His real-estate holdings were extensive: they included his residence, office lots, other miscellaneous parcels of land in town, and several quarter sections of land in Madison County. Some of this he sold at a loss in order to liquidate, other portions he was able to sell at a profit. The original cost of his property had been $14,500. He sold it for $17,650,[45] but difficulty in collecting after he left Alabama resulted in substantial loss.

There was also the matter of his slaves to be settled. A few years later Colonel W. L. Stone, editor of the New York *Spectator,* was to make the charge that Birney had been careful to sell his own slaves before he turned abolitionist.[46] This charge gained credence, growing into the story that Birney had been a large slaveholder when he left Alabama and had at that time sold all of his slaves. It was in 1824, however, that he had sold his plantation slaves, two years before his conversion and long before he took an antislavery stand. Since 1824 he had become the owner of a few additional slaves, not, however, for his own profit, but because he was appealed to by these slaves to help them out of their degraded circumstances.

The first case was that of a pious old Methodist whose master, for amusement in fits of drunkenness, would compel him to play tunes of vulgar songs on the fiddle. This violated the old man's religious scruples, and he asked Birney to buy him and his wife. Not long afterwards, desirous of moving to Kentucky, where they had relatives, the old couple asked to be resold to a gentleman they knew who was moving there. To this Birney obligingly agreed, even accepting a pecuniary loss in order to accede to their wishes.

The second instance of his purchasing a slave occurred on the way home from his visit to the free states in the autumn of 1831. As he sat on the porch of an inn in Tennessee one evening, he was startled by the

[45] Madison County Deed Records, Books F, K, L, M, N, O, P, Q, S, and U, 1819–1841, Courthouse, Huntsville, Alabama.

[46] Birney to Col. Stone, in William Birney, *op. cit.,* Appendix D.

cries of a woman and the sound of a whip being wielded in an out-building. Unable to stand the sound, he interfered. A Negro woman, about twenty-five years old, stripped to the waist and tied by her wrists to a joist overhead so that she reached the floor only with her tiptoes, was being beaten by a white woman, the wife of the innkeeper. A small mulatto girl about five years old cowered in a corner. The slave woman, thankful to her benefactor, sought him out later and implored him to buy her and her child to remove them from their misery. The child was hers by the innkeeper, and as a consequence, the outraged wife took every opportunity to wreak her vengeance on the slave and her child. Birney found the master willing to sell and took the two along back to Huntsville.

This woman and her child, together with Michael's family of five, who were his house servants, were the only slaves Birney owned at the time he moved from Alabama. The slave labor for working his second farm in Madison County had been hired. Birney had long contemplated giving his slaves their freedom and had proposed that they might go as colonists to Liberia. All had expressed strong fear and disinclination. Michael had known for several years that he would have his freedom on condition that he control his love for drinking; but Birney was afraid to free him and then have him become a public charge. It was decided that Michael and his family would be taken along to Kentucky. The woman and her child were given the choice of going to Liberia or of being taken to Kentucky, where she would be paid for her past services and manumitted. The woman, however, had formed an attachment for a Negro man in the vicinity of Huntsville and chose to be sold to his master despite Birney's attempts to convince her of the injudiciousness of her decision. The little girl, with her mother's approval, was taken along to Kentucky, given a good common-school education, and taught to be a seamstress.

Birney was not yet an abolitionist when he left Alabama. He was not fully convinced that slavery was a sin which must, therefore, be completely given up. He found himself unable to answer satisfactorily the Southern defense of slavery on Biblical grounds. He was still a colonizationist, though, it is true, he had begun to doubt that colonization could be a final solution to the problem; and he was still of the opinion that in Alabama and Mississippi, where blacks would eventually outnumber the whites, free Negroes did constitute a real problem. Even in 1833 he supported a petition of the Huntsville Colonization Society to the Alabama legislature asking for an appropriation, with the stipulation that emancipation was to be accompanied by colonization.[47] It was necessary for Birney in moving from Alabama to resign his agency for the Colonization Society, but wherever he was, Birney informed Gurley, he would continue to be interested in the cause.[48]

By November, 1833, Birney had settled his business affairs in Alabama and was ready to join his family in his home town of Danville, on land which he had purchased adjoining his father's property. Like Agatha, he realized that there would be some dark days ahead; yet his was a more optimistic nature. Surely in Kentucky there was enough anti-slavery feeling which, if organized, might accomplish great things.

[47] *Democrat*, Oct. 3, 1833.
[48] Birney to Gurley, Sept. 24, 1833, Am. Col. Soc. Papers.

Chapter V

Gradualist to Abolitionist

BIRNEY returned to Kentucky with the great hope that something could be done in the border states which might lead to a solution of the slavery problem and prevent the calamity which must otherwise be inevitable. The prospects seemed good. In the first place, Kentucky had a tradition of comparative liberalism in regard to slavery. Her economic system was not nearly so dependent on it as was that of the cotton-growing region of the deep South, and through the years there had remained a good deal of the antislavery sentiment of the post-Revolutionary era. As an outgrowth of the activities of the antislavery Baptists associated with David Barrow, a Kentucky Abolition Society had been organized in 1808. It had established, in 1822, an antislavery newspaper, the *Abolition Intelligencer,* edited by John Finley Crowe at Shelbyville.[1] After the discontinuance of the *Abolition Intelligencer,* two other papers in the state, the *Western Luminary* at Lexington, and the *Russellville Messenger,*[2] had continued to support plans for gradual emancipation.

[1] Asa Martin, *The Anti-Slavery Movement in Kentucky Prior to 1850* (Ithaca, 1918), pp. 44–46.

[2] A proposed gradual emancipation plan was printed in the Russellville *Messenger* in 1827. Benjamin Lundy reprinted it in his *Genius of Universal Emancipation,* April 14, 21, and 28, 1827.

During the last half of the 1820's the Abolition Society gradually passed out of existence as antislavery sentiment was absorbed into the colonization movement. By 1832 there were thirty-one auxiliary colonization societies in Kentucky,[3] and Birney knew that many of the leaders had strong antislavery leanings. Here, he hoped, he would not have to appeal to the slaveholders' selfish motives, but he could instead discuss the duty of Christians to manumit slaves. On whom could he count for support?

Robert J. Breckinridge had delivered an address to the Kentucky Colonization Society in 1831 that had more of an emancipation than a colonization theme. He had said that hereditary slavery was at odds with the principles of every species of social system and inconsistent with Christianity and had pointed out that ever since the Quakers in Pennsylvania had expressed disapproval of slavery, as early as 1698, there had not ceased to be "men of large and just views" who had pleaded with the country "to wipe from her escutcheon the stain of human tears." In 1831 he had boldly run for re-election to the state legislature on a platform that included antislavery principles.[4] Surely he was a man to be counted on, and the fact that he was of one of Kentucky's illustrious families would give weight to his opinions. There was also Judge Joseph R. Underwood, who, in an address before the Bowling Green Colonization Society on July 4, 1832, pointed not only to the dangers of slavery in case of foreign invasion or insurrection, but also to the unprofitableness of slave labor and the extent to which it promoted indolence in the whites.[5]

Two of the men in whom Birney placed a great deal of hope were the former president and the then president of Centre College, Gideon Blackburn and John C. Young, both Presbyterian ministers. Gideon Blackburn had won a reputation for fearlessness by daring to stand up to Andrew Jackson while serving as his army physician. As a man of God he was equally fearless, and he was an eloquent preacher.

John C. Young had succeeded Blackburn as president in 1830. He

---

[3] Alice Dana Adams, *The Neglected Period of Anti-Slavery in America 1808–1831* (Boston, 1908), p. 106.

[4] Robert J. Breckinridge, *An Address Delivered before the Colonization Society of Kentucky, at Frankfort, on the 6th Day of January, 1831* (Frankfort, 1831); Clement Eaton, *Freedom of Thought in the Old South* (Durham, 1940), pp. 275–276.

[5] Joseph R. Underwood, *Address Delivered before the Colonization Society of Bowlinggreen, on the 4th July, 1832* [n.p., 1832].

had publicly decried the deleterious effects slavery had on education. Not only were the colored people shut out from all benefits of knowledge, but none of the slave states, he felt, had devised an efficient system of education for the whites. Young was to come close to being an abolitionist as time went on and was probably restrained only by the position he held as head of an educational institution in a slave state. In 1835 in his letter to the Rev. Samuel Steele and Samuel Crothers, while arguing for gradual rather than immediate emancipation, he admitted that he did not think "that the danger from the worst kind of emancipation, is as much to be dreaded, as that which threatens us from the continuance of slavery." [6] Writing to Birney some years later he was to express great concern over his duty:

My mind has been perplexed and wavering, at one time fixed in the belief of the duty of remaining as I am, and again strongly inclined to take a position which would involve the necessity of my departure. . . . I believe that no man can hold a public station at the South and engage actively and *directly* in the promotion of abolition.[7]

Another of the men who Birney felt could be depended on was his cousin, John Green. Green had begun sounding out public opinion on the question of gradual emancipation back in 1831, but then the cholera epidemic had taken men's minds off everything else, and organization had not been carried through.[8] Green was an elder in the Presbyterian Church in Danville and might have some influence with the Kentucky synod as well.

Birney was pleased with the situation he found. The men to whom he intended to look for support were ready to welcome him as a colleague in an enterprise they had already begun, the revival of the sentiment for a gradual emancipation society. Almost immediately he was invited to an organizational meeting to be held in Lexington. Hav-

---

[6] *The Fourth Annual Report of the Kentucky Colonization Society, with an Address . . . by Rev. John C. Young* (Frankfort, 1833); John C. Young, "The Doctrine of Immediate Emancipation Unsound," Appendix to *An Address to the Presbyterians of Kentucky Proposing a Plan for the Instruction and Emancipation of Their Slaves* (Newburyport, 1836).

[7] John C. Young to Birney, Aug. 4, 1837, Birney Papers.

[8] *The Genius of Universal Emancipation*, March, April, and May, 1831; Charles Kerr, ed., *History of Kentucky by William Elsey Connelley and E. M. Coulter* (Chicago, 1922), p. 800; James G. Birney, "Prospective Gradual Emancipation," *African Repository and Colonial Journal*, X (April, 1834), 43–46.

ing come to the conclusion that a society based on gradualism was "the strongest that could be brought into action," Birney accepted.[9]

On December 6, 1833, the "Kentucky Society for the Gradual Relief of the State from Slavery" was formed. Its aim was eventual total abolition. Although its founders may not have been willing to admit it, or perhaps did not even know it, its goal was identical with that of the American Anti-Slavery Society. The latter's aim was interpreted by its leaders as future emancipation immediately begun. The Kentuckians even went so far as to say that those who were responsible for continuing slavery were as guilty of injustice as those who had introduced it. Any person could be a member of the society who would pledge to free any slaves born to his slaves when they attained the age of twenty-five. In the case of a female slave, her children were to be freed with her. An address was written by Birney, and signed by John Green as secretary, to accompany the publication of the constitution.[10]

As spokesman for the group, Birney pointed out in the address that slavery had already been condemned by the civilized world, and as it was hastening to its termination in the United States (three-fourths of the voters in Kentucky were not and never would be slaveholders), the group felt that its plan would accomplish that end safely and peaceably. Most of the group were colonizationists but had become convinced that colonization was not enough. First the decision must be made that slavery must cease to exist, "absolutely, unconditionally and irrevocably." Only then would the community feel a common interest in the means, whether colonization or preparation for emancipation here. The society suggested that in the interim the Negroes should be prepared for freedom by an apprenticeship system. This time would

---

[9] Asa Martin and William Birney attribute the revival of the gradual emancipation plan to Birney. Birney's own statements, however, give no indication that he took the initiative. In a manuscript memoranda reviewing the discussion of the slavery question in Kentucky, he says that "a few gentlemen who were determined to go forward," issued the call, and that he became a member at its commencement. To Gurley he wrote that he had been invited to Lexington to help form the society; and in his letter to Colonel Stone he says he assisted at its formation. See Martin, *op. cit.*, p. 69; manuscript memoranda on slavery in Kentucky [ca. 1835], Birney Papers; Birney to Gurley, Dec. 3, 1833, American Colonization Society Papers; and Birney to Col. Stone, in William Birney, *James G. Birney and His Times*, Appendix D.

[10] *Olive Branch*, Extra (Danville, Ky.), Dec. 24, 1833.

also give the whites an opportunity to dispense gradually with the services of slaves. The group admitted that dependence on the slaves for personal services had fostered habits of indolence, extravagance, and pride in the masters. Judge John Boyle, of Mercer County, was invited to become the president of the new society and was favorably considering it when his death occurred in January, 1834. The post was then offered to John J. Crittenden, who had already consented to be a vice-president.[11]

Writing to Gurley after his return from the meeting at Lexington, Birney expressed the doubts that he as well as so many Kentuckians were coming to have about colonization, that it was "impracticable to arouse the South sufficiently to make it the means of ridding us of slavery."[12] Birney was, in fact, moving rapidly toward the position that colonization was not only inadequate but that it was a real impediment to emancipation. As usual, however, he was not ready to express this idea publicly until his mind was completely made up on the question. Unaware of the change in his attitude, the Kentucky Colonization Society proceeded to elect him one of its vice-presidents at its annual meeting in January. Birney was not present at the meeting; he was in Frankfort at the time, hoping for a chance to address the state legislature in the interests of the gradual emancipation society. His attempt to obtain the use of the Hall of Representatives failed; but he did deliver two lectures.[13]

During the early months of 1834 Birney was busy, along with John Green and President Young, giving lectures recommending the Gradual Relief Society. His address delivered in the courthouse at Lexington in

[11] Birney to John J. Crittenden in Mrs. Chapman Coleman, ed., *The Life of John J. Crittenden, with Selections from His Correspondence and Speeches* (Philadelphia, 1873), I, 86–87. This letter was misdated in printing. It should be Feb. 11, 1834, instead of 1836. The date of Judge Boyle's death is incorrectly given as 1835 in both the *Dictionary of American Biography* and the *Biographical Encyclopedia of Kentucky*. See *Commonwealth* (Frankfort), Feb. 4, 1834.

[12] Birney to Gurley, Dec. 11, 1833, American Colonization Society Papers.

[13] Manuscript memoranda on slavery in Kentucky, Birney Papers. Reports conflict as to whether or not Birney attended this colonization meeting. William Birney, *op. cit.*, p. 140, says that he did not and was not notified of his election. A letter in the Cincinnati *Standard* of June 13, 1834, signed only "X," reported that Birney did attend the meeting and made a speech. This was reprinted in the *African Repository*, X (1834), p. 147. His name is not listed as a delegate in the annual report, however, so it seems probable that "X" was confused by the fact that Birney was in Frankfort at the time, but for a different reason.

March was even stronger than the address published with the constitution. He dwelt particularly on the growing sentiment of the civilized world against slavery and pointed to the abolition of the slave trade and to emancipation in the West Indies. Virginia, Maryland, and Kentucky were castigated for supplying the victims for the infamous domestic slave traffic. Slavery, declared Birney, was an impediment to education, hindered scientific development, and degraded the poor white man. If the system continued, slaves would eventually outnumber the free men, and even standing armies could not keep them in subjection. Men were already leaving Kentucky for the free states of Ohio and Illinois to escape the curse of slavery. Colonization, though a valuable auxiliary to emancipation, was not enough. The black man must be "raised in the scale of respectability and improvement" so that he could continue to live in this country.[14]

While still not outwardly opposing colonization and while speaking publicly for gradual emancipation, Birney was becoming more and more convinced that slavery was a sin. Although certain passages in the Bible might be used to rationalize the holding of slaves, no matter how Birney argued within himself he always came in the end to the Golden Rule; and in reading "whatsoever ye would that men should do unto you, do ye even so to them," he was unable to reconcile the system of slavery with the spirit of Christ. Ever since his return to Kentucky, Birney had been reading antislavery literature and studying the progress of the British antislavery movement and the debates in Parliament which led to emancipation in the West Indies. Besides sending to London for the *Anti-Slavery Reporter* he had read the works of the leading British abolitionists, Wilberforce, Clarkson, George Thompson, as well as Charles Stuart, who was Theodore Weld's friend and benefactor. To the English publications he added the current works of several American abolitionists, among them Elizur Wright on the sin of slavery, Beriah Green's *Four Sermons*, and Amos A. Phelps's lectures on slavery, as well as subscriptions to the *Emancipator* and the *New York Evangelist*, a Presbyterian paper with an antislavery viewpoint. All together they marshaled an imposing array of evidence.

It was in the *Emancipator* in the spring of 1834 that the letters from the Lane Seminary students, Theodore Weld among them, appeared.

[14] James G. Birney, "Prospective Gradual Emancipation," *op. cit.*, pp. 43–46.

At Lane the students had become so excited about slavery that for eighteen days running they held debates on the issue of immediatism as opposed to colonization. Students from the South, including William Allan of Huntsville, testified to the cruelties and horrors of slavery, relating incidents which one of their listeners, Harriet Beecher, was later to use in *Uncle Tom's Cabin.* A revival spirit swept the campus; students experienced a personal conviction of the guilt of slavery and were converted to the idea of abolition. Excitement grew so intense that President Lyman Beecher, fearful of repercussions against such radicalism, tried to discipline the students for introducing seditious ideas into the college.

Birney followed the Lane dispute carefully. Here was just the argument that he had been having within himself. The students had gone to the very heart of the matter and were continuing their search for the truth despite the efforts of the college authorities to put them off. Birney resolved that he must go to Lane to talk this thing out.

It was late in the spring of 1834 when he arrived at Walnut Hills, just outside of Cincinnati, and was met by his old friend Theodore Weld. He was not disappointed. The intellectual ferment had not died away. Disciplinary action by the trustees was still pending, and some of the students were already considering withdrawing from Lane unless their freedom of discussion was respected. Weld, one of the leaders in the debates, was as persuasive as Birney had found him in their talks of two years previously. He and the other students took Birney in hand and "expounded unto him the way of God more perfectly." [15] It was not really necessary to convert Birney; he had already advanced far enough in his own thinking so that all that was needed was the encouragement of like-minded men. Before Birney left he confided to Weld that he was ready to abandon colonization.

Birney set out for home persuaded that he must now declare publicly that he was an abolitionist. What would the repercussions be? Could he persuade his friends in the Gradual Relief Society to take this last step along with him? Would he still have the respect of the people among whom he hoped to work, or would they now turn against him? Kentucky was, after all, a slave state. Yet he had to be true to his own conscience, which told him that slavery was sinful. An honest application of this belief could lead to but one conclusion, that it was

[15] W. G. Ballantine, ed., *The Oberlin Jubilee 1833–1883* (Oberlin, 1883), p. 63.

as illogical to recognize the evil of slavery and still continue to be
a slaveholder as it was to repent of a sin and then try to give it up
gradually. He was ready to make a full admission:

The only means of succeeding at all is to apply the *whole truth* to the conscience. If less be done, it will be as inefficient as would be the preaching of
gradual and *partial* repentence toward God. . . . It is the total failure of
gradualism to lay hold of men's consciences, that must render it ineffectual for
the extermination of slavery in our country. . . . Colonization has done more
to rock the conscience of the slaveholder into slumber, and to make this slumber soft and peaceful, than all other causes united.[16]

In May, 1834, Birney resigned his offices in both the Colonization
Society and the Kentucky Society for the Gradual Relief of the State
from Slavery. Rumors as to what his motives were, as well as his own
sincerity, made it imperative that he make known his reasons. To this
end he decided to write an open letter to the Rev. Thornton Mills,
corresponding secretary of the Kentucky Colonization Society. He was
particularly anxious that it be more than a vindication of his personal
actions, that in a larger sense it might strike a blow of "deep and extensive effect" for the antislavery cause.[17] Meanwhile, he had completed preparations for the step which would be his first public testimony of complete conversion, the manumission of the slaves he still
held. Kentucky law required that a bond with surety be posted as
security against their bad conduct or pauperism.

On the morning of June 2 all the members of the Birney household
were assembled.[18] It was a solemn occasion, a scene which Birney
wanted implanted in his sons' minds. James, Jr., and William, now
college youths of seventeen and fifteen, were serious with the importance of being their father's witnesses along with Joshua Fry Bell
and William Miller. Dion, aged eleven, and David, nine, were also old
enough to understand the significance of the proceedings, although
neither of them, on that bright June morning, could foresee that one
day both of them were to lay down their lives for the sake of other
slaves whose masters would not thus voluntarily free them. Only the
baby, George, a toddler of two, was oblivious of the fact that six peo-

[16] Birney to Gerrit Smith, Nov. 14, 1834, Birney Collection.

[17] Weld to Birney, May 28, 1834, Birney Papers.

[18] William Birney, *op. cit.*, p. 139; Mercer County Deed Book 19, p. 32, Mercer
County Courthouse, Harrodsburg, Kentucky.

ple in that room were about to be given gifts of immeasurable price
—their own lives. Michael and his wife were still in the prime of life,
with many years ahead of them as free people; their two daughters,
Mary and Betsy, were almost exactly the ages of the two oldest Birney
boys; and their son, Edwin, was fourteen. All three of the children
were at the ages when the yoke of slavery would have begun to feel
its heaviest. Their carefree childhood was past. To them, even more
than to their parents, this was a triumphant moment. Lastly, there was
the little mulatto girl, now between six and seven, who, more than any
of the others, had a full life of freedom ahead of her, but who was
doomed to carry with her through that life the sound of a whip cutting into flesh, the memory of fear, of horror, alone in a dark corner.

The actual ceremony of manumission took little time. Birney had
already drawn up the deed of emancipation which contained his
confession that slavery was "inconsistent with the Great Truth that all
men are created equal, upon which as I conceive our Republican institutions are founded—as well as with the great rule of benevolence
delivered to us by the Savior Himself that in all things whatsoever ye
would that men should do unto you do ye even so to them." The signatures of the witnesses were affixed, and it was done. All of the former
slaves were to remain with the Birney family on wages. To Michael,
now forty years old, back wages with interest were given for all the
years he had worked as a slave. This sum was eventually used to set
him up in a livery-stable business in Louisville. Edwin was apprenticed to a blacksmith in Ohio, and one of the daughters was found
a place as a housemaid. The little mulatto girl was apprenticed to
Birney until she became of age.

Yet Birney was troubled in his conscience. There was one of his
fellow men to whom he had not made, and seemingly now never could
make, restitution. After the death of Judge Boyle in January, one of his
young Negro men had come to implore Birney to buy him lest the
executors of the estate sell him to a stranger. Birney at first had refused,
saying he would never again buy a slave. The man, however, had
returned to plead with Birney, who finally had relented, with the
understanding that the slave should receive wages to be applied to
earning his freedom, provided his conduct was good. Unfortunately,
he had proved to be "trifling, lazy and troublesome" and had provoked
Birney especially by his harsh manner toward the little mulatto girl.

As a consequence, he had been returned to the Boyle estate. Despite the special circumstances of the situation, this case gave Birney much uneasiness of mind, and he later wrote to try to repurchase the slave to give him his freedom. Unfortunately, he had been sold to a Southern planter. "While most persons would probably have acted as I did, yet I do not seek to justify it," wrote Birney two years later. "The influences which warped and obscured my moral vision I ought to have resisted." [19]

Birney's emancipation of his slaves and his letter to Mills which came out the following month marked him openly as an abolitionist. The letter had been sent to Weld who, together with Professor John Morgan and two Lane students, read it carefully and suggested more emphasis on certain points and editorial changes on others. Weld proposed that it be sent to the *New York Evangelist* to be printed as an extra; but Birney was particularly anxious that it be done by a Kentucky printer so that there could be no cry of connection with radical Northern abolitionists.[20] Consequently, he sent the letter off to Abraham T. Skillman, former editor of the *Western Luminary*, who took it to the current editor, the Reverend John F. Coons. Coons was dubious; he felt it would be imprudent to publish it at the time. Not to be dissuaded, Skillman next tried Clarke and Bryant of the Lexington *Intelligencer*, who promised to consider it. They were both in favor of emancipation but were not yet ready to turn their backs on colonization completely, and Birney had used some strong language in speaking of the Colonization Society. After consideration, however, they consented to print it as an extra, provided they could affix a statement of their own as a preamble. In it they assured the public that they still believed in colonization and regretted the loss of "so efficient and talented" an adherent as James G. Birney, and they affirmed that they were printing his article "by way of a JOB," being in no sense responsible for its content.[21]

Meanwhile, Weld and his colleagues at Lane Seminary had collected

[19] Birney to Col. Stone, in William Birney, *op. cit.*, Appendix D.

[20] James G. Birney, *Letter on Colonization, Addressed to the Rev. Thornton J. Mills, Corresponding Secretary of the Kentucky Colonization Society* (New York, 1834), p. 46; also, Gilbert H. Barnes, *The Anti-Slavery Impulse*, p. 227, n. 13. It was the Garrison group with which Birney did not want to be associated.

[21] Abraham T. Skillman to Birney, June 27 and July 12, 1834, Birney Papers; Lexington *Intelligencer*, Extra, July 22, 1834. William Birney is in error in stating that it was first published in the *Western Luminary*. Clarke later told Henry B. Stanton that he was an abolitionist, but was afraid to come out openly. Weld to Birney, Aug. 7, 1834, Birney Papers.

one hundred dollars to spread one thousand copies of the letter through the West and Southwest. Henry B. Stanton, by whose side Birney was to work for many years in the antislavery cause, was sent to Lexington to take charge of the extras. Each of the students going home from Lane for summer vacation was to be an agent of distribution. William Allan, the son of the Rev. John Allan who had been Birney's pastor in Huntsville, had been elected president of the Lane Anti-Slavery Society. He would carry the letter back to Birney's old friends and acquaintances in northern Alabama. If enough names and addresses could be procured, they had hopes of scattering eight thousand copies throughout the length and breadth of the Mississippi Valley.[22]

The significance of the letter lay not so much in the novelty of Birney's arguments as in the position he held as an individual. Here, for the first time, was a native Southerner, himself a former slaveholder, not of the poor-white, have-not class, but of the aristocracy, and one who had firsthand acquaintance with the workings of the Colonization Society, coming out strongly, directly, and with no reservations against slavery and against colonization. Although his several arguments were not new to Northern abolitionists, many of his readers in the South, especially, were seeing colonization in this new light for the first time.

Birney's arguments can be reduced to two main indictments: (1) the failure of the Colonization Society in practice because of its inadequacy; and (2) its false basis as a philanthropic organization. Aware of the unresponsiveness and apathy in the majority of the population toward the movement, Birney explained, he became convinced that it lacked a basic principle which could excite "to strenuous—to enduring action." Appeals to motives which were "unsound, imperfect, and repugnant" could never bring about a change in men's minds sufficient to extinguish slavery. Colonization left slavery unshaken as a system. It inculcated the principle that although slavery might be wrong in the future, it was not so for the present. This idea had the effect of an opiate, taking men's minds from its sinfulness. Consequently, another of its effects was to paralyze the power of ministers of the Gospel in the South, putting them in a position of defending rather than attacking a system so contrary to the spirit of Christianity. In spite of the inadequacy of colonization, it demanded a monopoly of the country's support; yet, Birney feared, it

[22] Huntingdon Lyman to Birney, July 11, 1834; Weld to Birney, July 14, 1834, Birney Papers.

might be using its influence with state legislatures and other influential associations "to encourage, and not to check, this heartless and grinding oppression." To him it was a strange paradox that our nation, which had before it continually "the purest principles of liberty" and the most unequivocal affirmations of the rights of man, as man, could be so far behind the other nations of the world in the practice of slavery. Its antirepublican tendency was "opposed to the very essence of our government."

In examining the Colonization Society as a philanthropic enterprise, Birney's conclusion was that it had not been in practice what it purported to be in theory. He did not doubt the sincerity of the benevolent motives of the men who founded it, nor did he criticize its aim as stated; but to him it seemed evident that it had degenerated into a scheme for serving the policy and self-interest of the whites rather than continuing to be primarily concerned with the welfare of the blacks. Slaves were often freed only on condition that they go to Liberia; sometimes their consent was gained by unfair pressure, often the same kind of "consent" which Birney had seen extorted from the Indians who moved to the West. In order to "encourage" free colored people to emigrate, more restrictive laws were passed against those who chose to remain. One of the arguments for colonization was that it would be an instrument for Christianizing Africa. If, however, Americans used the colony as a means of getting rid of those colored people who were degraded, vicious, and unhappy, how could we expect them to accomplish such an end?

For seventeen years colonization had been given a trial; it had barely touched the problem of slavery as a whole. Although Birney was willing to concede that many of the evils he pointed out were the fault of slavery, not solely of colonization, yet the latter had *"taken up* and *sustained* the vital principles of slavery by declaring *slavery now is right."* Its leaders were shortsightedly attempting "to convey away the bitter waters, whilst they left in full flow the fountain that was continually renewing them."

It was not to be expected that the American Colonization Society should remain silent after the blow Birney had dealt it. In July the *African Repository* had printed a correction of the rumors that he had withdrawn from the organization and had avowed his opposition to its principles.[23] Now they were in a position of having to correct the correction. In fact, they stated, they had been about to undertake a defense against the imputation that Birney's essays on colonization which he had written in Alabama were too proslavery; but now, "Instead . . . of defending the officer of the Society against his adversaries," they found themselves "in the sudden necessity of defending the Society against the Parthian warfare of the fugitive officer." Yet the task had been undertaken "with a strong feeling of regret at the loss which the cause of Colonization has sustained in the desertion of an adherent conspicuous for official zeal and diligence, and enjoying a high reputation for his literary attainments, moral respectability and ardent piety."

Unable to refute Birney's arguments and fearful of his influence in the future, the Colonization Society resorted to trying to discredit him on the grounds of inconsistency. Outwardly his shift to abolitionism had been sudden, yet their charge that it had been done with no intimation to them can scarcely be sustained in the light of Birney's frequent letters to Ralph R. Gurley expressing despair over the cause of colonization in the South and his growing conviction of the sinfulness of slavery.

Birney's letter to Mills was termed "an accumulation of trite commonplaces against Colonization; in collecting which, a sharp pair of scissors was quite as important as a sharp intellect," and the reviewer attempted to sow the seeds of suspicion as to his reliability:

Palpable as this misrepresentation is, Mr. Birney's character forbids the conclusion that it is wilful [sic]. But it displays such gross inaccuracy, as to require from every reader, whose object is "the advancement of truth," suspicious scrutiny into all the statements and reasonings of a writer who can, in any instance, fall into such "indefensible error."

The final charge was that Birney criticized one plan without putting forward an alternative one. Abolition, they protested, could not be proposed without a method of accomplishing it.[24]

Gerrit Smith added his protests to those of the *African Repository*'s editors. Birney's own eyes, he argued, and rightly, would not have been opened to his present ideas on the subject of slavery had it not been

[23] *African Repository and Colonial Journal*, X (1834), 147.
[24] *Ibid.*, pp. 257–279.

for the Colonization Society. Smith's explanation for Birney's "mistake" about its nature was that his heart had been hardened and his understanding perverted by being a slaveholder himself. Consequently, he had viewed the institution "through the medium of a slaveholder's passions and prejudices and interests," and it was not surprising that he had misinterpreted it.[25] Interestingly enough, Smith was shortly to make the same about-face as Birney.

Birney's old friends in Alabama had yet another interpretation. An editorial in the *Southern Advocate* of August 10, 1834, feared that "the want of regular employment, and a too intense and exclusive devotion to one subject have induced a state of morbid and gloomy sensibility upon the subject of slavery, and kindled and deluded his fancy with strange and visionary projects." [26] Birney's old law partner, Arthur Hopkins, wrote that he had read the publication. Although he did not doubt Birney's sincerity and purity of motive, he saw no reason for withdrawing his own support from the Colonization Society. He suggested that the question might be solved by dispersion if the nonslave states would admit black emigrants from the slave states. He would free his own slaves if he thought he could better their condition by so doing.[27]

In the abolitionist camp Birney's letter was hailed with shouts of joy and sanguine hopes for its success in winning adherents. It reached New York just in time to cheer the Tappan brothers, leading abolitionists in that city, after the antislavery riots early in July. Churches with antislavery ministers had been attacked, the colored people had been intimidated, and Lewis Tappan's house had been ransacked.[28] The latter read Birney's article, he wrote to Weld, "with tears of joy and gratitude," and expressed the decided opinion that the American Anti-Slavery Society should employ Birney to work exclusively in the cause.[29] Elizur Wright, secretary of the American Anti-Slavery Society and one of its outstanding editors, wrote to Weld that he was "electrified by

[25] Gerrit Smith, "Essay on Colonization," *African Repository and Colonial Journal,* XI (1835), 64–67, 105–119.

[26] *Southern Advocate,* Aug. 10, 1834.

[27] A. F. Hopkins to Birney, Aug. 25, 1834, Birney Papers.

[28] Lewis Tappan to Weld, July 10, 1834, in Gilbert H. Barnes and Dwight L. Dumond, eds., *Letters of Theodore Dwight Weld, Angelina Grimké Weld and Sarah Grimké, 1822–1844* (New York, 1934), I, 153–156. Hereafter cited as *Weld-Grimké Letters.*

[29] Weld to Birney, Aug. 25, 1834, Birney Papers.

that noble letter of Birney," which would be the weapon to pierce the heart of slavery "through all its brazen shields." [30] He wrote personally to 110 antislavery societies, urging them to make a "great and simultaneous effort" to circulate the letter.[31] It was hoped that one hundred thousand copies could be printed in the East, with telling effect.

Birney had taken his stand; now he must brace himself for the onslaught.

[30] Elizur Wright to Weld, Aug. 14, 1834, in *Weld-Grimké Letters,* I, 166–167.

[31] Wright to Amos A. Phelps, Aug. 20, 1834, Wright Papers, Manuscript Division, Library of Congress.

Chapter VI

Border State Abolitionist

IT WAS a lonely man who poured out his heart to Weld in the summer of 1834:

I have not one helper—not one from whom I can draw sympathy, or impart joy, on this topic! . . . My nearest friends . . . think it very silly in me to run against the world in a matter that cannot in any way do me any good. . . . Even my own children . . . appear careless and indifferent—if anything, rather disposed to look upon my views as chimerical and visionary. . . . My nearest friends here are of the sort that are always crying out "take care of yourself—don't meddle with other people's affairs—do nothing, say nothing, get along quietly—make money." [1]

It was the cry of a man who had advanced beyond the views of his time and place, the misunderstood radical, the disturber of the peace, who was upsetting the comfortable smugness of the *status quo.* Wherever Birney went, in Danville or in neighboring towns, he had come to expect to be lectured to by old friends, to be "roundly abused" by others. Even groups of ladies accosted him on the street to assail him verbally. There was no chance now that his hope of an appointment to the faculty of Centre College would materialize; parents would

[1] Birney to Weld, July 17, 1834, Birney Collection.

refuse to send their sons to an institution where they might imbibe such dangerous ideas as he held.

In the summer of 1834 when Lewis Green, professor of belles lettres, went to Europe to study, Birney had expected to be named to fill his position. It would have been an appointment in recognition of services as well as of merit. Birney had been an original trustee, had continued in that position even while in Alabama, had sent his sons back for their education, and had been re-elected a trustee when he returned to Kentucky in 1833.[2] Birney had thought he would like college teaching. Moreover, the year's appointment would have enabled him to support his family until the question was settled as to what form his full-time work for the antislavery cause should take. Besides, discussions of slavery and emancipation were already exciting the interest of the Centre students. President Young needed someone to strengthen him; otherwise, Birney feared, instead of encouraging free discussion he would capitulate to the dictates of public opinion, as President Beecher had already done at Lane Seminary. Nonetheless, Birney had insisted that if he did teach at Centre, the trustees must make the appointment in the full knowledge of his abolitionism. As was to be expected, he was not offered the position.[3]

Meanwhile, negotiations were under way between Weld and the group of abolitionists in New York led by the Tappan brothers to decide how Birney could best be used in the service of the American Anti-Slavery Society. Weld was sure that given Birney's Southern background, experience with colonization, maturity, intimate knowledge of the subject, and character, he would be able "to accomplish more, far more, for the termination of the system of slavery and the elevation of the free colored race than any other man in the Union." Weld had two definite plans to suggest: that Birney travel and lecture on slavery, either as an agent of the American Anti-Slavery Society or independently with his salary paid by private arrangement; or that he edit a weekly antislavery newspaper either in Lexington or in Cincinnati. If

[2] Early Correspondence of the Trustees of Centre College, Centre College Library, Danville.

[3] Birney to Weld, July 17, 1834, Birney Collection; *African Repository and Colonial Journal,* XI (1835), 26–28. Professor Howard K. Beale, in his *History of the Freedom of Teaching in American Schools* (New York, 1941), erroneously cites Birney as one of the cases of college dismissals in the slavery controversy. See pp. 146, 149.

Cincinnati were chosen, the Lane students could give considerable help.[4]

Birney had been back in Kentucky less than a year, but already he was beginning to doubt how effectively an abolitionist could work even in one of the border states. The incident at Centre College strengthened his premonition that he might not be able to remain long in Kentucky; for if free discussion were restrained, what hope was left? The thought of leaving, especially after the death that summer of the woman his father had but recently married, worried him; yet he felt that even for him he could not remain "at the cost of having fetters put upon every attempt . . . for the advancement of God's cause." If an agency for the Anti-Slavery Society did not materialize, he would have to go to Illinois, "scuffle along" in his profession, doing what he could as occasions might arise "to advance the kingdom of God on earth." [5]

Birney's pessimism was the result of the first shock of realization of what it meant to be an abolitionist in a slave state, but he soon recovered his fighting spirit. His situation would not be an easy one, but he could not give up. There was work to do; and as long as the possibility of some success remained he had to exhaust that possibility. First he had to try to get those few who supported emancipation to come out openly and to organize their forces. The meeting of the Kentucky Synod of the Presbyterian Church in Danville in October would give him an excellent opportunity to sound out ministerial opinion. Already he had begun to prepare an address to the ministers and elders. This would keep him busy until the matter of an agency for the American Anti-Slavery Society was decided. Elizur Wright was already working to round up men who would be willing "to give the cause the talents and influence of Birney without delay" by subscribing personally to his support. Arthur Tappan was ready to give a part of the yearly $1,500, plus traveling expenses, which Weld had suggested. During the summer, however, so many of the antislavery leaders were absent from New York that no permanent decision could be made. Arthur Tappan and the few who were there were willing to guarantee Birney's support as an agent in Kentucky in the interim.[6]

[4] Weld to Birney, June 19, 1834, Birney Papers.
[5] Birney to Weld, July 17, 1834, Birney Collection.
[6] Elizur Wright to Amos Phelps, Aug. 20, 1834, Wright Papers; Weld to Birney, Sept. 4, 1834, Birney Papers.

Early in September, Weld and Birney decided to meet again to talk over plans of operation. They were to start out on horseback and meet at a point on the Cincinnati Road north of Georgetown, Kentucky. Birney decided this was an excellent chance to sound out the opinions of some of the Presbyterian ministers, and with this in mind he left home on September 10, six days before he was to meet Weld.[7] The first day he rode only to Harrodsburg, where he stayed the night with the Rev. Thomas Cleland, who, however, declared himself against any synodical action on the slavery issue as it would alienate so many women church members whose husbands were slaveholders. The next day was more encouraging. At Salvisa Birney found the Rev. Robert Holman, who was visiting his father there. Birney had known him in Alabama, where he worked as a missionary among the Cherokee Indians. Holman was a slaveowner but had expressed to Birney his concern over the matter. After the two men talked and prayed together for two hours, Birney, "shedding tears of joy" left him, convinced that he would free his four slaves when he got home to Alabama. There were several more stops on the way to Lexington, but Birney was discouraged to find that most of the pastors and elders seemed opposed to any resolution in synod which might disturb slavery. He found that Henry Thompson, of Lane Seminary, who had turned abolitionist and had manumitted his two slaves, was as unpopular in Jessamine County as he himself was getting to be in Mercer County.

Riding the least weary miles into Lexington, Birney determined to act on an idea which had been revolving in his mind—to go to see Henry Clay, who was home from Washington. Clay had spoken out against slavery in 1799; perhaps he could be persuaded to do so again. His popularity and prestige would command a hearing in Kentucky. Acting on his resolution, Birney penned a note to Clay and sent it out to Ashland, his home. The answer to his message did not come until late that evening. Clay had returned home too late to talk to him that night but would be happy to have the pleasure of Mr. Birney's company at breakfast the next morning.

It was a long time since the days of Birney's political activity on Clay's behalf. To meet a hero of one's adolescence after long years of absence was a frightening prospect at best. Birney was well aware of the changes that had taken place in his own thinking and of the extent to which politics and religion had switched places in his scale

[7] See Birney's diary, entries Sept. 10–Sept. 22, 1834, Birney Collection.

of values. But what of Clay? Would he still be the old politician, or would the years have tempered his ambition so that he would not look at everything from the point of its political effectiveness? Could he be expected to support a cause for the sake of the cause? Which arguments would tell with him?

The next morning, September 16, Birney rode out to Ashland, just on the edge of the city, and was greeted by Clay, Mrs. Clay, and one of their sons. Clay, in his fifty-seventh year, was Kentucky's most famous son and one of the men to be reckoned with in the legislative halls of the nation. His suave, affable manner blended well with the quiet beauty of Ashland. Kentucky gentlemen both, neither he nor Birney allowed the subject of their interview to breach the sociability of the breakfast table. There were inquiries about James Birney, Sr., questions of old friends in Danville, and much news to exchange on the years which had intervened since their last meeting. Only when the morning meal was over and they rose from the table did Clay invite Birney into the parlor where they could converse alone.

Birney had indicated in his note the subject that he wanted to discuss. Clay was ready with his answer and did most of the talking for about an hour; but before much of it had passed, Birney knew he had nothing to hope for in the way of support. He was hearing a glib politician rationalize his action, or lack of it, with the same, well-worn excuses. Slavery in Kentucky, Clay protested, was in so mitigated a form that it could scarcely be termed an evil. Direct efforts would but stir up contentions. Men's interests in property rights had been an insurmountable barrier in 1799; now they were even more formidable. One must not rush into things; the question would settle itself as liberal principles gradually pervaded the country. "Look at Robert Breckinridge and John Green," he went on—and here he tipped his political hand, "two gentlemen of great worth, who have lowered themselves in the popular estimation and disqualified themselves for political usefulness by the part they have taken in reference to slavery."

Birney realized there was no point to be gained by further argument. The man talking to him, it was now apparent, was a man with no conscience in the matter, someone who seemed "never to have gone beyond the mere outer bark of the subject." And that outer bark was his own political skin. He did not mention the slave, the right of a man to possess his own body and soul, or even the dangers inherent in the slave system. He spoke only of "political usefulness" and "popular estimation" as factors to be considered. Clay was a man who swam with the popular current, the current which presented a smooth surface to the outward eye, but which hid the deepening chasm underneath it.

This was the last time Clay and Birney were to meet. As Clay shook hands with his departing guest that morning, little did he dream that James Gillespie Birney was one day to stand between him and his highest aspiration, the presidency of the United States.

It was a relief for Birney to catch sight of Weld approaching on horseback from the North and to hear his cheery greeting. The prospect of a long talk with someone who shared his hopes, his own values, was what Birney needed to restore his faith in mankind after his disappointment of the morning. After finding a "quiet house of private entertainment," the two travelers sat down to talk over what would be the best and most effective course for Birney to pursue. It was four o'clock the next afternoon before they had finished, for theirs were two minds which stimulated each other. Birney was much encouraged by Weld's faith. "I have seen in no man," he wrote in his diary that night, "such a rare combination of great intellectual powers with Christian simplicity. He must make a powerful impression on the public mind of this country, if he live ten years."

Weld and Birney had agreed that Birney's first concentrated effort should be to persuade the Presbyterian churches in Kentucky to throw the weight of their influence behind the antislavery movement. Although the Presbyterians were not so numerous in Kentucky as either the Methodists or the Baptists, they numbered among their communicants many of the leading men in the state and in community affairs. If the autumn synod could be persuaded to take a public stand against slavery, the other churches would be disposed to follow suit.

On his way back to Danville, Birney continued to canvass opinions among the ministers, with more encouraging results. The Rev. Simeon Salisbury, in Georgetown, favored action against slavery; Thomas P. Smith, an elder in Paris, to whom Birney had written on the matter early in April, and the Rev. William W. Hall, in Lexington, were also favorably disposed, though not yet ready to forsake colonization entirely. In Georgetown, Birney renewed his acquaintance with an old friend, John Johnson, now a Campbellite preacher, and left him with the assurance that Johnson would emancipate his eight or nine slaves that winter and would impress the duty upon his congregation. At one point on his route home Birney had the pleasure of actually drawing up a deed of emancipation.

When Birney arrived home on the afternoon of September 22, he found young James Allan, brother of William Allan, who had come from Lane Seminary with over three hundred copies of Birney's *Letter to the Churches to the Ministers and Elders of the Presbyterian Churches in Kentucky.* Birney had tried to get the *Western Luminary* to publish it, but again Coons feared its content was "too strong for the times—rather too high wrought a picture of the sin of slavery in the Presbyterian Church." Even President Young's recommendation that it be published was unavailing.[8] It had then been accepted by the *Cincinnati Journal,* where it had been sent accompanied by a letter from Dr. Luke Munsell, of Danville. Birney and his Danville friends were to pay half the cost of printing extras, and the Lane Seminary students would make up the rest.[9]

Birney's indictment of slavery on religious grounds was fourfold: it originated and was maintained by violence utterly at variance with the spirit of the Gospel; it wrested from the members of one group, without offense on their part, the fruits of their toil, which it gave to another group; it stupefied and benumbed the mind and consciences of its victims to the exclusion of knowledge of God or any preparation for life to come; and it bred in those who maintained it indolence, passion, and contempt for their fellow creatures.

Birney tried to answer some of the arguments in the Biblical defense of slavery, concentrating chiefly on the development of society since Biblical times. Men then, he pointed out, had complete authority over women and over their children. A creditor had the power of life and death over his debtor. These practices, however, were no longer accepted in the United States, so why should slavery be? The reason Jesus did not condemn slavery, he thought, was that He did not preach to the Romans, but to the Jews, among whom it was already nearly, if not entirely, extinguished; and because Peter and Paul admonished

[8] MS memoranda on slavery in Kentucky, Birney Papers; Abraham Skillman to Birney, Aug. 25, 1834, Birney Papers.

[9] Birney to Weld, Sept. 2, 1834, Birney Collection; Weld to Birney, Sept. 10, 1834, Birney Papers.

servants to be obedient to their masters, it did not follow that they would approve slavery, nor condone its concomitant evils. Birney also attempted a distinction between the servants of Old Testament days and American Negro slaves.

Birney's challenge to the church was that it had done nothing to meet the argument that slaves were unprepared for freedom. Thirty years before in Kentucky there had been a movement to educate them, but the work had stopped with only a few Sunday schools established. Too many church members said they would be willing to emancipate if everyone else did. It would be as logical to repent from sin on that condition. His arguments ended with a rejection of the fears of amalgamation and of freed slaves seeking vengeance upon their former masters. His conclusion was a plea for ministerial leadership in abolishing slavery. "You may, it is true, be called madmen," he admitted, "but Paul was so called before you. You may be called fanatics, fools, and knaves; but Sharp, Clarkson and Wilberforce were so baptised by the enemies of humanity; you may at first obtain but little honor from men; but you will win an eternal weight of glory from God."

After the first printing of the letter, the Lane students managed to obtain a press and continued to print copies of the part of the *Cincinnati Journal* containing it. These copies were mailed to ministers of all denominations throughout the Mississippi Valley. The Rev. Robert Holman acted as distribution agent in Alabama but reported no reformations from it in that area. Since his return from Kentucky he had already begun to waver in his decision to manumit his own slaves. He feared, as did so many antislavery Southerners, that the act would identify him with the North and nullify his work in the South.[10]

The *Southern Advocate* of October 7, 1834, had its bit to say on this last production of Birney's. It termed his project "wholly incompatible with the security of the whites and the happiness of the blacks themselves," and accused him of not even being revolted by the idea of future amalgamation. The editors claimed that they used to think Cervantes extravagant in making Don Quixote tilt at windmills; but noting Birney's recent activities, they now found Don Quixote's actions credible.

The Presbyterian synod was to meet in Danville early in October. Birney's work all summer had been directed toward that meeting, and

[10] Robert Holman to Birney, Oct. 9, 1834, Birney Papers.

he approached it full of both hope and fear. The "new" and "old" school disputes seemed to be dominating everyone's attention, to the exclusion of slavery as well as other matters. "Christian action will still be hindered by angry dispute," wrote Birney in his diary. "Oh! Lord! let it not be so, but let this branch of the Church shake out this sin from her skirts!" [11] There were few out-and-out abolitionists who could be counted on. At Centre College there were only about fifteen among the students. Professor Buchanan was one in principle and might soon be one in practice. Luke Munsell was, decidedly. Abraham T. Skillman was said to be an abolitionist, but Birney feared he was too timid. The only other men in the state whom he could name were the Rev. Mr. Calvert of Bowling Green; Hervey Woods of Glasgow, who was already preparing to move to a free state; the Rev. Simeon Salisbury of Georgetown; the Rev. Eli N. Sawtell of Louisville; and the Rev. L. W. Cole of Augusta. "And this is the whole number," lamented Birney. "Most of us very obscure—many very young and without influence, to do this mighty work in which we have to meet the strongest prejudices as well as the strongest interests and talents."

On October 6, two days before the synod met, a Presbytery meeting was held in Danville. Birney, a member of the Danville church, was allowed to attend as a spectator. John Green committed himself in favor of a declaration by the synod on the sin of slavery and advocated that the Presbyterians should see that slavery be not continued beyond the present generation. Slavery was not a new issue at the synod meetings. In 1832 the following resolution had been proposed:

That in the view of this Synod, Slavery as it exists within our bounds is a great moral evil, and inconsistent with the word of God. And we do therefore recommend to all our ministers and members who hold slaves, to endeavor to have them instructed in the knowledge of the gospel; and to promote in every peaceable way the interests of the Colonization Society; and to favour all proper measures for gradual voluntary emancipation.

The resolution had not been acted on in 1832, however, but was carried over to the next year, when it had been defeated by a substitute resolution: "Inasmuch as in the judgment of [the] Synod it is inexpedient to come to any decision on the very difficult and delicate question of Slavery, as it exists within our bounds; Therefore *Resolved*, that the

[11] Diary of James G. Birney, entry for Sept. 30, 1834.

whole subject be indefinitely postponed." This motion had been carried by a vote of forty-one to thirty-six.[12] There was sure to be a sharp division at the 1834 meeting.

Birney was on hand when the synod organized, conversing with the members and trying to persuade them to take action.[13] On the second morning John Green presented his resolution and declaration against slavery. Immediately the Rev. J. K. Burch rose to oppose it. President Young, in turn, demolished his arguments. The dispute was under way. Col. Thomas Howard, of Richmond, backed Burch; the Rev. Samuel Lynn, of Springfield, supported Green; and Professor Marshall, of Lexington, though ambiguous in his arguments, was thought to be against the resolution. When the discussion from the floor was finally concluded for the day, it was decided to refer the matter to a special committee. Fortunately for the emancipationists, they secured a majority on the committee, which, the next morning, reported the resolution with but slight alteration. Nonetheless, debate continued in a "tumultuous manner" for another whole day.

On the eleventh the resolution was finally, and triumphantly, passed by an overwhelming vote of fifty-six yeas, seven nays, and eight *non liquet's*, with the added stipulation that each pastor was to read the whole document to his congregation. It declared slavery to be "repugnant to the principles of our holy religion" and its continuance "any longer than is necessary to prepare for its safe and beneficial termination" to be sinful. All Presbyteries, church sessions, and people under their care were to commence immediate preparation for its termination among them. In addition, the synod "would not be understood as excluding those now living [slaves] from the operation of the benevolent principle above recommended," but because of the difficulty of laying down a general rule to cover each individual case, this was left to "the operation of the Christian law of love on the conscience of men." Finally, a committee of ten was appointed for promoting harmony of action which should include the drawing up of a plan for instruction and emancipation. Before adjournment a resolution of support for colonization was also passed.

Joyous over this victory, Birney decided to capitalize on the prevail-

[12] Records of the Synod of Kentucky, Presbyterian Seminary Library, Louisville, V, 50–52.
[13] Diary of James G. Birney, see entries Oct. 6–Oct. 15, 1834.

ing mood by giving a public lecture and obtained permission to speak in the church the evening of the eleventh. He talked for one and three-quarters hours to a "tolerably well filled" church, making, he thought, a favorable impression. Though the synod had not gone so far as he might have wished, yet "good was promoted."

Birney's efforts for emancipation were being waged at home as well as in the community and state. Having freed his own slaves, he was now trying to persuade his father to take the same step. James Birney, Sr., had long recognized the evil of slavery and had favored an anti-slavery clause in the state constitution. He felt, however, that not much could be accomplished until the state took legal action for general emancipation. As he grew older he became more conservative, less inclined to any move which would stir up dissent or disturb the *status quo*. During the summer and autumn of 1834, however, he seemed to be more responsive to his son's ideas and intimated that he might manumit at least some of his slaves. The death of his second wife early in the fall and his considered retirement made this seem even more probable.[14] To his son's disappointment the step was not taken, and when James Birney, Sr., went off to Louisville to live with his daughter for the winter, the son's hopes fell. "My sister," wrote Birney in his diary, "is very far from being an abolitionist, and I fear, she will have considerable influence upon my father's views."

The new arrangement, which necessitated Birney's moving from his small farm back to take care of Woodlawn, embarrassed him on account of the slaves that were left. To add to his mortification, he discovered that before leaving for Louisville his father had promised to give a Negro woman and her four children to a Mrs. Polk, in Danville. Birney wrote to his father, offering to pay Mrs. Polk any sum satisfactory to her instead of giving her the Negroes; but he knew his father's inflexibility in regard to promises too well to entertain much hope of success. "I lament much," confided Birney, "that he had thought proper to leave such a memorial behind him." [15] Birney did arrange to give the slaves wages for their services for the time they were under his control.[16]

[14] Birney to Weld, Sept. 2, 1834, Birney Collection; James Birney, Sr., to Birney, Nov. 27, 1834, Birney Papers.

[15] Diary of James G. Birney, entries Sept. 25–Sept. 30, 1834.

[16] John C. Young to Reverend Samuel Steele and Samuel Crothers, *An Address to the Presbyterians of Kentucky*, Appendix.

There was still another distressing incident in regard to one of his father's slaves. Louisa, a woman on the plantation, had fallen in love and wanted to marry Milo, the slave of Birney's brother-in-law, George C. Thompson. A few days before the marriage was to take place, Thompson refused to consent unless Louisa be sold to him. Otherwise, if Milo were to visit Louisa at the Birneys, he might imbibe the notions about liberty that the Birney slaves were known to have. "I am brought to reflect," wrote Birney, "upon the horrible power which slavery gives to one man over another's happiness. Here, for mere convenience, or from an apprehension that Milo would be impaired in value by hearing something of liberty, two persons young and loving each other are, perhaps forever, separated." Major Thompson used the occasion also to express his frank disapproval of Birney's course in regard to slavery, which, he was sure, could lead only to "unfortunate results." Already, he warned, there was increased insolence and discontent among the blacks around Danville.[17]

By the end of October the news came from the Tappans in New York that Birney could consider his agency as permanent and that four hundred dollars, his first quarter's salary, would be deposited for him.[18] This settled, Birney could proceed to sound out sentiment on organizing an antislavery society and establishing an antislavery newspaper. Dr. Luke Munsell and Professor James Buchanan were already privy to the plan and ready to co-operate. The next step was to write to friends in the surrounding area to ascertain the number of potential subscribers.

The *Olive Branch,* a Danville newspaper, made no objections to another paper being started in town, even one which would advocate emancipation. Its editor announced:

We have understood that our fellow citizen and neighbor, James G. Birney, Esq., has it in contemplation, during the ensuing year, to commence the publication of a Newspaper, dedicated chiefly to the cause of Emancipation. From what he has hitherto written on this subject, we presume he will occupy the ground of duty as well as the policy of the measure. Howmuchsoever we may

---

[17] Diary of James G. Birney, entries for Oct. 17 and 18, 1834; Milo to Louisa Bethley, Oct. 15, 1834, George C. Thompson to Birney, Oct. 18, 1834, Birney Papers. Mrs. Thompson was the sister of Agatha Birney.

[18] Weld to Birney, Oct. 20, 1834, Birney Papers.

differ with him—in some of his main grounds—we are assured of one thing, that whatever cause this gentleman may deem it his duty to support, he will do it with candor, moderation, and Christian feeling.[19]

While ground was being broken for organized effort in Kentucky, Birney was entrusted with another mission, the winning of Gerrit Smith, wealthy philanthropist of western New York, for the antislavery cause. Smith had been an ardent friend of, and contributor to, the American Colonization Society; but word came to Weld that he had been much impressed by Birney's letter to Mills, despite his arguments against it in the *African Repository*. Weld wrote to Birney in October urging that he write a private letter to Smith, whose conversion to abolition would secure "an immense and incalculable influence."

Birney complied, addressing Smith as a colleague because of his interest in the Christian charities of the day.[20] His emphasis, however, was on the failure of the colonization movement. Birney wrote as one who himself had been devoted to colonization but had realized that it was insufficient because it left the conscience of the slaveholder undisturbed. Smith, because of his powerful influence, was helping to continue this very obstacle, Birney argued. On the other hand, if he were to come out publicly for "the great and soul-stirring principle that *man* cannot be made the *property* of man," he could do more for liberty than any one in the country. Smith's response satisfied Birney that he was moving in the right direction. Their correspondence continued, Birney trying to convince Smith to take the step and Weld encouraging Birney to "hold on to him by all means." It was a correspondence which was to result in a lifelong friendship. It was not, however, until after mobs broke up an antislavery convention in Utica in the autumn of 1835 and Smith offered his home as a place to continue the meeting that he came out fully for abolition. Smith was to become one of the most generous contributors to the cause in both time and money. He was indefatigable in writing articles and making speeches, particularly after the movement entered its political phase.

Meanwhile, Birney was busy with the movement of events in Kentucky. In January, 1835, when the legislature met, there was talk that something might be done to amend the constitution on the subject

---

[19] *Olive Branch,* Nov. 1, 1834, quoted in Lexington *Intelligencer,* Nov. 7, 1834.

[20] Weld to Birney, Oct. 20, 1834, and Feb. 16, 1835, Birney Papers; Birney to Gerrit Smith, Nov. 14 and Dec. 30, 1834, Birney Collection.

of slavery. There was also a bill under discussion which would prevent the manumission of slaves unless they were sent out of the state. If found at large after six months, they could be resold as slaves.[21] Birney, believing that "with the political action of political men, and the holy action of religious men, there is . . . no inconsistency that is irreconcilable," decided to go to Frankfort to see what could be done. He found the city changed since his own days as a state legislator; but men's hearts had remained the same. Not one legislator could he find who believed a slave was entitled to his freedom or who would even think of emancipation without compensation. If this was the attitude of the top men of the state, he despaired, what of "the great mass yet to be penetrated by the truth?" [22]

While Birney was in Frankfort, Judge Joseph R. Underwood delivered an address at the annual Colonization Society meeting in which he proposed a scheme for taking four thousand colored people a year out of Kentucky, thus removing them all within fifty years. "Have you any . . . hope," asked Birney, "that the people of Kentucky will give up, for the purpose of Col'n. *this* year 4000 slaves at the ages when they are most valuable, when human flesh is selling in the Ky. market for about $4 or $5 per pound?" Such schemes of "arithmetical benevolence" were only "beguiling the Slave States from that repentance which would save them." [23]

Another anodyne to men's consciences was furnished, Birney thought, by a recent article of President Young's, published in the *Cincinnati Journal*, in which he expressed the idea that although slavery, generally speaking, was sinful, it was not sinful to retain authority over slaves unfit for freedom.[24] Birney had tried to persuade Young not to publish the article, but to no avail. "My soul is moved within me," wrote Birney to Lewis Tappan, "when I see such quacks as 'Desire to Conciliate' and 'Fear of Prejudice' ministering to a patient whose life is fast ebbing and Death stands ready at the door." [25]

[21] *A Bill to Amend the Law Concerning the Emancipation of Slaves* [Kentucky, 1835].

[22] Birney to Lewis Tappan, Feb. 3, 1835; Birney to Gerrit Smith, Jan. 31, 1835, Birney Collection.

[23] *Ibid.*

[24] *African Repository and Colonial Journal*, XI (1835), 119–123. Young's ideas are more completely given in the *Address to the Presbyterians of Kentucky* and in the letters printed in the appendix thereto.

[25] Birney to Lewis Tappan, Feb. 3, 1835, Birney Collection.

Early in March Birney was scheduled to deliver a lecture before the Danville Lyceum, and he decided that he would use the occasion to discuss Young's article. A few days prior to the Lyceum meeting he inserted a notice in the paper that all who were coming should read Young's article first, the better to judge what he had to say. Eagerness to hear the debate which would develop, as well as interest in the subject itself, brought out a goodly number of people. Young and Birney were personal friends, but Birney's criticism of his friend's views was severe, "though decorous." As was expected, President Young was on his feet as soon as Birney was through and "with more feeling than he ordinarily exhibited" asked that the meeting be adjourned until the next evening when he could reply.[26]

A large audience awaited the return engagement. Abolition could never secure liberty for the blacks, Young argued; because the abolitionists excited too much prejudice against themselves, few slaveholders would listen to a doctrine they considered so radical. To get results, the slaveholder's interests as well as his conscience must be appealed to. Birney, on the other hand, contended that it was time something drastic was done to arouse the South from her lethargy. People had repeated long enough that "the system" was wrong, but "the system" was always made up of the reported cruelties of others; their own never entered into it. As for Northern abolitionists, Birney's answer was that the South should spend less time attacking them and more time taking care of the problem of slavery so that Northerners need not feel the necessity of interfering:

Whilst our dwelling is on fire, and a large & deep stream (abolition) is at hand, with an ample supply of buckets, at once to raise the water and extinguish it— our doctors of all sorts & sizes are discussing the capabilities of a distant engine, sending for it, & uttering learned lectures on its powers, its proportions, its materials, its beauty, its symmetry & its cost:—Before it can be made ready to play upon the flame, the house is a heap of smoking ruins.[27]

Birney was satisfied that he had come off well in the debate and that Young had failed to vindicate his position successfully. He had made the mistake of accusing all abolitionists of being Garrisons, and, in

[26] Manuscript memoranda on slavery in Kentucky, Birney Papers; Danville Literary and Social Club, "Anaconda," *History and Semi-Centennial Celebration, December 27, 1889, 1839–1889* (Danville, 1889).

[27] Birney to Lewis Tappan, Feb. 3, 1835, Birney Collection.

speaking of Garrison, he had "out-Garrisoned G. himself." [28] Of most significance, however, was that the debate and the discussion it stimulated among Danville's citizens helped to focus attention on the forthcoming organization of the antislavery society toward which Birney had been working. Birney immediately set to work to circulate a pledge, with the understanding that as soon as twenty-five signers were obtained, the society would be organized. Invitations to a meeting to be held on March 19 were sent out three weeks in advance.

Although the weather was bad, twenty of the forty signers came by horseback or other conveyances from the neighboring towns and villages to gather in the First Presbyterian Church in Danville. Methodists and Baptists as well as Presbyterians were among the number, and even a few who were not members of any church. Professor James Buchanan of Centre College presided. Luke Munsell was appointed secretary, and Birney opened the meeting with prayer. The previously signed pledge was read, following which the Committee on Resolutions, composed of Birney, Harrison Walker, and Thomas Cowan, reported the resolutions for adoption.

The resolutions were obviously framed in an attempt to remain free of the taint of Garrisonian abolitionism. The members took care to declare they were not advocates of amalgamation. They believed rather that amalgamation would be arrested by giving colored people the dignity of free men. They were not trying to create unrest among the slaves. They urged upon them patience, submission, and good conduct as requisite to the acquisition of rights now withheld from them. The orderly conduct and religious improvement of the free colored would also facilitate emancipation of the slaves. The society did not intend to oppose colonization of those who freely consented to emigrate but believed the plan of colonization to be too slow in operation to be effectual. Slaveholding was declared sinful; and the defense of slavery from the Bible "the most formidable barrier to the progress of the Redeemer's kingdom in our State." On the professors of religion rested the responsibility for not setting the right example. The members of the society expected to be labeled fanatics, yet would, as good Christians, forbear from recrimination.

The remainder of the resolutions were directly connected with Birney's work. Organization of county auxiliaries was encouraged, the

[28] Birney to Gerrit Smith, March 21, 1835, Birney Collection.

publication of a weekly paper was approved, and Birney was appointed as delegate to the American Anti-Slavery Society Anniversary meeting in New York in May. In addition it was resolved, "That our brother, JAMES G. BIRNEY, be requested to deliver Lectures upon the subject of Immediate Emancipation, whenever and wherever he can find a proper occasion to do so; and we pledge ourselves individually and collectively to do all in our power to assist and encourage him in the performance of that duty."

In addition to the resolutions, the constitution itself explicitly stated the reasons, aims, principles, and plan of operation of the society. The indictment of slavery was severe. It deprived the slaves, though free moral agents, of serving God as they should. It brought moral pollution into the families of slaveholders. It enfeebled the energies of the entire nation. It was opposed to the spirit in which our government had been founded and thereby made us hypocrites before the world. It produced a monopoly of land and labor. It erected a barrier to an effective educational system. Finally, as Thomas Jefferson had so solemnly warned, it exposed the nation to the judgment of God.

The principle of operation for the goal of abolition was to be brotherly love; the mode of operation, appeals to truth, presentation of facts, persuasion, and prayer. There was to be no encouragement of slave riots, no advocacy of force, no appeal for Congressional action. Immediatism did not mean to turn the slaves loose upon the nation, instantly invest them with civil rights, or expel them from the country as the price of their freedom. They should receive the protection of the law, be paid as laborers, have the right to obtain secular and religious knowledge, and be allowed to worship God according to the dictates of conscience. The document concluded with a solemn pledge and an avowal that "our trust for victory is solely with God. We may be personally defeated—our principles, never."

Professor Buchanan was chosen permanent president. Vice-presidents were the Rev. Jonathan Stamper, Andrew A. Shannon, James Shannon, Dr. John O. T. Hawkins, and Birney. Buchanan, William M. Riddle, Luke Munsell, Thomas Cowan, and Harrison Walker comprised the Executive Committee. Luke Munsell was made corresponding secretary; Thomas Cowan, recording secretary; and Joseph Jackson, treasurer.[29]

[29] *Proceedings of the Kentucky Anti-Slavery Society, Auxiliary to the American*

Twenty-two names were immediately affixed to the constitution, and the list soon increased to forty-five. Both of Birney's oldest sons were among the Centre students who signed. Birney had been apprehensive that there might be some objection to becoming affiliated with Northern abolitionists, but fearing the consequences of division, he had decided to press for that end. To his "unspeakable delight" there was no opposition, and the organization was officially named the Kentucky State Anti-Slavery Society, Auxiliary to the American Anti-Slavery Society.[30] The fifty dollars that Gerrit Smith had sent to Birney for the cause of immediate emancipation was used to publish the proceedings of the organizational meeting.

Birney was rightfully proud, and he rejoiced, albeit "with trembling," over the successful organization of an antislavery society in a slave state. If only Southerners and Northerners could continue to work in a spirit of co-operation and brotherly love to eradicate an evil for which the whole nation was responsible, slavery could be abolished without violence and without a separation of the Union. The accomplishment of this end would be his great purpose. He was encouraged by messages like the following one from Hervey Woods:

It is just what I have wanted to hear ever since I left Ky. Such a Society in a *Slave State* will have more influence than a doz. in Free States. You have made a fine start, in so daring an enterprise—it is one of the boldest in modern times—it is carrying the war into an enemy's country—go with it Sir, go with it, to the gates of Carthage. With the courage of Caesar you have crossed the Rubicon. May God grant you greater success than attended him in less commendable expeditions.[31]

Now that there was a publicly acknowledged connection between Birney's work in Kentucky and that of the American Anti-Slavery Society, it seemed wise that he should become personally acquainted with the other leaders in the movement. Besides, he was eager to meet his

---

Anti-Slavery Society, at Its First Meeting in Danville, Ky., March 19th, 1835 [n.p., 1835].

[30] J. Winston Coleman in *Slavery Times in Kentucky* (Chapel Hill, 1940), p. 298, says that Birney succeeded in getting Garrison to include the Kentucky Anti-Slavery Society "within the scope of his American Anti-Slavery Society." Birney had no correspondence or contact with Garrison. He had, in fact, objected to Garrison's methods. All of his arrangements to make the Kentucky society an auxiliary were with Weld and the New York group.

[31] Hervey Woods to Birney, June 23, 1835, Birney Papers.

fellow workers in the cause, the better to judge of accusations of radicalism and of Northern interference with the South's "peculiar institution." Weld was urging him to come to Ohio to be present at the formation of the state society there. From Ohio he could go on to New York for the anniversary meeting to which he had been appointed a delegate. Not only was Birney eager to meet his colleagues, but they were on "tiptoe curiosity" to see and hear this Southerner who had spoken out so strongly.[32] In Ohio, especially, he could discuss his proposed paper and see what support he could get for it. The one thing that might keep him at home was the health of Mrs. Birney. She had not been well since the birth of their daughter, Florence, in January. By April, however, she was much improved, and he felt that he could leave her.

Birney set out in time to have several days with Weld before the Ohio convention met at Putnam on April 22. They had much to talk over. On the matter of the paper, they considered the possibility of making some arrangement with the editor of the *Olive Branch,* leaving Birney time for other work in addition to helping with publication. Asa Mahan, who had recently been made president of Oberlin, had suggested that perhaps Birney could spend about four months out of the year lecturing in civil and ecclesiastical jurisprudence at Oberlin.[33] Charles Grandison Finney had just accepted the professorship of theology to teach the young men who had "seceded" from Lane Seminary. Weld also wanted to discuss the advisability of a convention to form a Mississippi Valley Anti-Slavery Society.

Birney arrived in Cincinnati on April 17 to discover that his visit had been publicized in the city newspapers as well as among the local abolitionists themselves. The city's residents were familiar with Kentuckians who came across the river to recapture fugitive slaves, but this one was different. Here was a Southern slaveholder who not only had freed his slaves, but who had given up his profession, a wealthy practice, and probably his chance to become a respected pillar of his community in order that he could devote his time to an unpopular and much-abused cause. Upon his arrival in Cincinnati, Birney registered at the Henry House downtown, where he was promptly welcomed by a delegation of antislavery leaders. Popular demand that he give a pub-

[32] Weld to Birney, Jan. 23, 1835, and Feb. 16, 1835, Birney Papers.
[33] Asa Mahan to Birney, Jan. 12, 1835, Birney Papers.

lic lecture in the city had to go unsatisfied, however, as within two days he was to leave for the state convention with the Hamilton County delegation.[34]

Local antislavery societies had been flourishing in Ohio for several years. Now delegates from these organizations had come together at Putnam to co-ordinate their efforts by the establishment of a state society. There were several veteran abolitionists among them. John B. Mahan, a "tall, muscular, raw-boned, stalwart, and swarthy man of middle age" had been helping fugitive slaves across the Ohio River since the 1820's; the Rev. Samuel Crothers had been opposed to slavery when he moved north from Kentucky in 1810; and John Rankin had been an early associate of Benjamin Lundy and the abolitionists in eastern Tennessee. His home near Ripley, Ohio, was on a hill high enough so that its lights at night were visible from the Kentucky shore and could guide runaway slaves in their crossing. Some years after the Civil War, when Henry Ward Beecher was asked, "Who abolished slavery?" he was said to have answered, "John Rankin and his sons did it."[35]

Among the younger men at the convention were several of the Lane Seminary group who had moved to Oberlin: Henry Stanton, who was to become one of the most effective organizers in the movement and the husband of the famous suffragette, Elizabeth Cady Stanton; Augustus Wattles, who was busy establishing schools for the free colored people in Cincinnati; Hiram Wilson, later to be well-known for his missionary work among the fugitive slaves in Canada; Elizur Wright, one of the best editors in the antislavery ranks and the "father" of actuarial insurance; and Theodore Weld, whose eloquence had already made him the most outstanding winner of converts to abolitionism in the whole West.

These were the first abolitionists with whom Birney had had direct contact in a group. He was deeply impressed. Instead of finding them to be fanatics or misguided radicals, they were, for the most part, sincere, serious-minded Christians. Many of them were men of property and respectable standing in their communities. Instead of rantings and ravings he heard sensible and moderate discussions, although

[34] William Birney, *James G. Birney and His Times*, p. 163.
[35] *Ibid.*, pp. 163–172.

throughout the meetings he was aware of the deep undercurrent of feeling amongst these men who were persuaded that their convictions were of God.

Birney announced his intention to begin the publication of an anti-slavery paper about the first of August. The convention formally approved, and the members agreed to act in assisting circulation.[36]

Speaking engagements had been made for Birney in Columbus, Pittsburgh, Harrisburg, and Philadelphia. Advance publicity had awakened interest and curiosity about this ex-slaveholding abolitionist so that good audiences turned out to see and hear him. He arrived in New York much encouraged. In addition, news from home that Mrs. Birney continued to improve contributed to his peace of mind. At the New York meeting he would be "the observed of all observers," [37] and Weld had warned him that the Yankees would keep him speaking as often as his health would permit.

The second anniversary meeting of the American Anti-Slavery Society was opened on May 12, in a large Presbyterian church, with delegates present from most of the Northern states. William Lloyd Garrison was there; and the wealthy Tappan brothers, who had been attacked by mobs the previous summer, were among the central figures; but Birney was the man most of the people present wanted to see. The abolitionist leaders were prepared to capitalize on the popular curiosity. On the very first day of the convention Arthur Tappan, president of the society, introduced him to a full church and crowded galleries. A burst of applause greeted him as he stepped forward to speak.

Birney, in middle age, was still a handsome man. His brown hair was beginning to gray, and he had added weight, but the years had given him even more self-assurance coupled with a more serious dignity. He was not above enjoying the limelight; but he was also conscious of the fact that on him lay the chief responsibility for attempting to co-ordinate the activities of these Northern abolitionists, some of them impatient and fiery, with what he hoped would develop into an abolitionist movement in the slave states, beginning with the Kentucky organization.

[36] *Proceedings of the Ohio Anti-Slavery Convention Held at Putnam . . . 1835* ([Cincinnati], 1835).

[37] The phrase was used by Garrison in the *Liberator*, May 9, 1835, and quoted by William Birney, *op. cit.*, p. 173.

In response to Tappan's introduction, Birney offered the first resolution of the meeting: "*Resolved,* that for the permanent safety of the Union it is indispensable that the whole moral power of the free states should be concentrated, and brought into action for the extermination of slavery among us." It set the keynote for his speech, which was really a call for, and a defense of, Northern action to help the South in a final solution to the slavery problem. It was, he emphasized, not the responsibility of the South alone. Foreigners were judging our whole nation for this evil so contrary to the magnanimous and noble-spirited ideals of our country. Northerners were jointly responsible for the existence of slavery in the District of Columbia and in the territories and equally guilty in the treatment of free colored people. Besides, he pointed out, reforms must often come as a result of outside pressure. The temperance movement, to use a comparison, did not begin among the hard drinkers but among those who had already given up drinking, or who could see its undesirable effects on individuals and on society.

Birney did not agree that the Union might be rent by Northern interference with the South's "peculiar institution." As long as the method employed was constitutional, which freedom of discussion certainly was, there should be no danger. Surely, he thought, the South would not be foolhardy enough to separate, for then the slaves would escape that much easier. If freedom of discussion were curtailed, freedom-loving people would also leave; and if the system continued, more and more of the whites would go as the large slaveholders bought out the small ones. Eventually the blacks held in bondage would so outnumber the whites that military force would be required to prevent a servile insurrection. "The thing must come to a head," he warned, "and when it does, it will burst over the land with tremendous and desolating violence." [38]

This was the first chance many of the Northern delegates had had to talk directly to a man who knew slavery at first hand. They had many questions for him. Was there a real danger of insurrection if the slaves were freed? What problems of vagrancy might result? Would all the Negroes migrate to the North? What was the reaction of the slaves themselves to the idea of colonization? Birney was optimistic that emancipation could be accomplished with little disruption of the

[38] *Second Annual Report of the American Anti-Slavery Society; with the Speeches Delivered at the Anniversary Meeting . . . 1835* (New York, 1835).

Negro population. Even if freed, the Negroes would be inclined to stay in the South, since they were acquainted with the type of labor there and the Southern climate suited them better. Moreover, their family ties would hold them, and many of them would prefer to work for their old masters. As a matter of fact, there was no less antagonism toward the Negro in the North than in the South, and the colored people would soon learn this.[39]

Busy as he was with private conversations and eager questioners, Birney was also given official duties. He was chosen to be one of the vice-presidents and appointed to one committee with Arnold Buffum and Joshua Coffin to try to influence repeal of all laws recognizing the principle of property in human beings and to another to put the Bible in colored homes. The American Anti-Slavery Society promised to give five thousand dollars for this project. Birney strongly advocated the measure for Tennessee and Kentucky, where there were no legal restrictions against it.

Birney remained in New York about ten days as the guest of the Tappans and of Judge William Jay, son of the former chief justice, who was an influential member of the antislavery group. Then, having received numerous invitations to lecture in New England, he decided to accept an appointment as a delegate to the anniversary meeting of the Massachusetts Anti-Slavery Society. Again he was well received. The annual report of the society commended him for his "untiring assiduity" and "unshrinking fortitude." "He was mild; yet firm," they reported, "cautious, yet not afraid to speak the whole truth; candid, but not compromising; careful not to exaggerate in aught, and equally careful not to extenuate and conceal." [40]

Engagements had been made for Birney to lecture in several cities of New York and Ohio on his way home. By the time he returned from Boston to New York, however, he was so worn out with traveling and speaking, and so anxious about his wife and family at home, that he determined to go directly back, giving up even his long-desired visit

---

[39] Questions of a similar nature were addressed to Birney in a letter from several members of the Society of Friends. Their queries, together with his answers, were published as *Correspondence between James G. Birney, of Kentucky, and Several Individuals of the Society of Friends* (Haverhill, 1835).

[40] *Fourth Annual Report of the Board of Managers of the Massachusetts Anti-Slavery Society, with Some Account of the Annual Meeting, January 20, 1836* (Boston, 1836).

with Gerrit Smith at Peterboro. To add to his uneasiness, there were
indications that a storm was brewing in Danville. James, Jr., had writ-
en that Grandfather Birney had received an anonymous letter inform-
ng him of a plot to seize his slaves and those of Mr. Gillespie. Murder
was threatened if there was opposition. Consequently, Birney was not
returning to peace and quiet at Woodlawn. Alignment with Northern
abolitionists was to bring its repercussions.

Birney returned home from the East to find community opinion
sharply divided on the subject of his proposal to establish his paper. It
was one thing for Kentuckians to organize their own societies to try
to do something to solve the problem of slavery; but it was quite another
openly to encourage Northern interference in something which was a
matter for state, not national, legislation. And even though the citizens
of Danville had known James Birney all his life and knew that he was
not really a radical himself, they could not tell what would happen now
that he was mixing with such people as the Tappans and William Lloyd
Garrison. They were taking no chances of having a *Liberator* in their
midst, urging slaves to escape or even to rise against their masters.
This could be even more dangerous in Kentucky than in the deep South,
or in Kentucky, thanks to the efforts of such men as Birney, many of
the slaves had been taught to read.

Before Birney. had time to take any step beyond the publication of
a prospectus, a letter signed by thirty-three citizens was delivered to
him by Colonel Will C. Cowan. Their aim was to express their regret
and their dread of the consequences should Birney proceed as he had
proposed. Although there was no existing law which would punish
him for such action, they felt it would come under the classification of
disturbance of the peace. Protesting that their only motive was a desire to avoid violence, they appealed to him not to bring civil strife
in the community which had given him birth by trying an experiment
which no American slaveholding community had heretofore found itself able to bear. If he would postpone publication, the delay would
give the legislature time either to make a positive law for his observance, or, by nonaction, "admonish" the objecting citizens of their
duty. If Birney should proceed before the legislature could take action,
damage would be done which no penalty could erase. Already, they
charged, Birney's teaching of his father's slaves to read had resulted in

the whole community's being secretly infested with dissatisfaction among slaves who used to be happy and contented. "You injure yourself," they wrote. "You injure society at large—you injure the slaves themselves— *you do good to none*." [41]

These were harsh words for Birney to read, and they placed him in a position which was not an easy one. The implication in the letter that harm might come to him was easier to bear than the hurt of his wounded spirit. He confided to Gerrit Smith:

I am at times greatly perplexed. To have alienated from us those with whom we [went] up from Sabbath to Sabbath to the house of God—many· of our near connections and relations estranged from us, and the whole community with but here and there an exception, looking upon you as an enemy to its peace, is no small trial. [42]

Sensitive as he was to the opinions of his friends and neighbors and to social ostracism, Birney could not compromise his principles. The issue had grown beyond difference of opinion on slavery and the proper means of dealing with it. It now included the constitutional right of freedom of the press also. Were he to defer to public opinion until the legislature could act to deter him, he would be tacitly admitting the authority of a state to restrain a right secured by the Constitution to every citizen "to speak, write and print on any subject."

Birney's reply to the attack was a carefully formulated defense of freedom of discussion in general as well as an argument for the need to discuss the problem of slavery in particular. It appeared in the form of an open letter in the *Olive Branch* of July 25. There was nothing, he declared, in the propositions or principles laid down in his prospectus which could be alleged to create dissatisfaction among slaves. His whole aim was to influence the master, in whom, he insisted, slaveholding was producing an aristocratic spirit potentially as vicious and cancerous as a system of nobility or a state religion. Freedom of discussion was a constitutional right. It was the only way of arriving at the truth. Actually, discussion of slavery had already begun and could not, "anymore than the winds, be chained upon our frontiers. . . . It is the mysterious silence—the timid secrecy with which it is invested that produces danger."

[41] C. H. Talbot and others to Birney, July 12, 1835, Birney Papers.
[42] Birney to Gerrit Smith, July 14, 1835, Birney Collection.

In Mississippi, where a purported insurrection had just been nipped in the bud, discussion had been kept down, instruction had been forbidden to slaves, and freedom of assembly had been restrained. It was when the master was associated only with unwilling toil and punishment, asserted Birney, that

all is gloom and sullenness and silence, save when passion is roused to deeds of vengeance, and hope gives energy to the struggles of despair. They who brutify their fellow men, and shut up the intelligence of the soul, must always look for a recoil of brute force upon themselves—and of a brute force goaded into convulsive action, and animated by a love of liberty that no man can quench.

Slavery was being abolished in all parts of the civilized world, Birney continued. It was only natural that people of the North should want action in their country. But if only Southerners themselves would give evidence of taking action, Northerners would not be inclined to interfere. On the other hand, if the South refused to face the problem, it would be the duty of the North to do so.

Public reaction to Birney's stand and to that of the thirty-three citizens was immediately evident. John Jones, of Glasgow, Kentucky, sent a list of eight subscribers to the forthcoming paper but reported that in his community there was "overwhelming opposition" to anti-slavery principles. Peter Vanarsdall sent twenty-one subscriptions from Harrodsburg and Salvisa. An anonymous person calling himself "Anti Abo Lition," in a letter to the editor of the *Olive Branch*, expressed his opposition to Birney's course but could not concur in putting a gag law into effect. His advice was that of Gamaliel to the Jewish Sanhedrin, "Now I say unto you refrain from these men and let them alone; for if this counsel or this work be of men, it will come to naught. But if it be of God, ye cannot overthrow it, lest haply ye be found even to fight against God." An article in the *Olive Branch* emphasized Birney's right to freedom of speech and press and deplored the fact that a few people in the community had threatened violence. The writer was confident that the "decent and orderly part of the community" was opposed to any such measure and would "frown upon any attempt to put a check upon the freedom of the press." The "thirty-three" took exception to this statement, printed a handbill quoting it, and added a refutation. They denied that they were a minority in the community and to prove it called a meeting to be held at the Baptist Church on Saturday, July 25, at three o'clock. The people of the town and surrounding community were urged to come to express their sentiments toward the publication. This notice was signed by nineteen men, some, but not all, of whom were among the thirty-three.[43]

Four or five hundred gathered at the church at the appointed time. James Barbour, a trustee and treasurer of Centre College and the husband of Birney's cousin, was called to the chair, and Major Robert Tilford was appointed secretary. John G. Miller offered a preamble and resolutions, for which supporting speeches were made by C. H. Talbot, author of the letter from the thirty-three, John Kincaid, and the Rev. James K. Burch, the minister who had opposed the antislavery resolution in the Kentucky synod. Burch's purpose in speaking was particularly to deny that the Presbyterian clergy were backing Birney, as had been rumored.

The preamble stated that the resolutions were the result of Birney's insistency on publishing an abolitionist paper. Those who opposed them, therefore, viewed his attempt, "sustained as it is by persons unknown to, and at a distance from us," as a direct attack upon, and a "wanton disregard" of, their domestic relations. His scheme was "wild, visionary, impracticable, impolitical and contrary to the spirit of our laws," which view was concurred in, they said, by nine-tenths of the people of the town and vicinity.[44] Thomas Ayres reported the meeting to Birney, giving him the substance of the speeches. His opinion was "that if any speeches would be calculated to infuriate a multitude, these on that occasion were—the speakers indeed seemed desirous to be ahead of the current of popular excitement." [45] Evidently there was some talk of mobbing Birney when he rode into town, as was his morning habit, but while a crowd was gathering, young Joseph J. Bullock mounted a box and declared that no attack should be made unless the assailants were ready to march over his dead body and those of many others. When Birney rode up the street a few minutes later, not a hand was raised against him.[46]

---

[43] Printer's proof-sheet of a handbill.
[44] Lexington *Intelligencer,* Aug. 1, 1835.
[45] Thomas Ayres to Birney, [Aug., 1835], Birney Papers.
[46] William Birney, *op. cit.,* pp. 181–182.

Birney had hoped to begin publication of the *Philanthropist,* as his paper was to be called, by the first of August, but this became impossible. When he had returned from the East, Samuel S. Dismukes, editor of the *Olive Branch,* had approached him about becoming his publisher. The arrangement had been made, and Dismukes, who had been a charter member of the Kentucky Anti-Slavery Society organized in March, expressed himself as not very apprehensive of violence. Even after the Baptist Church meeting of July 25, he said he was fully determined to proceed. Consequently, on the morning of July 29, when Birney came to the editor's office, he was much surprised to find Dismukes in the midst of negotiations to sell the printing establishment back to J. J. Polk, from whom he had bought it. When Polk left and Birney expressed his astonishment, Dismukes confessed that he was afraid the press would be attacked. He wanted to get out of the business and go to Missouri. Dismukes did offer to sell Birney the press and the office furniture, but having no knowledge of printing and not knowing anyone else whom he could hire, Birney did not buy it. Polk's version of the story was that on the morning in question a mob had already assembled to destroy the press. In order to save the town the disgrace of violence and perhaps bloodshed, he called on Dismukes, demanding of him the key to the office, since the payments for it had never been completed. When the crowd was informed that he was once more the editor and proprietor of the *Olive Branch,* they quietly dispersed.[47]

Looking backward in 1866, Polk commented in his *Autobiography* that "for years and years multiplied, the laws of the state in which I lived gagged the press and the freedom of speech upon the subject of slavery. It was as much as a man's life was worth to say he was in favor of emancipation." Although when he was still a child Polk had determined to do "every act that the Constitution and the laws of my country would allow for the emancipation of the colored race," he had been one of the promoters of the anti-Birney meeting at the Baptist Church and one "whose opposition to the discussion of the subject of

[47] For three accounts of the whole incident, see Birney to the Patrons of the *Philanthropist* [July 29, 1835], Birney Papers; William Birney, *op. cit.,* pp. 182–183; and Jefferson J. Polk, *Autobiography of Dr. J. J. Polk; To Which Is Added His Occasional Writings and Biographies of Worthy Men and Women of Boyle County, Ky.* (Louisville, 1867), pp. 34–35, 144–145, 153. William Birney is incorrect in saying Dismukes disappeared in the night before Birney could see him.

immediate Emancipation,—by no means of the silent character,—had made him somewhat distinguished." [48]

Despite the loss of a press, Birney would not admit defeat and announced only a delay in publication, not its abandonment. Heated discussions continued. From New Providence came a request, also bearing thirty-three signatures, that Birney deliver a public address at the home of David Young in that community. Major Thomas P. Moore publicly pronounced in Harrodsburg that if any violence were attempted, he would collect three hundred men to march up to Danville to protect Birney and his press. [49] From Weld and his co-workers in Ohio also came encouragement to stand firm and the gates of Hell would not prevail. That the "slavery demon is becoming rampant in and about Danville," wrote Weld, showed that "the probe has touched the *quick*." [50] On the other hand, the Lexington *Observer and Reporter* of August 1 advised that although Birney's determination showed firmness and fixedness of purpose, it was neither wise nor prudent, and he was advised to defer to public opinion. James Harlan, candidate from the Fifth Congressional District, felt it necessary to issue a handbill denying that he was a subscriber to the *Philanthropist* in order not to jeopardize his election. [51]

Birney was aware of apprehensions that Centre College might be injured by the discussions of immediate emancipation and might lose some of its students, especially as many of them came from the deep South. To show his good faith toward the college, Birney offered ten fifty-dollar scholarships to young men "of good moral character, otherwise unprovided for, who desire the advantages of education and are unable to meet its expenses." No other strings were attached. Yet such was the antipathy against Birney that the editor of the *Olive Branch* refused to publish the offer, even as a paid advertisement; and Coons of the *Western Luminary*, feared it would "excite an unfavorable prejudice against Centre College, particularly in the southern states" [52] even to accept the donation. By the middle of August the *Olive Branch*

[48] Birney to the patrons of the *Philanthropist* [July 29, 1835], Birney Papers.

[49] Peter Dunn and others to Birney, Aug. 6, 1835, Birney Papers.

[50] Weld to Birney, Aug. 4, 1835, Birney Papers.

[51] Handbill, To the Voters of the 5th Congressional District, Aug. 1, 1835.

[52] Birney to the editor of the *Olive Branch* [n.d.], Birney Papers; the *Philanthropist* (Cincinnati), April 8, 1836.

had announced that its columns would no longer be open to the discussion of abolition.

Events elsewhere in the country in the summer of 1835 contributed to the heightened agitation in Danville. In Mississippi, fears of an extensive conspiracy led to the hanging of five white men and more than a dozen Negroes. Evidence was extracted from the Negroes by whipping, and one of the white men, a "steam doctor," signed a confession accusing the outlaw, John A. Murrell, of planning an uprising from Maryland to Louisiana.[53] Lewis Bond, of Clinton, Mississippi, who had read the letter of the thirty-three to Birney and his reply, wrote to urge him to desist. "What motive can you possibly have in view in the publication of your journal," he asked, "other than that of stir[r]ing up the Negroes in rebellion against the whites?" [54] In Nashville, Tennessee, Amos Dresser, a Lane Seminary student who was distributing Bibles, was seized by a vigilance committee and given twenty lashes in the public square because he was suspected of circulating literature of the American Anti-Slavery Society which he had in his possession. In giving an account of the Dresser episode, the Louisville *Journal* warned its readers:

These are times of peril. The emissaries of rebellion are abroad, concocting in secresy [*sic*] and darkness their schemes of anarchy and death. The slave States cannot be too vigilant. They are reposing upon a volcano, and ever and anon they may feel the tossings of that sea of flame, that heaves and welters beneath them.[55]

One of the expressions of vigilance in the South was the withholding of antislavery publications from the mails on the grounds of their being incendiary. On July 29, the very day violence was averted in Danville, mobs in Charleston, South Carolina, forced open the post office, rifled the mail, and made a huge bonfire of all the antislavery materials they found. The postmaster then took upon himself the responsibility of arresting circulation of such items until he should receive orders from Washington. In Danville, Birney was having difficulties of the same kind. As early as May he wrote to Postmaster General Kendall pre-

[53] Clement Eaton, *Freedom of Thought in the Old South*, p. 97.
[54] Lewis Bond to Birney, Aug. 31, 1835, Birney Papers.
[55] Louisville *Journal*, Aug. 14, 1835.

senting several instances of official delinquency in his subordinate officers. Kendall replied that in the case Birney cited, where a newspaper was sent to a person who was not a subscriber and who did not want it, the sender had no cause to complain if the postmaster did commit the papers to flames. Kendall did not reply to Birney's answer, in which he cited the law forbidding postmasters to take such action.[56] Kendall's views were made known in the much-publicized letter to the Charleston postmaster sanctioning this arrogation of power unto himself. Its consequence was, of course, the assumption of like power by postmasters throughout the South. The Danville postmaster, whom Birney termed "one of the most ignorant, unlettered and mobocratical of our citizens," decided to become his "intellectual caterer." After a month in which neither President Young nor Birney received their papers, Birney threatened suit convincingly enough to frighten the postmaster into delivering them.[57]

Other evidences of uneasiness in the South took the form of threats against Sabbath schools for the colored, stricter enforcement of black codes regulating slave conduct, and the formation of local patrols. In Alabama public antiabolition meetings were held, at several of which Birney's former friends and neighbors singled him out for censure. At one such meeting in Huntsville on August 18, Birney's old friends, Thomas Fearn, Leroy Pope, Jr., C. R. Clifton, and Arthur F. Hopkins, among others, were present. At a similar meeting at Triana on the same day, William I. Adair, Birney's former law partner, was the chairman. Committees of vigilance were appointed to apprehend any person circulating incendiary material.[58] At Athens, in Limestone County, a resolution referred to the "abolition fanatics of the northern states headed in part by *Garrison, Tappan, Cox, Thompson, May,* and JAMES

[56] Memoranda on the Postmaster General—Official Delinquency, Birney Papers.

[57] Birney to Gerrit Smith, Sept. 13, 1835; James Buchanan to Birney, Sept. 24, 1835, Birney Papers; Birney to Joseph Healy, Oct. 2, 1835, in Dumond, ed., *Letters of James Gillespie Birney,* I, 249–251. President Jackson upheld Kendall's action and asked Congress for a law to prohibit the sending of incendiary publications through the mails. Calhoun drafted such a bill, and it was presented to the Senate on Feb. 4, 1836, but it failed when it came up for final passage on June 8. The most complete and careful answer to Calhoun's arguments was made by William Plumer, former senator from New Hampshire, and published under the pseudonym "Cincinnatus" as *Freedom's Defence; or, A Candid Examination of Mr. Calhoun's Report on the Freedom of the Press, Made to the Senate of the United States, Feb. 4, 1836* (Worcester, 1836).

[58] *Southern Advocate,* Aug. 25, and Sept. 1, 1835.

G. BIRNEY of Kentucky with others, whose sole and avowed object, is to sow the seed [of] *discord, rapine* and *murder* among the slaves of the South." "We deeply regret," wrote the editor of the Huntsville *Democrat* about Birney, "that he has made himself the victim of such a cause. We cannot suppose him the *incendiary*—we must then suppose him the deluded *enthusiast,* and sorrowfully call to mind Pope's celebrated line, as true in this instance: 'The worst of madmen is a Saint run mad.' " Money for the abolitionist movement, the article continued, came from the "rich, fanatical, free-Negro-amalgamation Tappans, and their crew in New York." [59]

The Flag of the Union, a Tuscaloosa paper, attributed to mental hallucination or monomania on the subject of slavery Birney's "retrograde progression" from slaveholder to colonizationist to abolitionist, charged him with "bigoted blindness," and labeled him as one of the most bitter and violent of the Tappan school. Liberty of the press, the paper declared, must never be used as a machine to batter down dearest privileges and possessions.[60] A group meeting at Bellefonte, Jackson County, resolved on October 9, "That we view with feeling of abhorrence and contempt, the exertion of James G. Birney, in behalf of the abolitionists, even in a higher degree than we do the notorious A. Tappan." The resolution then repeated the unfounded charge that Birney had sold his slaves before he became an abolitionist in order not to lose any money by espousing the cause.[61] At the time a price of $20,000 was put on the head of Arthur Tappan in New Orleans, while the parish of East Feliciana in Louisiana was offering $50,000 for his delivery. The legislature of Georgia was ready to pay $5,000 for the delivery of William Lloyd Garrison to any county sheriff in Georgia.[62]

Fearful lest Birney might perchance come to Huntsville to collect some of his debts still outstanding, Arthur F. Hopkins wrote to warn him that the excitement was so great in the community that "no one actively engaged in the cause of abolition would be safe." Although he still retained his personal friendship for Birney, he regretted most deeply that Birney's sense of duty was leading him in his present course. An unidentified friend who visited Birney in the autumn

[59] Huntsville *Democrat,* Aug. 26, 1835.
[60] *Flag of the Union* (Tuscaloosa), Sept. 19, 1835.
[61] *Democrat,* Nov. 4, 1835.
[62] *Flag of the Union,* Nov. 14, 1835; *Southern Advocate,* Sept. 8, 1835.

cautioned him that he would be in danger of death were he to visit Huntsville.[63]

Liberty in the slave states was fast ebbing, and to Birney all the evidence seemed to indicate that repentance of slavery was far off. Surely they would be visited with God's judgment and it was time for Christians to leave. Despite these apprehensions, he wrote to Gerrit Smith:

And yet it is not time for us to sit down and do nothing. It is as much as all the patriotism in our country can do to keep alive the spirit of liberty in the *free* states. The contest is becoming—has become,—one, not alone of freedom for the black, but of freedom for the white. It has now become absolutely neces- sary, that slavery should cease in order that freedom may be preserved to any portion of our land. The antagonist principles of liberty and slavery have been roused into action and one or the other must be victorious. There will be no cessation of the strife, until slavery shall be exterminated, or liberty de- stroyed.[64]

Birney was now convinced of the impossibility of establishing an abolitionist paper in a slave state, even in a border state or in his own community, where he had the backing of many personal friends and where his opponents knew him to be a man moderate in action. Why was this so? Fear was the answer. Fear of self-examination, fear of free and critical discussion, fear that probing beneath the surface might dis- close how deadly a cancer the South's "peculiar institution" really was. And where fear ruled, men were governed by their emotions, their passions, rather than by reason.

What was his next step to be? Perhaps he could take a strong stand; but this was even more difficult among people he knew, with friends and family urging him to desist, than if he were among strangers. It was not easy to be labeled a traitor to his community, a fomenter of strife, among old associates. He might bear it for himself, but no matter how much he wanted to take all the odium upon himself, it was im- possible. His father, his wife, and his children would inevitably share it. Already the boys had been taunted and jeered at by playmates.

The only alternative was to move to a free state. Cincinnati had al- ready been suggested by Weld as a promising place for an antislavery

---

[63] Arthur F. Hopkins to Birney, Aug. 15, 1835, Birney Papers; Birney to Gerrit Smith, Nov. 11, 1835, Birney Collection.
[64] Birney to Gerrit Smith, Sept. 13, 1835, Birney Collection.

newspaper; and he would still be close enough so that his work might have some good effect in Kentucky. It would be hard to leave his father, but at least he would be leaving him in peace—something he would not have were his son to stay in Danville.

Birney's decision to move was made before the end of August. It was not until October, however, that he had sold his farm, bought a home in Cincinnati, and completed preparations for moving his family.[65] There were now six children. James and William he proposed sending to Oberlin; Dion and David were still of elementary-school age; George was only three and one-half; and Florence was not yet a year old. For the children, moving to a new home in a large city was an exciting adventure; but for Mrs. Birney it was resignation to the fact that from now on their lives could not be called their own. All considerations of comfortable living, of a quiet home life, of a settled future, would be subject to the needs and the call of the antislavery movement. She had had no bright illusions when they left Alabama, but at least then she was going back to live amidst her own family and old friends in Kentucky. Now she would be really setting out for a land of strangers. She could have felt more optimistic if her health had been better, but there were few days now when she felt well and vigorous. Although she was only thirty-six, she was worn out from child bearing. Yet in a free state she would not have to feel a constant worry that her husband might be the victim of a mob; and her sons could grow up without the contaminating influence of the slave system.

It was in October, a time of year when the Kentucky hillsides lay warm and mellow with the brilliant colors of the autumn foliage, that the Birneys left Kentucky. Farewells were said, and the family was "affectionately recommended to the care and affection of all Christians wherever God in his providence may cast their lot." [66]

So Birney left his native South, sorrowful that even in his own state he had been denied the right to act on his convictions, yet hopeful that from across the river his shots at slavery might reach their mark. The Louisville *Journal*, taking note of his departure, was forced to admire

[65] James Birney, Jr., to Birney, Aug. 16, 1835, Birney Papers; Birney to Joseph Healy, Oct. 2, 1835, in Dumond, ed., *Letters of James Gillespie Birney*, I, 249–251. There were rumors that Birney fled town, and also that he was forced to leave Danville. Neither was correct. His decision was made at least two months in advance, and preparations for moving were deliberate and unhurried.

[66] Certificate of Dismissal from the Danville Presbyterian Church, Birney Papers.

his resoluteness but could not forego a parting jibe: "Not having been permitted to open his battery in this State," the paper taunted, "he is determined to cannonade us from across the river. Isn't it rather too long a shot for execution, Mr. Birney?" [67]

[67] Louisville *Journal*, quoted in *Philanthropist*, Jan. 8, 1836.

Chapter VII

Defense of Civil Rights

IT was with renewed optimism that Birney crossed the river which had come to symbolize for him, as well as for the slaves, the dividing line between the land of bondage and the land of Canaan:

Among the reasons persuading me to assume a permanent residence here, it was not, certainly, among the least, that the rights of the Citizens are so nobly set forth in the Constitution. In no other form, are religious and civil rights . . . more unambiguously and fearlessly guaranteed and proclaimed to the world than in the Constitution of Ohio.[1]

But any move, whether to Alabama or to Ohio, was, for Birney, exhilarating. A pioneer in spirit, his life was to be a constant looking toward far horizons, a pursuit of the never-fading but elusive dream that by starting out anew in a different place, happiness and fortune would smile on him. Many old cares could be left behind; new ones always seemed much lighter by comparison. Yet at the time each move was made, that one, he thought, would be permanent.

In moving to Cincinnati, Birney purchased property even before moving his family and before he was certain that Cincinnati was the

[1] Birney to Charles Hammond, Nov. 14, 1835, Birney Papers.

125

best place for him to establish an antislavery paper. The "Queen City of the West" was Birney's own choice, provided he could find safety there; but Cincinnati, he knew, had strong social and commercial ties binding her to the South. Weld thought that perhaps Hillsborough, in Highland County, might be a good place, since it was near the slave states yet surrounded by strong abolitionist influence. Eli Taylor, of the Cincinnati *Journal,* had proposed a joining of forces; but because his was a Presbyterian paper, it was feared that Birney might lose the sympathy of the other denominations were he to accept the offer.[2]

The Executive Committee of the American Anti-Slavery Society made the decision still more difficult by suggesting that Birney might accomplish more by working in New England, where the people were already aroused to inquiry and needed a speaker to settle them on the right side. The illness of Amos Phelps's wife was handicapping his work in that area, and George Thompson, the Englishman, was so frequently mobbed that many were afraid to invite him to speak. Only George Storrs and Henry B. Stanton remained as full-time lecturers in New England, and they could not cover the whole six states.[3]

R. H. Rose, of Silver Lake, Pennsylvania, was promoting the idea that a fund should be raised to send Birney to the West Indies to study the progress of emancipation there and write a book comparing the achievements there with the progress of emancipation in the United States. Such a book should have a large sale and do much good in both England and the United States.[4] Still another invitation came from Beriah Green for Birney to edit a paper for the New York State Anti-Slavery Society at Utica. This offer was especially appealing because it would furnish an opportunity of working with Gerrit Smith, who had recently come over fully to the abolitionist camp.[5]

Birney, however, preferred to stay in Ohio to try to publish his paper in Cincinnati. It would take perhaps until the first of the year to get organized and to settle his family; but meanwhile there would be some time to give to preparing public opinion by means of lectures and written articles.

[2] Weld to Birney, Aug. 19 [1835], and Sept. 26, 1835, Birney Papers.

[3] Elizur Wright to Birney, Nov. 5, 1835, Birney Papers.

[4] R. H. Rose to Birney, Sept. 28, 1835, Birney Papers. The following year Rose inaugurated a communal association of colored people on his large estate at Silver Lake, Pa.

[5] Beriah Green to Birney, Dec. 30, 1835, Birney Papers.

He had not long to wait for indications of public opinion on any antislavery publications in Cincinnati. One evening, early in November, three distinguished men of the city called at his house on Race Street. They were the mayor, the city marshal, and Charles Hammond, editor of the *Gazette*. The immediate object of their visit was to complain of the distribution of a handbill, the "Declaration of Sentiment of the Cincinnati Anti-Slavery Society," which they held to be "incendiary"; but their real purpose was to impress Birney with the imminence of violence against him or the printing office should publications continue. In fact, such was the popular opposition and excitement, they reported, that they feared there might be an outbreak of some sort that very night.

Birney thanked them for their personal interest as evidenced by the warning; but he also took the occasion to make clear his position in refusing to surrender his civil rights "whatever might be the madness and folly of those who might choose to assail them." He also tried to indicate, in as diplomatic a manner as possible, that with efficient men in control of the city authority, mob action could easily be suppressed.[6]

The night passed without a mob, but after the visit of the evening, Birney was certain that in case of real emergency he would not be able to count strongly on Mayor Davies. He decided to make his own preparations for defense, for he had no intention of standing idly by while a mob overran his property and frightened his family. The threat of a mob in Cincinnati was quite a different prospect from the threat of one at home in Danville. There, even had the threat been carried out, there would have been no real danger to his life, and certainly none to his wife and children. But a mob of city hoodlums goaded into action was quite another matter. There would be no personal feelings whatsoever to restrain them. So, with the help of his sons, Birney planned the defense of his home. About forty muskets and double-barreled shotguns were collected and placed strategically about the house, on the landing of the front staircase and at other points which commanded the approaches. Birney was confident that if worst came to worst, a few well-placed shots would turn back any would-be depredators.

So the Birney family was to live for almost two years, with the ever-present apprehension of danger hanging over them. Any noise in the

[6] Birney to Gerrit Smith, Nov. 11, 1835, Birney Papers; William Birney, *James G. Birney and His Times*, pp. 207–208.

street, any sign of commotion, might be the indication that the posts of defense must be taken. It was enough to shake anyone's nerves, and Mrs. Birney, far from well and again pregnant, was in a constant state of worry. Her chronic cough and recurrent fever had begun to give unmistakable signs of tuberculosis.

Birney, meanwhile, proceeded with his preparations to publish. A short time after the visit from the city authorities, he addressed a long letter to Hammond, to be printed in the *Gazette,* which set forth his position.[7] Confiding in the protection of those rights so "unambiguously and fearlessly" guaranteed by the constitution of Ohio, he intended to establish a paper which would be the "medium of calm and gentlemanly and generous discussion." He had not done so immediately because he was aware of some opposition and did not wish "hastily to provoke to effervescence an erroneous public sentiment."

Birney insisted that it was not only expedient but necessary that he go ahead. Northern abolitionists were always discredited by the charge that they knew nothing about slavery; he knew firsthand both its milder aspects, as in Kentucky, and its severities, as in the lower South. Besides, his extensive acquaintances and close family connections in the slave states were ample reason for him to treat the subject with "candor and fairness, and with a strict regard to the well-established proprieties of amicable discussion." Slaveholders must be awakened to the fact that slavery was as harmful to those who wielded power as to its victims. Societies based on slavery could never become permanently prosperous. The subject of slavery had become one of world-wide discussion which could not be stopped. Mobs might demolish a house or dismantle a press, but they could not destroy truth; they only gave a fresh impulse to its propagation. A body of people such as the antislavery group, with objects of vast importance to the whole nation, needed a paper in the West in order that its principles be clearly known, understood, and properly considered.

Hammond refused to print Birney's letter as it was but suggested instead a series of pieces that would begin a long way back and "trace the premises so artfully" that the readers would not suspect it was going to be abolitionism. Birney considered such a procedure a waste of time.

Although stanch in maintaining his civil rights, Birney was no radical. Desiring to avoid, if possible, any occasion for a breach of the peace,

[7] Birney to Hammond, Nov. 14, 1835, Birney Papers.

he decided to establish his press at New Richmond, a small town twenty miles up the river from Cincinnati. It would be more expensive, and certainly more inconvenient, because it would mean that he would have to travel by stagecoach or go on horseback all that distance. On the other hand, it would reduce the chance of danger to his family, and it would give him a chance to get some numbers of the paper out without violence. Once the people of Cincinnati had seen how moderate a paper it was, their fears of incendiarism, he hoped, would be allayed. He had given up, for the time being, any hope of making a profit; but he was willing to go ahead if he could only break even, in order to get antislavery views before the people.[8] He had hoped to secure the aid of his Danville friend, Professor James Buchanan, as assistant editor. This arrangement would free Birney for lecturing as well as editing and would enable him, provided Mrs. Birney's health improved, to make a lecture tour of New England with Amos Phelps. Unfortunately, domestic problems prevented Buchanan from moving.[9]

The first number of the *Philanthropist* was published on January 1, 1836. It contained none of the vituperative language of Garrison's *Liberator,* but rather invited discussion on both sides of the slavery question. Its motto, "We are verily guilty concerning our brother . . . therefore is this distress come upon us," indicated Birney's belief that the North as well as the South was responsible for slavery and should share in its solution. Part of the issue was taken up with Birney's "Vindication of Abolitionists," an answer to the resolutions of the mass meeting at Athens, Alabama, which had been sent to him.

After explaining the Christian motives and peaceful purpose of the antislavery societies, he denied that they had violated the laws of a single Southern state or had incited the slaves to rebellion. On the other hand, he charged, slaveholders had not only restrained freedom of speech and press in their own states, but had gone to the North, stirred up the disorderly and lawless, prevented peaceable assembly, and violated the constitutional right of people to be secure in their persons and property. Why would not the people of the South discuss and argue the matter? Did it not concern them? Were they afraid of a truthful decision? On them, above all, should fall the duty of investigat-

[8] Birney to Gerrit Smith, Nov. 25, 1835, Birney Collection.
[9] James Buchanan to Birney, Dec. 21, 1835; Weld to Birney, Dec. 22, 1835, Birney Papers.

ing the truth, for they had an inexhaustible store of facts and professed to be alone able to understand and interpret them. He invited them, therefore, to use the columns of the *Philanthropist* without charge to present their side of the argument. To demonstrate his sincerity, the recent message of Governor McDuffie of South Carolina was printed on the front page.

The Cincinnati *Whig* of December 21, however, had already called the *Philanthropist* an insult to Cincinnati's slaveholding neighbors and an attempt to browbeat public opinion. Even the move to New Richmond left Birney so close as to make "the pestiferous breath of his paper spread contagion among our citizens." Birney could see what was happening. The hope was, of course, to arouse a wave of opposition that would force him to abandon publication. It was also, and inevitably so, a refined invitation to mob violence. The Cincinnati *Republican* spoke of a malignant spirit abroad which was cloaking itself under the guise of philanthropy and benevolence. It compared the abolitionists to the fallen angels of Milton's *Paradise Lost,* who could not appreciate order and peace but wanted strife, turmoil, and anarchy.[10] From across the river the Louisville *Journal* voiced expectations of violence but hoped no personal harm would come to Birney.[11]

It was the *Whig* which took the leadership in suggesting a mass meeting to oppose Birney, and some of the city's most prominent citizens organized it. It was called for the evening of January 22, in the courthouse.[12] Prior to the time for the formal meeting at the courthouse, however, men recruited to do the actual mob work were gathered together at another spot, in a store on Front Street, to be given their instructions. As soon as rumors of this unannounced meeting began to spread through the city, Birney's friends urged him to take refuge in some other part of the town or in the country. He declined. The time had come, he decided, when a bold stand must be taken. The issue must be faced head on, or all hope for freedom of the press would have to be abandoned.

After taking dinner at home, making no mention of the impending

[10] Cincinnati *Republican*, Jan. 15, 1836, quoted in the *Philanthropist*, Jan. 22, 1836.

[11] *Philanthropist*, Jan. 8, 1836.

[12] See *Philanthropist*, Jan. 29, 1836, for a complete account; also, William Birney, *op. cit.*, pp. 212–219.

trouble so as not to alarm his wife, Birney took William, the oldest of the boys at home, into the study and announced that he was going to attend the mass meeting. William resolved to stand with his father, and together they walked down the street to the courthouse. The place was already thronged with people crowding to get in, and some had taken up perches on the window sills in order to get a view of the proceedings. With difficulty the father and son made their way inside and proceeded, unobserved and unrecognized, to find seats near the judge's bench in the front.

Outwardly, the meeting seemed to be conducted in an orderly, parliamentary fashion; but those who knew what had gone on at the earlier meeting on Front Street knew that it was intended to be climaxed with violent action. When the crowd of over five hundred was quieted, Mayor Samuel W. Davies was elected chairman. Vice-chairmen were William Burke, postmaster and Methodist minister; Jacob Burnet, wealthy lawyer, former senator, and judge of the State Supreme Court; and Morgan Neville, receiver in the land office. One of the secretaries was Robert Buchanan, president of the Bank of Cincinnati. A committee of fifteen was appointed to prepare resolutions which denounced abolitionism as a doctrine of a few misguided men entirely at variance with the views and feelings of a majority of the population. As it was "affecting . . . social relations," and "jeopardizing . . . internal commerce," they resolved to "exert every lawful effort to suppress the publication of any abolition paper in this city or neighborhood." Moreover, they continued, these "deluded men" must be warned "of the odium they are creating."

Quietly listening from his seat near the judge's bench, Birney was amused when Henry Starr, a lawyer, suggested that the constitution of the Ohio Anti-Slavery Society be read in order that the people might know what they were opposing. It was read; and to the astonishment of many of those present, they could find nothing to which to object. One man was so impressed with what it did contain that he withdrew from the meeting. Then, to arouse what spirit might be lagging, speeches were given by Judge Wright, Colonel Pendleton, R. T. Lytle, and Colonel Charles Hale, the latter two especially emotional in appeal. Birney was charged with approving amalgamation, incendiarism, and treason. The citizens of Cincinnati, demanded Hale, must not allow such a man to make their city the center of his intrigues to stir up the slaves to massacre their masters. Such a man was a threat to the Constitution and to the Union.

It was when the fervor of the crowd had reached a high pitch that a voice toward the front of the courthouse was distinguishable above the din:

"Mr. President, my name is Birney. May I be heard?"

Astounded at such a request, from such a source, the crowd appeared stupefied. Then, realizing that their prey was in their midst, there were shouts of "Tar and feather him!" and "Kill him!" Before he could be caught up, to Birney's own great surprise Colonel Lytle, who had made one of the most rabid speeches against him, rose and shouted above the tumult:

"Hear before you strike!"

A vote was hastily taken, and the meeting decided to hear Birney. A man of such cool courage deserved to speak.

Birney talked for three-quarters of an hour. He emphasized that he was not an enemy of the South, was not indifferent to her problem. He had lived in the South all of his life, had numerous friends and relatives there, and was certainly not advocating insurrection. But unless action were taken, destruction would surely come upon the South. If the number of slaves increased and there was no amelioration of the slave system, an explosion was inevitable. Birney was not usually an eloquent or an impassioned speaker; but that night in the courthouse, facing a mob against which he had no protection except his power of persuasion, he delivered a more eloquent plea for the cause of the slave than ever he had as a lawyer defending an accused man before the bar of justice.

Further attempts to rouse the mob to their previous pitch were unavailing. As Birney and his son walked out, the men respectfully made way for them. Mob action had once more been averted; but the fact that respectable men of high standing in the community would even participate in such a procedure was to Birney a realization filled with "mournful solicitude" for the cause of liberty.

The *Whig* of January 25 declared that should the editor of the *Philanthropist* and his coadjutors "be so mad as still to persist in their present course, they assume an awful responsibility and the consequence must be upon their own ill-fated heads." It was clearly an attempt to confuse the public mind by placing the responsibility on the assailed rather than on the assailants should violence occur.

Birney was not one to let the challenge go by. Immediately he began to consider the best means of converting the occasion into a victory that would be recognized. He was sure the cause had gained support, especially among the working classes. In the *Philanthropist* he began a series of articles considering the resolutions of the mass meeting.[13] The nature of the articles varied from constitutional interpretation, to satire, to an eloquent plea for freedom of the press; but the objective of them all was to point up the danger of meetings which advocated action contrary to the principles upon which a republican structure is founded.

But even that was not enough. Now, it seemed to Birney, was the propitious time to move the press from New Richmond to Cincinnati. There were, of course, other factors involved in the decision. The mails out of New Richmond were irregular and uncertain. During all sorts of weather he had been going the twenty miles, often on horseback, plowing through mud and snow, drenched and frozen by storm and ice, carrying papers in his saddlebags for subscribers. And more and more often he returned home exhausted to sit all night with Mrs. Birney, by this time bedridden. The constant pressure of worry, writing, lecturing in neighboring towns, and attending to the business of the Anti-Slavery Society was beginning to tell on his own health.

Above all other considerations was the principle involved. Just as Quakers insisted on wearing their hats in the presence of the king, declared Birney, so liberty of the press must be asserted where it was most disputed. He was determined to demonstrate that the people of Ohio were stronger than the group whose commercial interests lay in catering to the South.[14] The *Philanthropist* was moved to Cincinnati in April,[15] and in May it became the organ of the Ohio Anti-Slavery Society. No violence accompanied the move.

While the opposition in Cincinnati seemed quieted, wherever Birney and his antislavery colleagues lectured they were greeted with tangible

[13] These articles run from Feb. 19, 1836, to April 22, 1836.
[14] Birney to Lewis Tappan, March 17, 1836, Tappan Collection; *Philanthropist*, March 4, 1836.
[15] Beginning with the issue of Feb. 5, 1836, the paper carries Cincinnati as the place of publication, but it was not actually printed there until April.

evidence of disapproval. Objections of the townspeople at Granville
forced the Ohio Anti-Slavery Society to hold its annual convention
in a large barn outside the village. Attempts to lecture in the village
were broken up by mobs, the delegates' horses were disfigured by
having their manes and tails shaved by a group of drunken pranksters,
and Birney himself was egged as he left town. At Xenia, in Greene
County, he was egged again; and at Columbus he spoke for an hour
despite a steady discharge of apples, pebbles, and other missiles. Although he was not harmed, the mob followed him to his lodgings, and
the next day he found it impossible to obtain a place to speak again.[16]
Such instances served only to increase antislavery zeal. "We fight,"
wrote Birney, "not with the courage of despair, but with the calmness of
certain victory; with the strength of those who feel that their power is
from the Almighty; with the weapon of truth prepared by him who is
the friend of truth, for the destruction, the final and utter destruction of
its adversary, error." [17]

One of Birney's aims in Cincinnati was to enlist the churches in the
fight against slavery. In May the general conference of the Methodist
church convened in the city, and Birney attended to report their discussions on abolition. The majority did not favor it, and resolutions were
passed censuring two of their members, George Storrs and Orange
Scott, both of New England, who had spoken publicly at antislavery
gatherings. Busy in the gallery taking notes, Birney was suddenly
aware that he had become the focus of attention. Afraid of an unfavorable report in the *Philanthropist,* the delegates were objecting to his
presence. The Rev. Mr. Sorin, of Philadelphia, moved a resolution that
such note taking was "highly indecorous," and Dr. Bangs, of New York,
was of the opinion that it was as much a breach of gentlemanly conduct as reporting a conversation from another man's parlor. The motion
to exclude Birney from the house was not put to a vote, however, but a
resolution of censure was passed against the publication of Birney's and
Orange Scott's report on the conference. Paradoxically, one of the men
introducing the resolution was the Rev. Jonathan Stamper, who had
been a charter member of the Kentucky Anti-Slavery Society but had
since renounced abolitionist principles. Birney could only conclude that
the Methodist church was "staggering more and more under the life-

[16] Birney to Lewis Tappan, April 29, and May 2, 1836, Tappan Collection.
[17] *Emancipator,* May 12, 1836.

destroying influence of the pestilent atmosphere with which it [slavery] has enveloped her."[18] He was beginning to realize, like Luther and Wesley, that the only hope of reform was in separation.

Yet, on the whole, Birney was encouraged by the prospects in Cincinnati. There had been no demonstrations of violence against his press, and the number of subscribers had more than doubled by July. John Jones reported from Kentucky that much of the heat manifested on the paper's first appearance had cooled because of Birney's mild and Christianlike course.[19] The Athenian Society of Ohio University elected Birney an honorary member for his piety as a Christian, his taste and reputation in literature, and his philanthropy "in boldly asserting the doctrine of Equal and Unalienable Rights, and perseveringly advocating the cause of *Human Liberty.*"[20] Judge William Jay sent a contribution to express his satisfaction with the "gentlemanly and Christian spirit" of the paper;[21] and Benjamin Lundy, pioneer antislavery publisher, wrote to extend his decided and unqualified approbation. "Thy plan of proceeding," he wrote in his gentle Quaker fashion, "accords more strictly with my own views, than those of any of our editorial contemporaries."[22] Even Birney's brother-in-law, John J. Marshall, although disagreeing "radically and irreconcileably [*sic*]" in viewpoint, commended him on his manner of publishing.[23]

At home things were more cheerful, too. Although the baby, a daughter, had lived only two months, Mrs. Birney's health had been much better. There was no hope of a complete and permanent recovery, but

[18] *Debate on "Modern Abolitionism," in the General Conference of the Methodist Episcopal Church . . . 1836* (Cincinnati, 1836); *Philanthropist,* May 27, 1836.

[19] John Jones to Birney, April 30, 1836, Birney Papers. Information on Birney's lecture trips is taken from the *Philanthropist.*

[20] Athenian Society of Ohio University to Birney, June 18, 1836, Birney Papers. In 1832 the Philomathic and Erosophic Societies of the University of Alabama had elected Birney to honorary membership out of regard for him as "an individual whose literary and scientific attainments will reflect great honor upon the Society." By 1837 their regard for him was considerably subdued, and they both expelled him, "being unwilling to claim membership with a man whose only study is to distinguish himself by constantly proclaiming that the people of the South are oppressors and tyrants, and not worthy of the name of a free and independent people." See B. Boykin to Birney, Nov. 24, 1832; Committee of the Philomathic Society to Birney, Nov. 12, 1832, Birney Papers; Tuscaloosa *Intelligencer* quoted in *Philanthropist,* Aug. 11, 1837.

[21] William Jay to Birney, April 22, 1836, Birney Papers.

[22] Benjamin Lundy to Birney, March 27, 1836, Birney Papers.

[23] John J. Marshall to Birney, June 18 and 24, 1836, Birney Papers.

she was now able to be up and about the house and even to walk out occasionally.[24] Although his father had declined the copies of the *Philanthropist* which Birney had tried to send to him, he had strongly defended his son against the imputations of ungentlemanly and dishonest conduct made by the Methodist ministers; and the Marshalls had been cordial in their invitation to him to visit them. Perhaps there was yet hope that the family could be won over.

All of these factors combined to make Birney optimistic. By July he was beginning to feel assured that the cause had gained complete tolerance. And, if the battle were completely won in Ohio, perhaps there was still hope for Kentucky too.

Then, without warning, the storm broke. On the night of July 12 the office of Achilles Pugh, Birney's printer, was broken open, the issue of the *Philanthropist* for that week torn up, and the press taken to pieces and its smaller parts carried away. The following night a handbill was stuck up on the street corners with the warning "Abolitionists Beware." The language and ideas it expressed were not those of a rabble mob but represented the opinions of the merchant class. "The citizens of Cincinnati," it began, "embracing every class interested in the prosperity of the city, satisfied that the business of the place is receiving a vital stab from the wicked and misguided abolitionists, are resolved to arrest their course." Then followed the warning to those engaged in "the unholy cause of annoying our Southern neighbors," the appeal for them to pause before provoking a crisis, and lastly, the threat:

If an attempt is made to reestablish their press, it will be viewed as an act of defiance to an already outraged community, and on their heads be the results which will follow . . . longer patience would be criminal, the plan is matured to eradicate an evil which every citizen feels is undermining his business and property.[25]

An anonymous letter from Covington, Kentucky, warned Birney: "Sir, there is a band organized for to take you prisoner if you set your feet on the Kentucky side. For to tar and feather you. Three persons come from our town on the 12th and destroyed your press. As I am a friend of Abolitionist I would give you warning not to come over on our side." [26]

One hundred dollars was deposited by the Anti-Slavery Society with

[24] Birney to Lewis Tappan, July 4, 1836, Tappan Collection.
[25] Handbill.   [26] "Alpha" to Birney [n.d.], Birney Papers.

Mayor Davies as a reward for the detection of the rioters; but the latter's proclamation, which appeared the next morning, was as much an admonition to the abolitionists not to "inflame the public mind" as it was to the rioters to maintain peace.[27] Although Birney had no thought of backing down, it was not so easy to persuade Pugh to continue printing. On Friday afternoon, July 15, he refused to go on, and before the next issue, that of July 22, was completed, the Executive Committee of the Anti-Slavery Society had to guarantee his property to the amount of two thousand dollars. The society had decided, should a second attack be made, to abide by Pugh's Quaker belief in nonresistance, though Birney himself thought a show of force would effectively stop any rioters.[28] On July 17 another handbill appeared, offering a reward of one hundred dollars for the "delivery of one James G. Birney, a fugitive from justice. . . . Said Birney in all his associations and feelings is *black*, although his external appearance is white. The above reward will be paid and no questions asked, by Old Kentucky." [29]

The threats were growing unmistakably stronger in tone. Again the Birney family went to bed at night fearful that they would be routed out before morning; and again the muskets on the staircase were regularly inspected to be sure they were ready for any emergency. But to lie awake at night listening to each small noise which might indicate the approach of ruffians, or even of a lone assassin, was too much for Mrs. Birney's nerves. Although far from well, she was able to travel, and it was arranged that she should go to her family in Kentucky. To make traveling as easy for her as possible, friends in the country offered to take care of Florence during her absence.

Worried about the safety of his son, James Birney, Sr., sent John J. Marshall to plead with him to give up his foolish and stubborn resistance to public opinion. Marshall resorted to every plea that might sway him, but Birney remained firm. Worn out by sleepless nights and anxiety, Birney did consent to go to the Franklin House to stay, hoping that in a few days the emotional pitch of public indignation would die down. So strong was the belief that wherever Birney was there would be

[27] Ohio Anti-Slavery Society, Executive Committee, *Narrative of the Late Riotous Proceedings against the Liberty of the Press in Cincinnati. With Remarks and Historical Notes, Relating to Emancipation* (Cincinnati, 1836). This was written by Birney, who was a member of the Executive Committee.

[28] Birney to Lewis Tappan, July 15 and 22, 1836, Tappan Collection.

[29] *Philanthropist*, July 22, 1836.

an attack, however, that no sooner had the other boarders learned the identity of the new guest than they descended upon the landlord in a fury. Birney must go, they demanded, or they would all leave. Fortunately for Birney, Mr. Johnson stood his ground despite the fact that twelve of the protesters promptly packed their valises and walked out.[30]

During this time the Executive Committee of the Ohio Anti-Slavery Society was preparing an address to the citizens of Cincinnati which stated the society's full determination to maintain unimpaired the principle of freedom of the press and to refuse to surrender to the "spirit of misrule and oppression." The *Whig* and the *Republican* continued the assault, with the *Whig* playing up the angle that the abolitionists were led by "an English emissary," were "fanatical refugees," "hirelings of the despots of Europe," and "fugitive amalgamationists." Under such conditions, said both papers editorially, action by the citizens was necessary for the preservation of themselves and the interests of the city. The *Republican* of July 21 advised some of the prominent anti-slavery men of the city to "eschew the society of James G. Birney" and "avoid him as you would a viper." James C. Ludlow, Reese E. Price, and William Donaldson, prosperous businessmen, were warned to be more careful of the interests of the community from which they had acquired their fortunes.

Birney boldly reprinted the handbills as well as the articles against him, adding a challenge of his own:

Must we trample on the liberty of white men here because they have trampled on the liberty of black men at the South? Must we forge chains for the *mind* here, because they have forged them for the *body* there? Must we extinguish the right to *speak*, the right to *print* in the North, that we may be in unison with the South? No, never.[31]

Furious at being unable to frighten Birney into silence, the citizenry decided to take the law into their own hands and called a meeting for Saturday evening, July 23, to decide whether they would permit the publication or distribution of abolitionist papers in the city. Its leaders were the same as those of the January meeting. Nicholas Longworth and Morgan Neville declared the paper would be put down, "peaceably

[30] *Philanthropist*, July 22, 1836.   [31] *Ibid.*

if it could, forcibly if it must." These same two men prepared a set of resolutions and planned the meeting at a time and place best suited to get the laborers from the foundries and shipyards just as they came from work. William Burke, the postmaster, acted as chairman. The resolutions, very similar to those of the January meeting, again expressed commercial motives. Only the absolute discontinuance of the *Philanthropist* could prevent violence. A committee of twelve was appointed to wait upon Birney and his associates to request them to desist "and to warn them that if they persist, we cannot hold ourselves responsible for the consequences." [32]

On Monday, the committee addressed a note to Birney asking him to meet them for a "free conversation" on the matter. Birney immediately replied that since his paper was the organ of the Ohio Anti-Slavery Society, he could not act singly. Accordingly, the Executive Committee was approached, and its members expressed their willingness to meet at the house of one of their number, Dr. Isaac Colby, to discuss the situation. Negotiations began that evening. James C. Ludlow, William Donaldson, Thomas Maylin, John Melendy, C. Donaldson, Gamaliel Bailey, Dr. Colby, and Birney represented the Anti-Slavery Society. Twelve men had been appointed by the Saturday mass meeting to speak for the opposition: Jacob Burnet, Josiah Lawrence, Robert Buchanan, Nicholas Longworth, John C. Wright, Oliver M. Spencer, David Loring, David T. Disney, Thomas W. Bakewell, Stephen Burrows, John P. Foote, and William Green. John C. Wright left the city on Sunday, however, and Burrows declined to serve.

Judge Burnet assumed the initiative in presenting the danger involved if the *Philanthropist* was continued. Nineteen-twentieths of the people of Cincinnati opposed it, he protested, and 160 men were already drilled and ready to destroy it should the meeting that evening be unavailing. The city was too close to the slave states. Kentuckians were as opposed to an abolition paper in Cincinnati as they were to one within their own state. Again, most of the arguments centered on the business of the city. Robert Buchanan said his Southern correspondents had told

---

[32] Complete accounts of the proceedings of July, 1836, are to be found in the Cincinnati *Gazette*, quoted in the Frankfort *Commonwealth*, Aug. 10, 1836; articles from the Cincinnati *Republican and the Public Advertiser* reprinted in the Huntsville *Democrat*, Aug. 16, 1836; *Narrative of the Late Riotous Proceedings;* and William Birney, *op. cit.*, pp. 240–249.

him that trade was being withdrawn because of the abolitionists. They had no criticism of the manner and spirit of the *Philanthropist* but only of the subject discussed.

Before parting, the Executive Committee promised to deliver its answer by the next day. It was unequivocal. The right to discussion could not be surrendered to "highhanded dictation." The *Philanthropist,* as the mouthpiece of twelve thousand Ohio citizens, had been conducted with fairness and moderation. The attempt to silence it was an attack on the fundamental freedom of speech and press, which, the committee felt, the people of Cincinnati did not really want to see prostrated. Birney's editorial in that day's issue was as firm:

As to ourselves, we have but one course to pursue. We are not more the advocate of freedom for the slave than we are of liberty for those who are yet free. Whatever others may do, we have but one duty. Believing the government under which we live, to be the best on earth—the only one which is founded in reason—the only one which can secure to us and our offspring, the proper blessings of government—our last cry to its friends will be "To the rescue."

Burnet's committee saw nothing left to do but to report failure, which it did—to the newspapers. Regard for peace, commented Hammond in the *Gazette* later, should have postponed publicizing the news. He refused to print it until Monday. Not so the *Whig* and the *Republican.* The result was the mob of Saturday night, July 30, which this time did its work more completely.

About six o'clock the crowd began to gather in front of the Exchange Hotel on Front Street and proceeded, with due observance of the parliamentary niceties, to elect a chairman and a secretary and to pass formal resolutions to violate the laws protecting life and property by demolishing the antislavery press and tarring and feathering its editor. Joseph Graham, a salesman in the Southern trade and an active member of the Texas Aid Committee, was the leader. He had been active in the mob of July 12, also, and had been one of the authors of the antiabolition handbills.

Shortly after dark the mob reassembled on the corner of Main and Seventh to get the real work of the evening under way. A rush at the printing office quickly broke it open, and in a minute the people in the crowd below were pushing and trampling in retreat to avoid the books, type, pieces of the press, and other office equipment which came hurtling out of the windows. The whole printing office was torn apart. For a minute there was a lull while all shoulders were bent to the big job, and then with a tremendous heave the press itself was pushed out and a great shout went up from the approving throng. Strong hands hurriedly hitched a rope to it, and as the onlookers moved back to make way, it was triumphantly dragged down the street to the river. Not a policeman was visible along the whole line of march, and this despite the fact that the meeting at the Exchange had been advertised in the newspapers and the resolutions adopted at it publicly made. The absence of policemen, however, was no stranger than the presence of Mayor Davies as a silent spectator of the proceedings. Only one courageous young man offered to restrain the depredators if six other men would volunteer to help him. None did.

As the water of the Ohio River closed over the sinking press, shouts of "Birney! Birney!" were raised and quickly taken up. Tar and feathers were next on the agenda. On the way to Race Street an unsuccessful raid was made on Pugh's house to search for more printing materials, and then a rush was made for Birney's house. They approached quietly, but as they came near, a boy of seventeen stepped out, closing the door behind him. Joseph Graham took the command in questioning.

"Who are you?"

"My name is William Birney."

"Where is your father?"

"In Warren County."

"Is anyone else in the house?"

"No."

As Graham turned to consult with his cohorts, William stepped quickly inside again, turned the key in the lock, and with a bound was on the stair platform ready "to give a due reception to the expected intruders." Evidently they believed him, however, and his grip on the rifle relaxed as he saw them turn to go. Birney, fortunately, was in Lebanon, Ohio, for the third in a series of Saturday night lectures, and Mrs. Birney was still in Kentucky.

From the Birneys' the crowd surged on to William Donaldson's, but there only the ladies were at home. Frustrated at losing their prey at two places, the patience of the mob ran out. Turning to Church Alley, the Negro part of the city, they indulged in an orgy of destruction.

Windows and doors of houses were ripped off, some whole houses were practically torn down, other houses were entered and their interiors demolished as their occupants fled into the street. Only about midnight, after four hours of destruction without any attempt on the part of the city authorities to interfere, did the mayor finally speak to the mob, advising them, "We have done enough for one night. . . . The abolitionists themselves must be convinced by this time what public sentiment is."

Still the mob was not satisfied to let Birney escape. The next evening, Sunday, they gathered again in front of the Franklin House, thinking Birney had hidden there. When a search, this one also supervised by the mayor, failed to produce him, they dispersed.

Fearing the situation was getting out of hand, on Monday Mayor Davies called for a restoration of peace. Several volunteer companies were organized which checked further attempts at violence, including another attack on the Negro section. On Tuesday, August 2, Charles Hammond, of the *Gazette*, who saw the issue as one of fundamental civil rights, took the lead in calling for a public meeting to oppose the action of mobs. He pointed out that while it was praiseworthy to respect the rights of slaveholders, fellow citizens of Cincinnati also had rights, among them, free discussion.

Those who responded to Hammond's call met at the appointed place, only to find the "mob" there first. Nonetheless, an orderly discussion was conducted in which both groups participated, and a resolution was passed which stated that full co-operation would be given to the city officials in maintaining peace. A parting thrust at the abolitionists, however, was a declaration that their press had been the cause of all the recent difficulties.[33]

Birney, out on his week-end lecture trip, was oblivious of the disturbances which had been upsetting the city. It was not until Tuesday evening on his return trip, when he stopped for the night about fourteen miles out of Cincinnati, that he learned the alarming news of the destruction of the press and the outburst against him personally. Ignorant of whether peace had been restored or whether some of the most determined might still be waiting for him, he decided that per-

[33] Cincinnati *Gazette*, quoted in Frankfort *Commonwealth*, Aug. 10, 1836; *Aurora* (New Lisbon, Ohio), Aug. 13, 1836; *Independent* (Cincinnati), undated clipping in the Birney Papers; *Narrative of the Late Riotous Proceedings.*

haps discretion was the better part of valor. He took what rest he could before midnight, then stole out quietly about one o'clock, saddled his horse, and set off to reach the city under cover of the darkness and at a time when no one would be expecting his return. In the quietness of the early morning hours, however, any watch posted could hear from a long way off the hoofs of his horse on the hard dirt road, and at any point in the darkness ahead an ambush might be ready to seize him. Only when the first early glimmers of dawn were apparent in the eastern sky could he somewhat relax his tense watchfulness. Shortly after daylight he entered the city, and, without incident, arrived safely at home before other people were stirring.

By the afternoon Birney had contacted his antislavery colleagues, who were unanimous in their persuasion that for him to stay in his own house was folly. Before nightfall he was secretly taken from the city to the farm of a friend about three miles in the country; but even that was not considered safe enough, and he was driven on by "a circuitous and private way" to another place about five miles from the city. There he remained until Saturday. By that time Hammond's strong campaign against mobs had produced a public reaction which insured the effectiveness of the volunteer companies. Even after Birney returned to the city, however, it was as much as his life was worth to venture into the business district near the river front, and for some time he took the precaution of not sleeping regularly in the same place.[34]

As so often happened in such instances, the mob perhaps did more to help than to hinder the cause. Antislavery books and other publications which had been pitched out of the windows were carried away and read. Birney's *Address to the Ladies of Ohio* found its way into a family of four and converted them all to abolition. Another man got Jay's *Inquiry* and declared if that was abolition, he was an abolitionist. A mechanic carried off a whole pile of books, read them, and later returned them to Birney. Many people such as Hammond, although not converted to abolitionism, were ready to support the abolitionists in their fight for the preservation of freedom of the press. Birney wrote that the action of the mob had won people to the cause by the thousands where only tens had been added before.[35]

---

[34] Birney to Lewis Tappan, Aug. 10, 1836, Tappan Collection.
[35] *Philanthropist,* Sept. 23, 1836; American Anti-Slavery Society, *Fourth Annual Report* (New York, 1837), pp. 82–87.

Recruits were not gained in the ranks alone. It was this incident which brought Salmon P. Chase to stand openly with the abolitionists when his own sister, the wife of Dr. Colby, took refuge in his house during the riots.[36] William T. Allan's wavering between preaching the Gospel, as Finney wanted him to do, or becoming an antislavery worker was resolved by the Cincinnati mob.[37] Birney's own son, William, who faced the mob when it came to his family's house, became a stanch worker in the cause, champion of the rights of the free colored people in Cincinnati, and commander of Negro troops during the Civil War.

Birney's stand for freedom of the press elicited a powerful expression of praise for the abolitionists from William Ellery Channing. He thanked them for being true to rights others were willing to betray.

I earnestly desire, my dear Sir, [he wrote] that you and your associates will hold fast the right of free discussion by speech and the press, and, at the same time, that you will exercise it as Christians, and as friends of your race. That you, Sir, will not fail in these duties, I rejoice to believe. Accept my humble tribute of respect and admiration for your disinterestedness, for your faithfulness to your convictions, under the peculiar sacrifices to which you have been called. . . . I look with scorn on the selfish greatness of this world, and with pity on the most gifted and prosperous in the struggle for office and power; but I look with reverence on the obscurest man, who suffers for the right, who is true to a good but persecuted cause.[38]

Publication was, of course, resumed, and the growing success of the paper enabled Birney to bring in Gamaliel Bailey as his assistant and to train him for the editorship, thus giving Birney more time for lecturing in addition to his writing. From all over the country came letters cheering him on and urging a firm stand. The Executive Committee of the New York Anti-Slavery Society had heard the shout of his "ruthless persecutors" and were cheered by the "calm and firm tones" of his "unchanged voice." [39] Lewis Tappan was confident that the *Philanthropist* would "rise Phoenix-like from its ashes." Daniel Henshaw, a Lynn,

[36] Albert B. Hart, *Salmon P. Chase* (Boston, 1899), pp. 48–52.

[37] William T. Allan to Weld, Aug. 9, 1836, in *Weld-Grimké Letters,* I, 323–325.

[38] William E. Channing to Birney, Nov. 1, 1836, in *Philanthropist,* Dec. 9, 1836.

[39] Executive Committee, New York Anti-Slavery Society, to Executive Committee, Ohio Anti-Slavery Society, August 26, 1836, in *A Collection of Valuable Documents, Being Birney's Vindication of Abolitionists—Protest of the American A.S. Society— To the People of the United States, or, To Such Americans as Value Their Rights* . . . *Outrage upon the Southern Rights* (Boston, 1836).

Massachusetts, editor, called Birney "one of the noblest sons of the West" who had "dared to lift up his voice in favor of liberty when all around him seemed given over to corruption, to slavery, to moral destruction." [40] Even out of the deep South came the voice of Alva Woods, whom Birney had hired as president of the University of Alabama. In a baccalaureate address of December 17, 1836, Woods deplored mob action, the trampling underfoot of civil authority, and the placing of both life and property at the mercy of unbridled passions.[41]

On the other hand, the *Southern Advocate* of August 11, 1836, refering to Birney, spoke of the "wild, dangerous and fantastic extremes into which a spirit of bigotry will sometimes hurry even an amiable and intelligent man." That he had been so highly respected in Huntsville was all the more reason to deplore his "present pernicious associations." Reports circulated that in Cincinnati the Union Society of Coloured Persons had held a meeting at which resolutions were passed condemning the actions of Birney and the other abolitionists as prejudicial to the interests of the colored people. Thirty-five names were attached; but a few days later a disclaimer signed by twenty-eight people appeared in the *Gazette,* with the explanation that their names had been used without their consent.[42]

To withstand mob pressure was not nearly so difficult for Birney as to feel obliged to turn a deaf ear to the entreaties of his family. "Suffer me to approach you once more," wrote his sister, Anna Marshall, "and with affectionate solicitude beseech you to check the prosecution of this fearful warfare with opinion, fearful in all its phases." And for her father she pled, "Is nothing to be yielded to the evening of his days, can that service be acceptable to God, which in its pursuit, brings sorrow, nay unmingled grief, upon a tender, aged parent?" She reminded him also of his wife and children, "driven from point to point." James Birney, Sr., broke his long period of nonintercourse with his son to warn him that he was entailing on his children a "most destructive heritage." "I dislike and disapprove [*sic*] of slavery as much as you or any person can do," he wrote, "but to abolish it at present in this Country

[40] William Birney to James G. Birney, Aug. 22, 1836, and undated clipping, Birney Papers.

[41] Alva Woods, *Baccalaureate Address Delivered December 17, 1836. At the Fifth Annual Commencement of the University of the State of Alabama* ([n.p.], 1836).

[42] *African Repository and Colonial Journal,* XII (1836), p. 322; *Narrative of the Late Riotous Proceedings.*

by the efforts of a few sanguine or fanatical men shews I think a very limited view of human nature and a Great want of understanding the prevailing passions of man." [43]

Although torn by his sense of duty to his family and in constant apprehension of danger for several months, Birney could still address the readers of the *Philanthropist* with unwavering faith:

We have lost no confidence in the rectitude of our principles, nor in the judgment which you, and those which may succeed us, will pass on our conduct. . . . We shall still continue to maintain, and publicly to inculcate the great principles of liberty incorporated in the constitution of our state and general governments—believing, that if ever there was a time, it is now come, when our republic, and with her the cause of universal freedom is in a strait, where everything that ought to be periled by the patriot should be freely hazarded for her relief.[44]

Men must "themselves die freemen [rather] than slaves, or our Country, glorious as has been her hope, is gone forever." [45]

Suits were begun by Pugh for damages to his press and office and by Augustus Wattles, as agent for the Ohio Anti-Slavery Society, for damages of three hundred dollars to the papers, pamphlets, and books in the depository. Salmon P. Chase and Harvey Hall were counsel for the plaintiffs. The first time the cases came up they were postponed because necessary witnesses were absent. Finally, on February 15, 1838, the case of *Wattles vs. Joseph Graham, Joseph S. Bates, Joseph Talbot, John C. Clark and Others* was tried. Chase delivered a fervent vindication of the abolitionists, reading parts of Channing's letter to Birney, but Judge Este awarded the plaintiff only fifty dollars. An appeal to the Supreme Court was later withdrawn. The case of *Pugh vs. Joseph Graham, Archibald Gordon, Joseph S. Bates, Julien Neville and J. A. D. Burroughs* was tried for three days beginning June 19, 1838, but the jury could not agree. The trial was not concluded until July, 1839, when Pugh received $1,500 damages.[46]

In July, 1836, Birney received his commission for another year as

[43] Anna Marshall to Birney, Aug. 3, 1836, and James Birney, Sr., to Birney, Aug. 13, 1836, Birney Papers. Birney to Lewis Tappan, Sept. 26, 1836, Tappan Collection.

[44] *Narrative of the Late Riotous Proceedings.*

[45] *Philanthropist,* Sept. 23, 1836.

[46] *Philanthropist,* Feb. 27, and June 19, 1836; Birney to Tappan, July 17, 1839, Tappan Collection.

agent of the American Anti-Slavery Society. He had been lecturing only when he could spare the time from his editorial work; but now that he had Bailey to help him, he was relieved for other active duty in the field. Most of the autumn was spent in lecture tours. In September he visited Lebanon, Springboro, Batavia, Bethel, Georgetown, Goshen, and Wilmington, surviving disorders and disturbances with equanimity, and organizing antislavery societies wherever there was enough interest. In October he made an extended trip up the Miami Valley as far as St. Mary's, stopping at Dayton both going and coming and at various other towns. Many of his lectures were held in churches—Methodist, Baptist, Presbyterian, or Quaker, depending on the locality.

It was a strenuous life of riding on horseback from place to place, meeting the demands of speaking engagements almost every night, and adapting himself to all varieties of accommodations in the way of rooms and meals, often "boarding around" with different families as itinerant preachers did. Yet it was stimulating and rewarding to find people from all walks of life willing to give whatever they could to support the principle of liberty for all men. Farmers from the middle of Ohio, many of whom had never seen a slave and never would, became convinced that only with the abolition of slavery could the dream of a happy and prosperous America be fulfilled. And so they came, even after a long day's work behind the plow or clearing the land, with their wives, their sturdy sons, and their babies, to sit sometimes for as long as two hours listening to stories of the sufferings of the slaves, to the arguments on the sinfulness of slavery, and to the warnings of calamity which would overtake the nation which persisted in this evil.

Overwork, both physical and mental, began to take its toll of Birney's health to the extent that he began to worry about his family's welfare in case anything should happen to him. Expenses had mounted dreadfully with his wife's ill health and with the cost of educating his sons. William and James were both at Miami University in Oxford, and Dion and David were in boarding school. In addition, there had been the losses on the *Philanthropist*. Moreover, as long as he continued an active abolitionist against the wishes of his father, there was little chance of an inheritance. By the spring of 1837 James Birney, Sr., had commanded that if he did not at once give up the *Philanthropist,* all intercourse between them must cease. It was also futile to count on the payment of the money due him in Alabama.

The solution which presented itself to Birney was the purchase o western lands selling at $1.25 an acre, which, he estimated, would be worth about $5.00 an acre in five years. Despite his father's warning against speculation and despite his own bitter experience in Alabama he proposed to both Lewis Tappan and Gerrit Smith that if they would advance him anywhere from five thousand to ten thousand dollars, he would give the whole of his land purchase as security for double the sum in five years. Neither was willing to make the investment; but on his own Birney did buy about one thousand acres in Darke County Ohio, and about three thousand in Randolph and Jay counties in Indiana.[47]

It was inevitable that in writing articles and preparing lecture Birney should be led to a serious consideration of the constitutiona powers and legislative duties of the government in regard to slavery. He had come to Ohio firmly convinced that slavery was antithetical to re publican government and incompatible with the Declaration of Inde pendence, but he was not then ready to advocate direct political action In his *Address to the Ladies of Ohio* he had stressed the fact that the movement was religious, not political; and in one of his first editorial in the *Philanthropist* he warned against the dangers of "assuming a party-posture" which might lead to compromise of principle in the interest of expediency. He had advocated a refined form of pressure politics, moral suasion. With the old parties nearly balanced, he had argued, antislavery sentiment would be respected by both. A full de velopment of his fundamental theses that slavery was antagonistic to the structure of republican government and that no society based on slavery could be permanent and prosperous could lead, however, to only one end—a swing to political action when the failure of persuasion to change the old parties should be evident. His experience with the violence of mobs in the summer of 1836 convinced him that abolition ists, as the trustees of civil rights, must throw their political weigh against lawless opponents, particularly at the ballot box.[48]

Birney's constitutional theories were carefully developed through

---

[47] Birney to Lewis Tappan, Nov. 2 [or 7], 1836, Tappan Collection; enclosures i Virginia R. Heiss to Betty Fladeland, July 10, 1954.

[48] *Philanthropist,* Jan. 8, and Dec. 10, 1836; Birney to Lewis Tappan, Dec. 1 1836, Tappan Collection.

articles in the *Philanthropist*. He considered the power of Congress to abolish slavery in the District of Columbia, the argument that the Constitutional Convention guaranteed slavery by leaving its determination to the states; and the harmony of antislavery principles with international law and the federal Constitution. His inquiries were directed, also, to the constitutionality of state "Black Laws," and especially to the federal fugitive slave law of 1793.[49] His interpretation developed the thesis which was to be expounded five years later by Justice Story in *Prigg* vs. *Pennsylvania*. The states, he said, were forbidden by the Constitution to pass laws which would prevent the return of fugitives escaping from labor; but neither the states nor individuals were required by it to use physical force to aid the slaveholder in regaining his slave. His major conclusion on the unconstitutionality of the law of 1793 was, of course, different from Justice Story's. Congress, according to Birney's view, had been given no power to legislate on this matter. It could not create a slave, and, therefore, in a state such as Ohio, where neither the state constitution nor the Northwest Ordinance recognized the existence of slavery, all persons were free unless they had escaped from a slave state. Slaves brought by their masters to free soil became free. He went even further in interpreting the Ordinance of 1787 as a compact between the original thirteen states and the Northwest Territory. Fugitives escaping from those states only were bound to be returned. These interpretations formed the basis of the arguments used by Salmon P. Chase and Birney when, in March, 1837, Birney was himself indicted for harboring and concealing a fugitive.

The day began as an ordinary one in the Birney household. Birney had gone on an overnight trip to give a lecture; the children, all but Florence, were in school; and Mrs. Birney was resting as she could while directing the household duties of the maid, Matilda. It was in the afternoon, after Mrs. Birney had sent Matilda up the street on an errand, that she heard running steps, the slam of the door, and then hysterical sobbing. Bit by bit she pieced together the story that the trembling, frightened Matilda was trying to tell her. A rough man had accosted her in the street and had told her he knew that she was a runaway Negro slave.[50]

[49] *Philanthropist*, Feb. 12, Feb. 19, April 29, Oct. 28, Nov. 25, Dec. 9, 1836, and Feb. 24, 1837.
[50] *Philanthropist*, March 17, March 24, and March 31, 1837; Birney to Lewis Tap-

Matilda had come to the Birney home late the previous summer looking for work, and Mrs. Birney herself had hired her when Mr. Birney was away on a lecture trip. To all outward appearance completely white, Matilda had awakened no suspicions with her story that she had come from Missouri to work because her family was too poor to support her. Her mother was dead, she said, and she had left home to earn her own living. An industrious worker and a pleasant girl, she had quickly won the affections of the Birney children and the confidence of Mrs. Birney. Only then did she tell her secret to Mrs. Birney, who also revealed it to her husband, although none of the children knew the truth. As several weeks had passed since her arrival and there had seemed to be no effort to recapture Matilda, she had been allowed to remain instead of being sent on.

Matilda was an octoroon, the slave of Larkin Lawrence of Missouri (and said to be his daughter). She was an attractive brunette in her early twenties, and on a trip with him to the East, being allowed to act as her father's daughter and to pose as a free woman for the first time in her life, she became aware of the admiration she excited and of the possibilities which might be hers if she were really free. Before they arrived at Cincinnati, their last stopover to wait for a boat to St. Louis, Matilda had begun to plead with her father to set her free. She promised that if he would only give her a certificate proving that she was legally free, she would return home with him and serve him faithfully as long as he lived.

As her pleas were of no avail, Matilda resolved to seize her last opportunity to escape while in free territory. Without taking any extra clothes or belongings, which might excite suspicion, she slipped out of the hotel and made her way to the colored people of Cincinnati whom she hoped would take her in. For several days she remained hidden in the home of a colored barber until watchers reported that the river boat to St. Louis had left with Larkin Lawrence on it. He had made no effort to find her, and there had been no publicity about her escape. It seemed safe to conclude that if he had not acted immediately, he did

---

pan, April 18, 1837, Tappan Collection; Salmon P. Chase, *Speech* . . . , *in the Case of the Colored Woman, Matilda, Who Was Brought before the Court of Common Pleas of Hamilton County, Ohio, by Writ of Habeas Corpus; March 11, 1837* (Cincinnati, 1837); William Birney, *op. cit.,* pp. 261–265. The accounts differ slightly in some of the details. I have accepted Birney's own contemporary statement that he and Mrs. Birney knew Matilda was a fugitive prior to Riley's appearance.

not intend to seek her. So it was that she stayed in the city and had set out on her own to find employment, ending up in the Birney household.

When the man on the street detected her, not only was her own freedom in jeopardy, but she was endangering the lives of people who had befriended her. There was nothing Mrs. Birney and Matilda could do until Birney came home the next day except to keep an anxious vigil at the window so that they might have warning of the approach of any strangers or the authorities. Upon his arrival, Birney was hastily apprised of what had occurred. There was no escaping the serious implications of the situation, but for Birney there was only one thing to do. He determined "to take a high stand on the ground of humanity in assisting the oppressed—to strike at the very root of the prevailing prejudice about aiding slaves to escape." Hitherto Birney had played no active part in the Underground Railroad. In fact, the antislavery group in Cincinnati felt it was wisest, as long as he was editing the *Philanthropist,* that other hands should manage such matters. Usually the fugitives were taken care of by the colored people, and Birney was informed of the escape only when it was safely accomplished. Now it would be necessary to hide Matilda until she could be secretly taken out of the Birneys' house and out of the city. This, he quickly discovered, would not be easy. The house was being watched.

On March 10, before Matilda could be moved, E. V. Brooks, a constable of Cincinnati, appeared at the door to announce her arrest. He carried a warrant issued by William Doty, a justice of the peace, who had been presented with an affidavit by John M. Riley, purporting to be the agent of Lawrence. Riley was known in Cincinnati for his unsavory reputation as a Negro hunter. Without more ado, the young girl was taken before a magistrate and summarily committed to the Hamilton County jail until the next day. No cause of capture or detention was named in the commitment.

Although he could not admit it in Matilda's presence, Birney had little faith that her freedom could be legally obtained. Nonetheless, he was determined to use every argument which might swing the scales of justice to the right. He considered defending her himself but dismissed the idea as injudicious. To do so would automatically prejudice her chances. It would be far better to secure someone to defend her who was not an active abolitionist. It was not necessary to consider at length who this should be. Salmon P. Chase was the obvious choice. He was not an abolitionist himself, but his sister and brother-in-law were, and he had taken a strong stand at the time of the riots the previous summer. Moreover, he was steadily gaining the reputation of being one of the outstanding lawyers of the city.

Chase agreed to defend Matilda with the help of his partner, Samuel Eells; but time was at a premium. With less than twenty-four hours to prepare the case Birney and Chase sat down, Birney as teacher, Chase as pupil, to a concentrated lesson on the legal and constitutional aspects of the fugitive slave law as it applied in Ohio. By the next day, Birney's interpretations had been incorporated into Chase's arguments to be used before the court.[51] Meanwhile, the defense had applied to Judge Este for a writ of habeas corpus, which was issued by William Henry Harrison, at the time clerk of the Court of Common Pleas.

At 9:30 A.M. on March 11, Matilda was brought before the court, Judge D. K. Este presiding. M. N. McLean, R. T. Lytle, and N. C. Read represented the plaintiff, Riley, who sat ready, with three rough-looking men he had hired, to take Matilda away as soon as the decision should be rendered in his favor. Birney and Chase had hoped that the sight of the attractive girl would arouse the sympathy of the crowd gathered to watch the proceedings and hence of the court also. Instead they were revolted by the undercurrent of sadistic expectation that she would be turned over to men who made their living by "brutifying" their fellow men.

Chase made an able plea, stressing the awful responsibility resting upon the court, "not to the community alone—not alone to the humble individual who sues for protection here;—but to conscience and to God." He called attention to the "helpless and almost friendless woman who sues for this protection" by disclaiming that he sought aid for his argument by invoking sympathy for her, and then he launched into the specific legal and constitutional arguments. He maintained that (1) the warrant and affidavit were void because the fugitive slave law authorized no issuing of a judicial process and there was no such law among the state statutes; (2) the commitment was void because it was in the name of the State of Ohio but not authorized by any law of Ohio; (3) the fugitive slave law was repugnant to the Ordinance of 1787 and could have no jurisdiction over justices of the peace in states

[51] Hart, *op. cit.*, pp. 52, 65–66.

formed from the Northwest Territory; (4) the laws of Ohio gave no jurisdiction to justices of the peace, and, if they did, they would be unconstitutional; and (5) at the time Matilda left her master she was not held to service in one state from which she escaped into another. She had been brought by her master to Ohio.

Chase concluded with an appeal to civil liberty:

Vitally important as the issue of this cause is to the petitioner—for liberty is sweet even to the humblest, and slavery, disguise it as you will, is still a bitter draught,—the community has in it even a deeper stake. If she may be held in custody, though charged with no crime, upon a commitment, which shows, upon its face no cause of caption or detention, and which, even when aided by reference to every paper within reach of the court, still fails to show any legal or sufficient cause, then is it manifest that the habeas corpus act—that grand bulwark of personal liberty,—is virtually repealed. If such a commitment is a sufficient warrant for imprisonment, the whole legal security of personal freedom is gone.[52]

Judge Este's decision was a foregone conclusion. Matilda, he held, was legally a slave. She must be delivered up to the claimant's agent. Before there was time for any move to help her escape, Riley and his men went forward to seize her. She was whisked out of the courtroom, pushed into a waiting carriage, and driven to the river, where a ferry stood ready to take her and her captors to Covington. The next day she was put on a boat bound for New Orleans to be sold at public auction. The Birney family never heard of her again.

Matilda's defense had been useless; the decision of the judge had been known before it was uttered. At no time had there been any real proof that Larkin Lawrence had authorized Riley to claim Matilda; the whole case rested solely on Riley's oath. She was never returned to Lawrence. Yet public opinion supported the decision. "It was deplorable," wrote Hammond in the *Gazette*, "to witness such an excitement unfavorable to the liberty of an unprotected fellow creature, and a woman!"[53]

No sooner was Matilda remanded to slavery than a bill of indictment was brought against Birney for violating an Ohio law of 1804 against harboring or concealing a black or mulatto person who was the property of another. McLean, Lytle, and Read again conducted the prosecu-

[52] Chase, *Speech . . . , in the Case of the Colored Woman, Matilda.*
[53] Reprint from the *Gazette* in *Philanthropist*, March 31, 1837.

tion; Chase and Henry Starr, the defense. Lytle was the same man who had delivered the tirade against Birney at the mass meeting of January 22, 1836. He now justified the mob of the previous summer, openly declared that popular impulse was superior to law, and threatened that an even greater destruction was being prepared for Birney. Again the verdict was a foregone conclusion. Birney was found guilty and fined fifty dollars.

Birney and Chase, however, decided that this was a good opportunity to test the constitutionality of the 1804 law and appealed the case to the Ohio Supreme Court on a writ of error. Their contention was that in Ohio it was impossible to harbor or secrete a person who was the property of another. Matilda had ceased to be a slave the moment she was brought by her master to free soil. She was not escaping, merely exercising that freedom which the constitution of Ohio conferred upon her.

The Supreme Court, wishing to reverse the decision of the lower court but reluctant to face the real issue squarely, gave the opinion on a technicality. Judge Wood, handing down the decision of December 20, 1837, held that color afforded no presumption of condition; there was no evidence, therefore, that Birney had knowingly harbored a fugitive slave.[54] Not until the next decade did the Supreme Court of Ohio recognize that a slave brought by his master to free soil became free. This decision was given in another case defended by Chase, William Birney, and William Johnson, and, paradoxically, it was tried before Judge N. C. Read, who had been Chase's opposing counsel in the Matilda case.[55]

By 1837 the name of James G. Birney had become a familiar one to people all over the country who were interested in the cause of abolition, both to those who were supporting it and to those who were fighting it. It was unusual enough to have as a leader a man who was

[54] *Philanthropist*, Jan. 2 and 30, 1838; Charles Hammond, Reporter, *Cases Decided in the Supreme Court of Ohio in Bank at December Terms, 1837, 1838* (Cincinnati, 1872), VIII, 230–239; Chase to J. T. Trowbridge, March 16, 1864, quoted in Robert B. Warden, *An Account of the Private Life and Public Services of Salmon Portland Chase* (Cincinnati, 1874), pp. 282–284.

[55] *Reports of Cases Argued and Determined in Ohio Courts of Record as Published in the Western Law Journal* (Norwalk, O., 1896), p. 279; Jacob William Schuckers, *The Life and Public Services of Salmon Portland Chase* (New York, 1874), p. 77.

himself an ex-slaveholder. The Cincinnati riots had further publicized his name; and the *Philanthropist* had attained the rank of one of the leading antislavery newspapers. Birney was much in demand as a lecturer and was rapidly gaining the reputation of being one of the outstanding interpreters of the antislavery position on legal and constitutional issues.

Consequently, in the spring of 1837, Birney was approached by the Executive Committee of the American Anti-Slavery Society with the proposal that he come to New York to act as the corresponding secretary of the society. This office was a key position in the society, and a strong man was needed to fill it, particularly in view of the fact that there seemed to be danger of a growing rift in the ranks of the eastern abolitionists. A few New England ministers were even contemplating forming an antislavery society of their own.

The move to the East was being considered when Birney went to New York in May to attend the annual meeting of the national Anti-Slavery Society. Mutterings and mumblings of discontent behind the scenes were very much in evidence. They formed an anti-Garrison current, arising out of opposition to the latter's advocacy of such unpopular doctrines as women's rights and Christian anarchism. The fear was that the introduction of such subsidiary causes would frighten away possible converts to the antislavery cause and detract from the single-mindedness of purpose of those already in it. Birney's role, if he accepted the position offered, would be to conciliate the developing factions.

All of the men whose opinions he respected pressed him to accept: the Tappans, Gerrit Smith, Henry B. Stanton, and above all, Theodore Weld. Weld wrote to Birney:

In the present stage of the cause somebody must fill that office in whom the whole Abolition Community have perfect confidence and who will be greatly respected by the Church and heeded by the world—some one whose wisdom, for[e]cast, prudence, thorough going principle, firmness, fearlessness, and piety afford the assurance of *firm anchorage.*[56]

There was no one, he went on, in whom all abolitionists of all denominations had such confidence as they did in Birney, and there was no one more feared by their opponents. Birney's maturity, wide ac-

[56] Weld to Birney, May 23, 1837, Birney Papers.

quaintance in the South and West, legal knowledge, courteous manners, gentlemanliness, and style of writing and speaking all pointed him out as the best man. Stanton dwelt on the importance of making the Executive Committee the link between the "ultras" and the too prudent. Stanton's own influence was negligible because of his youth, but Birney carried weight with both groups and might prevent a schism.[57] It was true, as Weld had pointed out, that Birney would not be leaving a critical situation in Ohio. The *Philanthropist* was firmly established, the mob spirit seemed vanquished, and Ohio was well on the road to being abolitionized. There was a real need for Birney's talents in New York, where they would influence the whole field; they should not be confined in Ohio.

If Birney would not accept, the second choice for the position was John Greenleaf Whittier. Although Whittier was a devoted man, much beloved by his friends, he had no influence with the churches because of his Quakerism. Besides, he never spoke in public, had no business experience, and was timid. His poetic temperament would be an obstacle to his gaining the confidence of those with whom he would have to work.

Again Birney was faced with the necessity of making a decision on another move, a move which would be expensive and difficult, particularly in view of Mrs. Birney's health. She probably would be reluctant to be so far from her family, especially when it meant settling in so large a city as New York, where she would not know even her nearest neighbors. There was another question in his mind, too. Did he want to undertake the responsibility of the job he would have to do? It would not be an easy assignment to try to get someone like William Lloyd Garrison to modify what he had to say or print, and if this were impossible, how could a schism be prevented? He would probably incur the irritation of both sides in his attempt to reconcile them.

With the explosiveness of the New England situation in mind, Birney decided to go from the New York convention to Boston to attend the meeting of the New England Anti-Slavery Society. He had been appointed to a committee with Whittier and Charles Follen to communicate to John Quincy Adams a resolution commending his defense in Congress of the right of petition.[58] The Boston meeting would be a good opportunity to deliver the message personally and to get a first-

---

[57] Henry B. Stanton to Birney, Aug. 7, 1837, Birney Papers.
[58] American Anti-Slavery Society, *Fourth Annual Report.*

hand impression of how things stood in the quarrel which had developed between the New England ministers and Garrison. He was much relieved, consequently, to find the convention a harmonious one. Large crowds gathered for the meetings, which were held in the Salem and Park Street Congregational churches. Even Governor Everett honored the abolitionists with a visit, although he had to listen to some sharp remarks about his own gag-law opinions. Not only did Garrison refrain from interjecting controversial doctrines, but, as a fellow member of the business committee with Birney, he actually implied that he supported political pressure to oppose the annexation of Texas.[59]

John Quincy Adams had been invited to attend the Boston convention to receive the public thanks of the antislavery people for his fight on petitions, but Adams was politician enough to be circumspect about hobnobbing with people who were still considered radicals by many of his constituents. "The most insignificant error of conduct in me at this time would be my irredeemable ruin in this world," he confided to his diary.[60]

Instead of mailing the resolution of the American Anti-Slavery Society to Adams, Birney chose to deliver it in person to his house in Quincy. He was graciously received and much impressed by the "republican plainness and simplicity and dignity of this venerable champion of our liberties." They talked for two hours. Birney reported to Gamaliel Bailey:

When I review, what Mr. A. has done in defense of the liberties of his fellow citizens—and this too, with but little aid from those who ought to have stood by him—in the face of a majority whose opposition may well be termed *savage;* and when I see him at this late period of his life with the alacrity and determination that usually belong to younger men, defending the outposts and the citadel of his country's freedom, he has not only my highest admiration, but my sincerest gratitude. He will at least have the consolation of saying, *if Rome must fall that I am innocent.* May every abolitionist be enabled to say the same, and with equal conscientiousness.[61]

Another call was made at the home of William Ellery Channing, who, upon hearing that Birney was in town, sent a special letter inviting him to visit. Channing had been moving in the direction of

[59] *Philanthropist,* June 16, 1837; William Birney, *op. cit.,* p. 269.
[60] Allan Nevins, ed. *The Diary of John Quincy Adams, 1794–1845* (New York, 1929), entry for April 19, 1837.
[61] Birney to Gamaliel Bailey, June 3, 1837, in *Philanthropist,* June 16, 1837.

abolition ever since his public letter in praise of Birney's defense of freedom of the press. Now he was casting about for some new topic to which his writing ability might be directed. Birney suggested that he write a letter on Texas to some distinguished politician, such as Clay, who was not already committed on the question of annexation.[62] Not long after, Channing's *Letter to the Hon. Henry Clay, on the Annexation of Texas to the United States* was published.

Birney was kept busy lecturing all the way from Boston back to Cincinnati. He addressed the students at Andover at their request; lectured in the Congregational Church at Hanover, where he was the guest of President Lord of Dartmouth; and spoke at Hartford, where the meeting was broken up by noisy intruders.

It was a relief after weeks of traveling, attending conventions, and lecturing to arrive at the hospitable Gerrit Smith home in Peterboro. Here was the kind of life which appealed strongly to Birney, still a country gentleman at heart. The tiny village, completely dominated by the large Smith mansion on the corner of its square, offered the needed peace and relaxation after the bustle, noise, and heat of New York and Boston; and Gerrit Smith, often described as one of "nature's noblemen," was a genial host. With a large fortune at his command, he entertained easily and bountifully. This was Birney's first visit; but the Smith home was to become, in later years, a haven of refuge for him.

Birney gave a lecture in the Methodist Church in Peterboro, and, in the pleasant company of Smith, Beriah Green, and William Goodell, he made a trip into Chenango and Oswego counties. At Oswego the sight of white and colored children walking hand in hand at a Sunday-school picnic was to him "one of the most pleasing and certain proofs that the cause of human rights is also on the advance." [63]

Before catching a boat from Buffalo, Birney made another excursion, up into Canada, and was again much encouraged by the progress of the colored fugitives who had settled there and by the work being accomplished by Hiram Wilson. There were two lectures in the Baptist Church in Buffalo, spiced by the throwing of some eggs and a few pebbles; then the boat trip to Erie; the rough ride by stage to Pitts-

---

[62] Birney to Salmon P. Chase, June 5, 1837; Chase Papers, Manuscript Division, Library of Congress.

[63] Birney to Lewis Tappan, July 5, 1837, Tappan Collection.

burgh, where he delivered an evening lecture to a large audience in the Methodist Church; then another exhausting stagecoach ride to Wheeling; and, finally, the last lap of the journey home by boat.[64]

Home meant rest and recovery from his physical exhaustion, but there could be little mental relaxation until he had made up his mind what was to be done about the New York offer. Mrs. Birney was, as he had anticipated, reluctant to move. She was pregnant again and would have little strength and less heart for another uprooting, even though, as William told her in trying to boost her spirits, she might be happier away from the "democratic, mobocratic West." [65]

Yet there was duty. Having dedicated his life to the cause of anti-slavery and having joined forces with the American Anti-Slavery Society as the most effective means of working for the cause, Birney could not refuse to accept responsibility where he was most needed. Men like Lewis Tappan and Theodore Weld, who understood his family problems, felt that he should go, despite the initial opposition of his Ohio antislavery colleagues to his leaving them. As for Agatha and the family, they could make living arrangements which would relieve her of the housekeeping duties. Another argument in favor of moving was the greater educational opportunity his sons would have.

So by the end of July the Birney house and lots were up for sale, and Lewis Tappan was authorized to choose a place in New York for them to live. With the four oldest boys in school, the family would be reduced to four, and arrangements were made to board out. James, Jr., was to stay on as an instructor at Miami University, William's plans were to enter Yale, Dion would go to Mr. Guthrie's school at Putnam or to Middlebury, and David was to be sent to his grandfather in Kentucky.

When Birney was considering the move to New York, he decided that he would risk a farewell trip to see his father in Kentucky, even though the old gentleman had declared that he wanted no more intercourse between them. It would be a dangerous trip, for the threats to mob Birney should he set foot across the river had not been forgotten. To avoid publicity, he rode about eight miles down the river instead of trying to cross at Cincinnati. Once landed on the Kentucky shore, he proceeded the sixty miles by horseback, talking to no one, instead of

[64] Birney to Lewis Tappan, July 14 and 18, 1837, Tappan Collection.
[65] William Birney to Agatha Birney, July 26, 1837, Birney Papers.

going by stage, where he might be more easily recognized and his presence reported. Everything went well, and best of all, his father could not conceal his pleasure at seeing him. For two days they visited, and Birney left with a much lighter heart than he had carried for a long while. His father was in good health, seemed contented, and, above all, was so pleased with the New York proposal, which would remove his son from the danger of violence, that he never once mentioned anything about abandoning the antislavery cause.[66] It was as a result of this reconciliation that Grandfather Birney had asked that David be allowed to come to live with him for awhile, and permission had been granted. Birney's farewell with his sister was also affectionate. Mrs. Marshall made the trip from Louisville to Cincinnati to bid the family goodbye.

Once more the Birney family was setting out for a new life. This time not even Birney himself was completely optimistic. Doubts and forebodings were pressing him as he wrote:

I know my own powers, I think, better than anyone else, and I fear their insufficiency for what is before me. My health is not generally so good as it was two or three years since. I am not capable of such continuous mental or physical effort as I used to be. Add to this, I have a large family of children and a sickly and dispirited wife, who is unable to control and educate them. Besides these circumstances embarrassing to myself—I apprehend, and I did from the first, that the salary I am to receive, will create some jealousy and jarring. Notwithstanding, I hope for the best. Should my hope not be met I shall most cheerfully yield to circumstances that may point out to me an humbler sphere.[67]

[66] Birney to Lewis Tappan, Aug. 8 and 23, 1837, Tappan Collection.
[67] Birney to Lewis Tappan, Sept. 14, 1837, Tappan Collection.

Chapter VIII

Secretary of the American Anti-Slavery Society

THE problem of maintaining unity which faced the Executive Committee of the American Anti-Slavery Society in 1837 was threefold: (1) a growing fear that subsidiary causes such as women's rights and Christian anarchism which were being advocated by William Lloyd Garrison and his followers were a detriment to the effectiveness of the antislavery cause; (2) the question of the organizational and financial relationship which should be maintained between the parent antislavery society and its auxiliary state societies; and (3) disagreement over the degree to which political action should be supported.

At the time Birney arrived in New York to take up his duties as corresponding secretary, the first of these issues was uppermost. In addition to his advocacy of "no-human government," or Christian anarchism, Garrison had been hurling invectives against the church. As a consequence, several New England clergymen were ready to secede from the old antislavery organization and form a new one of their own. The Rev. Charles Fitch and the Rev. Joseph H. Towne, Congregational ministers of Boston, took the lead in publishing a severe castigation of Garrison in what was known as the "Clerical

Appeal." [1] It was hoped that Birney could help smooth the troubled waters, as his appointment had been approved both by the ministers and by such men as Samuel J. May, Ellis G. Loring, Henry C. Wright, and Francis Jackson, who could be said to speak for the "Garrisonites." Birney, as well as most of the Executive Committee, felt that the clergymen were right in substance but injudicious in making public the schism in the ranks. On the other hand, if Garrison could not be "reduced to moderation," Birney said "his departure from us" might "be the best thing he could do for the cause of Emancipation." [2]

The labors of Birney, Stanton, and Elizur Wright, Jr., as corresponding secretaries were divided with an eye to the explosive situation in New England. Wright was to take care of foreign correspondence and have editorial charge of all society publications except the *Emancipator;* Stanton would manage the financial department and the correspondence relating to legislative objectives; while Birney was to take care of general domestic correspondence and to supervise the agencies. This assignment would enable him to travel, particularly in New England, where he could exert his influence for peace. Birney's acquaintance with such men of importance as William Ellery Channing, President Nathan Lord, of Dartmouth, and President Justin Edwards, of Andover Theological Seminary, could be counted on for increased support from them. By this time many of the state legislatures, particularly in New England, were considered receptive to antislavery persuasion, especially on the question of the annexation of Texas. Birney's legal training and experience in state government admirably qualified him for such an assignment.

The arrangement at the society's office in New York was such that Birney and Stanton could alternate lecture trips, each of them being gone about half the time. During the latter part of 1837 Birney did make short trips, but since Mrs. Birney's approaching confinement made her health very precarious again, much of his time was spent in writing. On December 1, 1837, Birney sent out from the Anti-Slavery Society's office letters to the governors of all the slave states, informing them that the American Anti-Slavery Society would send them, without cost, all of its publications, thereby furnishing them "the current information of the

[1] "Appeal of Clerical Abolitionists on Anti-Slavery Measures," *Liberator*, Extra, Aug. 19, 1837.
[2] Birney to Lewis Tappan, Aug. 23 and Sept. 14, 1837, Tappan Collection.

condition and prospects of a cause in which the slaveholders have so deep an interest." Governors Campbell, of Virginia, Cannon, of Tennessee, and Bagby, of Alabama, all refused to receive the literature, while Governor Butler, of South Carolina, merely returned Birney's own letter. Governor Bagby, an acquaintance of Birney, professed the greatest respect for him personally, but not for the opinions of the society.[3]

In January, 1838, Birney sent a tract, *Why Work for the Slave?*, accompanied by a note, to John C. Calhoun and other southern Congressmen. He was pleased when, instead of ignoring it or refusing it, they evinced enough interest to appoint Representative Elmore, of South Carolina, to write on their behalf to secure more information. Elmore's letter of February 16 to Birney contained fourteen questions concerning the number of antislavery societies, their membership, recent increase, connection with societies outside the United States, number of presses and publications, source of funds, aims, and means of effecting their aims. Birney's reply was as thoroughly informative as he could make it, yet to the point. He wisely refrained from a philippic against the slaveholder. The aims of the antislavery societies, he said, were the "re-animation of the Republican principles of our Constitution" and the "establishment of the Union on an enduring basis." He admitted that Congress had no power over slavery in the states, but he explained that the societies would continue to try to influence Congress to abolish the slave trade, end slavery in the District of Columbia and the territories, and prevent its extension. If the South chose to dissolve the Union on this ground, it would bring only ruin upon itself. The Southern people should be informed of the storm gathering over their heads; all the abolitionists asked was for access to the popular mind. Twenty-five thousand copies of this correspondence were published by the American Anti-Slavery Society.[4]

It was at the anniversary meeting of the American Anti-Slavery Society in New York in May, 1838, that the question of the relationship between the national and state societies came to a head. For several years agents had operated without conflict as to who should receive the

[3] James G. Birney, *Correspondence between the Hon. F. H. Elmore, One of the South Carolina Delegation in Congress, and James G. Birney, One of the Secretaries of the American Anti-Slavery Society* (New York, 1838), Appendix H.

[4] *Ibid.;* Minutes of the Executive Committee of the American Anti-Slavery Society, Boston Public Library, entries for Feb. 15, 1838, and June 7, 1838.

money collected for the cause. But as state and county societies multiplied, a decentralization movement set in. County societies felt that all money collected within their limits should be allocated by them; the state societies, in turn, took this position toward the national society. Scarcity of money after the panic of 1837 served to augment the trend, as did, also, local differences on the political question and, in Massachusetts, on "Garrisonism." [5] As a result of the strong stand taken by the delegates to the meeting in New York, a resolution was passed by which each state or other auxiliary society so electing could take complete charge of the cause within its own field. This would include direction of lecturers and agents in forming local societies, collecting funds, circulating petitions, and establishing libraries. The parent society would not send its agents into states adopting this plan without the concurrence of the state executive committee. The state society, however, would have to guarantee to the national treasury "such stated payments as may be judged reasonable." [6]

The Massachusetts Board of Managers decided to adopt this plan, with a pledge of $10,000 to the parent society. Almost immediately the Massachusetts society asked for the aid of Henry B. Stanton in lecturing and collecting funds. Stanton sensed, however, that there was more than finances involved. "There is a disposition on the part of some of the Board at Boston, to cramp us at N.Y. all they can," he reported to Birney; and he advocated that the Massachusetts society be required to fulfill its part of the arrangement to the letter.[7] Garrison organized a peace convention in Boston in September, whose Declaration of Sentiments proclaimed nonresistance for both individuals and nations. Its supporters expressed the opinion that they could not acknowledge allegiance to any human government.[8] This declaration added to the general feeling of mistrust that the cause in Massachusetts was being sidetracked.

[5] Gilbert H. Barnes, *The Anti-Slavery Impulse,* pp. 149–151.

[6] Massachusetts Anti-Slavery Society, *Seventh Annual Report of the Board of Managers . . . 1839* (Boston, 1839), pp. 5–6; Minutes, Executive Committee, American Anti-Slavery Society, entry for June 21, 1838.

[7] Henry B. Stanton to Birney, Aug. 11, 1838, Birney Papers.

[8] Wendell Phillips Garrison and Francis Jackson Garrison, *William Lloyd Garrison, 1805–1879, The Story of His Life Told by His Children* (New York, 1885), II, 230–234.

By the autumn of 1838, personal and family concerns were uppermost in Birney's mind. Agatha had been confined to the house most of the time since the move to New York. A vacation in the country at the Gerrit Smith home during the summer had seemed to improve both her health and her spirits, but there was no hope that she could completely recover from tuberculosis. The loss of the baby, Ellen, in August, was perhaps the final blow to her spirit. Agatha died scarcely three months later, in October.

By the time she was thirty-nine she had borne eleven children, six of whom were living. Since the family's return to Kentucky in 1833 she had been a semi-invalid. The fear of personal danger to her husband and children, estrangement from friends, family, and home were a constant drain on her diminishing strength. As the wife of an active abolitionist, she, with her children, were often torn from familiar surroundings to follow Birney to a new assignment. Although her husband had often expressed a wish to take his family to "some little glen or hollow" where they could spend their days in peace, Agatha knew that his sense of dedication to the antislavery cause would not permit it. She was a dutiful wife, but she never really shared Birney's crusading zeal.

It was impossible for Birney to keep the children with him. James had left teaching to study for the ministry at Andover Seminary, and David was at Phillips Academy. William's ill-health had forced him to drop out of Yale, and he and Dion were trying their luck as farmers on some of the land Birney had bought in Darke County, Ohio. The older boys were able to take care of themselves, but a home had to be found for George and Florence. Mrs. Marshall wrote from Louisville offering to take them, but Birney was reluctant to have them raised in a slave state. Consequently, he was deeply grateful for the generous offer of the Gerrit Smiths to care for them. In the Smith home the children would be raised as Birney wished, and they were near enough so that he could visit them regularly.

Once the children were settled, Birney proceeded to sell the Brooklyn house and furniture and to find rooms for himself. Despite the fact that his wife had been sickly and his children often unruly, the new existence was barren and cheerless by comparison. His depression is reflected in the entry in his diary for February 4, 1840: "I am this day 48 years old,

& living in this great city, alone, a widower, & without any of my children with me. Were it not for my constant engagements as one of
the Cor. Secs. of the American Anti-Slavery Society, it would be a lonely
life. But I am not allowed leisure to feel solitary."

The year 1839 opened with portents of troubles to come. The meeting
of the Massachusetts Anti-Slavery Society in January was stormy. The
Garrison forces, who were most numerous in Boston and Lynn, sent
enough delegates to outvote easily those who came from elsewhere in
the state. It was charged that a new city society had been organized in
Boston in order that additional delegates might be appointed to the
state meeting. As a result, Garrison succeeded in swinging the vote
in favor of his nonresistance and women's-rights views and against
abolitionist action at the ballot box. Stanton wrote to Birney that whenever anyone rose to speak from an opposite point of view, "Men would
cry out, 'no matter what they say—no matter what they propose—let
us vote them down!'" "The split is wide," he reported, "and can never
be closed up. . . . Our cause in this state is ruined unless we can
seperate [*sic*] the A.S. Society from everything which does not belong
to it." [9]

The group in Massachusetts which refused to go along with Garrison's ideas seceded to form the Massachusetts Abolition Society, distinct from the Massachusetts Anti-Slavery Society. By February the
members of the new society had established a new paper, the *Abolitionist*, which they felt would more correctly represent their views than
the *Liberator* had been able to do. Its mottos, "Supremacy of the Laws"
and "Liberty, the right of all—law, its defence," indicated its disavowal
of "no-human government" ideas.

Birney and the other men in the national office were faced with the
problem of what course of action to follow. Garrison and many of the
men associated with him had been among the pioneers in the organized
antislavery movement. To break with them openly was not easy from
a personal standpoint and would result in much unfavorable publicity.
Ellis Loring, one of the founders of the New England Anti-Slavery
Society, wrote an appeal to Birney to prevent the national society from
departing from a neutral course; if a stand were taken, he felt that the

[9] Stanton to Birney, Jan. 26, 1839, Birney Papers; Massachusetts Abolition Society, *The Second Annual Report . . . : Together with the Proceedings of the
Second Annual Meeting . . . 1841* (Boston, 1841), pp. 7–8.

split would spread to the other states and become a national one.[10] A majority of the Executive Committee of the American Anti-Slavery Society, including Birney, agreed with Stanton, however, that the anti-slavery cause must be stripped of any extraneous dogmas.

It was at this point that the financial problem became definitely interwoven with the problem of the society's policy on Garrisonism. The Massachusetts Anti-Slavery Society had defaulted on the first two payments due on its pledge to the national society and gave little sign of meeting the third. Believing that the default was, as Stanton had concluded, to "cramp" the New York authority, the American Anti-Slavery Society announced that it considered its financial arrangement with Massachusetts terminated. Agents would once more be sent to Massachusetts to collect money directly for the American Anti-Slavery Society.[11] The money which had come in on the pledge had been raised mostly by Stanton, a national agent; and the pressure of the debts of the national society, they felt, justified their action.

The Massachusetts Board of Managers responded with a reply addressed to the abolitionists of their state terming the action of the Executive Committee hasty and violent. The Massachusetts group was split, however. Four of the Board, Amos Phelps, Amasa Walker, Joseph Eayrs, and Simon Shipley refused to sign the letter. The Executive Committee of the American Anti-Slavery Society protested that its step had not been taken as a measure of censure against the Massachusetts Society, but they were unable to convince the state society.[12] In June, 1839, the Executive Committee recognized the schismatic Massachusetts Abolition Society as auxiliary to the American Anti-Slavery Society.[13] The rift was becoming a chasm.

Birney spent most of February and March in Connecticut and Massachusetts and was on hand, together with Stanton and Lewis Tappan from the Executive Committee, for a meeting with the Massachusetts

[10] Ellis Loring to Birney, Feb. 16, 1839, Birney Papers.

[11] Minutes, Executive Committee, Am. Anti-Slavery Soc., entry for Jan. 29, 1839.

[12] *Christian Journal* (New York), Extra, March 20, 1839. This contains the letter from the Executive Committee of the American Society to the Massachusetts Board of Managers, the protest of the Massachusetts Board, the reply of the Executive Committee, and the statement of the Rev. A. Phelps and others; Minutes, Executive Committee, Am. Anti-Slavery Soc., entries for Jan. 3, 17, 29, Feb. 18 and 21, and March 7, 1839; Garrison and Garrison, *op. cit.*, II, 287–288.

[13] Minutes, Executive Committee, Am. Anti-Slavery Soc., entry for Nov. 6, 1839.

society at Marlboro Chapel in Boston on March 26. The financial arrangement and the obligations of the abolitionists at the polls were again debated, with nothing gained but increased ill feelings on each side. Birney returned from the meeting to pen an article called "View of the Constitution of the American Anti-Slavery Society as Connected with the 'No-Government' Question," which was later published as *A Letter on the Political Obligations of Abolitionists*. The constitution of American Anti-Slavery Society stated that Congress was to be "influenced." How, Birney asked, could this be done except at the ballot box? It was absurd to advocate petitions to Congress yet oppose voting for persons who would hear and act on such petitions. The Declaration of Sentiments also explicitly stated that there were "the highest obligations resting upon the people of the free states, to remove slavery by moral and political action, as prescribed in the Constitution of the United States." [14] Now, however, a no-human government group had arisen in their midst whose policies would strike at the root of the social structure, throw society into confusion, and renew scenes of anarchy and license which had heretofore been the offspring of the rankest infidelity and irreligion. According to Birney's point of view, abolitionists who did not agree to assume their obligations, moral and political, as stated by the basic documents of the society, should withdraw from membership. It was unjust to try to compel those who joined in order to abolish slavery to be part of a crusade to abolish government. Although he avowed his friendship for individuals who advocated the no-human government doctrine, he honestly felt that they were driving people away from the antislavery cause.[15]

Garrison replied to Birney, calling his arguments

truthless, slanderous, cruel—caricatures of the pacific precepts of the Gospel —phantasms of a distorted imagination—satires upon the obligations of Christianity—libels upon the character and conduct of the Prince of Peace— unsupported by any show of reasoning, any appeal to the scriptures, any presentation of evidence.

[14] *The Constitution of the American Anti-Slavery Society: With the Declaration of the National Anti-Slavery Convention at Philadelphia, December 1833, and the Address to the Public, Issued by the Executive Committee of the Society, in September, 1835* (New York, 1838).

[15] James G. Birney, *A Letter on the Political Obligations of Abolitionists . . . : With a Reply by William Lloyd Garrison* (Boston, 1839), pp. 3–13.

Publication of Birney's article in the *Emancipator* was termed a "prostitution of the official organ of the Parent Society to party purposes," especially as it had been done just before the annual meeting without allowing time for a reply. Garrison insisted that Congress could be influenced by other than political actions, such as petitions, remonstrances, facts, and arguments. He attempted to make a rather dubious distinction between the duty of abolitionists to influence Congress and that of creating a Congress. Their work was not to put people into office, but to set right those who did, he insisted. Birney was attacked as a disorganizing spirit who was creating a schism in the ranks by trying to force everyone to swallow his own political dogmas. Stanton, Elizur Wright, Amos Phelps, and Orange Scott were named as his partners in a "belligerent crusade" against the nonresistants.[16] Birney refused to take any public notice of Garrison's reply, deeming it "replete with sophistry and unfair dealing."

The factions were pretty well aligned by the time of the annual meeting in New York in May, 1839, and the break was evident as soon as the first session began. If the Garrisonites could first introduce the question of women's voting and win on the issue, they could control a majority of the votes to win on the others. Oliver Johnson, Garrison's right-hand man, moved to substitute the word "persons" for "men" in making up the roll of delegates. As the votes of the women present were counted on this issue, the victory of the Garrisonites was assured. An immediate counterresolution offered by Tappan, Phelps, and Charles Torrey was voted down. A protest signed by 123 members and presented by Birney later in the convention was equally unavailing.[17] Many of the delegates were not opposed to women's rights per se, indeed, women such as the Grimké sisters had been giving antislavery lectures for several years. Their objection was to making the issue of women's rights an adjunct of the antislavery movement. Birney himself, however, was still an old-school southern gentleman on the woman question. Although he preferred that the women in the movement work only among women and not publicly address mixed audiences, he was quick to their defense when remarks against them bordered on the improper. When the Rev. Leonard Bacon, of New Haven, compared Sarah Grimké to a fanatical Quaker woman of early New England who

16 *Ibid.*, pp. 13–36.
17 Am. Anti-Slavery Soc., *Sixth Annual Report* (New York, 1839).

had walked nude through the streets, Birney immediately addressed a letter of reproach to him.[18]

The report of the Executive Committee to the convention emphasized the gains of the past year which were due to political pressure, among which were counted the prevention of the annexation of Texas and favorable elections in Ohio, New York, and Massachusetts. The Garrison group triumphed, however, when its resolutions were adopted and Birney's resolution "That to maintain that the elective franchise ought not to be used by abolitionists to advance the cause of emancipation, is inconsistent with the duty of abolitionists under the Constitution" was tabled.

Ever since Birney had left Cincinnati, his friends there had been urging him to come back to pay them a visit and give some lectures. With the New York convention over, he decided to make the trip. He would attend the Ohio convention and at the same time visit his sons in Darke County and his aging father in Kentucky. The trip was not without its political significance. Birney was to call on Senator Thomas Morris and urge him to attend the national convention which was being planned and he was to try to secure a strong delegation from the West.[19] Birney attended not only the Ohio anniversary meeting at Putnam at the end of May but also the first anniversary of the Indiana society at Greensburg early in June. At both he introduced the topic of political action, which was discussed and "harmonious conclusions" reached. At Greensburg there was still so much opposition to abolitionism that no meeting place could be secured and benches had to be put up in a grove out of town. "When men and women, too, are content to assemble for two days in the woods," wrote Birney, "to consult on the best means of carrying on an unpopular cause, you may be sure the root of the matter is in them."[20]

James Birney, Sr., was pleased that his son was coming for a visit and thought there would be no danger if prudence were exercised and if Birney refrained from conversing with Negroes on the way.[21] Nothing

18 Birney to the Rev. Leonard Bacon, Dec. 24, 1838, Birney Papers; manuscript memorandum, Dec. 22, 1838, Birney Papers.

19 Stanton to Birney, June 10, 1839, Birney Papers; Birney to Tappan, June 12, 1839, Tappan Collection.

20 *Philanthropist*, June 11, 1839; Birney to Joshua Leavitt, June 11, 1839, in *Emancipator*, June 20, 1839.

21 James Birney, Sr., to Birney, June 8, 1839, Birney Papers.

untoward occurred, and Birney was happy to find that he still held much of the respect and good will of his old friends and of many of the influential men of the state. He intended to go from Louisville to Lexington with his sister "by way of trying the temper" of his "old countrymen," but an attack of chills and fever prevented it.[22] This was the last meeting between father and son, and Birney later regretted that even then he had not been able to convert his father to abolition. The elder Birney died a cynic, without hope that the South would repent or that the North would try to be tactful and practical. Birney knew that he had greatly disappointed his father by advocating a radical cause, by being maligned and persecuted instead of respected and honored by the public.

Birney was hardly back in New York before word followed him that his father had died on July 24.[23] There was no will, but during Birney's recent visit his father had expressed the intention of leaving his slaves to his son, who might, if he chose, set them free. This arrangement was agreed to by the Marshalls, and Birney received the slaves in lieu of other inheritance. The twenty-one slaves, some of them skilled rope-makers, would have brought about $12,000 in the market. Birney demurred against any undue laudation for this act of emancipation, which, he protested, was but "rendering *their own* to those who are entitled to it,—it having providentially come into my hands." [24] The *Protestant and Herald* of Louisville, one of whose editors was William L. Breckinridge, praised this proof of Birney's sincerity. Giving up $12,000 was a "rather heavier argument than those with which the most of people back their opinions." [25] Yet there was the hair-splitting northern abolitionist who questioned whether Birney had not, by accepting the slaves as his portion of the estate, made himself a slave-holder and thereby departed from the principles of antislavery! [26]

Birney did not return to New York until late in October and then was not sure that he could continue his work as corresponding secretary for the national society. He had had an attack of fever in the spring. Then, while he was going from Cincinnati to Louisville after

[22] Birney to Lewis Tappan, July 17, 1839, Tappan Collection.
[23] John J. Marshall to Birney, July 24, 1839, Birney Papers.
[24] Birney to Lewis Tappan, Sept. 12, 1839, Tappan Collection. The act of emancipation is printed in the *Emancipator*, Sept. 26, 1839.
[25] Reprint from the Louisville *Protestant and Herald* in *Philanthropist*, Sept. 24, 1839.
[26] *Emancipator*, Nov. 21, 1839.

his father's death, the boat grounded and all the passengers had to get out. When the yawl to which they were transferred overturned, Birney had to swim to shore. This overtaxed his strength, and the fever returned.[27] In addition to his own health, there was the problem of whether the national society should continue in existence or whether, especially in view of the fact that it was likely in the future to be under the control of Garrisonian ideas, there should be a complete transfer of controls to the state and local societies. In that case, all national agents would become state agents. The national society was definitely in a financially embarrassing position. Its agents no longer collected money in states having state societies, yet their expenses remained the same. Birney had declined receiving his salary while he had been away settling his father's estate, and most of the others of the Executive Committee had felt it necessary to resort to other means of supporting themselves.[28]

In May, 1837, Arthur Hopkins declined to act any longer as Birney's agent in collecting his still outstanding claims in Alabama. This was not only a personal blow, but it meant that the money might never be recovered. Resorting to lawsuits would be futile, since he was convinced that no Alabama jury would give him the verdict.[29] With Mrs. Birney's doctor's bills to pay at that time, and five sons to be educated, something had to be done. After investing in Ohio lands, Birney bought more land in Indiana and then undertook the project of raising multicaulis mulberry trees. It turned out to be a complete failure. By 1840 he had mortgaged all of his Indiana land for a debt of over $6,000.[30] In view of the whole situation, he considered retiring to the farm in Darke County, where he might gather his family together and try to recoup both his health and his financial independence.

By February, 1840, only the Eastern Pennsylvania Anti-Slavery Society had responded to the call of the parent society for money, but the Executive Committee felt that for psychological reasons, at least,

[27] Birney to Lewis Tappan, Sept. 12, 1839, Tappan Collection.
[28] Minutes, Executive Committee, Am. Anti-Slavery Soc., entry for Nov. 6, 1839; Birney to Arnold Buffum, Nov. 8, 1839, Birney Manuscripts, Boston Public Library; Birney to Stanton, Nov. 27, 1839, Wright Papers.
[29] Gamaliel Bailey to Birney, May 27, 1837, Birney Papers; Birney to Lewis Tappan, July 5, 1837, Tappan Collection.
[30] Luther J. Cox to Birney, Feb. 13, 1840; Indenture between Birney and Cox, March 24, 1840, Birney Papers.

it had to hold out until the anniversary meeting in May. Then, if the nonresistants could be foiled, the present committee reappointed, and the restrictive regulation on collecting money rescinded, all might again go well. In March, Joshua Leavitt offered to buy the *Emancipator* if the Executive Committee would provide for its continuance to the close of the current volume, three or four issues. In April the subscription books were sold to the New York City Anti-Slavery Society for one year, to be published by Leavitt under its charge. The rest of the property of the American Anti-Slavery Society was transferred to Lewis Tappan and S. W. Benedict to be held in trust.[31] This transfer of property was interpreted by the Garrison group as a move to prevent its falling into their hands should they gain the ascendancy at the annual meeting in May. It continued to be a point of bitter contention after the split occurred. Birney felt the society was doomed if the Garrisonians gained control.[32] In that case, it would have to disband or form a new organization.

By the time the meeting convened on May 13, Birney was on his way to England as a delegate to the World Anti-Slavery Convention, but Lewis Tappan wrote him the details.[33] The Garrison group had arranged for a chartered steamboat to carry its supporters to New York in large enough numbers to control the meeting. Fearing that something of this sort might eventually happen, the Executive Committee had proposed that the constitution of the society be amended so that no state society could send voting delegates in excess of the number of men that state sent to the House of Representatives. If there were two state societies, as in Massachusetts, the delegates should be equally divided; where the number was uneven, the one with the most auxiliaries should get the extra vote. Of course nothing could be done to amend the constitution until the annual meeting, and as the Garrison men now controlled it, the effort was fruitless.[34]

[31] Minutes, Executive Committee, Am. Anti-Slavery Soc., entries for March 26 and April 16, 1840.

[32] Birney to Amos Phelps, Feb. 4, 1840, Birney Manuscripts, Boston Public Library.

[33] Lewis Tappan to Birney, May 13 and May 16, 1840; also, Tappan to Weld, May 26, 1840, Tappan Collection. See also Garrison and Garrison, *op. cit.*, II, 344–49.

[34] Minutes, Executive Committee, Am. Anti-Slavery Soc., entry for March 19, 1840.

Although the same old issues were all contributing causes to the
ensuing split, the actual break came over the appointing of women to
offices in the society. Francis Jackson, a Garrison man, presided. He
appointed Lydia M. Child, one of the most active antislavery writers,
to a business committee. As Mrs. Child was absent, Lewis Tappan tried
to avoid the issue by suggesting that her husband, David Child, be
substituted. His attempt failed, and Abby Kelly, one of the most radical
of the women in the movement, was chosen instead. Tappan then asked
to be excused from serving on the grounds that he believed it to be
unconstitutional for women to be appointed to committees. Amos
Phelps joined Tappan in leading a secession.

That evening about thirty of the secessionists met at the Tappan home
to consider the situation. The decision was for complete separation. At
a meeting the next day a new society, the American and Foreign Anti-
Slavery Society, was formed. Arthur Tappan was elected president;
F. J. LeMoyne and John T. Norton, vice-presidents; Birney and Stanton,
secretaries; and Lewis Tappan, treasurer. The schism was complete.

The disagreements and bickerings in the antislavery ranks by men
who should be pulling together for the good of the cause were disheartening to Birney. Sometimes they were enough to make him question the labor and sacrifice which had been put into the antislavery
movement. Such moments of depression were temporary, however.
Even with Garrison's no-human government vagaries to contend with,
even if the American Anti-Slavery Society had split, good had still been
accomplished. The cause had become respectable throughout the North.
Prominent men in the government and in the literary field were now
contributing the weight of their influence and talents. Antiabolition
mobs were a thing of the past, and the battle for freedom of the press
had been won. If the antislavery cause could move forward steadily
but slowly in the area of political action, there were surely great gains
ahead.

Chapter IX

Advocate of
Political Action

BIRNEY was well aware of the difficulties involved in uniting all of the abolitionists in political action. There was still a great deal of opposition to changing the character of the antislavery movement from a religious to a political basis, and this opposition came not only from the Garrison group but from the ministers, and even from leaders such as Weld and Tappan. Yet Birney was convinced that coalition of all people with antislavery views into one great party was inevitable. It had taken a long while for abolitionists to realize that the churches would not take strong and united action against slavery and would refuse to acknowledge openly that slaveholding was sinful and that the consequence of continuing in that sin would be excommunication from the church. Now it was taking some people just as long to realize that it was visionary to hope that either the Whig or the Democratic party would espouse antislavery principles and campaign on such a platform.

Everyone opposed to slavery favored some sort of political action— everyone, that is, except the Christian anarchists. And the more the no-human government adherents confused antislavery doctrine with their own peculiar political ideas, the more conservative men felt they must disclaim the alliance by taking more definite political steps.[1] Even so, political action would have come eventually. It had been inherent in Birney's thesis that slavery was incompatible with a republican form of government, a view he had expressed in his letter to Mills on colonization in 1834.

Birney's early advocacy of political action had not meant that he then favored partisan action, however. While in Ohio he had feared that the abolitionists might be driven by persecution to organize a party. If they did so, there would be grave danger that they might sacrifice "that sacred regard for *duty*" in the interests of expediency. Consequently, he felt, they should keep themselves free to act as a pressure group upon all parties. Many of his articles and editorials in the *Philanthropist* had been devoted to this question of political responsibility, which at that time had comprised, for him, responsibility along two lines: (1) influencing Congressional legislation where Congress had the constitutional power to legislate, as for the District of Columbia and the territories; and (2) refusing to vote for any candidates who would contribute to the continuance of the evil of slavery. Political weight should be exerted especially against anyone who upheld or condoned the actions of lawless mobs. Besides discussing the political issue in the *Philanthropist*, he had presented his ideas in the form of resolutions to the Ohio Anti-Slavery Society's convention as early as 1837 and they had been supported.[2]

Men who opposed slavery on religious and moral grounds could hardly be expected to vote for proslavery men if there were antislavery men who met the requirements in other respects. The next obvious step after voting for antislavery men was to bring pressure to bear on legislative bodies as well as upon individuals and churches. How could a line be drawn between influencing legislators already in office and electing legislators who would respond favorably to that influence?

The petition campaign of the 1830's had served to focus attention upon the votes of individual senators and representatives. Thomas Morris, of Ohio, in the Senate and John Quincy Adams in the House of Representatives were repeatedly singled out for resolutions and

[1] Dwight L. Dumond, *Antislavery Origins of the Civil War in the United States* (Ann Arbor, 1939), pp. 86–87.

[2] *Philanthropist*, Jan. 8 and Dec. 30, 1836, and May 12, 1837.

otes of gratitude for upholding the right of petition against the supporters of gag laws. When Birney attended the anniversary meeting
n the spring of 1837, he reported back to Bailey in Cincinnati, "Wher-
ver I have been, since I parted with you, our friends are unanimous
s to the propriety and necessity of political action." They were especially determined to oppose the annexation of Texas and would
question candidates for public office on the matter before giving them
their votes.[3] It was on this trip East that Birney had visited both John
Quincy Adams and William Ellery Channing, encouraging the first
o continue the fight on petitions and urging the latter to come out
with a letter to Clay against annexation.

Almost immediately after his move to the East, Birney set out to at-
end the Vermont Anti-Slavery Society's convention. Besides speaking
t several of the society's meetings, he was invited to sit in on committee hearings in the Vermont legislature, then in session. Several
petitions had been received against the annexation of Texas and against
the slave trade in the District of Columbia. To Birney's delight they
were favorably reported in resolutions. Vermont's Governor Silas H.
ennison, Lieutenant Governor David M. Camp, and Secretary of
State Chauncy L. Knapp were all abolitionists. For several years a
Vermont representative, William Slade, had been the only abolitionist
n the United States House of Representatives. Birney had been much
encouraged. "Should the slaveholders succeed in banishing liberty from
the free states," he had written then, "the last refuge would be in
the hearts and hills of these noble Vermonters."[4]

On December 20, 1837, Slade addressed the House of Representa-
ives on the subject of abolition in the District of Columbia. He was
followed the next day by Representative John M. Patton, of Virginia,
speaking for the Southern congressmen, who introduced what came
o be known as Patton's gag law, proposing the tabling of all memorials
or petitions on the subject of slavery. On the twenty-seventh of the
same month, John C. Calhoun introduced into the Senate his famous
resolutions which set forth the Southern position on the question of
slavery and the Union.

[3] Birney to Gamaliel Bailey, May 18, 1837, in *Philanthropist*, June 2, 1837.
[4] Birney to Joshua Leavitt, Oct. 30, 1837, in *Philanthropist*, Nov. 28, 1837. For a
complete account of the antislavery work in Vermont, see David M. Ludlum, *Social
Ferment in Vermont, 1791–1850* (New York, 1939), chs. v and vi.

They began with a restatement of the compact theory of government. Each state had entered the Union voluntarily to gain security against both foreign and domestic dangers. Each state retained the right to control its own domestic institutions. Any intermeddling in these institutions tended to weaken the Union. The federal government, as the agent of the states, should not only refrain from such interference itself but should prevent any such attempts from other portions of the Union. As slavery was such an institution, the federal government must prevent attacks on it in the states where it existed and also in the District of Columbia and the territories.[5] This denial of the right of Northerners to work against what they saw as the greatest evil in the nation roused anew antislavery sentiment for political action.

Birney threw his whole effort into getting a renewed flood of petitions while the gag law and Calhoun's resolutions were under debate. In the Anti-Slavery Society office he and Stanton prepared a circular which could be sent out to the auxiliary societies or to individuals, giving proper forms to use in sending petitions to Congress and to the state legislatures. "The Doughfaces will have to be put out of Congress," he wrote to Amos Phelps. "The proceedings in Congress only serve the purpose of revealing to us who they are." [6]

At the annual meeting of the American Anti-Slavery Society in New York in May, 1838, Alvan Stewart went so far as to propose that the part of the national society's constitution which recognized a state's exclusive control over slavery within its own limits should be struck out. Stewart argued that the Constitution of the United States did not protect slavery and that Congress had the power to abolish it, even in the states. He based his arguments on three parts of the Constitution: the Preamble; the clause granting power to Congress to regulate commerce between the states so as to regulate the slave trade, and consequently slavery, out of existence; and the due-process clause. Negroes were persons and could not be deprived of life, liberty or property without due process of law.[7]

Stewart's position was too advanced for Birney, who declared that the theory of Congressional power over slavery in the states could not

---

[5] *Congressional Globe*, 25 Cong., 2 Sess., pp. 41–55.

[6] Birney to Amos Phelps, Jan. 9, 1838, Birney Manuscripts.

[7] See Luther R. Marsh, *Writings and Speeches of Alvan Stewart on Slavery* (New York, 1860).

)e maintained even speciously. The society must be careful not to
;o from a power which was conceded to one which was not or it
vould destroy the whole foundation of the campaign against slavery
n the District of Columbia and the territories. Stewart's resolution
ailed to receive the necessary two-thirds majority for passage. Fol-
owing this annual meeting, the Executive Committee did appoint
a subcommittee on political action composed of Birney, Henry B.
;tanton, Lewis Tappan, Samuel Cornish, and Joshua Leavitt.[8]

By the autumn of 1838 the Executive Committee felt the time was
ipe for some statement of political action which would clarify and
inify the purpose of the antislavery societies. Such a statement was
lrawn up and signed by Birney, Elizur Wright, and Henry Stanton.
They declared themselves opposed to the organization of an abolition
)arty but in favor of questioning candidates. Already the abolitionists
aeld the balance of power in several Congressional districts, and they
hould let it be known they would support only antislavery men. If
neither party put up suitable candidates, abolitionists would refrain
rom voting. The motto should be, "Form alliances with no political
)arty, but enstamp our principles upon all." [9]

New York and Ohio, especially, entered into this new area of anti-
slavery endeavor with zeal. Gerrit Smith, in western New York, had
aandbills drawn up entitled "Freeman's Ticket," which contained the
names of candidates whom antislavery men could conscientiously sup-
)ort. "We as Anti-Slavery men, and citizens of this republic," the an-
nouncement read, "do not calculate to be disfranchised because we
:hoose to 'live out' the principles, to sustain which this government
vas organized. We believe in political action, and action without
lefiniteness is folly." [10] From the Western Reserve in Ohio an anti-
slavery Whig, Joshua R. Giddings, was elected to Congress. Even in
Massachusetts where there was anything but unanimity on the polit-
cal issue, several local societies resolved that slavery could be abol-
shed only by electing antislavery men to Congress.[11]

Although the Garrisonians were able to dominate the annual meet-
ng of 1839, Birney and Stanton did their best to emphasize the good

[8] *Emancipator,* June 7, 1838; Minutes, Executive Committee, Am. Anti-Slavery
;oc., entry for May 10, 1838.
[9] *Emancipator,* Sept. 20, 1838.   [10] Broadside, "Freeman's Ticket."
[11] *Liberator,* Extra, [n.d.].

results of political action. Stanton laid down specific suggestions for
the states: they could take discriminatory clauses from their constitutions; give judicial decisions in harmony with the thesis that free
soil made free men; provide trial by jury for fugitives escaping from
slave states; give protection to their colored citizens who visited the
South; and throw the weight of legislative remonstrance on the side
of freedom. He believed that the political power of the free states, if
properly exercised, was enough, ultimately, to exterminate slavery in
the nation. Should the South maintain herself against all these influences, the North, he declared, "has a *dernier resort*. We will alter
the Constitution and bring slavery in the States within the range of
federal legislation, and then annihilate it at a blow."

The annual report of the Executive Committee was of the same
tenor:

The Committee would solemnly inquire, whether it is not time for every
man who regards the eternal laws of right and wrong, which God has im-
posed upon the moral universe, to cast off the cords which slavery has thrown
around us all, whether they be political or ecclesiastical. Let us contribute
our political strength to the election of only those men who will bring slavery
to an end. . . . In regard to the President, we may not succeed this term
or the next, but succeed we ultimately must if we now seize the right
principle and persevere.[12]

Another fruit of this anniversary meeting in May was a decision to
hold a national convention at Albany in July for the purpose of discussing those principles which formed the foundation for the abolition
enterprise, especially "those which relate to the proper exercise of the
right of suffrage by citizens of the free states." The groundwork was
carefully laid and pains taken to make sure that enough men favoring
political action would be present so that any attempt by Garrison to
gain control of the meeting could be thwarted.

On Birney's trip west early in the summer, one of his main purposes
was to stimulate interest and to secure a good delegation to the Albany meeting. At the Ohio anniversary meeting at Putnam he succeeded in the passage of the following resolution:

That the elective franchise is a power conferred in the providence of God
on the citizens of the United States for good—which they ought to use, and

[12] Am. Anti-Slavery Soc., *Sixth Annual Report* (New York, 1839).

invariably, for the election to legislative and other stations of trust, of those only who, being of good moral character, are known to be favorable to human rights, and to the abrogation of all distinctions in right founded on color.[13]

Birney also visited Senator Thomas Morris to persuade him to come to the Albany meeting. Morris owed his re-election to the Senate to the balance of power held by the abolitionists in Ohio, and they, in turn, meant to make the most of the advantage this gave them.

As had been expected, Garrison showed up in Albany, clearly for the purpose of trying to swing the convention to his own views. No sooner was the meeting under way than it was apparent that he was employing the same strategy which had worked so well at the May anniversary in New York. This time the advocates of political action were ready for him; and his attempt to substitute "all persons" for "freemen" in the admission of delegates failed. He had lost his bid for control. To emphasize the victory, the convention then proceeded to elect Alvan Stewart president and Birney one of the vice-presidents. Stewart was perhaps the most advanced of the antislavery men on the political question.

Also despite the objections of Garrison the question of the formation of a distinct political party was discussed, although no formal vote was taken on the issue. The delegates did resolve that they would not vote for any man for a state or national office who did not favor immediate abolition.[14] This was a decidedly advanced stand, because if neither the Democratic nor the Whig party nominated abolitionists as candidates, there would be no one for whom to vote unless independent nominations were made. Independent nominations would mean, eventually, a new party. The men who engineered the convention were well satisfied.

Having advanced thus far, the society held a meeting at Cleveland on October 23 to test sentiment on the final step. Under the guiding hand of Myron Holley, two significant resolutions were introduced. The first would have provided for independent nominations when none of the other candidates was satisfactory; the second, "That when

[13] *Philanthropist*, June 11, 1839.
[14] *Philanthropist*, Aug. 20, 1839; William Goodell, *Slavery and Anti-Slavery; A History of the Great Struggle in Both Hemispheres; With a View of the Slavery Question in the United States* (New York, 1855), p. 470.

existing parties directly oppose or purposely overlook the rights of the slave it is time to form a *new political party.*" The prolonged debate which followed indicated that the abolitionists present, largely from Ohio, were not yet ready for such a move. Both resolutions were defeated.[15] This defeat was, to a great extent, a result of the influence wielded by Gamaliel Bailey, Birney's successor as editor of the *Philanthropist,* who declared himself against the movement "tooth and nail" and continued to oppose it in his editorials throughout the autumn and winter.

Yet another attempt was made. Myron Holley succeeded in calling another meeting at Warsaw, New York, on November 13, at which enough advocates of political action were present to carry his proposal of independent nominations. Birney was named for president, and Dr. Julius LeMoyne, a prominent physician and philanthropist from Pennsylvania, was named for vice-president. After the Cleveland meeting, however, Birney had grave doubts that the time was ripe for independent nominations. To forge ahead too recklessly without sufficient popular support might set the movement backward instead of forward. Consequently, he decided to decline the nomination. In his letter to the nominating committee, he expressed agreement "that the great Anti-Slavery enterprise can never succeed without independent nominations," but cautioned that action was being taken too hastily before the subject had been fully discussed and unity achieved. That unity would be achieved he had no doubt; to act prematurely would only distract and divide.

Actually, Birney's personal sensitivity was another reason for his declining the nomination. There had been rumors and intimations that some of the leaders for political action such as Joshua Leavitt, Gerrit Smith, and Elizur Wright thought that a more effective nomination could be made. Thomas Morris, for example, had more political experience; or there was Judge William Jay, the son of Chief Justice John Jay, whose name and family prestige would lend weight to his candidacy. Yet, despite the fact that he had written a public declination of the nomination, Birney knew he did not really want to put himself out of the running entirely, and in a private letter to Myron Holley, he indicated his willingness to withdraw his refusal "if the

[15] Theodore Clarke Smith, *The Liberty and Free Soil Parties in the Northwest* (New York, 1897), p. 36.

Committee think it would be best for the cause." [16] Meanwhile, he had allowed himself to be named as candidate for the New York Senate.[17]

Dr. LeMoyne had also declined his nomination, believing the action to be inexpedient as well as premature. His arguments were that the abolitionists were too heterogeneous to form a unified political group and not yet numerous enough to give respectability and influence to such a measure. It would only expose them to ridicule. Besides, he feared the "bright standard of Emancipation" might be "blurred and smutted at the demand of time serving politicians." [18]

Antislavery newspapers throughout the country took up the issue, and during the autumn and winter all sides of the question were fully aired. Bailey continued to lead the opposition in Ohio, although he had facetiously expressed the hope that when Birney was elected president he might be appointed secretary of state. Bailey felt very strongly that the abolitionists' best chance of being politically effective lay in exerting pressure as a group on the two other parties. He argued in his letters and articles that one of the factors in the Whig nomination of William Henry Harrison, instead of Clay, was that Harrison would be less offensive to the abolitionists. To defeat the Democratic candidate, Van Buren, by supporting Harrison would be, he urged, the most telling blow that could be given the slaveholding interests. In the event of a Whig victory, the Democrats would also begin to modify their policies with the demands of the abolitionist voters in view.[19]

Stanton's report from Massachusetts was discouraging. He was afraid that hasty political action was driving more people in that state to rally around Garrison. A thousand subscribers had already canceled their subscriptions to the Massachusetts *Abolitionist*, the organ of the anti-Garrison society. He estimated that forty-nine fiftieths of the Massachusetts abolitionists were Whigs, and nineteen-twentieths of them opposed independent nominations.[20]

Within the Executive Committee of the American Anti-Slavery Society itself there was disagreement. Leavitt and Wright were among

[16] Birney to Myron Holley, Joshua H. Darling, and Josiah Andrews, Dec. 17, 1839; Birney to Myron Holley, Dec. 26, 1839, Birney Papers.
[17] Campaign poster, Nov., 1839.
[18] F. Julius LeMoyne to Birney, Dec. 10, 1839, Birney Papers.
[19] Bailey to Birney, Feb. 21 and March 3, 1840, Birney Papers.
[20] Henry B. Stanton to Birney, March 21, 1840, Birney Papers.

the foremost advocates of a party organization; Stanton and Birney agreed in principle but wanted to wait until the time was ripe; while Lewis Tappan was resolutely opposed to such action because he believed it would violate the society's constitution. At a meeting of the Executive Committee on November 7, 1839, he had proposed that a resolution be adopted disapproving Leavitt's advocacy in the *Emancipator* of a distinct antislavery party. It was tabled, however, as was also another resolution:

That while this Committee feel a deep interest in the subject of "Political Action" which agitates many of our auxiliaries, and has enlisted still more of our members, yet we, as AN EXECUTIVE BODY have taken no measures, nor will we commit ourselves, or the Am. Society over whose interests we preside, in any way what ever on the subject of politics.[21]

While questioning the timing, Birney defended political action as wholly in accordance with the constitution of the society. If the right of the abolitionists to vote be conceded, he asked, "Where is the ground of his obligation to vote for candidates presented to him by two parties—both, *as such*, hostile to him—any more than to vote for such as he may himself select without any reference to these parties, but simply with a view to *principles?*" The constitution had stated that moral and political action would be employed. Actually, Birney argued, political action in this case was but a species of moral action. The term moral action, as used in the constitution, was synonymous with peaceful, as opposed to forcible, action. This was evident in the society's Declaration of Sentiment, in which the projected antislavery movement was contrasted with the forcible character of the American Revolution. If the constitution were to be interpreted according to strict constructionist views, many activities of the society would have to be given up, for it nowhere authorized even the sending out of financial agents or the raising of money.[22]

Despite opposition the tide of political organization continued to rise, and at the end of January, 1840, the call for a new national nominating convention was issued, under the leadership of Gerrit Smith, from a meeting at Arcade, in western New York. In a letter to Wil-

[21] Lewis Tappan to Birney, Dec. 6, 1839, in *Emancipator*, Dec. 12, 1839; Lewis Tappan to Birney, Dec. 20, 1839, Tappan Collection; Minutes, Executive Committee, Am. Anti-Slavery Soc., entry for Nov. 7, 1839.
[22] Birney to Lewis Tappan, Dec. 9, 1839, in *Emancipator*, Dec. 12, 1839.

liam Goodell soon after, Smith suggested the name "Liberty" for the new party.[23] Between the autumn of 1839 and the spring of 1840 Birney was convinced that party organization at that time would not be too precipitate. Leavitt and Wright did their part in persuading him as they worked together in the antislavery office; but it was the long talks with Smith and William Goodell around the fire in the Smith home at Peterboro in February that had really confirmed his position.

On that trip to western New York Birney addressed the judiciary committee of the legislature at Albany on the nine months' law and trial by jury for persons claimed as slaves. The nine months' law, for whose repeal the abolitionists had long been agitating, allowed slaveholders, with their slaves, to travel or reside in the state nine months. Although not feeling well at the time, Birney had agreed to speak, and a meeting was arranged for the evening of March 5.[24]

It was undoubtedly Birney's best speech since the one he had helped Chase write for the Matilda case.[25] Bolstered by some strong coffee and a prayer for "composure of mind, quickness of thought and readiness of utterance" despite his ill-health, he faced the legislators. He was at his best when he spoke as a lawyer.

"I am aware, gentlemen," he began, "that I am not speaking in a forum for constitutionality, but the poor, uninformed and unfriended sufferers whom I defend have been declared unqualified to take their cause to a tribunal." It was true, he continued, that the law in question did not violate the letter of the New York constitution, but, he asserted, a legislature is morally bound to observe the spirit as well as the letter of its fundamental documents. "In one sense, there are laws by which even the makers of the Constitution as well as the legislators are bound—those rules of right existing in the public mind prior to the Constitution." Birney was antedating Seward's "Higher Law" speech by fifteen years.

[23] Ralph V. Harlow, *Gerrit Smith, Philanthropist and Reformer* (New York, 1939), p. 147; William Birney, *Sketch of the Life of James G. Birney* (Chicago, 1884), p. 29, says that during the campaign of 1840 the party was known by different names: Antislavery, Abolition, True Democrat, and Republican, in addition to Liberty.

[24] Diary of James G. Birney, entries for Feb. 29 to March 6, 1840.

[25] Manuscript notes of speech on the nine months' law and the residence law, Birney Papers.

On the basis of these "rules of right" the Declaration of Independence should be as legally binding as the Constitution. New York had adopted the Declaration of Independence in its first constitution but had omitted it in the last. Why? Not because its principles were less binding but because it was unnecessary, "they having become, as it were, an atmospheric medium under the influence of which every part of the political machine was to be propelled." He reminded them of the inalienable rights conferred on men by the Creator, rights which can not be legislated against, not because the Constitution forbids it but because if these rights pertain to men, as men, they are indestructible.

"Let these principles be applied to the nine months' law," he went on. How could the state of New York say to a slaveholding citizen of Virginia who has destroyed these inalienable rights in one or more of his fellow men: "We cannot initiate the deed of destruction in New York, but we will recognize the destruction as committed by you here, and on your entering into our state we will assist you in continuing or perpetuating it"? The existing relation between New York and the slave states, he pointed out, was a one-sided comity. New York was allowing citizens of the slave states to displace its constitution; yet New York citizens traveling in the South were not granted equal freedom to uphold their views on slavery. Fifty thousand of the population, from whom the right of suffrage was withheld, were liable at any time to be claimed as slaves and hurried away into bondage.

Why? Were they aliens? No. Were they hostile to the country and its institutions? No. Were they poor? Yes, but did poverty predicate slavery? Were they ignorant? Yes, but was ignorance alone a justification for bondage? What then was the cause? "I will tell you, gentlemen. The cause is that their complexion is different from yours; and unlike poverty or ignorance which may be overcome, complexion is a fault from which there is no appeal. These people must be helped to elevate themselves," he concluded. "We owe it to the South—to the Union—to the cause of Human Liberty throughout the world." Before the legislature adjourned, it had passed one law securing a trial by jury to persons claimed as slaves and another designed to protect free citizens from being kidnapped or reduced to slavery.[26]

[26] *American and Foreign Anti-Slavery Reporter* (New York), July, 1840.

On April 4 Leavitt returned from Albany with the news. The die had been cast for independent nominations by a vote of 44 to 33, and Birney had received all but a few of the votes for first place on the ticket, those going to Gerrit Smith. Thomas Earle, of Philadelphia, was selected as his running mate to replace LeMoyne. Birney approved; Earle was a good choice. He was a Quaker, a young man—only forty-three—a man of good character and good mind, although unfortunate in business, "rather inclined to thin refinements," and a democrat in principle.[27] The call of the convention was for abolitionists to rise above all parties and "unite as patriots, philanthropists and Christians, to put down the slavery of all parties, and put up the principles of the Declaration of Independence, at the ballot box and everywhere, by every lawful, Constitutional, moral and religious influence." [28]

As soon as he received the news, Birney wrote to Earle urging him to accept. They both, he agreed, had already borne and suffered enough for the cause not to be afraid of assuming the candidacy, yet this was not the time to draw back. They must stand by their friends "who have ventured on so bold a step." If the independent movement should fail, it might well mean failure for the whole antislavery movement. Their only other means of salvation would be to rely on foreign influence.[29]

Again there was pressure on Birney to decline the nomination, pressure from men like Bailey and Whittier who hoped such action from Birney would prevent political organization. But this time his mind was fully resolved, although his letter of acceptance was not penned until May.[30] The letter was an attempt to convince wavering fellow abolitionists of the necessity of political organization. He reviewed the reasons that antislavery men could not conscientiously vote for the candidates of the two other parties. He pointed to the increased control of the federal government by the slave power and to the loss of essential rights because of such policies as censorship of the mails and the gag law. All the concessions, he charged, were being made by the North to the South, but a harmonious whole could never be made

[27] Diary of James G. Birney, entry for April 4, 1840.

[28] *Philanthropist*, May 5, 1840.

[29] Birney to Thomas Earle, April 4, 1840, in *Liberty Party: Thomas Earle* [n.p., n.d.].

[30] Birney to Myron Holley, Joshua Leavitt, and Elizur Wright, May 11, 1840, in Dwight L. Dumond, ed., *The Letters of James Gillespie Birney*, I, 562–574.

from parts which were, in principle and essence, discordant. Even the hard times of the country were to be laid at the door of the Southern economic system of "expense, waste, credit, and procrastination." [31] He ended with a call for unity among abolitionists. Some of them, he realized, would persist in voting for Harrison; but he was confident they would see their mistake in thinking Harrison to be an antislavery sympathizer. It would be evident, he predicted, before Harrison had been in office a year.

The Liberty party made its debut with the nomination of presidential and vice-presidential candidates but with the full realization that it was a party of protest, with no chance of winning the election. The campaign was certainly unusual, in view of the fact that the candidate was in England from May to late November of the election year. Entertaining no hopes of winning, the party consequently set up no particular campaign organization. Antislavery societies, which were essentially moral in character and formed according to the pattern of religious organizations, could not be converted overnight into political rallying grounds. Birney's candidacy was also singular in the respect that he had more active opposition from his antislavery friends than from the rival parties. There were the no-human government Garrisonians who declined to go to the polls, many Christian abolitionists who deplored the shifting of emphasis to political action, and, above all, large numbers of antislavery men who had always voted Whig and who could not bring themselves to the point of "throwing away" their votes on a candidate who had no chance, thus paving the way for a Democratic victory. In many places an insufficient number of ballots were prepared, or there were no Liberty ballots distributed, and friends of the cause thought the candidates had been withdrawn.

In the final returns, Birney received only 7,059 votes out of an estimated potential of 70,000 from eligible voters who were members of antislavery societies. Even in Massachusetts and Ohio, two of the most highly abolitionized states, he did not receive over one per cent of the total votes. Gamaliel Bailey had finally thrown the weight of the *Philanthropist's* influence behind Birney in the summer of 1840, but even that was not enough to overcome the handicaps.

---

[31] For a discussion of this argument of the abolitionists, see Julien P. Bretz, "The Economic Background of the Liberty Party," *American Historical Review*, XXXIV (1928–1929), 250–264.

Outside the ranks of the abolitionists themselves, the efforts of the Liberty party in 1840 were drowned amid the tumult and shouting of the log-cabin and hard-cider campaign; but those few who had their ears to the ground heard in it the distant rumble of mighty thunder.

Chapter X

Delegate to World

Anti-Slavery Convention

THE American reform movements of the first half of the nineteenth century, of which antislavery was one, were phases of world-
wide humanitarian and democratic trends. The first three decades of
the century had witnessed the abolition of slavery in most of the Latin
American republics, the attempts to outlaw the African slave trade by
Great Britain and the United States, and the development of organized
antislavery movements in both Great Britain and France, as well as
in other countries of western Europe and their colonies. The international character of the movement had been, in fact, one of the strong
arguments of American abolitionists. They argued that the United
States, whose Declaration of Independence had expressed with such
dignity the doctrine of the equality of man, should have been a leader
in the liberation movement. Slavery exposed the nation to ridicule and
scorn. One of the oft-repeated arguments for the abolition of slavery
in the District of Columbia was the national disgrace of permitting
distinguished foreigners to see human beings bought and sold in the
very shadow of the Capitol.

In the controversy between Mexico and Texas, abolitionists sympa-
thized strongly with Mexico because by her laws slavery was outlawed

190

in Texas. Benjamin Lundy made several trips to Mexico for the purpose of obtaining a grant of land on which a Negro colony could be established; and in 1840 Birney addressed a letter to the Mexican legation at Washington with a similar plan. He proposed that if Mexico granted land to the free colored people of the United States, many of them could be induced to emigrate. Their colonies would form a buffer state between Mexico and the United States which would prevent further encroachments on Mexican territory. Birney delivered the letter to Mexican Vice-Consul Granja, in New York. Granja agreed to the efficacy of the plan but was convinced that Mexican affairs were too deranged to permit its acceptance.[1]

Co-operation between the British and the American antislavery movements had existed for many years. After the British victory at home with the passing of the Emancipation Act of 1833, additional support was available for the movement elsewhere. To this end the British and Foreign Anti-Slavery Society was organized. Two well-known English lecturers, Charles Stuart and George Thompson, were particularly active in the American movement. Charles Stuart was a retired British army captain from Jamaica. When emancipation was accomplished there, he turned his attention to the movement in the United States. As early as 1825 he became acquainted with Theodore Weld, helped finance his education, and looked on him as his protégé. The American Anti-Slavery Society passed a special resolution at its annual meeting in 1834 welcoming Stuart's aid in the cause. The so-called "interference" of the British with America's "peculiar institution" was not, of course, without its repercussions. George Thompson, a very fluent orator, was so often mobbed in the United States that local antislavery organizations were afraid to invite him to speak. English travelers such as Harriet Martineau and, later, Charles Dickens, who were severe critics of America in the matter of slavery, evoked violent anglophobic reaction. The charge of leadership by foreigners, especially by the English, was used effectively to stir up the Cincinnati mob in July, 1836, and was used again against Birney in the presidential campaigns of 1840 and 1844.

English antislavery publications obtained wide circulation in this country. For years antislavery Quakers in the United States had been distributing pamphlets written by their English brethren. Even in his

[1] Birney to the Mexican Legation, April 1, 1840, Birney Papers.

early days in Alabama Birney read, and was undoubtedly influenced by, the works of Clarkson and Wilberforce. Among the better-known writers, in addition to Clarkson and Wilberforce, were Granville Sharp, John Wesley, Elizabeth Heyrick, and, in the later period, Harriet Martineau and Daniel O'Connell, but a host of others contributed a flood of pamphlets on the slave trade, slavery and emancipation in the British West Indies, and slavery in the United States itself. Some of them dated back to the era of the Revolution. Among these were John Wesley's *Thoughts upon Slavery* (1774); Clarkson's *An Essay on the Impolicy of the African Slave Trade* (1788); and John Newton's *Thoughts upon the African Slave Trade* (1788). Several of those by Granville Sharp were even earlier. The published argument of the counsel for the Negro Sommersett in 1772, which resulted in a decision that slaves brought to English soil became free, was an especially welcome legal precedent to antislavery people in America.[2]

Pamphlets on the slave trade were numerous throughout the first two decades of the nineteenth century. The 1820's and '30's brought an increase of those on the subject of emancipation in the West Indies. Among them were Elizabeth Heyrick's startling *Immediate, Not Gradual Abolition; or, An Inquiry into the Shortest, Safest, and Most Effectual Means of Getting Rid of West Indian Slavery* (1824); Thomas Cooper's *Facts Illustrative of the Condition of the Negro Slaves in Jamaica* (1824); George Thompson's *Three Lectures on British Colonial Slavery;* and Charles Stuart's *The West India Question.*

Once emancipation had been accomplished in the West Indies, attacks on slavery in the United States became more direct. Harriet Martineau's views of slavery from her *Society in America* were published for distribution as separate pamphlets. The Edinburgh Emancipation Society's *A Voice to the United States of America, from the Metropolis of Scotland; Being an Account of Various Meetings Held at Edinburgh on the Subject of American Slavery, upon the Return of Mr. George Thompson, from His Mission to That Country,* was typical of many letters of appeal sent from antislavery societies throughout the British Isles. It was hoped that *The Testimony of Daniel O'Connell,*

---

[2] Francis Hargrave, *An Argument in the Case of James Sommersett, a Negro. Wherein It Is Attempted to Demonstrate the Present Unlawfulness of Domestick Slavery in England. To Which Is Prefixed, A State of the Case, By Mr. Hargrave, One of the Counsel for the Negro* (London, 1772).

the Liberator of Ireland, against the Infamous System of American Slavery would have great effect on the Irish people in America.

It was no hasty alliance, then, which led to the decision to call a world antislavery convention in London in the summer of 1840. State societies in the United States, as well as the American Anti-Slavery Society, were invited to send delegates. Birney and Stanton were chosen to represent the parent organization. The extreme embarrassment of Birney's financial situation at the time made him hesitate about consenting to go, but the Executive Committee decided that the society would assume the expense.[3] The opportunity offered Birney a welcome release from the disagreements and wranglings of the abolitionist factions.

The American abolitionists had high hopes that the resolutions of an international antislavery gathering would not only increase the prestige and dignity of the American movement but might actually carry weight in American policy making. Judge William Jay urged Birney to bring Calhoun's Resolutions of 1837 to the notice of the conference. A vote protesting them might have a good effect on the Senate. A point of international law was currently being agitated in the case of the Amistad captives; the issue was whether or not a slave landing on free soil became free. Discussion of this question at the convention could lend weight to a favorable court decision in the United States.[4] Joshua Leavitt urged that Birney try to get the conference to appoint a committee to consider what bearing the corn laws might have on slavery. It would have tremendous implications if Birney could be instrumental in opening a market for western flour which might challenge the economic tie between Britain and the cotton-producing South.[5] William Ellery Channing sent wishes for the formulation of "broad and efficient plans of action in which the friends of freedom may everywhere take part" and included letters of introduction to a member of Parliament and to the former mayor of Liverpool.[6] Antiabolitionists, on the other hand, interpreted the mission of "the mad abolitionist of Ohio" as an attempt to seek "alliances with

[3] Diary of James G. Birney, entries for March 13 and April 3, 1840.

[4] William Jay to Birney, April 20, 1840, Birney Papers. For a complete account of the Amistad Case, see John B. McMaster, *A History of the People of the United States*, VI, 605–609; *House Executive Documents*, 2 Cong. 1 Sess., No. 185.

[5] Joshua Leavitt to Birney, May 19, 1840, Birney Papers.

[6] William E. Channing to Birney, April 14, 1840, Birney Papers.

Royal Dukes" and to enlist the aid of a "hostile people" in behalf of the slaves.[7]

Birney and the Stantons sailed on the English packet *Montreal* on May 11, 1840.[8] Henry Stanton had just been married to Elizabeth Cady, a cousin of Gerrit Smith, and they were taking advantage of Stanton's appointment as a delegate to the London convention by making it their honeymoon trip. Although Elizabeth was a fine, strong-minded woman, Birney was somewhat shocked by her lack of restraint in the company of other people, especially by the fact that she addressed her husband as "Henry" instead of as "Mr. Stanton." Feeling that she needed to be "toned down" before being launched into English social circles, Birney adopted the devious method of pointedly criticizing the other passengers in her presence.

Elizabeth Stanton was much too intelligent a woman not to sense what was going on. Secretly amused herself at Birney's "excessively proper and punctilious" manners and conversation and perceiving that his remarks had a "nearer application" than he intended she should discover, Mrs. Stanton one day turned the tables on him by inquiring in her forthright manner whether it was good breeding "to make fun of the foibles of our fellow-men who have not had our advantages of culture and education." Conscious of her rebuke, Birney desisted in such remarks. Elizabeth, however, suggested that he should take her "squarely in hand," and thereafter they held a daily polishing session, often after a game of chess in the saloon in the evening.

The crossing took twenty-two days. They had sailed on May 11 from New York, and they landed in England on June 1. The voyage was not a rough one, but Birney was seasick much of the time. He was not, as he put it, "brought to cascading," however, and was able to take daily walks on deck with Stanton while they discussed the importance of the forthcoming convention. Nevertheless, he was glad to see land and offered no objections to Mrs. Stanton's suggestion that they board the pilot boat which came alongside with an offer to take passengers in to shore more quickly than the big ship could get in.

[7] Huntsville *Democrat*, Aug. 22, 1840.

[8] For information on the whole English trip see Birney's diary, entries from May to November, 1840; Notebook of English Trip, Birney Papers; Elizabeth Cady Stanton, *Eighty Years and More* (1815–1897); *Reminiscences of Elizabeth Cady Stanton* (New York, 1898).

The Stantons and Birney were lowered into the small boat with a luncheon of cold chicken, bread, and a bottle of wine. The six hours the pilot had promised it would take to get them in lengthened, however, into a whole day. They had been out eleven hours and it was already getting dark when it was finally necessary to transfer again, two miles out from shore—this time to a rowboat, with Birney and Stanton at the oars. "The woman tempted me and I did leave the good ship," was Birney's report of the adventure. It was a bright, moonlight night, however, the air balmy, and the coast waters smooth. Few travelers had the chance to enter England in so romantic a way.

Their landing was at Torquay, where, although the hour was late, they found rooms in a comfortable little hotel. The next day, in high spirits, they were off by stage for Exeter. The soft green English countryside, with its blossoming trees and shrubbery, was at its loveliest. The coachman in his white gloves and with his dignified air and a postman in red who blew his horn as they passed through villages gave the trip the air of a ride through fairyland. The setting sun was just streaming through the stained glass windows as they arrived at Exeter Cathedral, and the deep tones of the organ reverberating out into the twilight air. "As if moved by the same impulse to linger there awhile, we all sat down," wrote Mrs. Stanton, "silently waiting for something to break the spell that bound us."

It was June 4 when they arrived in London, where they took lodgings in a rooming house on Queen Street where most of the other American delegates were also staying. As the convention was not to begin until the twelfth, they had six days of sight-seeing. They crowded as much as possible into the time: St. Paul's, the British Museum, London Tower, Windsor Castle, St. James Palace, Westminster Abbey, the Parliament Houses, the zoological gardens, prisons, hospitals, art galleries, and courts. They even went down into the excavations which had been begun for a tunnel under the Thames.

Birney had been overoptimistic in hoping his trip to London would take him away from the abolitionist troubles at home. Even before the world convention met, news arrived from Lewis Tappan in New York that the feared split in the antislavery ranks had taken place at the annual meeting in May. But, as Birney well knew, this did not mean that the trouble with Garrison was all over. It would be characteristic of him to publicize the dissension among the American abolitionists by introducing the same issues at the international conference. Leavitt had, in fact, sent Birney warning that Garrison was coming over with the determination "to rule or ruin." But perhaps, as Leavitt had also suggested, they could depend on John Bull to "dispose of the matter in his own way, very quietly." [9] Birney hoped there would be no unpleasantness.

The World Anti-Slavery Convention opened on June 12 in the Great Hall of the Freemason's Tavern.[10] There were about five hundred delegates. Most of the state antislavery societies in the United States were represented, as well as the national society. The delegates came from all the cities and shires of England, from Scotland, Ireland, and Wales, from Barbados and Jamaica, from Sierra Leone, the Isle of Wight, Spain, Switzerland, and France. Joseph Sturge, as the representative of the British and Foreign Anti-Slavery Society, the host organization, opened the meeting by nominating Thomas Clarkson, the venerable champion of emancipation, for the position of president of this first world convention. Birney, as the ranking representative of the American national society, seconded the motion. It was purely an honorary gesture, for Clarkson was unable to preside. Birney was himself honored with one of the vice-presidencies; and Stanton, along with Wendell Phillips, from Massachusetts, was chosen a secretary.

From the beginning of the convention Birney nervously waited for the Garrison delegation to tip its hand as to what it intended to do about the seating of women delegates. The Massachusetts Anti-Slavery Society had sent Lydia M. Child. The answer came at the very first meeting, in the form of a resolution introduced by Wendell Phillips that a committee be appointed to prepare a list of the convention members and that it include all persons bearing credentials from any antislavery body. Determined not to let the convention get the impression that the whole American delegation backed the motion, the Rev. Nathaniel Colver and Birney both spoke in correction of Phillips. Once the issue had been introduced, Birney decided that

[9] Leavitt to Birney, May 19 and June 1, 1840, Birney Papers.

[10] For the complete accounts see *Proceedings of the General Anti-Slavery Convention Called by the Committee of the British and Foreign Anti-Slavery Society, and Held in London . . . 1840* (London, 1840); London *Sun*, June 13, 16, 18, and 19, 1840; Dublin *Weekly Herald*, June 27, 1840.

frankness would probably be the best policy. In a brief speech he explained how the question had led to a split in America, but he emphasized the fact that there were sincere abolitionists on both sides.

At this convention the Garrisonians were badly outnumbered, and victory went to the conservatives. The convention voted overwhelmingly against the seating of women delegates. As the decision was announced, Garrison rose from his seat on the main floor and made his way up the stairs to the gallery, where he dramatically took his place with the women.[11] If he had hoped there would be protests against the losing of so eminent a delegate, he was disappointed. He remained in the gallery for the rest of the conference. At the lodging house on Queen Street, where delegates of both factions were staying, the argument continued. Even at mealtime the discussions became so heated, and finally so bitter, that Birney "packed his valise and sought more peaceful quarters."

Birney played an active part in the whole convention. At the second meeting he spoke briefly in reply to a question on the sinfulness of slaveholding; and on June 15, a day set aside for the consideration of slavery in America, he talked at length on the relationship between the state and national governments in the United States as it affected the existence of slavery under them. Stanton also addressed this meeting, on the subject of the great influence English literature had on American public opinion, and encouraged use of this vehicle as a means of making antislavery converts. John Keep, from Oberlin, talked on slavery and the churches; and Wendell Phillips spoke on the difficulties of getting antislavery articles accepted for publication in America. Although by no means the most eloquent speaker in the American group, Birney aroused the most interest among the audience because of his own background as a slaveholder.

Birney acted as chairman for the meetings of June 16, which were devoted to a discussion of slavery in the French and Dutch colonies and in Mohammedan countries. The problems of the African slave trade, Cuban slavery, slavery and the churches, free and slave labor, and abstinence from the use of products of slave labor were other

[11] At a meeting of colored people before Garrison left for London, the suggestion was made that they pass a resolution expressing trust in him as a delegate. Most of those present wanted to include all the American delegates in the resolution, but as Garrison objected to having his name coupled with Birney's and Stanton's, none was passed. Charles B. Ray to Stanton and Birney, May 20, 1840, Birney Papers.

topics on the agenda. There was much discussion on the subject of British encouragement of cotton production in India, which would make it unnecessary for Britain to sustain the slave system by her trade with the planters of southern United States.

Although presiding again on June 20, Birney relinquished it long enough to offer resolutions against British recognition of Texas as one of the family of nations so long as she countenanced slavery. Another resolution deplored the fact of French recognition. In this speech he reviewed territorial arrangements on slavery from the time of the Missouri Compromise and explained the political significance of the South's gaining more slave territory. His last speech, at the afternoon session on June 22, was on the inadequacy of colonization.

The convention, which had been in session both morning and afternoon for nine days, terminated on June 23 with the adoption of an address to be sent to the heads of governments, requesting aid against slavery and the slave trade. Few of the delegates went home when the convention was adjourned, however, for the anniversary meeting of the British and Foreign Anti-Slavery Society was to open the very next day.

Its meeting was in Exeter Hall, the Duke of Sussex in the chair. Again Birney was singled out from the other Americans present by being invited to sit on the platform with such notables as Thomas Clarkson; the Duchess of Sutherland; Elizabeth Fry; Monsieur Guizot, ambassador from France; Monsieur Isambert, deputy from the French Anti-Slavery Society; and Daniel O'Connell, from Ireland. O'Connell, in a speech, paid special tribute to Birney as head of the American delegation, and Birney replied briefly in praise of the antislavery efforts in the British Isles.[12]

Birney had made a great impression on his English colleagues. "By his solid and varied attainments, rich fund of information, courtesy, candor, and fine debating powers," reported Stanton, he "inspired confidence in his statements and reflected credit upon his country."[13] During the meetings invitations to speak in various parts of the country were so numerous that he and Stanton decided to make a lecture tour of the British Isles before returning to America. First they were to have a period of rest, but sight-seeing and social demands kept them almost constantly occupied.

[12] London *Sun*, June 25, 1840.
[13] Henry B. Stanton, *Random Recollections* (New York, 1887), p. 48.

Samuel Gurney, a wealthy Quaker banker and abolitionist, entertained the entire American delegation. Seven barouches were sent
to take the guests to his elegant home a few miles out of London.
After the banquet, at which the Duchess of Sutherland, Lord Morpeth,
and Haydon, the artist, were also present, Birney and Garrison were
called on for short speeches.[14] The meeting with Haydon resulted
in the latter's making sketches of several of the delegates, including
Birney, which were incorporated into a composite painting of the
World Anti-Slavery Convention.[15]

Birney had been presented to Lord Brougham, also an active abolitionist, when he first arrived in London. Later a special occasion was
arranged at which Birney gave him a carved inkstand made from the
wood of Pennsylvania Hall, which had been burned by the antiabolitionists in the mob of 1838. Several invitations were extended to
Birney to meet some of the figures in London literary circles, including Lady Byron, who had expressed a particular desire to know him.[16]
Amelia Opie, a novelist of note who prepared the convention speeches
for publication, wrote to Mrs. Sturge, at whose home Birney had
stayed, that she was "so interested in that sound-minded, and
doubtless sound-hearted man that I should like to hear of him all I
can." [17]

Birney's pride and vanity dictated that if such invitations were
to be accepted, he should be properly dressed. A shopping trip into the
city resulted in the careful purchase of black silk cloth boots and a
black suit consisting of trousers, a silk waistcoat, and a dress coat
with a velvet collar. It had been many years since he had indulged
his taste in such handsome fashion, and it made him feel quite the
aristocrat again.

By the middle of July, Birney had started out on a lecture tour
with John Scoble, an active member of the British and Foreign Anti-
Slavery Society. This trip would, he thought, give him a chance to see

---

[14] Wendell P. Garrison and Francis J. Garrison, *William Lloyd Garrison, 1805–
1879*, II, 387.

[15] Haydon's diary entry for July 14 reads: "Hard at work. Birney and Alexander,
both fine heads, all good hearts. . . . These delegates are extraordinary men in
head, feature, and principle." See Tom Taylor, ed., *The Autobiography and Memoirs
of Benjamin Robert Haydon (1786–1846)* (New York, [1926]), II, 684–686.

[16] Elizabeth Reid to Birney [n.d.]; Dr. R. R. Madden to Birney, June 29, 1840,
Birney Papers.

[17] Amelia Opie to Sophia Sturge, Aug. 23, 1840; Sophia Sturge to Birney, Sept.
5, 1840; Amelia Opie to Birney, Sept. 9, 1840, Birney Papers.

the country at the same time. The two men were so much in demand for lectures, however, that they hurried on from place to place too rapidly to have time for more than meals and rest, and hardly enough of the latter. Cambridge, Northampton, Leicester, Nottingham, and Derby were covered in a week. At Birmingham, where "Mr. Birney spoke admirably," they were guests at the Joseph Sturge home before setting off again.[18]

The northern tour continued with stops at Manchester, Leeds, York, Hull, Durham, Darlington, Shields, and Newcastle. Good crowds turned out to see Birney, the former slaveholder, and to hear his speeches, which stressed mostly the moral and religious aspects of the cause. The only disturbance occurred when Chartists broke up the assembly at the Friends' Meeting House in Newcastle; but Birney had already finished his address on the need for English churches to exert pressure on those in America. Another project he and Scoble were pushing was the formation of a North England auxiliary to the British and Foreign Anti-Slavery Society.[19]

By August 25 Birney and Scoble had moved westward to Liverpool, while Stanton went out on a separate tour in Sussex and Essex with G. W. Alexander, treasurer of the British and Foreign Anti-Slavery Society. After six weeks of this pace, however, Birney was too exhausted to continue, and it was decided that he should return to London to "rusticate" while Stanton went out with Scoble. Then Birney would take up again while Stanton rested.[20]

There was little time for rest even then. A consequence of having

---

[18] John Scoble to J. Tredgold, July 18 and 21, 1840, in Annie H. Abel and Frank J. Klingberg, eds., *A Side-Light on Anglo-American Relations, 1839–1858* (Lancaster, Pa.: Association for the Study of Negro Life and History, 1927), pp. 71–72; Birney to Lewis Tappan, July 23, 1840, in *American and Foreign Anti-Slavery Reporter*, I (1840), 31; London *Sun*, July 27, 1840.

[19] *Gateshead Observer*, Aug. 15, 1840; *American and Foreign Anti-Slavery Reporter*, Oct., 1840. Thomas P. Martin, in "The Upper Mississippi Valley in Anglo-American Anti-Slavery and Free Trade Relations: 1837–1842," *Mississippi Valley Historical Review*, XV (1928–1929), 204–220, concludes that Birney and Stanton "spoke much" for free trade and against the corn laws. I have discovered no specific evidence to support this. Leavitt was the chief advocate in America of such a plan and did express the hope in a letter to Birney on May 19, 1840, that the London convention might appoint a committee to consider the bearing of the corn laws on slavery. He also wrote in favor of it in the *Emancipator*, as well as made it the subject of several public addresses.

[20] *American and Foreign Anti-Slavery Reporter*, Oct., 1840.

the Garrison split brought up at the London conference was that everywhere Birney went it was necessary to answer questions and offer explanations. Another worry was that too many of the American delegates had stayed to lecture in England with the purpose of gaining contributions for local and state phases of the cause at home. Eventually Birney, as the representative of the national organization, had to take action to restrict such activity.

Still another problem was the revival of the old rivalry with the American Colonization Society. Sir Thomas Folwell Buxton, an English abolitionist, had recently undertaken the organization of the Society for the Civilization of Africa. Its object was to civilize the natives of Africa, teach them how to utilize their own resources, and show them the crime of co-operating with slave traders by exporting their own people. To accomplish this the society planned to establish model farms and schools.[21] The American Colonization Society, hearing of this project, claimed it as a group having a common aim with its own, and Ralph R. Gurley was sent to England to effect an alliance between them.

Upon his arrival Gurley also solicited an interview with a committee of the British and Foreign Anti-Slavery Society to try to remove any unfavorable impressions its members might have of the Colonization Society. Although most of the British abolitionists were well aware of the American abolitionists' stand on this question, Birney and Stanton were afraid that some of the popular backing in England might be diverted to colonization. They were, however, invited to attend the committee's meeting with Gurley and were satisfied that no erroneous impressions were left. To make certain that Gurley should have no grounds for public statements of half-truths, Birney and Stanton addressed a request to Sir Thomas Buxton that he define his position clearly and in writing. Buxton avowed his faith in immediatism and his distrust of colonization as an aid to achieving it, using in substance the same arguments which Birney had so often presented.

There the affair ended for the time being, but its effect on Birney was to stir up his old feelings on the subject to the extent that he even contemplated a trip to Liberia before returning home in order to be able to speak from a firsthand view. He wrote to Lewis Tappan:

[21] William Forster to Birney, Aug. 15, 1840; Sir Thomas Buxton to Birney and Stanton, Oct. 14, 1840, Birney Papers.

I am sick to death almost of quarreling with those, or rather of being quarreled with *by* those who profess to have the same object in view that I have. The war against open adversaries I can wage tolerably well—but I will neither use devices to undermine others, nor can I trouble myself to guard *against* devices or to counteract those who practice them.[22]

Besides dealing with Gurley during the time that he was supposed to be resting in London, Birney busied himself with writing. His article on Texas, which appeared in the London *Times* of September 8, 1840, was an argument against British recognition. It would, he asserted, neutralize the good influence of British emancipation in the West Indies as far as British example to the United States went and render ineffectual any antislavery efforts in Texas. Great Britain's antislavery policy, the result of a half-century of consideration, must not be lightly relinquished. The article continued with a severe indictment of Texas for her proslavery policy, her ingratitude toward Mexico, and her injustice to the Indians, all of which characterized her more as a buccaneer than as a civilized nation. If Britain recognized Texas as a slave nation, Birney charged, she would be responsible for a revived international slave trade that which would develop between Texas and the United States.

Birney was busily engaged also in compiling materials on the stand of American churches in regard to slavery. The results were published first in England under the title *The American Churches the Bulwarks of American Slavery* and later went through three American editions. The idea for such an article was suggested in a letter from William Jay to Birney which was read at the London convention. In his letter, Jay, who was an Episcopalian, expressed the hope that the English could be induced to use their influence against slavery through the medium of the church, which in America was the "great buttress" of slavery. To support his charge, he cited several examples of proslavery attitude in the Episcopal church.[23]

Birney's pamphlet included information about the Episcopal, Methodist, Baptist, and Presbyterian churches, with notice that the Society of Friends and the United Brethren did exclude slaveholders from communion. Most of the churches, he pointed out, had taken anti-

---

[22] Birney to Lewis Tappan, Sept. 3, 1840, in *American and Foreign Anti-Slavery Reporter*, I (1840), 43; Stanton to Birney, Aug. 15, 1840, Birney Papers.
[23] Jay to Birney, March 28, 1840, in London *Sun*, June 19, 1840.

slavery positions in the early days of the republic but were now in the opposite camp of the slavery defenders. Churches, in a corporate character, could hold slaves themselves, and slaves who were church members were sometimes sold by white men who were fellow members. Negro pews were maintained in nearly all churches. Not only did the churches use the excuse that they could not legislate on what was a civil and political problem, but they failed even to remonstrate against laws forbidding slaves to be taught to read the Bible. Moreover, church members and ministers had been active participants in antiabolitionist mobs which denied the rights of freedom of speech and press.

Birney sent copies of this pamphlet to the archbishops of York, Canterbury, and Dublin. Enclosed with each was a personal letter requesting that the Anglican church should do all in its power to lead the American church to purify herself. The responses of the archbishops evinced personal sympathy, but the Archbishop of Canterbury explained that he had neither the right nor the authority to inquire into the proceedings of the ministers of a church independent of his jurisdiction.[24] After Birney's lectures in Scotland, the Congregational Union of Scotland did address a remonstrance to fellow Christians in America.[25] Thomas Clarkson added his voice of entreaty with *A Letter to the Clergy of Various Denominations and to the Slave-Holding Planters, in the Southern Parts of the United States of America.*

Birney had hoped to make a trip across the Channel to France before returning to lecturing, but he was too busy. After taking advantage of the invitation of Quaker friends, the Braithwaites, to visit them at Kendal in the Lake Country, he set out again with Scoble. This trip took him to western and southern England, to Devizes, Bath, Bristol, Taunton, Exeter, Plymouth, and Oxford. At Plymouth the audience was so large that the Mechanics' Institute would not hold them all; and at Oxford Town Hall they had "such a meeting as was never before held in Oxford," with several "gownsmen" present.

[24] Birney to the Archbishop of Canterbury, Oct. 12, 1840; F. B. Wells for the Archbishop of Canterbury to Birney, Nov. 2, 1840; E. Norwich to Birney, Oct. 19, 1840; the Archbishop of Dublin to Birney, Oct. 19, 1840; the Archbishop of York to Birney, Oct. 20, [1840], Birney Papers.
[25] *American and Foreign Anti-Slavery Reporter*, Nov., 1840. Congregational Union of Scotland, *Address . . . to Their Fellow Christians in the United States, on the Subject of American Slavery* (New York, [1840]).

On October 12 Birney set out from London for Liverpool, where he took a steamer for Scotland to join Scoble and Stanton, who had gone by land. The deputation was given a warm welcome by their Scottish friends despite, as Scoble wrote, "all the Garrison party have been doing to produce a contrary state of things." George Thompson and Charles L. Remond, a Negro lecturer of the Garrison delegation, were there ahead of them, but instead of working at odds, the two groups wisely joined forces. By the end of the visit, Scoble reported "that Garrisonism has made but little way in Scotland, and that even his warmest admirers are by no means prepared to advocate his extreme views—indeed I may say that they are more inclined to repudiate them." [26] Ralph R. Gurley was also in Scotland at the time, but he was able to obtain an audience of only fifteen at his lecture. Birney and Stanton spoke at meetings in both Edinburgh and Glasgow and did manage to steal some time to visit Scotland's historic castles, including the scenes of Sir Walter Scott's novels.

On October 22 they left for Carlisle but were disappointed to find that fear of the Chartists prevented other than a private meeting there. After another stop at Kendal, they embarked at Liverpool on the twenty-fourth for Dublin. This was a visit to which Birney had looked forward with great anticipation because of his Irish parentage. Prior to going, he had made inquiries about relatives who might still be alive, and he took time from antislavery activities to visit the old family homestead at Cootehill, where he saw the house in which his father had been born.

In Dublin, besides speaking at an antislavery meeting, Birney attended one of O'Connell's repeal meetings. Upon seeing him enter, O'Connell introduced him to the crowd, referring to him as "Judge Birney." When Birney promptly declined the honor of being so addressed, O'Connell replied, "If you are not, you well deserve to be one." When the audience learned that Birney was Irish, their cheers redoubled. Throughout their speeches in Ireland, Birney and Stanton both stressed the significant role of the Irish vote in the United States, especially in New York, and appealed to their audiences to help see to it that every future Irish emigrant would be a stanch abolitionist.

The speeches at the Dublin meeting brought down upon Birney's

[26] J. Scoble to Tredgold, October 15 and 30, 1840, quoted in Abel and Klingberg, *A Side-Light on Anglo-American Relations*, pp. 71–76n.

head the wrathful criticism of the Washington *Globe*. R. R. Madden, an Irish abolitionist, had, they charged, misrepresented the facts in speaking of the Amistad case, and "the more than infamous, the parricidal Birney" had sat by "hearing his country thus calumniated." Both Madden and Birney were accused of trying to create prejudice against the United States.

Birney later answered the charges of the *Globe*, declaring that its account of the Dublin meeting was incorrect. Madden knew his facts thoroughly and had reported them accurately. As for himself, he denied that he had behaved in an unpatriotic manner. Slavery must be attacked wherever it existed, in the British Empire, in the United States, or anywhere else in the world. "They who see the crisis and cry not out," he challenged, "are unworthy of the liberty they enjoy and recreant to the manhood Heaven has given them." [27]

Before he left Ireland, Birney received the promise that O'Connell would prepare an address to the Irish people of America on the subject of slavery. The address from O'Connell, Father Mathew, Dr. Madden, and sixty thousand Irishmen arrived in 1842, at which time Birney was called upon to defend its genuineness after Bishop Hughes of New York declared it the duty of every naturalized Irishman to reject it with indignation.[28]

The Irish trip concluded Birney's lectures in the British Isles. He had worked as long and as hard there as he did at home, and again he was worn out. "I have had but little to give to the cause besides personal efforts," he wrote to Tappan, "and the power of making them any longer to much effect is beginning to be exhausted." [29] Another year or two of such a pace would kill him, he feared. It was with mutual regret, however, that he parted from his English friends. "High and cordial is the esteem which he has acquired wherever he has become known," was the appreciative comment of the *British and Foreign Anti-Slavery Reporter*. He had, declared its editors, done more than any other person to make England aware of the enormities of the

[27] Washington *Globe*, Dec. 23, 1840, and Birney's reply to the editors of the *Globe*, Jan. 1, 1841, quoted in *American and Foreign Anti-Slavery Reporter*, Jan., 1841.

[28] Birney to the editor of the *Free Press* (Detroit), reprinted in *Signal of Liberty* (Ann Arbor), April 20, 1842.

[29] Birney to Lewis Tappan, Sept. 3, 1840, in *American and Foreign Anti-Slavery Reporter*, I (1840), p. 43.

American slave system, "while at the same time, he has uniformly evinced the truest love, and the deepest tenderness for his Country." [30]

A formal resolution of thanks for his efforts was written by the British and Foreign Anti-Slavery Society and signed by Thomas Clarkson:

Resolved, that this Committee are deeply sensible of the services rendered to the Anti-Slavery Cause by their esteemed friend and coadjutor James Gillespie Birney Esq're. whilst in this Country, in a course of laborious efforts in which his accurate and extensive information, his wise and judicious counsels, his power of calm and convincing statement, have become eminently conspicuous. [31]

Although John A. Collins, one of the Garrison men who remained in England, made every attempt to place both Birney and Stanton in a bad light and to deprecate their antislavery reputations, Birney's friends assured him that "all who know you have too much confidence in your honorable character to pay the slightest attention." [32] Two years later, when the Rev. Hiram Kellogg, president of Knox College in Illinois, visited England, he found it refreshing "amid the many complaints against my countrymen . . . to hear James G. Birney so frequently spoken of and always in terms of unqualified approbation and respect." [33]

Birney secured passage home on the *Great Western,* one of the best and fastest ships of her day, sailing from Bristol on November 7. Unfortunately, the voyage home was so rough that he was too sick the whole seventeen days to New York to enjoy either his time for relaxation or the ship itself, and he was relieved to set foot on land on November 24.

[30] *British and Foreign Anti-Slavery Reporter,* quoted in *American and Foreign Anti-Slavery Reporter,* Jan., 1841.

[31] J. H. Tredgold to Birney, Jan. 2, 1841, Birney Papers.

[32] Scoble to Birney, Jan. 2, 1841; M. C. Braithwaite to Birney, Feb. 3, 1841, Birney Papers.

[33] William Birney, *James G. Birney and His Times,* p. 369.

Chapter XI

"Out of the

Peopled World"

BY THE time Birney landed in New York, he had already come to one important decision: he wanted to remarry and to be able once more to gather his children about him in a home of their own. The lady he had in mind was Elizabeth Fitzhugh, sister of his old college friend, Dr. Daniel Fitzhugh, of Geneseo, New York, and of Mrs. Gerrit Smith.[1] Birney had met Miss Fitzhugh on his frequent trips to Peterboro. She was an attractive lady, seemed to have a happy and cheerful disposition, and completely shared his antislavery views. She was ten years younger than he but had never married. Her father, Colonel William Fitzhugh, and her brothers, Dr. Daniel Fitzhugh and Henry Fitzhugh, were men of property and some wealth. They were originally a Southern family from Maryland before they moved to western New York.

Birney had not spoken of his regard for Miss Fitzhugh before going to London; but it was she who was in his thoughts whenever they were unoccupied enough with antislavery matters to choose their own paths.

[1] In 1839 he had been interested in a widow in Cincinnati, a Mrs. Garrard, the daughter of Israel Ludlow. Bailey had encouraged a marriage proposal, but meanwhile Birney had met Miss Fitzhugh.

According to Mrs. Stanton, whenever he felt depressed and discouraged, the mention of her name in conversation could restore his spirits. By the time he returned, he had made up his mind to speak to her. Within a month Miss Fitzhugh had been won; on December 17 they became engaged to marry.[2]

The next few months were busy ones for Birney. The wedding was to take place in March, but meanwhile he could make no definite plans for a home until the American and Foreign Anti-Slavery Society should decide what it could do in the way of financial arrangements and salaries for its agents. Birney's situation was an especially complicated one. The problem of funds to keep him active in antislavery work was one thing. In addition, as long as he was the titular head of the political movement and as long as the abolitionists were divided on the propriety of political action, there was a question of the extent to which the national society should back him. Lewis Tappan was still against political organization, as was also Theodore Weld. Another schism must be prevented.

Early in December the Executive Committee held a meeting to discuss the problem of what to do about Birney. As he was about to leave for western New York, he could not be present himself, but he urged upon Tappan the necessity of placing political action at least on equal grounds with the other questions connected with the cause. All the supporters of political action really wanted, he insisted, was that the Executive Committee not be considered as constitutionally barred from approving them.[3]

Leavitt sent a report on to Birney at Peterboro as soon as the meeting was over. It had been a harmonious session, in which the members agreed that the Executive Committee itself would "abstain from all the machinery of party arrangements" but would urge upon all abolitionists the duty of exercising their political power at the ballot box. This was conservative enough to satisfy Lewis Tappan, and he gave no indication of withdrawing, as they had feared. A circular was adopted stating this position and also Birney's readiness to remain active in the field provided immediate funds were available. His employment by the society would depend on the responses to the

[2] Diary of James G. Birney, entry for Dec. 17, 1840.
[3] Birney to Lewis Tappan, [Dec., 1840], Tappan Collection.

ircular. If these were favorable, he would be employed at a salary
f two thousand dollars a year.[4]

Birney's time from December to March was spent mostly in west-
rn New York, partly in seeing Elizabeth, but also in delivering anti-
lavery lectures. Early in January he attended a convention of the
'resbyterian and Congregational churches of western New York in
'enn Yan, where he gave an account of the London convention. He
vas appointed, along with Beriah Green and several others, to pre-
)are three letters, one to Southern Christians, one to Northern Chris-
ians, and a third in response to that from the Congregational Union
f Scotland. At the meeting Birney introduced several resolutions
vhich would provide more equality for the colored people in the
hurches, among them the abolition of the Negro pew. His censure of
he churches for failing to discuss the issue of human rights, for re-
)ressing the spirit of freedom in their theological schools, for receiv-
ng slaveholders in communion and in their pulpits, and for accepting
ifferings "wrung from the toil of the slave" aroused so much dis-
ussion that it held the attention of the convention for the rest of the
ession.[5]

Attendance at conventions at Nunda, in Allegheny County; at Perry,
n Genesee County; and at Rochester, in Monroe County, was sand-
viched in between visits with Elizabeth. Political organization was
he main issue for discussion at both Nunda and Rochester, and Birney
vas much pleased with the harmony of sentiment.

On February 10 and 11 Birney went over to Albany to a convention
or the purpose of choosing state delegates to a national convention in
May. On the last evening the use of the representatives' chamber was
ibtained, and Birney addressed a full house. As many legislators were
)resent, he submitted a series of resolutions bearing on the consti-
utional view, one of which commended Governor Seward for his
ecent refusal to extradite to Virginia three men accused of slave
tealing.[6] While in Albany, Birney also made arrangements for a

---

[4] Joshua Leavitt to Birney, Dec. 4, 1840, Birney Papers.

[5] *The Friend of Man* (Utica), Jan. 26, 1841.

[6] Three sailors, Peter Johnson, Edward Smith, and Isaac Gansey, had induced a
lave belonging to John G. Colley of Virginia to escape by stowing away on their
hip. Two Virginians claimed the fugitive when the vessel docked at New York,
nd he was taken back to Virginia. The three sailors were arrested, but released on

Rev. Garnett, of Troy, and Dr. James McCune Smith, a prominent
Negro doctor of New York City, to speak to the Judiciary Committee
of the legislature on the nine months' law and the extension of the
franchise to free colored people.

The well-occupied weeks passed quickly. March 25 had been set
as the wedding day. The ceremony was performed at the home of
Judge Carroll at Groveland, in Livingston County, in the presence
of Elizabeth's family; the Birney children with the exception of
William and David, who were in Ohio; and some antislavery friends.
It was a happy day for Birney, a day of new beginnings with a help-
meet who would make his cause her own. Florence and George would
have a mother, and the older boys would have a home.

It was ironic that just when Birney was looking ahead with new
vision, just when he had found a wife who was wholeheartedly in
sympathy with his antislavery views, who would encourage him and
strengthen him in his work, other circumstances prevented the continuation of that work. The hoped-for salary could not be raised by the
American and Foreign Anti-Slavery Society; it would be impossible for
the society to keep him on as an agent unless he could get along on
less.

Birney's debts made this impossible. With the Alabama accounts
still not settled, his losses because of the mulberry tree project, and
the recent default of his brother-in-law, John J. Marshall, on a debt,
it was necessary for him to borrow money from several of his anti-
slavery friends. His second wife owned some property, but Birney was
too proud to appropriate it for his own use or that of his children. Consequently, his resignation was tendered to the Executive Committee
in April.[7]

The old group of leaders was breaking up. Stanton, too, found it
necessary to retire and begin the practice of law; while Elizur Wright

---

a writ of habeas corpus because of a defective affidavit. The Governor of Virginia
demanded that they be extradited to Virginia for slave stealing. Seward's refusal was
on the grounds that neither common law nor the laws of New York recognized
slavery, therefore, the crime charged was no crime. The Democratic Senate of New
York passed a resolution censuring Seward's refusal; but he remained firm in his
decision. See Frederic Bancroft, *The Life of William H. Seward* (New York, 1900),
I, 101–104; Albany *Argus*, April 24, 1841; *Journal of Commerce* (New York), Feb.
20, 1841.

[7] *American and Foreign Anti-Slavery Reporter*, April, 1841.

ngaged in the translation of French fairy tales. With the removal of
oshua Leavitt and the *Emancipator* to Boston at the end of the year,
nly the Tappans, of the old policy-making committee, remained in
New York.

Until the Birneys could decide where to make their permanent
ome in an attempt to get on their feet financially, they settled down
emporarily in western New York to await the results of the political
onvention to be held in New York in May. The convention was
lanned to be in conjunction with the anniversary meetings of both
he old American Anti-Slavery Society and the new American and
Foreign Anti-Slavery Society.

It opened on May 12, with delegates present from all the free states
xcept Michigan and Illinois. Birney was renominated for the presi-
lency and Thomas Morris, of Ohio, for the vice-presidency. The
hoice of Morris over Earle was a diplomatic one. Morris was from
he West, had risen from poverty, and had attained prominence for his
peech on slavery in answer to Henry Clay in 1839. It was true that
p to this time he had been a Democrat, but he had displeased his
arty colleagues by his antislavery stand and was now known as a
ull-fledged Liberty man.

The Liberty convention's appeal to the rank-and-file voter reflected
recognition of the rising of the common man. In the letter of the
Committee of Nomination to Birney, the evils of the country were
lamed on the "prevailing contempt of labor," which implied dis-
egard for the working classes by the maintenance of "a system of
alse political economy" which permitted some to live in idleness sus-
ained by the labor of others, "depriving industry of its just reward
nd entailing upon the country the wicked system of slavery—a system
t variance with . . . the Declaration of Independence, . . . true
Democracy . . . Religion . . . Nature, and the best interest of the
ommunity." [8]

The convention's *Address to the Citizens of the United States,*
written by William Goodell, embodied what could be termed the
latform of the new party. It contained an indictment of the late ad-
ninistration as "chained to the car of the slave power" and expressed
he conviction that nothing more could be expected from the new one.
t announced that the Liberty party would take no definite stand other

[8] Committee of Nomination to Birney, May 12, 1841, Birney Papers.

than advocacy of emancipation. Because slavery was the cause of most of the evils of the nation, curing it would automatically cure other ills. Other issues, such as the tariff, land policy, and the banking system, were incidental. The party would (1) try to find markets for the products of free labor rather than for the products of slave labor; (2) allow tax-free cotton from other parts of the world as well as tax-free manufactured goods for the benefit of the South; (3) oppose an "artificial" or "forced" equalization of exchanges between the "free-laboring North" and the "spendthrift, dependent, and poverty-stricken South" by means of a subtreasury or national bank; (4) prevent the disposal of public lands for the benefit of the slaveholders at the expense of free immigrant settlers; (5) put an end to all needless, wicked, and disgraceful wars such as those against the Indians; (6) uphold human rights and republican principles; (7) seek to make education available to all, regardless of color or caste; and (8) consider the propriety of changing the Constitution to allow for the direct election of the president and vice-president by popular vote, eliminating the Electoral College.[9]

Immediately after the convention Birney left with Mrs. Birney for Ohio, but their moving west was postponed until after Birney had made a trip to Michigan in the autumn, where his brother-in-law, Daniel Fitzhugh, had already invested in some land. The infant town of Saginaw, on a bay of Lake Huron, was his destination, and thither he decided to move his family, after concluding a trade of some eight hundred acres of his Indiana lands. He would take Dion, George, and Florence, and David would come from Ohio to join them. William, however, had plans for studying law in Cincinnati; and James had accepted a pastorate in Clyde, New York, and was on his way to becoming established. In June he was to marry Miss Amanda Moulton, of New Haven, a stepdaughter of Nathaniel Bacon.

Birney's antislavery friends protested that he was burying himself in the wilderness. It was, Birney admitted, almost "out of the peopled world . . . but I can't help it. I must go where I can live cheap[ly] and where I can put my boys to doing something to support themselves. I have so long neglected my private affairs, that they will no longer

---

[9] Address of the National Anti-Slavery Convention to the Citizens of the United States, *Philanthropist*, June 16, 1841.

endure it." [10] Those who knew him well realized, too, that a continuation of his strenuous and wearing public labors would but lead to ill-health. He was urged to find a country place closer to the civilized world, just outside New York, as Weld had done, or near Cincinnati, close to his old friends and relatives; but the lure of the frontier and great optimism for the development of the virgin lands of the West had always been strong in Birney.

He had grown up with the state of Kentucky, had helped to build Alabama, and would have gone to Illinois had he not entered anti-slavery work. Since then he had made investments in the unsettled parts of both Indiana and Ohio. He was now enthusiastic about the future of Michigan, pronouncing its people "intelligent, imbued more than is common in their circumstances, with religious sentiments—law-abiding, hospitable, and generous. This is the mental and moral soil on which the shoot of Liberty naturally springs and grows." [11] At the same time, he realized that moving into the Michigan woods meant enduring privations and giving up comforts to which he had become accustomed.

The Birneys arrived in Saginaw the first week of November, 1841. It was a thinly settled region, with log cabins scattered through the woods at wide intervals. During the winter months, when navigation was closed on the Great Lakes and most of the roads were impassable, it was isolated indeed. Supplies were obtained from Indian traders.

After staying temporarily as guests of the James Frazer family, the Birneys moved into an old inn, the Webster House, which they soon converted into a comfortable home for the winter, making a sitting room and study out of the old bar. Occasionally during that first winter groups of Indians came by looking for a drink of whiskey. No farming could be begun at that time of year, of course, but Birney made preparations to resume his law practice and also to act as land agent to make investments for others and to give information or advice to immigrants.

He immediately, as was his habit, began to concern himself with

---

[10] Birney to Lewis Tappan, Oct. 4, 1841, Tappan Collection. The information on the Birney children in this chapter is all found in the Birney Papers.

[11] Birney to the editors of the *Signal of Liberty*, Sept. 29, 1841, in *Signal of Liberty*, Oct. 6, 1841.

local affairs and the improvement of the community. His interest as well as his ability and knowledge soon gave him great influence with his neighbors, many of whom were Chippewa Indians. The place was without either a school or a church. Dion started a school; and Birney himself read sermons on Sunday in the schoolhouse. Meanwhile, he began correspondence to secure a minister, a missionary for the Indians, and a storekeeper. As in Alabama, he championed the cause of the Indians against unscrupulous traders.[12]

Busy as he was getting himself established in the wilderness, Birney was not allowed to fade completely from the antislavery movement. Michigan already had a state antislavery society [13] and since the previous April, an antislavery paper, the *Signal of Liberty,* which was published in Ann Arbor by Theodore Foster and Guy Beckley. Stanch antislavery pioneers such as Nathan Power, of Farmington, Seymour B. Treadwell, of Jackson, and Nathan Thomas, of Schoolcraft, greeted Birney's coming to Michigan with the expectation that his presence would give great impetus to the cause in their state. The *Signal of Liberty* immediately announced the necessity of changing the Liberty ticket to read, "For President: James G. Birney, *of Michigan,*" and added with pride, "Westward the star of empire takes its way." [14] Birney made his debut on his initial trip to Michigan by lecturing three times in Detroit, once in Ann Arbor, and once in Flint.

Despite the work of moving and getting settled, the winter of 1841–1842 was the most relaxed and peaceful that Birney had spent in many a long year. Although his health was not as good as he might have wished, he was strong and active, and he weighed 150 pounds. It was a long while since he had done manual labor, especially outdoors in subzero weather, but he enjoyed it. There was plenty of time to enjoy his children, too. On fine days George and Florrie were taken along on the ice jumper to Lower Saginaw or to the lighthouse; and in the long evenings he and the older boys read from the Greek

[12] Diary of James G. Birney, entries from Oct. 25, 1841, to Dec. 12, 1841; Birney to Daniel Fitzhugh, Dec. 10, 1841, Birney Papers; Birney to Lewis Tappan, Jan. 14, 1842, Tappan Collection; Theodore Foster, Notebook on the Liberty Party, Foster Papers, Michigan Historical Collections, Ann Arbor.

[13] See Arthur R. Kooker, "The Anti-Slavery Movement in Michigan," an unpublished dissertation, University of Michigan, for the complete background.

[14] *Signal of Liberty,* Nov. 3, 1841.

New Testament or Caesar's *Commentaries.* On January 9, 1842, Elizabeth had their first son, whom they named Fitzhugh for her family.

Although Birney had been nominated for the presidency in the spring of 1841, he did not write his acceptance until the next January. Part of the reason for this delay was his preoccupation with starting a new life. Beyond this, however, were some misgivings about the Liberty party itself. Birney was by nature and upbringing an aristocrat. He had been active in opposition to Jackson, and looking back over the years, he believed that most of the evils of the country, especially the ascendancy of the slave power, dated from his administration. If Jacksonian democracy were responsible for the evils he saw on every hand, what of the democratic tendencies which had been expressed in the Liberty platform? It had gone so far as to advocate direct election of the president. Could the people, who put up with censorship of the mails and press, curtailing of freedom of speech in a large portion of the country, unjust treatment of the Indians, persecution of the Mormons, and the maintenance of human slavery, be trusted to govern themselves?

Birney was not sure that they could, and feeling as he did, he was reluctant to accept the party's nomination unless he could do so with sincerity. His fears were confided to Weld and Leavitt, who both encouraged him to accept. Although Weld was still convinced of the inexpediency of party organization, he rejoiced to see that "a very large number of men are working in the political harness, who will not draw steadily in any other" and resigned himself to its inevitability.[15] Birney's acceptance, however, was made with the reservation that he would "cheerfully acquiesce" in the substitution of any other candidate who might be found who would be more serviceable.[16]

The letter of acceptance, which was mainly a pointing up of the ways in which our country had failed to live up to the ideals of the Declaration of Independence, was decidedly pessimistic, almost despondent. The Revolutionary War had freed us from colonial dependence, Birney wrote, but "not from the spirit of oppression; not from

[15] Theodore Weld to Birney, Jan. 22, 1842, Birney Papers.
[16] Birney to the Committee of Nomination, Jan. 10, 1842, in *Signal of Liberty,* March 16, 1842.

its companion spirit, hypocrisy." There would be, he feared, "other revolutions needed, revolutions whose processes will be sad, sorrowful, sanguinary, before these malignant spirits shall be cast out." Freedom, justice, and law were being sacrificed to the new god, Public Opinion. Congress, the courts, and even the church had prostrated themselves before it.

There was some regret in Liberty circles over the mournful picture Birney had drawn of the situation. Even William reminded his father, "If the trumpet of the leader give forth an uncertain sound, who shall arm himself for the battle?" Leavitt, however, was glad Birney expressed himself so strongly, since it would save the party from degenerating into a mere struggle for office and would prevent the sacrifice of its ultimate objective to present expediency.[17]

In Ohio, meanwhile, before Birney's acceptance was published, there was danger of just such a move in the interests of expediency. Salmon P. Chase took the lead, backed by Gamaliel Bailey and Samuel Lewis. Chase's idea was that, rather than have Birney as the Liberty candidate again, the party should choose someone who had already made a name for himself in national politics and so had a chance of winning, even though he were not an out-and-out abolitionist. At the Ohio State Anti-Slavery Society's convention in December, 1841, William H. Seward and John Quincy Adams were both suggested, and it was proposed that a new convention be called which would be more truly a national convention than the one in New York the previous May.

Chase himself wrote to Birney to inform him of their move, explaining that although all of them had the utmost confidence in him personally, they regarded his nomination as impracticable and knew he would gladly yield his position to one "whose name might be deemed more useful to the cause." In a letter to Joshua R. Giddings, written on the same day, Chase was even more frank in expressing his fears that Birney's nomination would be a little more successful in 1844 than in 1840 and in advocating a new convention which would be regarded as distinctly a Liberty convention rather than as a meeting of the national antislavery society.[18]

[17] William Birney to Birney, March 1, 1842; Leavitt to Birney, Jan. 18, 1842, Birney Papers.

[18] Salmon P. Chase to Birney, Jan. 21, 1842, Birney Papers; Chase to Joshua Giddings, Jan. 21, 1842, in George W. Julian, *The Life of Joshua R. Giddings* (Chicago, 1892), pp. 130–131.

It was exactly on this point that Chase made his mistake, in trying to make it seem that the Liberty party and the Anti-Slavery Society were separate movements and that one could be a Liberty man without being an abolitionist. To men such as Birney who had pioneered in the antislavery movement, who had given up fortunes and risked their lives against the mobs of the 1830's, this smacked of political opportunism. It was true one could be an abolitionist without being a Liberty party man, but the reverse was impossible if true antislavery principles were to be maintained. To digress from the moral within the political was to separate the body from the heart. Although Chase's sympathies had been on the antislavery side for some years, and although he had gained a reputation in the courts for defending fugitive slaves, he had steadfastly refused to be called an abolitionist. Moreover, he had clung to his Whig party affiliation even through the election of 1840. It was inevitable that this attempt by a "raw recruit" to determine party policy should be resented by those who had laid the party groundwork. "He seems," wrote Leavitt to Birney, "to have been much impressed with the idea that there is very little practical wisdom among those who raised the Liberty Standard while he was worshipping the Log Cabin, and that therefore all that has been done, needs undoing that it may be done right." [19] Gerrit Smith openly charged Chase with ambitious motives.[20]

Birney's reply to Chase was frank and straightforward. It was true he was still willing to acquiesce in the substitution of another candidate who might be more serviceable, but he could not conceive of going out of the abolitionist ranks to find such a man. It was to avoid such action that the party had been formed. Birney expressed strong hopes for Governor Seward but thought that until Seward was willing to be called an abolitionist in name as well as in feeling it would be a "gross disparagement" of the cause to nominate him. Birney had high respect for Adams, also, and was conscious of the debt of grati-

[19] Leavitt to Birney, Feb. 14 and June 19, 1842, Birney Papers.

[20] Gerrit Smith to the editor, *American and Foreign Anti-Slavery Reporter*, Nov. 1, 1842. An entry in Birney's diary for Oct. 4, 1851, contains the following comment on Chase: "While he is a man of very handsome talents, and, no doubt, supports what he thinks will, in the long run be best, he has appeared to me ambitious of individual precedence and prominence—not relying so much on the strength of his principles as on the strength of the party by which he is supported—uneasy when left to himself with nothing to lean on and unwilling to [bear] with any contempt of caste, or with any neglect of it, for the sake of his principles."

tude the abolitionists owed him for championing the right of petition and for defending the Amistad captives; but Adams still looked on the doctrine of immediate emancipation as ridiculous. Chase was chided on another score. Referring to the Columbus convention of December, Birney wrote, "in no A.S. convention that I remember has the opposition to slavery been considered so much a matter of money policy—so little a matter of religious duty." [21]

Alvan Stewart, chairman of the national Executive Committee of the Liberty party, wrote to beg Birney that "no consideration on earth" might induce him to resign or yield his nomination "in consequence of an unregulated spirit which inhabits a few bosoms in Ohio." His letter to the Ohio group reminded its members that Ohio had been well represented at New York when the nominations were made and that he would not permit them to ruin the cause by questioning those nominations. [22]

In the spring of 1842 it was necessary for Birney to make a trip to Ohio to take care of his land business there, and he took the occasion to visit Cincinnati. Immediately after his arrival Chase called on him to converse on the prospects of the Liberty party. Ward meetings were beginning in the city, and the party's "Liberty Roll" was gaining in signatures. Yet Birney was uneasy. The leaders of the party in Cincinnati wished it to be considered as purely a political one; real sympathy for the slave was not expressed. Three days later he met with a group at the Chase home, where he took the opportunity to express frankly and strongly the opinion that the efforts of the Liberty party in Ohio to separate from the abolitionists in order to avoid the unpopularity of abolitionism would be gravely injurious to the whole cause. Birney felt that he had won his point, and they parted with good feelings.

Both Chase and Lewis were given letters of recommendation from him to take along on their trip to the East. Leavitt reported, after having talked to Lewis in New York, that he thought he had been set right and would no longer favor "some of the over-wise fancies of Chase and Bailey." Bailey himself, who had been accused by Alvan Stewart of having "betrayed an unstable spirit on political abolition," wrote to

[21] Birney to Chase, Feb. 2, 1842, Chase Papers, Manuscript Division, Library of Congress.

[22] Alvan Stewart to Birney, April 14, 1842, Birney Papers.

Birney in November to vindicate himself and his colleagues. Both Chase and Lewis, he insisted, were now outright abolitionists, and as for him, he was what he had always been "since you introduced me to the tripod." [23]

Yet the issue was not settled. Chase and Bailey had given up the idea of nominating from outside the ranks of the recognized abolitionists, but they were still of the opinion that they could do better with a candidate other than Birney. Judge William Jay seemed to fill the bill. In addition to being an avowed and sincere abolitionist, he was the son of the former illustrious chief justice, and, as such, his name would bring in votes. Moreover, he had not associated himself with either faction in the antislavery split of 1840. The one difficulty was that, like Tappan and Weld, he had withheld his support from political organization.

Again Bailey wrote to Birney to state his position on the matter:

I have no doubt, as to your entire fitness for the presidential chair, so far as competency and perfect integrity are concerned. But, I have had doubts, as to your being the most eligible candidate. You have always appeared in the character of a Moralist, a reformer, rather than a Politician, or Statesman. [24]

Bailey also feared Birney's distrust of the ability of the people to govern themselves. Despite these doubts, Bailey declared he was willing to leave the decision to Birney. This willingness to put the responsibility for withdrawing on Birney was a psychological move. Bailey was well aware of Birney's sensitivity; he also knew Birney's sincerity would prevent his keeping the nomination if once he were convinced that someone else could really do more to further the success of the cause.

William Birney, who had begun the practice of law in Cincinnati and who had been elected to the Executive Committee of the Anti-Slavery Society there, was particularly disturbed about Bailey. Oversensitive concerning his father, he was convinced that Bailey was guilty of double-dealing. Recently Birney had sent to the Michigan legislature a memorial embodying his ideas on the return of fugitive slaves in the Northwest Territory. [25] William gave a copy of this memorial to

[23] Leavitt to Birney, June 19, 1842; Stewart to Birney, April 14, 1842; and Bailey to Birney, Nov. 16, 1842, Birney Papers.

[24] Bailey to Birney, March 31, 1843, Birney Papers.

[25] James G. Birney, *Memorial of James G. Birney to the Legislature of Michigan*, in *Signal of Liberty*, Jan. 30, 1843.

Bailey to publish in the *Philanthropist*, but, to his surprise, Bailey came out with an article using the arguments and illustrations as if they were his own.[26]

Besides, Bailey had tried to get support for a letter to Birney asking him to resign the nomination. Failing in this, he had prepared a circular to western Liberty men disparaging Birney's nomination with a view to defeating it in the convention which the Central Committee had called for Buffalo in August. In private conversation, William told his father, Bailey was insinuating that Birney was a monarchist and therefore unfit to hold office in a republic. William avowed that his own ideas of democracy were widely different from his father's, but he saw no point in introducing this topic. Bailey and Chase, he charged, were simply using it to distract Birney's supporters and gain their own point in the nomination.

In May, Samuel Lewis wrote a letter to Birney in order to put him on the spot. It was probably written at the suggestion of Chase and Bailey. He was asked whether he thought the right of suffrage as exercised in the free western states should be restricted and if so, to what extent; whether he favored making any department of the government more permanent by lengthening terms of office; and whether he advocated any other changes with the object of restricting direct popular power.[27]

Birney replied that too many people took the elective franchise for granted; he would have it forfeitable by those who violated their neighbors' rights of freedom of press, speech, and inquiry. Foreigners coming into this country who were ignorant of our civil institutions easily became the prey of demagogues. They should not be allowed to vote immediately, as they were in some states, even before they had citizenship papers. In reply to the second question, he said he would have senators eligible at a more advanced age and would lengthen their term of office to give the Senate more permanency. They should have more opportunity to give their advice and consent to presidential actions. This would curtail the powers of the executive and diminish the operation of the spoils system. The president should not, by attempting

---

[26] See *Philanthropist*, Feb. 24, 1843, for Bailey's editorial.
[27] Samuel Lewis to Birney, May 28, 1843, Birney Papers. See also the letters of William Birney to his father through 1843.

to impose policies on Congress, discourage Congressional deliberation and encourage party dictation. In addition, he advocated limiting the president to one term.

This answer took the floor from under any suspicions of Birney's being a monarchist. The trend was, he recognized, toward shorter terms and rotation in office, but he felt that these resulted only in disregard for high qualifications for public service. As for democracy, there need be no worries about it if justice were first established in the land. Otherwise the despotism of the multitude would but drive people to seek security under the despotism of one person. As for the form of government, he accepted ours as "the best mode . . . of protecting and promoting the solid happiness of the people."

In expressing his views to Lewis, Birney made it clear that he felt that no issues should take precedence over the antislavery motives of the Liberty party, and no issues should be introduced if there was a danger of their detracting from the primary one. Had Lewis (and this referred as well to Chase) participated in the early labors of the movement, he would be able "to estimate more correctly than one coming into the cause at a later period can, the magnitude of the obstacles . . . and the danger of again subjecting ourselves to their pressure." [28]

While Birney's nomination was being discussed and considered throughout 1842 and 1843, he was doing all he could for the cause under the existing circumstances of his isolation in Saginaw. Late in 1841 the case of the *Creole*, with its resultant debates in Congress in 1842, aroused the interest of all antislavery people. The brig *Creole* had sailed from Virginia bound for New Orleans with 135 slaves on board. Several days out at sea the slaves rose against the officers, wounding the captain, the first mate, and two of the crew, and killing one of the passengers. Having obtained possession of the vessel, they forced the crew to sail to Nassau in the Bahamas. There nineteen of them were held on murder charges, but the rest were set free. Anti-English excitement in the South was reflected in Congress under the leadership of Calhoun, who demanded that the president take immediate action. Secretary of State Webster responded by directing Edward Everett, our minister in London, to demand the return of the slaves as mutineers

[28] Birney to Lewis, July 13, 1843, Birney Papers.

and murderers.[29] While Southern senators and representatives were calling for satisfaction, the antislavery contingent in Congress, flushed with their recent victory in defeating the censure of John Quincy Adams, prepared to present their side.

Fortunately, Birney, the ablest of the antislavery lawyers on con-stitutional interpretation and international law, had already prepared a short article on the *Creole* case for the New York *American*. His argu-ments were summarized and introduced by Joshua Giddings in the House of Representatives as a series of nine resolutions.[30] Their argu-ment ran as follows: (1) exclusive jurisdiction over slavery within its own territory was reserved to each state; (2) this jurisdiction was not surrendered to the federal government as was jurisdiction over com-merce and navigation on the high seas; (3) slavery could exist only by force of positive municipal law and was confined to the territorial jurisdiction of the power creating it; (4) when a ship left the port of a state and entered upon the high seas, the persons aboard it ceased to be subject to the laws of the state, but were subject to the laws of the United States; (5) therefore, the persons aboard the *Creole* were no longer subject to the slave laws of Virginia and were but resuming their natural rights of personal liberty. To re-enslave such persons and to place the country in the position of maintaining a commerce in human beings would be incompatible with our national honor.

Giddings' resolutions were greeted with a storm of protest. He was accused of justifying murder and mutiny "in terms shocking to all sense of law, order, and humanity" and was therefore subject to the censure of the House of Representatives. A resolution of censure was introduced and passed by a vote of 125 to 69.[31] Giddings resigned his seat and returned to Ohio, only to be re-elected in triumph by his antislavery constituents.

On the local scene in Michigan, Birney was much in demand as a speaker and adviser. Guy Beckley and Theodore Foster, editors of the *Signal of Liberty* in Ann Arbor, looked to him for suggestions on style

[29] James Brown Scott, *Cases on International Law Selected from the Decisions of English and American Courts* (St. Paul, 1906), pp. 252–255; *Senate Documents* 27 Cong., 2 Sess., III, No. 137.

[30] New York *American*, Feb. 18, 1842; Seth M. Gates to Birney, April 4, 1842, Birney Papers. See *Congressional Globe*, 27 Cong., 2 Sess., p. 342, for the resolu-tions.

[31] Julian, *op. cit.*, pp. 120–124.

and mode of argument, as well as on content and policy; while abolitionists in the western part of the state consulted him on starting a
paper of their own and hiring an editor. When Prior Foster established
the Grand River Institute (in Ingham County), a manual labor school
for colored students, Birney was made one of its trustees. As soon as
he was settled in Saginaw, invitations for him to give speeches in the
surrounding community began to come in. These he accepted whenever possible, the only exception being his refusal to talk at Fourth of
July celebrations "until liberty be enjoyed by all the inhabitants of
the land." [32] In the summer and autumn of 1842 he addressed anti-
slavery conventions at Pontiac and Ann Arbor, speaking also at several
other towns along his route. At the Pontiac convention he was nominated
as Liberty candidate for the state Senate. [33]

Early in 1842 a movement had begun to run Birney for the governor-
ship of Michigan, and in February, 1843, he received that nomination
at a convention held in Ann Arbor on the occasion of the eighth anniversary meeting of the Michigan Anti-Slavery Society. Luther F.
Stevens, a lawyer of Kalamazoo, was chosen as his running mate. The
platform the convention adopted included, besides antislavery resolutions, other resolutions which favored the opening of new world markets so the free West would not have to trade with the slaveholding
South, the diffusion of education among all classes, sound and honest
currency of gold and silver, and the adoption of just commercial regula-
tions. The thesis of Birney's memorial to the legislature, that because
Michigan was in the Northwest Territory it was not bound to return
fugitive slaves, was approved. [34]

In the election Birney received 2,775 votes to 15,607 for the Whig
candidate, Pitcher, and 21,414 for the Democratic governor, Barry, who
was re-elected. Small though the vote was, it showed a decided increase in Liberty votes since 1840. In that year there were 328 Liberty
votes; in 1841, 1,214; and in 1842, 2,310. [35] It was a rate of increase
which augured well.

During the summer of 1843 the second World Anti-Slavery Convention met in London. Birney was urged by his many English friends

[32] Saginaw Committee to Birney, June 24, 1842, Birney Papers. A draft of Birney's
answer is on the back side.
[33] *Signal of Liberty*, Aug. 29, 1842, Sept. 26, 1842, and Oct. 24, 1842.
[34] *Ibid.*, Feb. 13 and Feb. 20, 1843.   [35] *Ibid.*, Dec. 11, 1843.

to visit them again, but his duties kept him at home this time. Besides, delegates would convene at Buffalo in August to settle the matter of national nominations. Morris had resigned his nomination as vice-presidential candidate, but Leavitt and Stewart were determined that Birney should not disregard the wishes of all the other states because of pressure from Ohio. Both had sent word that he must "stand his ground until shot down." [36]

Birney did not go to the convention himself, but he wrote to the chairman requesting that the convention consider the nomination an open one. If another candidate should be preferred, it would be a "mortifying reflection" to him to think he might stand in the way of a cause which more than any other had interested the prime of his life and whose "successful consummation" would be "one of the most precious consolations of its decline." [37] To Charles Stewart, delegate from Michigan, and to Joshua Leavitt, he wrote more fully and confidentially. If Judge Jay really came out for the party and if he would be the unanimous choice, should Birney's name be withdrawn, would it not be for the good of the cause, he asked, if he withdrew unconditionally? He would leave it to their judgment—theirs, and that of his other trusted and tried colleagues: William Goodell, Gerrit Smith, Beriah Green, and Henry Stanton. They must remember that "abolitionists, after all, have a good deal of human nature in them." Judge Jay was a distinguished man; while he himself was now a laboring man, "engaged daily in farming drudgery, and in discharge of menial offices. Could they well stand it to have as their candidate one seen hoeing potatoes or rolling logs, or chopping his own firewood or cleaning his own shoes?" Should someone else be chosen but his name suggested for second place, he must decline on the grounds that demoting him in position would destroy his effectiveness and influence as a candidate.[38] While antislavery newspapers were seriously discussing the relative merits of Birney and Jay, the editor of the Danville *Kentucky Tribune* rather amusingly declared his intention of remaining neutral "so as not to be disqualified for accepting a seat in the cabinet under either." [39]

[36] Leavitt to Birney, Feb. 28, 1843, Birney Papers.
[37] Birney to Alvan Stewart, Aug. 15, 1843, Birney Papers.
[38] Birney to Charles H. Stewart and Leavitt, Aug. 17, 1843, Birney Papers.
[39] *Kentucky Tribune* (Danville), Sept. 1, 1843.

The delegates gathered on August 30 in a vast tent, over one hundred feet in diameter, pitched in the park in front of the Buffalo courthouse. Seats were arranged for three thousand, but even that number was inadequate. The number of delegates totaled over a thousand, but visitors swelled the audience from two to five thousand. Each state was allowed voting delegates equal to its electoral votes, plus two delegates at large. Leicester King, Liberty candidate for governor of Ohio, was elected chairman; and several Ohio men were put on committees. By this time, however, the Ohio delegation was convinced that Birney had everyone's support; it therefore joined the others to make his and Morris' nomination unanimous on the first ballot.

Chase, Alvan Stewart, and Stanton composed the committee on resolutions and managed to compose a total of forty-four. Most of them were a reiteration of antislavery principles. The Liberty party was declared to be a national party, not a sectional one, for both candidates were native Southerners, Birney from Kentucky and Morris from Virginia. Neither was it a new party but the revival of the party of '76 and of the principles of that era. In an effort to tie together the separate phases of antislavery endeavor, voting was declared to be a moral and religious duty. The party owed it to the laws of God (the higher law doctrine) to treat clause three of Section Two, Article IV (the fugitive-slave clause of the Constitution) as unconstitutional and, therefore, null and void. In accordance with the recent decision of the Supreme Court in *Prigg* vs. *Pennsylvania,* which stated that state and local officers were not required to aid in the return of fugitives, the free states should place a penalty on so doing.[40] The direct result of agitation for this point was to be the passage of "personal liberty laws" throughout the North.

Leicester King conveyed to Birney the official notification of his nomination.[41] It was unfortunate that Birney was so sensitive to the Ohio dissension, for it was undoubtedly responsible for the aggrieved, even vindictive, tone which is evident in his letter of acceptance. The substance of the letter was an attack on John Quincy Adams, but it was not, in reality, intended so much as an attack on him as it was a chastisement of the Ohio group for their attempt to make a nomination

[40] *Facts for the People* (Cincinnati), Oct., 1843; *Signal of Liberty,* Sept. 18 and Sept. 25, 1843; Foster, Notebook on the Liberty party.
[41] Leicester King to Birney, Sept. 18, 1843, in *Signal of Liberty,* Jan. 29, 1844.

of expediency from outside the old abolitionist ranks. This was apparent even in his acceptance of the honor: "To learn that my constancy as an Abolitionist and my steadfastness in the Liberty party from the time of its being organized, have drawn toward me the confidence of that party, is too gratifying not to be acknowledged." In trying to emphasize his point by using Adams as an illustration, Birney overdrew his arguments. The letter, consequently, became entirely too anti-Adams and not enough pro-Liberty.

Birney charged the abolitionists with having been overly influenced by Adams' defense of petition and his opposition to the annexation of Texas. Adams owed most of his popularity and votes to the abolitionists; in fact, they had run no candidate against him in his legislative district. Yet he favored admitting Florida as a slave state, did not support abolition in the District of Columbia, opposed antislavery societies as such, and dismissed immediatism as a moral and physical impossibility. From the true antislavery view of no compromise of principle, Birney was correct. Unfortunately, he went further than was either necessary or wise by terming Adams' course "eccentric, whimsical, inconsistent" and defended by "frivolous arguments." [42]

Unlike 1840, this time the campaign was not to end with the nomination. Party organization would reach down to the local level, special efforts would be made to secure town and county offices, campaign tracts would be published and distributed, and committees of correspondence would keep every area alert and in touch with general developments.

[42] Birney to Leicester King, Jan. 1, 1844, in *Signal of Liberty*, Jan. 29, 1844.

Chapter XII

The Campaign of 1844

ALTHOUGH a Whig paper in Cincinnati predicted that Birney was more apt to become "a perfume peddlar in Hayti, or a shoeblack in Timbuctoo, than President of the United States," [1] the Liberty party men started off their campaign as if they really expected to put their candidate in the White House. Elizur Wright and Joshua Leavitt spearheaded the attack in New England and the East, Alvan Stewart and Gerrit Smith in western New York, Charles Stewart and the editors of the *Signal of Liberty* in Michigan, and Leicester King and Thomas Morris in Ohio.

Wright wrote immediately after the Buffalo convention to express the hope that Birney would consider the nomination a "voice from Heaven" and take the stump to inspire antislavery activity. Money would be provided for him to come to Boston at once; he should leave the city of Saginaw "to grow as it may for a season." While the abolitionists were on their road to victory, their leader must not be "browsing . . . among the reeds and alders and *weeping* willows." [2] Finally convinced that as a candidate he must be seen as well as heard, Birney con-

[1] Cincinnati *Daily Enquirer,* April 1, 1842.
[2] Elizur Wright to Birney, Sept. 16, 1843, Birney Papers.

sented to a lecturing tour in New England. From the middle of October and through the early part of November, he spoke at meetings in Boston, Cambridge, Lynn, Lowell, Worcester, Charlestown, Wrentham, Haverhill, East Arlington, Roxbury, Taunton, Northampton, and Pittsfield.

Wright took upon himself the duties of publicity manager through the *Emancipator and Free American,* writing up notices of meetings with spirit and enthusiasm, and promising that anyone who came would be "cured of voting the slaveocratic ticket." He reported afterwards that the meetings had infused new life into Massachusetts abolitionism and had resulted in adding hundreds to the ranks. "Who is James G. Birney?" asked Wright and answered, "The finest specimen of the glorious, erect, reasoning animal." He compared him to Washington in courage, patriotism, dignity, and self-devotion, adding, "Should he die this day, he has achieved more for the liberty and welfare of his country than all the presidents or other candidates for the presidency, that have lived since Washington died." [3] Another of his eulogies was reprinted in Liberty papers throughout the country:

Some heroic man, and I think it will be James Gillespie Birney, will take his place in history, as reviled and hated by lordlings, underrated and suspected by the poor, miserable shrink-aways of his generation, who has yet to lead his country to victory over despotism, which will be brilliant through time. Such a man I say will be written down, or our country will rot. I go for that man.[4]

On his way home from Massachusetts, Birney spoke at New Haven, where his son, James, now a Congregational minister, was active in antislavery work; addressed a large gathering at Albany; and made stops at Peterboro, Rochester, and Detroit. Even Lewis Tappan had been won over to the support of the organized antislavery political movement.

Plans had already been made to write a campaign biography of Birney. Leavitt began it as a sketch for the *Emancipator,* but when he was not able to finish, James C. Jackson, William L. Chaplin, and Beriah Green took up the work. For Beriah Green it was a labor of love, and the body of the work, which consisted largely of long quotations from Birney's writings, was interspersed with eulogistic phrases on his life of self-sacrifice and devotion to the antislavery cause.

[3] *Emancipator and Free American* (Boston), Oct. 26, 1843 and Nov. 16, 1843.
[4] *Signal of Liberty,* Oct. 30, 1843; *Western Citizen* (Chicago), Nov. 16, 1843.

The Liberty party was explained as an outgrowth of the realization that good men must not stay out of politics. It was an attempt to combine faith and works, the ideal and the actual, to embody the ideal in human form and human government.[5] The call to religious men to accept political responsibility provided the keynote for sermons of antislavery ministers throughout the North. That of James Birney, Jr., preached on Thanksgiving Day, 1843, was typical. Government, as an institution of God, he expounded, must be maintained by religious men whose principles were sound. Neglect of this duty was the reason for the low level to which politics had fallen.[6]

Wright, meanwhile, continued his newspaper publicity. The cedar of Lebanon had been chosen as the party symbol, and articles for Birney and Morris were printed with pictures and appropriate inscriptions: "The righteous shall grow like a Cedar in Lebanon"; and "The Cedar is the emblem of Constancy, of Protection, of Renown, of Immortality." Wright wrote:

When the Hickory of Tennessee, the Elm of New York, the Buckeye of Ohio, and the Persimmon of Virginia, shall have perished in oblivion our serviceable, fragrant, and ever-enduring Cedar will stretch its sheltering arms over the nation, and tower aloft, as a memorial of victorious deeds, and a witness to the latest ages that God loves the good, and those that honor Him He will honor.[7]

Wright's eleven-year-old son composed a "Birney March" for the campaign, while Wright himself wrote an "Ode to Birney" which he set to music. It became one of the popular campaign songs:

> We hail thee, Birney, just and true,
> The calm and fearless, staunch and tried,
> The bravest of the valiant few,
>   Our country's hope, our country's pride!
>   In Freedom's battle take the van;
>   We hail thee as an honest man.
>
> Thy country, in her darkest hour,
> When heroes bend at Mammon's shrine,
> And virtue sells herself to Power,

[5] Beriah Green, *Sketches of the Life and Writings of James Gillespie Birney.*
[6] *Christian Freeman* (Hartford), March 7, 1844.
[7] See *Emancipator* throughout the autumn of 1843 and 1844.

> Lights up in smiles at deeds like thine!
>   Then welcome to the battle's van—
>   We hail thee as an honest man.
>
> Thy own example leads the way,
>   From Egypt's gloom to Canaan's light;
> Thy justice is the breaking day
>   Of slavery's long and guilty night;
>   Then welcome to the battle's van—
>   We *hail* thee as an honest man.
>
> Thine is the eagle eye to see,
>   And thine a human heart to feel;
> A worthy leader of the free,
>   We'll trust thee with a Nation's weal;
>   We'll trust thee in the battle's van—
>   We *hail* thee as an honest man.
>
> An *honest man—an honest man*
> God made thee on his noblest plan
>   To do the right and brave the scorn
>   To stand in Freedom's hope forlorn;
> Then welcome to the triumph's van—
> WE HAIL THEE AS OUR CHOSEN MAN! [8]

Antislavery gatherings, which had always been opened with prayer and hymn singing, were often very similar in spirit and atmosphere to religious revival meetings. Rousing hymns were replaced by equally rousing campaign songs, and special songbooks were published and distributed for this purpose. Several other selections besides Wright's "Ode" paid tribute to Birney:

> Lo! all the world for Birney now,
>   Hurrah! Hurrah! Hurrah!
> See! as he comes the parties bow,
>   Hurrah! Hurrah! Hurrah!
> No iron mixed with mirey clay,
> Will ever do, the people say,
>   Hurrah! Hurrah! Hurrah!

---

[8] Philip Green Wright and Elizabeth Q. Wright, *Elizur Wright, The Father of Life Insurance* (Chicago, 1937), p. 146; the songs are taken from George W. Clark, *The Liberty Minstrel* (New York, 1846).

> Be Birney's name the one you choose
>   Hurrah! Hurrah! Hurrah!
> Let not a soul his ballot lose,
>   Hurrah! Hurrah! Hurrah!
> No other man in this our day
> Will ever do, the people say;
>   Hurrah! Hurrah! Hurrah!

"We're for Freedom through the Land" contained the Liberty call to battle:

> We are coming, we are coming!
> Freedom's battle is begun!
> No hand shall furl her banner ere her victory be won!
> Our shields are locked for liberty, and mercy goes before;
> Tyrants tremble in your citadel! Oppression shall be o'er.
>   We will vote for Birney! We will vote for Birney!
>   We're for liberty and Birney and for freedom through the land.

Copies of Birney's portrait were made and advertised at one dollar apiece, eight dollars a dozen, or fifty dollars a hundred. "Walk up to Duren's window," advertised the *Bangor Gazette,* "compare the heads of the different candidates for president, and buy the best one. There is no mistaking it." Women's auxiliary antislavery societies arranged huge picnics at which Liberty mottoes were displayed and cakes were inscribed to the candidates. Fifty thousand copies of the *Liberty Almanac* were planned to carry antislavery propaganda into as many homes.[9]

Back home in Saginaw, Birney was bombarded by queries of potential supporters as to how he stood on the various other issues of the day: Masonry, pacifism, naturalization of aliens, public lands, tariff, a national bank, internal improvements, and postage rates. He attempted to answer them all but also to maintain his position that each of these was subordinate to the main issue of slavery, and that if once slavery were abolished and righteousness in government established again, these other problems would settle themselves.

The question on his peace principles came from his old Quaker friend in Haverford, Pennsylvania, Abraham S. Pennock. Birney had

[9] *Christian Freeman,* March 7, 1844; *Bangor Gazette,* quoted in *Emancipator and Weekly Chronicle* (Boston), Aug. 14, 1844.

been thinking of the peace question for years and held war to be certainly one of the greatest evils. He considered wars of conquest to be "wholly iniquitous" but could not accept pacifistic doctrines to the extent of condemning strictly defensive wars. States must punish wrong-doers among nations, he believed, just as they punished wrongdoing members of their own societies. Governments ought to be God's "bracements" on earth; to be so, they must have substantial power or become useless. Adjustments among nations to avoid war should be the object of earnest and insistent negotiations.[10]

Tariff supporters of western Pennsylvania were particularly interested in Birney's stand on that question, especially since he was reputed to be in favor of free trade. Although he knew his answer would not be in accord with the hopes of those to whom he wrote, he stated his true position as one who favored a tariff for revenue only. He thought a tariff for protection smacked too much of "immunity or privilege conferred on a particular portion of the community" and, as such, savored of the "*aristocratical* in the most odious sense of the word." World trade would prosper best without a protective tariff; this freedom, in turn, would help to remove the obstacles in the way of labor's receiving its just due. Until the problem of labor—slave and free—in this country was settled, there could be no peaceful progress. As Birney was not, however, in favor of rash or violent changes in the existing order where lawful interests were involved, he would not have the existing tariff suddenly revised until it had been "fairly and fully tried." Russell Errett, to whom Birney addressed his discourse, was persuaded by friends that to publish Birney's adverse views would lose the Liberty party votes in Pennsylvania. Unaware of their decision, Birney allowed a copy of the letter to be published in the *Signal of Liberty*. Immediately the charge was made that Birney was making political capital by publishing his views only when and where they coincided with local sentiment.[11]

Birney agreed that Congress had the power to establish a national bank; but he did not favor one while there was slavery in the country, since he feared it would give advantages to the insolvent South at the expense of the "hard-earned" capital of the North. Under other cir-

[10] Abraham S. Pennock to Birney, Feb. 29, 1844; Birney to Pennock, March 31, 1844, Birney Papers.

[11] Russell Errett to Birney, July 13, 1844, Aug. 27, 1844, and Oct. 4, 1844; Birney to Errett, Aug. 5, 1844, Birney Papers; *Gazette and Advertiser* (Pittsburgh), undated clipping.

cumstances he would favor a national bank as a depository and fiscal agent of the government. He was against distributing to the states the proceeds from the sale of public lands. That money should rather be put into the national treasury to be used for the interests of states later admitted as well as those already existing.[12] He also opposed the plan of a group calling itself the National Reform Association, which advocated that public lands should not be sold but that settlers should be allowed to occupy them and pass on certain rights of occupancy only to other people not already owning land. Birney thought most settlers would prefer to call their land their own, and popular will would settle this question.

He had already expressed himself on the subject of requiring naturalization of aliens before allowing them to vote. Once naturalized, they should be allowed the same rights as others in civil and political affairs, regardless of their religion or national backgrounds. Discrimination against the foreign born and attacks on them by nativist groups could be laid at the door of slavery, according to Birney, for that evil had hardened the public mind to overlook trespasses and even violence.[13]

As for Masonry, his connection with it had been severed, though without any public renunciation, a long time before there had been any organized opposition to it. He denounced it now in unequivocal terms "as productive of no good which could not better be attained in some other way," for even its charities were discriminatory and expensive:

as inviting to habits of dissipation, chiefly gambling and intemperance; as giving to fraudulent and dishonest persons a passport to the confidence of the generous and unsuspecting; as, *in its secrecy*, inimical to what ought to be the open and straightforward course of a republican government; as inducing weak and unstable men to regard it as a sufficient substitute for the Christianity which it had profaned by its absurd and despicable imitations.[14]

Birney had, in fact, become so strongly antimasonic that when he discovered that his son, William, had joined the order, he refused for a long time to have any communication with him.

The main issue of the campaign of 1844 as far as the Liberty party

[12] Birney to the Hartford Ohio Committee, Aug. 15, 1844, in *Signal of Liberty,* Sept. 16, 1844.

[13] Birney to Committee of Naturalized Citizens of Dayton, June 10, 1844, in *Emancipator and Weekly Chronicle,* Aug. 14, 1844.

[14] Birney to Reese Fleeson, Jan. 20, 1844, in *Signal of Liberty,* June 3, 1844.

was concerned was the annexation of Texas; and it was on this question that the rivalry between the Whig and Liberty parties centered. The Democrats, with James J. Polk and Birney's old college friend, George Dallas, were definitely committed to annexation with their dual motto, "The re-annexation of Texas and the re-occupation of Oregon." They stood little chance of winning any abolitionist votes. The Liberty party realized full well that there was little danger that large numbers of antislavery men would backslide into the Democratic ranks; but as long as Clay could be represented as opposed to annexation there was a strong possibility that many antislavery votes would be deflected into the Whig column, especially as a large majority of antislavery people had been, or still were, Whigs.[15] The appeal of the Whigs was strong. If by voting Whig rather than Liberty, antislavery men could prevent the annexation of Texas, was that not their duty, rather than throwing away votes on Liberty candidates who had no real chance of being elected anyway?

Perhaps with any other candidate the Whigs could have won their point, and with it, the election; but to ask stanch antislavery men who antedated political abolitionism to vote for Clay was asking too much. In the first place, Henry Clay was himself a slaveholder. Back in 1834 Birney had visited him to try to induce him to take the lead in some plan of emancipation in Kentucky; but Birney had left with the conviction that nothing could be expected. The subsequent reaction in Kentucky in favor of slavery was credited to Clay's withholding the weight of his influence from the abolitionist cause. Once since then Birney's hopes for Clay seemed not entirely lost. In 1836, while he was editor of the *Philanthropist*, Birney praised Clay's speech in defense of the right of petition and the constitutional power of Congress over the District of Columbia. "We will not give up all hope of him in the great struggle that is to succeed the present skirmishes," [16] he wrote; but the flame of renewed hope flickered only briefly. Early in 1839 Clay made a strong proslavery speech which alienated even some of his own party.

An incident which added new cause for resolute opposition occurred at a public address by Clay in Richmond, Indiana, in 1842. During the

[15] See Dwight L. Dumond, *The Antislavery Origins of the Civil War in the United States*, p. 93, for a discussion of this point. George R. Poage in *Henry Clay and the Whig Party* (Chapel Hill, 1936), p. 112, agrees that nine-tenths of the abolitionists were drawn from the Whig party.

[16] *Philanthropist*, March 25, 1836.

meeting a Quaker named Mendenhall had presented Clay with a petition asking him to emancipate his slaves. Instead of accepting the petition and then disposing of it quietly, Clay answered that his slaves were as well shod, as well clad, as sleek and fat, and, he thought, as honest as Mendenhall or any of his associates who signed the petition. Pointing a finger at Mendenhall, he told him to go home and mind his own business.[17] This was the kind of incident which made good campaign material for the Liberty party.

On the subject of annexation itself, Clay tried to straddle the fence. He avoided the issue as long as he could, attempting, as George Bancroft reported to Van Buren, to "humbug the northern abolitionists and then humor the South." In April, 1844, Clay wrote his "Raleigh Letter," in which he said he considered the annexation of Texas at that time as dangerous, inexpedient, and "not called for by any general expression of public opinion"; yet to Alexander Stephens he had already privately acknowledged that he favored annexation if it could be done without endangering the Union and that such a step would be a leading object of his administration if he were elected.[18]

Antislavery men who held positions in the Whig party throughout the North, however, were eager to accept his "Raleigh Letter" without serious consideration of the phrase "at this time." Giddings and Slade, in Congress, retained their Whig allegiance rather than go over to the Liberty party. Zephaniah Platt, formerly Whig attorney general of Michigan, in a debate with Birney in Detroit in July, argued that the Whigs were an antislavery party and stood for the same things the Liberty party did.[19]

Cassius Clay, who was becoming famous as a fighting abolitionist in Kentucky, actively campaigned for his kinsman, even making a trip into the North to do so, but with what Theodore Foster described after his Ann Arbor visit as a "fatal efficiency." In attempting to gloss over Henry Clay's bad traits and glorify his good ones, he served only to diminish his own reputation and influence with Liberty men, even to the extent of impairing their faith in his antislavery principles. On the other hand, Henry Clay, fearing that Cassius' impolitic speeches identi-

[17] Theodore Foster, Notebook on the Liberty Party, Foster Papers; Poage, *op. cit.*, pp. 117–118.

[18] Poage, *op. cit.*, p. 134.

[19] *Emancipator and Weekly Chronicle,* Aug. 14, 1844.

fying opposition to annexation with abolitionism were doing more to alienate Southern votes than they were to gain Northern ones, felt compelled to repudiate his support. This repudiation, in turn, helped to paralyze the efforts of the more conservative antislavery Whigs such as Slade and Giddings.[20]

It was Henry Clay himself, however, who lost the abolitionist vote by the writing of his "Alabama Letters" in July. In these letters, addressed to John M. Jackson and Thomas M. Peters, he stated that he had no personal objection to annexation if it could be effected without jeopardizing the Union. He also attempted to divorce the slavery issue from annexation, an impossibility as far as the Liberty party was concerned. In New York, Washington Hunt wrote to Thurlow Weed, "We had the abolitionists in a good way, but Mr. Clay seems determined they shall not be allowed to vote for him." [21]

Birney's ideas on annexation were discussed in responses to inquiries from various persons and groups. According to his interpretation, annexation was unconstitutional. The government was one of delegated powers, none of which authorized the acceptance of a cession of foreign territory. If this were read into the treaty-making power, whole states could be transferred to other sovereignties, and integrity of the Union would be put into the hands of the president and two-thirds of the Senate. Birney favored liberal construction only when the object sought was allowable in the Constitution; otherwise, liberal construction today might become licentious construction tomorrow. He felt that the unauthorized purchase of Louisiana, which even Jefferson recognized as unconstitutional, was a disastrous event for the country. By the slower process of amendment before action, consideration could have been given to guarding against slavery. Birney refused to allow to any kind of human law the power to establish slavery. To enact slavery was no more right than to enact murder, blasphemy, incest, or adultery.

Birney's position was the opposite of Garrison's view that the Constitution was a proslavery document. In Birney's eyes, it was definitely antislavery, having as its object the establishment of justice and the blessings of liberty. Consequently, slavery was unconstitutional in every territory under the control of the federal government, and North-

[20] Foster, Notebook on the Liberty party. Poage, *op. cit.*, has a general discussion of this point.

[21] John B. McMaster, *A History of the People of the United States*, VII, 388.

ern congressmen had been betrayers of freedom in accepting the Missouri Compromise. If the free states demanded that no slaveholders be appointed to any offices under the government, slavery would die out quickly, without violating either the letter or the spirit of the Constitution. He opposed annexation on practical grounds, too. The country, he argued, was already large enough for the purposes of government. If Texas were added, the acquisition would but create an insatiable desire for more, perhaps Mexico or even the lands westward to the Pacific.[22]

As the summer of 1844 went on and the Whig and Liberty rivalry became more bitter, invectives were hurled from both sides. In the Detroit debate between Birney and Platt, the audience began to hiss to prevent Birney from speaking and had to be calmed down by the presiding officer, who reminded the listeners that the Liberty party had hired the hall and was their host. Ignoring the fact that out of three evening speeches on that Detroit trip Birney devoted one to the subject of the Democratic party and slavery, the main Whig charge was that Birney and the Liberty party acted as the disguised auxiliary of Polk and the Democrats.[23] The Detroit *Advertiser* informed its readers that Birney was receiving $2,200 a year besides his traveling expenses. "Who wouldn't be a candidate for President and sympathize with the poor darkey for twenty-two hundred dollars per annum?" the paper asked. The *Signal of Liberty* denied that Birney was being paid more than his expenses. Nor had he, retorted its editors, a plantation from which he could "derive wealth by the robbery of his fellow men, like his presidential competitors."[24]

Birney himself prepared a scathing campaign document entitled *Headlands in the Life of Henry Clay,* which summarized Clay's services to the slave power. These included securing a clause in the Treaty of Ghent protecting slave property in territory taken by the British during the war, fastening slavery on Missouri by "coaxing and dragooning" Northern members of Congress from their fidelity to liberty, and negotiating for the rendition of fugitive slaves from Canada. In Kentucky, Clay had "prosecuted to conviction for murder, a poor, friendless,

[22] Birney to William E. Austin, David Shields, and James Clarke, Feb. 23, 1844, in *Signal of Liberty,* April 29, 1844; Birney to Benjamin Hoffman, May 2, 1844, Birney Papers.
[23] *Emancipator and Weekly Chronicle,* Aug. 14, 1844.
[24] *Signal of Liberty,* Dec. 4, 1843.

yet faithful slave, who had at most been guilty of manslaughter" and had procured the passage of a bill to limit to two years the time in which a person illegally held as a slave could sue for freedom.

An old speech made in the debates over the Missouri Compromise, in which Clay had said if men did not have black slaves, they must have white ones to do the menial tasks, was again revived with insinuations that he favored enslaving the poorer classes. Besides his record on slavery, each of his duels was listed, and references were made which implied, rather than described, his gambling and drinking habits. Still another black mark on his record was that he had taken his seat in Congress before attaining the legal age of thirty, thereby taking an oath to support the Constitution "while he was violating it in his own case."

Birney soon learned that even his personal honesty and integrity were not immune from attack. One charge was that he was secretly a Catholic or else had sent one of his sons to a Catholic school in order to obtain Catholic votes. It was true that Dion, his third son, was enrolled at the time at St. Xavier's in Cincinnati. He had left home after a sharp disagreement with his father and had gone to Cincinnati, where William had taken him under his wing and was paying his expenses at school. In a period of intolerance toward Catholics the situation provided political ammunition for Birney's opponents, despite letters of explanation which Dion, William, and James, Jr., wrote to the newspapers. If Birney were not a Romanist, either secretly or openly, his opponents charged, he was at least aiding the Catholics by patronizing their institutions and so giving his influence to the advance of Catholicism.[25]

Another attack was originated in his home town of Danville, Kentucky, by a young editor, A. S. Mitchell, who brought up the old accusation that Birney had sold his slaves in Alabama in order to make money and then immediately had turned abolitionist. Mitchell's accusations took the form of implications and half-truths, omitting facts which Birney had already published in his letter to Colonel Stone in 1836.[26] The rumor was circulated, also, that in Alabama Birney had taken advantage of his law partner's absence to sell the firm's slaves and pocket the money,

[25] William Birney to Birney, July 18, 1843, Oct. 10, 1843; James Birney, Jr., to Birney, Dec. 12, 1843, Aug. 23, 1844, and Sept. 14, 1844; J. S. Brown to Birney, May 16, 1844; and O. Porter to Birney, Sept. 9, 1844, Birney Papers.

[26] R. H. Folger to Birney, July 12, 1844, and Birney to Folger, July 24, 1844, Birney Papers.

then had moved to the North to lecture on abolition. Still another un-founded charge was that he was not entitled to any credit for emancipat-ing his slaves because he had defrauded his creditors to do so.[27]

The wisest course of action seemed to be to republish the letter to Stone in order that the full facts should be known; and this the anti-slavery papers did in the autumn of 1844. Even John J. Marshall came to Birney's defense against such maligning. His published letter de-clared that although he differed absolutely with his brother-in-law on abolition, there was no doubt of Birney's "entire sincerity and highest purity." He had made great personal sacrifices for his opinions, had abandoned his patrimony, and had given up his native state as well as a host of friends and relatives. Despite the fact that Marshall's own relations with him had been severed, he still held a warm regard for him. "Any doubt as to Mr. Birney's devotion and sincerity to the cause he has espoused, is folly—is preposterous. . . . A man of more pure morality, more honest principles, and of warmer heart, does not exist." [28]

When Birney was speaking at Syracuse in the autumn of 1844, an unknown man called at the American Temperance House, where he was staying, and asked to see him alone. The stranger warned him that if he did not desist from traveling through the country trying to hurt Clay, he would expose Birney's past life to the people. Birney declared that there was nothing in his life that he was unwilling to have told; so the stranger left with the threat that he would confront Birney in the afternoon meeting. After delivering his intended lecture on the public acts of Clay, Birney outlined the story of his own early life, and called for the unknown person to stand forth and accuse him. No one stirred.[29]

The old charge of English influence in the antislavery ranks was also revived. In the House of Representatives, Representative Wise of Vir-ginia had charged Birney with being the candidate of the British aboli-tion societies.[30] It was said that both Birney and Morris had been picked by Joseph Sturge when the latter visited the United States in 1842. The often-cited dangers of an alliance of any American group with the

---

[27] *Christian Freeman*, March 7, 1844; *Emancipator and Weekly Chronicle*, Aug. 14, 1844.

[28] John J. Marshall to James Loughead, Sept. 1, 1844, in the *Signal of Liberty*, Oct. 14, 1844.

[29] *Signal of Liberty*, Dec. 2, 1844.

[30] *Congressional Globe*, 27 Cong., 2 Sess., pp. 173–176.

English were pointed to with alarm. Anglophobia, like anti-Catholicism, was easy to arouse.

Not all the attacks on Birney came from outside the abolitionist ranks. At the meeting of the Massachusetts Anti-Slavery Society at Faneuil Hall in January, 1844, William Lloyd Garrison offered a resolution which was subsequently adopted:

Resolved, that the man who has conspired to betray the anti-slavery cause into the hands of its most insidious foes, religious bigotry and sectarism [*sic*] —to drive from the anti-slavery platform all those who cannot conscientiously exercise the elective franchise—to gag the anti-slavery women of the United States in public meetings—to destroy the American Anti-Slavery Society, by withdrawing from it in a spirit of hostility, and giving his support to a rival association, organized expressly to cover that Society with infamy— and to convey away unjustly the official organ and depository of the American Society—is a man not deserving of the approval or support of any genuine abolitionist—and that James Gillespie Birney is that man; and that the political party, which sustains such a man for the Presidency of the United States, is demonstrably either corrupt or mis-guided, and in either case, unworthy of anti-slavery countenance.[31]

For some time after the Buffalo nominating convention. Gamaliel Bailey refused to support the Liberty ticket, objecting now to Thomas Morris rather than to Birney. There was danger, in fact, that an open break might come, as Bailey was threatening to bring charges of youthful indiscretions against Morris if he did not resign the nomination. Evidently Chase's political acumen saved the day, however, and he persuaded Bailey that peace must be maintained within the ranks.[32]

In Dayton the clergymen of most of the churches refused to read notices of antislavery prayer meetings on the grounds that they were political gatherings and had departed from their religious character. They declared that the abolitionists had publicly condemned the churches and that such men as Garrison would do away with the church as well as with the Constitution. Neither would they support such action as that of the recent Peterboro convention, which had expressed the opinion that it was not wrong for escaping slaves to steal whatever

[31] *Liberator*, Feb. 2, 1844.
[32] William Birney to Birney, Sept. 24, 1843, Jan. 12, 1844, Jan. 26, 1844, and Feb. 26, 1844, Birney Papers. I have found nothing in the records to indicate that there was any basis for Bailey's insinuations.

supplies they needed.[33] Birney himself had for years declared that the antislavery appeal was to God; now, the ministers said, it was but to the ballot box.

Toward the end of the summer of 1844 developments in local affairs in Saginaw had unfortunate repercussions on Birney's presidential candidacy. Birney had taken an active part in building up the community ever since his arrival there, and because of his education and experience the other settlers continued to look to him for leadership. When the people protested that township and county funds were being mismanaged and mishandled by the Board of Supervisors, Birney took the initiative in calling a meeting at the schoolhouse to ask for a report on receipts and expenditures.[34] As the result of his assuming responsibility to see that a corrupt situation was straightened out, several persons, previous party allegiance notwithstanding, voiced the opinion that he should be sent as their representative to the state legislature. In fact, in the autumn of the previous year, at a union convention of both the Whigs and Democrats, Birney's name had been proposed; but when it was reported that Birney would not run, another man had received the nomination.

Suggestions of Birney's nomination for the legislature in 1844 were made prior to his departure for another speaking tour in the East. Aware of the public sentiment in his favor, Birney suggested that, in the event of a nomination materializing, he should not be the candidate of one party, but the representative of the people, even if his name were put in nomination through the channels of a party convention. Everyone was well aware of his abolitionism, and no idea of compromising his principles was entertained. No pledge of party service was proposed, and none was given.[35] Raised in the tradition of the duty of assuming public service and responsibility when called, Birney felt he must accept if acceptance were compatible with his principles. His own frankness and forthright honesty made him unwary of stratagem and subterfuge

[33] New York State Anti-Slavery Society, *Address of the Peterboro State Convention to the Slaves and Its Vindication* (Cazenovia, 1842).

[34] James G. Birney, To the People of Saginaw County, Aug. 30, 1844; G. D. Williams, To the People of the County of Saginaw, Sept. 26, 1844.

[35] Birney to the editor, New York *Tribune*, Oct. 10, 1844, and Birney to the Liberty party, Oct. 15, 1844, in *Countryman*, Extra (Perry, N.Y.), Oct. 21, 1844; Birney to the Liberty party, *Signal of Liberty*, Jan. 20, 1845; Seth Willey to Birney, Dec. 12, 1844; Albert Miller to Birney, Dec. 18, 1844; and Sidney Campbell to Birney, Dec. 16, 1844, Birney Papers.

in others; as a result, he was a naïve politician. As he had written to Tappan in 1840, "The war against open adversaries I can wage tolerably well—but I will neither use devices to undermine others, nor can I trouble myself to guard *against* devices or to counteract those who practice them." Consequently, he had not reckoned with the possibility of the hue and cry which would be raised by men of his own party as well as of other parties.

Unfortunately the nomination came while Birney was in the East. It was doubly unfortunate that it came from a Democratic convention, for the national and state leaders of the Whig party were by this time eager to seize on any means for discrediting Birney. The sacrifice of the local interests of one county meant nothing in the light of what it might gain the party in the presidential race. Consequently, these Whigs completely disregarded the facts of the case, including the item that Birney was informed of his nomination by a Whig friend, who wrote that he should prepare to spend most of the winter in Detroit because it seemed to be the wish of "a goodly number of boath [*sic*] partys[*sic*]." [36]

The Whig newspapers immediately raised the cry of a bargain between Birney and Polk to defeat Clay. Birney was charged with having sought the Democratic nomination and with having pledged himself to support Democratic men and measures. Letters were secured from Saginaw Whigs declaring that they had never intended to support Birney, and the Whig Central Committee of Michigan issued a statement "confirming" the suspicion of Birney's coalition with the Loco focos.[37] Southern papers were able to refute anew any rumors of Clay' alliance with abolitionists. To add to the confusion, the Democrats realizing they had played into the hands of the Whigs, started a move to withdraw the nomination. The impetus for the movement wa probably dictated in Detroit. A mass meeting was subsequently held in Saginaw, and Birney was accused of trying to "impose himself upon the Democracy of Saginaw County as a Democrat," and of trying to break up their party. Three of the five members of the county committee had not signed their own names to the call for the meeting

[36] Seth Willey to Birney, Sept. 29, 1844, Birney Papers.
[37] Detroit *Daily Advertiser*, Oct. 26, 1844; New York *Tribune*, Oct. 8 and Oct. 1 1844; Rochester *Daily Democrat*, Oct. 8, 1844, *Union* (Detroit), Oct. 10, 1844.

however, and did not even know of it until it was already in circulation.[38]

Many Liberty men were thrown into a panic. A Detroit committee composed of Arthur L. Porter and others wrote to demand that Birney repudiate the nomination immediately, before its effect would drive the Whigs who had joined the Liberty party back into their old ranks.[39] Other friends from western New York and Ohio appealed to Gerrit Smith to use his influence in getting Birney to decline so that there would be no suspicion of coalition. Hundreds would believe the Whig charges; while others would be glad to use it as an excuse to vote for Clay. Others insisted that if Birney accepted the Saginaw nomination, someone else must be chosen as Liberty candidate for president. Everyone wanted a full statement of facts, whether or not Birney declined the nomination.

His decision was made public in a letter to the Liberty party, which was published as a handbill. He explained the circumstances surrounding the situation, his nonpartisan support, and his nonpartisan aims. To give way now, he declared, would indicate that he could be frightened from his purpose. There would always be such falsehoods circulated, all one could do was to steel himself against them. "To such of you, then, as feel disquieted," he wrote, "I say—be assured. Give me your confidence—command mine." He would abide by the position he had taken, "equally prepared to resist the shock of open enemies or the panic of real friends."[40]

Birney addressed another letter to the New York *Tribune* to answer some of its accusations against him. The paper had stated that his trip to the East, under the pretense of visiting his son, was at the suggestion of New York Locofocos as well as of the abolitionists, and that this could be verified by a disclosure of a conference between Birney and General Hascall at Flint, Michigan, before Birney left.[41] The im-

[38] Handbill signed by the Democratic Corresponding Committee of Saginaw County, Oct. 9, 1844; *The Mill-Boy of the Slashes* (Ann Arbor), Oct. 21, 1844; Elizabeth Birney to Birney, Oct. 19, 1844; Birney to the Liberty party, in *Signal of Liberty*, Jan. 20, 1845.

[39] Arthur L. Porter and others to Birney, Oct. 3, 1844, and Oct. 4, 1844, Birney Papers.

[40] Birney to the Liberty party, in *Countryman*, Extra, Oct. 21, 1844.

[41] New York *Tribune*, Oct. 10, 1844, quoted in Dumond, ed., *The Letters of James Gillespie Birney*, II, 850–851n.

plied invitation of the Locofocos was sheer fabrication, but it was not until he got back to Michigan that Birney could get a sworn statement from Hascall which could be presented publicly as proof.[42] Another rumor was that, on the boat to Buffalo, Birney had been heard to express a preference for Polk over Clay. Birney denied any personal hostility toward Clay, but stated that he opposed Clay's election on the same ground that he opposed Polk's—both repudiated "the paramount object of the UNION, the perpetuation of liberty to all." However, as Clay was the leader of his party to a much greater extent than Polk was of his, Clay was perhaps more to be feared.[43] The Rochester *Daily Democrat* and the Albany *Evening Journal* found evidences of coalition in the fact that Birney's view on the tariff coincided with that of the Democrats.[44] The *Clay Tribune* went even further by attributing to Birney a statement that he thought the annexation of Texas was the surest way of getting rid of slavery.[45]

The hard core of abolitionists, of course, had too much confidence in Birney to be swerved. At the Michigan State Liberty convention on October 9 they resolved "that this convention has unshaken confidence in Mr. Birney: his sacrifices to the antislavery cause have been too numerous—and his judgment too well proved, to permit any doubt either as to his integrity or discretion, on mere vague rumor, and in the absence of communication with him." [46] Many others were satisfied by his addresses at Albany, Rochester, Batavia, and Buffalo on the way home. A committee of the Utica Liberty Association issued a letter to the antislavery people of their state calling on them to remain firm and not to be seduced by the Whigs; [47] and the Ohio Liberty committee issued a similar address entreating the people, "For God and Duty stand! Stand this once!" [48] Although many who might have backslid were thus kept in the fold, enough doubts had been planted in their minds to make them even more receptive for the culminating stroke of Whig artifice which was to follow.

Just prior to the election, so as to preclude any possible chance of

[42] Charles C. Hascall to Birney, Nov. 30, 1844, Birney Papers.
[43] W. F. Brayton to Gerrit Smith, Oct. 9, 1844, Birney Papers; Birney to the editor, *Tribune*, reprinted in *Countryman*, Oct. 21, 1844; *Tribune*, Oct. 8, 1844.
[44] Rochester *Daily Democrat*, Oct. 8, 1844; Albany *Argus*, Oct. 26, 1844.
[45] *Clay Tribune* (New York), Oct. 26, 1844.
[46] *Signal of Liberty*, Oct. 21, 1844.　　　[47] Albany *Argus*, Oct. 29, 1844.
[48] Theodore C. Smith, *The Liberty and Free Soil Parties in the Northwest*, p. 74.

refutation, a paper, purporting to be an extra of the *Genesee County Democrat,* a Whig paper in Flint, Michigan, appeared, printing a letter purportedly written by Birney to Jerome B. Garland of Saginaw County. It contained proof of all the recent charges against Birney. The sentence, "My journey is indispensable, else a *DUELLIST* and GAMBLER will soon fill the seat of a Washington, a Jefferson, and a Jackson," was interpreted as evidence of his going East to confer with Locofocos on defeating Clay. Other parts were even more damaging: "I now and EVER HAVE BEEN, a Democrat of the 'Jeffersonian School.' . . . I hereby pledge myself to go for Democratic men and measures, and . . . will forego the agitation of the slavery question in our State Legislature." [49]

Several documents were affixed to the letter: a sworn statement of Garland, supposedly made before a justice of the peace, Robert R. Page; the statement of the county clerk, Thomas R. Cummings, attesting to the authority of Page; and another signed by James Birdsall, A. Thayer, and A. P. Davis, the Whig County Corresponding Committee, attesting to the character and good standing of Garland. Every part of the document from the caption "Genesee County Democrat" to the final signature was an absolute forgery.

The letter was released almost simultaneously in Ohio, Massachusetts, Connecticut, Maine, and New York. It appeared in the Columbus (Ohio) *Journal,* the Worcester *Spy,* the Hartford *Courant,* and the New York *Courier and Enquirer* on October 29; but it was withheld in the cities through which Birney was to pass on his way homeward until he had gone on and there was no possibility of obtaining a contradiction. It did not appear in Utica, Rochester, or Syracuse until October 31, and not in Buffalo until he had embarked on a boat on Lake Erie. Birney first saw it in the *Ohio State Journal* when the boat arrived in Cleveland on November 1. As the boat stopped there for a couple of hours, he did all he could to denounce it as an absolute forgery, but the election was already on, and much of the damage was done. [50] Liberty papers were caught unprepared, and even in places where there was time to get out an issue before the election, the most that could be done

[49] *Genesee County* (Mich.) *Democrat,* Extra, Oct. 21, 1844, reprinted in *Courtland County* (N.Y.) *Whig,* Extra, Oct. 31, 1844.
[50] Detroit *Daily Free Press,* Nov. 2, 1844; Birney to Elizur Wright, Nov. 1, 1844, Wright Papers, Manuscript Division, Library of Congress.

was to term it a forgery without having any concrete proof to present.

The number of votes lost to Birney because of the Garland forgery was impossible to compute. William Birney thought it cost his fathei about three thousand in Ohio alone. Many antislavery people gave their votes to Clay, and hundreds, maybe thousands, of others stayed away from the polls altogether. There was an actual gain in total votes over the 1843 returns; but the vote in a presidential election should have been much heavier. Birney's popular vote was 62,300 to 1,299,062 for Clay, and 1,337,243 for Polk.

The significant vote was that of New York, where Birney received 15,812 to 232,482 for Clay, and 237,588 for Polk.[51] Had a third of the Birney votes gone to Clay, he would have carried New York, and with it, the presidency. The election of Polk was a definite victory for the annexationists. From a short-sighted viewpoint, it seemed that the Liberty party was defeating its own purpose. Actually, it had struck the Whig party one of its mortal blows and, in so doing, had broken the ground for the antislavery party to rise from the rank of a third party to the status of a major one.

Clay's defeat and the Garland forgery insured the continuation of the Whig-Liberty rivalry and bitterness long after the election was over. Though forced to admit the forgery, the Whigs still accused Birney of having conspired to secure Polk's election, a conspiracy in favor of slavery! "Take it, Sir, *take all the credit of it!*" wrote J. M. Howard, chairman of the Michigan Central Committee for the Whig party. "Put the gains, if gains there be, into the same pocket where is now the price of human beings, whom you sold into perpetual bondage." [52]

The New York *Tribune,* in an article entitled "Birney and Birneyism," repeated the old arguments of Birney's selfish motives in not supporting Clay, and referred to the "confidential whisperings" with Locofoco managers in the cars between Albany and Buffalo. Refusing to recognize Clay's own lack of frankness on the subject of annexation and by-passing his "Alabama Letters," they condemned Birney for continuing to proclaim that annexation would come whether Clay or Polk were

[51] William Birney to Birney, Nov. 25, 1844, Birney Papers. T. C. Smith, *op. cit.,* p. 79. For votes by states and counties as well as total vote, see Horace Greeley and John F. Cleveland, compilers, *A Political Textbook for 1860* (New York, 1860), pp. 216–239.

[52] J. M. Howard to Birney, Jan. 15, 1845, in Detroit *Daily Advertiser,* Jan. 16, 1845.

elected.⁵³ Birney secured statements from Judge William M. Oliver and David H. Little, with whom he was supposed to have conducted the "confidential whisperings," denying the charges of the *Tribune*.⁵⁴

Birney was determined that the Garland forgery must be completely exposed in order to vindicate himself and the Liberty party. It is probable that the idea for the forgery was conceived just after the Saginaw nomination. At that time the Whig Central Committee dispatched William S. Driggs of Detroit to Saginaw to find out what he could about the situation. Driggs reported back that he had visited Garland, who said he had a letter from Birney but refused to show it. Driggs also called on a Mr. Eleazer Jewett, at whose house the local convention was held; and he said that both Jewett and Garland refused to supply affidavits of Birney's prior agreement to accept a nomination.⁵⁵

Upon receiving Driggs' report, J. M. Howard wrote to Robert C. Winthrop in Boston, stating that Birney was "fully committed to the Locos, except as to annexation, perhaps." "There is no earthly doubt of all this. Use it then!" Howard urged. "It will influence twenty thousand votes in the North."

On the basis of this letter, Joshua Leavitt, in the *Emancipator and Chronicle,* charged Howard with the forgery. While admitting the letter to Winthrop, Howard denied any knowledge of the forgery until after it was published and countered with the theory that it was a plot of the Democrats which they expected to use to discredit the Whigs. This argument was adopted by the Detroit *Daily Advertiser,* the chief Whig paper in the state. Leavitt retracted his accusation, but in the minds of most of the Liberty men, Howard was still not cleared of implication in the affair.⁵⁶

Birney set about to get affidavits from the other men whose names

⁵³ New York *Tribune,* Nov. 16, 1844, July 2 and 3, 1845. William Birney says that Horace Greeley probably knew of the Garland Forgery, and the evasiveness of his disclaimer put an end to friendly relations between Birney and him. He also states that Greeley gave orders that Birney's name was not to be mentioned in the *Tribune* thereafter. See *James G. Birney and His Times,* p. 355. The break was not so permanent as William thought. The two corresponded about the publication of several of Birney's later articles, and a letter from Greeley to Birney dated Jan. 5, 1852, indicates that Greeley was considering publishing one of them.

⁵⁴ William M. Oliver to Birney, Dec. 8, 1845, and David H. Little to Birney, Feb. 9, 1846, Birney Papers.

⁵⁵ Detroit *Daily Advertiser,* Nov. 2, 1844.

⁵⁶ Boston *Atlas,* Nov. 30, 1844; Detroit *Daily Advertiser,* Dec. 2, 1844.

had been used. Garland, besides designating the letter "an absolute, unmitigated forgery," went into detail on his relations with Birney and the background of the Saginaw nomination. He verified Birney's statement that both the Whigs and the Democrats wanted him to run as their representative after his exposure of the mismanagement of the county funds. At the schoolhouse meeting Birney had declared himself not a party Democrat, but a "democrat according to the Declaration of Independence." Garland had approached Birney on the subject of nomination, and both had agreed he should run as an independent candidate. No pledges were made, but Birney had told him that if he were elected, and in whatever way the slavery question came up in the legislature, "he would be found occupying the ground on which everyone knew he stood, in favor of human freedom."

The only letter Garland had ever received from Birney was published. It was dated September 3, 1844, and dealt with the county mismanagement. The only sentence of political significance was the last: "If the people intend to run another candidate for the House beside the regularly nominated one by the parties, they ought to let it be known as soon as possible;—at all events, before the regular nominations are made." It was, therefore, a surprise to Garland as well as to Birney when the regular Democratic convention nominated him. As for Driggs, he had talked to Garland twenty minutes, at the most, and during that time Garland had told him none of the things subsequently reported. It was untrue that Driggs had even asked him for an affidavit.[57]

J. Birdsall, A. Thayer, and A. P. Davis stated under oath that they had no knowledge of the *Genesee County Democrat* Extra of October 21 "being gotten up, had no agency in the matter, and in no instance authorized the same to be done, or their names to be used, and know the same to be a base forgery." A. P. Davis was not even a member of the committee, and there was no justice of the peace in the county by the name of Robert R. Page. The Whig County Corresponding Committee was composed of Birdsall, Thayer, and B. Rockwell, who issued a separate letter reiterating the fact that the whole handbill had been a "*base and infamous* FORGERY." William B. Sherwood, publisher and proprietor of the *Genesee County Democrat,* issued an Extra containing the above statements and added his own affidavit that "no handbill,

[57] Deposition of Jerome Garland, Nov. 12, 1844, Birney Papers.

extra, or other document, containing said letter" had ever been issued from his office.[58]

The forged handbill was dated October 21 and was first seen in Detroit sometime between the morning of October 22 and 24 in the hands of three members of the Whig Central Committee: J. M. Howard, D. Smart, and F. A. Harding. All declared it was a forgery. William Driggs was sent to the office of the Secretary of State to ascertain whether there was a justice of the peace named Robert R. Page, and David Smart was dispatched to Pontiac to see what he could learn there.

The Whig Central Committee had not written the forgery, but at least three of them did know of its existence and kept it a secret from the public until copies of it came back from Ohio by mail on October 31.[59] A package containing the forgery was put into the hands of an Ohio Whig, A. W. McCoy, in Detroit on October 23, for him to mail from Cleveland to the *Ohio State Journal* at Columbus. The editors were kind enough to send an original copy of the handbill to Birney in order that an attempt might be made to trace its origin by its print.[60]

Suspicion continued to center on J. M. Howard when it was revealed that, despite his statement to Leavitt that he had not seen the handbill until "several days after its publication and circulation," he had actually seen it early enough to have openly pronounced it a forgery before the election, had he wished to do so.[61] Joshua Giddings was also implicated in the charge of having known of the forgery beforehand, and he answered the charges with a blistering attack on Birney. Denying prior knowledge, he admitted he believed the forgery because he thought Birney capable of just such action. The reasons given were that he felt Birney showed insincerity in his letter to Colonel Stone; that his attack on John Quincy Adams in 1843 had been unprovoked; that Birney, by union with the Whigs, could have prevented the annexation of Texas; and that Birney had accepted the Democratic Saginaw

[58] *Genesee County Democrat,* Extra, Nov. 4, 1844.

[59] Information supplied by Hiram L. Miller, Birney Papers; Executive Committee, Detroit Library Association, to the editors, Detroit *Advertiser,* Nov. 27, 1844, in the *Signal of Liberty,* Dec. 9, 1844.

[60] *Ohio American* (Cleveland), Nov. 28, 1844; Birney to the editors, *Ohio State Journal,* June 3, 1845, Birney Papers.

[61] Information supplied by Hiram L. Miller, Birney Papers; Certifications of Silas M. Holmes, A. L. Porter, and Charles H. Stewart, March 12, 1845, in *Ohio American* [undated clipping].

nomination.[62] Howard also attacked Birney with venom, accused him of using the "low arts of the demagogue," "the little tricks of a paid harlequin," and of now complaining in the "whining, petulant tone of a charletan [*sic*], who has been detected in a dirty transaction." [63]

Once the responsibility for allowing the forgery to be sent out and used had been laid at the door of the Whig Committee, Birney let Charles Stewart take the initiative in tracing down its actual source. The refusal of the Whigs to supply information made this a difficult task, but eventually it was traced to the printing office of a Whig paper, the *Oakland Gazette,* in Pontiac, Michigan. The types used in the forgery were found in the office, and the editor, William M. Thompson, was indicted by the grand jury along with three others, H. H. Duncklee, Moses Wisner, and Charles Draper. The bill of indictment was presented at the 1845 autumn term of the District Court for Oakland County, with Charles Stewart as complainant; but the counsel for defense contended that the indictment was without lawful proof because the grand jury had been advised by a person who was not the county prosecuting attorney nor the attorney-general of Michigan. To this plea the prosecuting attorney filed a general demurrer, and Judge Witherall, at the request of the counsel for defense, reserved the question for an opinion of the Supreme Court.[64]

Some months later, in the early part of 1846, a young man named Joseph Beebe and another named Stimson, who worked in the *Oakland Gazette* office, disclosed that they had been in the office at the time the Garland forgery was printed and that they could furnish all the information about it. Further than obtaining their affidavits, however, the prosecution was not pushed.[65] All that Birney cared about was that the public be given the facts, not that the guilty be punished. They had gained nothing by their schemes; it had served only to discredit the Whig party.

While Birney was concerned with vindicating himself to the public,

[62] J. R. Giddings to the editor, *Ohio American,* April 5, 1845, in *Ohio American* [undated clipping].

[63] Howard to Birney, Jan. 15, 1845, in Detroit *Daily Advertiser,* Jan. 16, 1845.

[64] Birney to the Liberty party, *Signal of Liberty,* Jan. 20, 1845; Pontiac *Jacksonian,* Nov. 12, 1845; *Signal of Liberty,* Nov. 3, 10, and 17, 1845.

[65] J. C. Gallup to Birney, Jan. 26, 1846; Theodore Foster to Birney, Feb. 13, 1846; Birney to William Gray, Sept. 22, 1847, Birney Papers; Foster, Notebook on the Liberty party.

and especially in the eyes of the antislavery men, the Liberty party leaders were concerned with reassuring him that they had not lost faith in his sincerity and integrity. Birney's letter of explanation just after the election reached Joshua Leavitt at the Albany convention in December and was read aloud to the delegates, producing "the deepest sensation, even to tears in many cases." The effect was "deep and gratifying," Leavitt reported to Birney. "It showed, not only that you retain the full and perfect confidence of our friends, but that your services and the unmerited persecutions you have been subjected to have given you a strong hold on the best affections of their hearts." [66]

The Michigan State Anti-Slavery Society adopted two resolutions regarding Birney:

That James G. Birney, our late candidate for the Presidency, richly merits the thanks and full confidence of Liberty men for the wisdom, prudence, patience and firmness, with which he received the shafts hurled against *us and our principles* in his person during the late Presidential contest, and by which they were rendered powerless. . . .

and

That Mr. Birney has satisfactorily refuted the many charges brought against himself personally.[67]

[66] Leavitt to Birney, Dec. 18, 1844, Birney Papers.
[67] *Signal of Liberty*, Feb. 17, 1845.

Chapter XIII

"One of the
Rank and File"

THE Liberty party followed the pattern of all third parties. Once it obtained a balance of power in certain areas and so was in a position to force one or both of the major parties to adopt a favorable attitude toward antislavery, it became jealous of its exclusive right to advocate such principles and eager to maintain its separate identity rather than be absorbed into a larger group. To coalesce with the Whigs for some definite purpose, such as to defeat the annexation of Texas, would mean the loss of identity for the Liberty party with its one big goal, abolition. Instead of merging with the Whigs in areas where that party was definitely antislavery, it insisted that the Whigs must come over to the Liberty organization. Yet the campaign of 1844 had shown that great numbers of Whigs would not forsake their party unless they could be sure the Liberty candidates would favorably represent their political and economic interests as well as their antislavery viewpoint. Moreover, even antislavery men would not be willing to go on indefinitely voting the Liberty ticket unless they could see some actual gains. It was a problem that would have to be seriously considered before another election; and one which was certain to be the source of dissension.

Almost immediately after the election the question arose as to who should be the party candidate in 1848. New York was strongly for Birney, and a movement was begun to raise money so that he could leave the seclusion of Michigan to return to the East, where he might be once more in the thick of things, perhaps to help Leavitt with articles for antislavery publications.[1] Bailey and Chase, on the other hand, were again suggesting someone with more political shrewdness than Birney. Bailey had severely criticized Birney's acceptance of the Saginaw nomination as a grave error which exposed the party to misinterpretation; while Chase, whose contemporaries suspected he valued success more than principle, was said to have expressed regret that he had not voted for Clay to try to prevent annexation.[2] Fearful that Birney might yield to their pressure, Leavitt urged him to take no action toward withdrawing his name until the movement of the Ohio group, who were "getting bewitched after Seward," could be nipped in the bud.[3]

Birney himself, however, was determined not to run again. At the end of January, 1845, in a letter to the editor of the Albany *Patriot*, he announced that he wished to be considered "as no other than one of the rank and file." Although he appreciated the confidence of those antislavery journals which had been advocating his renomination, he was fully persuaded that it would be best for the harmonious interests of the party if such articles be discontinued, and he respectfully requested that thereafter his name be omitted.[4] This did not mean that Birney intended to give up all antislavery activity. Charles Stewart, chairman of the Liberty party in Michigan, planned a six weeks' series of lectures for him throughout the state; and at a convention at Marshall, Michigan, in July, he was again nominated as the Liberty candidate for governor.[5] Neither materialized, for in August the accident occurred which prevented Birney from continuing his public activity.

It was perhaps fitting that his last public appearance as the leader of the antislavery party should be in Cincinnati, where his firm stand had won the battle for freedom of the press. There, in June, a great "South-

---

[1] Joshua Leavitt to Birney, Dec. 18, 1844, and Jan. 25, 1845, Birney Papers.

[2] *Emancipator and Chronicle*, Jan. 1, 1845; William Birney to Birney, Nov. 25, 1844 and March 20, 1845, Birney Papers.

[3] Leavitt to Birney, Jan. 25, 1845, Birney Papers.

[4] Birney to the editor of the Albany *Patriot*, Jan. 31, 1845, in the *Signal of Liberty*, March 10, 1845.

[5] *Signal of Liberty*, July 21, 1845; Charles H. Stewart to S. B. Treadwell, Sept. 1, 1845, Treadwell Papers, Michigan Historical Collections, Ann Arbor.

ern and Western Liberty Convention" was held. The call had gone out in April inviting not only members of the Liberty party, but all who believed "that whatever is worth preserving in Republicanism can be maintained, only, by eternal and uncompromising war against the criminal usurpations of the Slave Power. . . ." Again they tried to emphasize the national character of the party by announcing that there would be delegates from at least two slave states, Kentucky and Virginia, and they hoped even more would be represented.[6] The name "Southern and Western" was indicative of their purpose.

The three-day convention of over two thousand delegates opened on June 10, and Birney was chosen chairman by acclamation. His short address, contrasting the prospects of the antislavery cause in 1845 with the situation when he arrived in Cincinnati ten years earlier, was accorded an ovation which made the walls ring and set the tone for an optimistic and stirring meeting. Many of the men who had fought Birney and the *Philanthropist* in 1836 were now advocating antislavery principles. By 1845 Ohio was one of the most completely abolitionized states.

The two problems of greatest importance to the party, the broadening of the platform and the nomination of candidates, were both postponed. Although the convention declared itself not indifferent to questions of trade, currency, and extension of territory, it subordinated them to the great question of personal rights. Another resolution favored keeping the presidential nomination open until 1847 or 1848. A proposal on the formation of a Mississippi Valley Anti-Slavery Society was adversely reported from committee.[7]

Salmon P. Chase was named chairman of a committee to prepare an address from the convention to the public.[8] It was a masterful summary of the position and aims of the antislavery people as embodied in the Liberty party; but the original address contained what Birney felt might be interpreted as overtures of coalition to the Democrats, especially in the light of Chase's known leanings toward the Locofocos.

[6] Salmon P. Chase to Birney, April 21, 1845, Birney Papers; Dwight Lowell Dumond, ed., *The Letters of James Gillespie Birney*, II, 934–935n.

[7] *Weekly Herald and Philanthropist* (Cincinnati), June 18, 1845; *Emancipator and Chronicle*, June 25, 1845; *Signal of Liberty*, June 30, 1845.

[8] *The Address of the Southern and Western Liberty Convention Held at Cincinnati, June 11 & 12, 1845, To the People of the United States. With Notes by a Citizen of Pennsylvania* (New York, 1845).

His fears were perhaps heightened by the fact that Joshua Leavitt had previously been approached by a prominent representative of the Northern Democrats to learn whether the Liberty party would support them if they should bring about the defeat of the annexation of Texas.[9] Leavitt's response that the Liberty party had been formed for "permanent and entire success and for nothing short," and that having resisted the Whigs they could not listen to proposals from the Democrats, undoubtedly carried great weight with Birney and represented the views of most of the party. Consequently, at Birney's counsel, the committee revised the objectionable parts.[10]

The most significant part of the address reviewed the antislavery sentiment in this country up to the framing of the Constitution and introduced an interpretation which was steadily gaining ground among abolitionists, the idea that the Constitution was not a proslavery document and was not meant to be so by its writers. It appeared to be proslavery because it had been misinterpreted and violated in practice. This was a position which Birney himself had not yet wholly adopted, but toward which he moved a few years later. The address ended with a double appeal to the faithful friends of Liberty, who had increased from a small handful of voters in 1840 to a great party, not to compromise or give up; and to people not yet in the party to co-operate on the one great issue rather than join parties with which they agreed on only minor points.

Despite Birney's earlier statement that he did not want his name mentioned as a possible candidate in 1848, his eastern friends were not willing to acquiesce. A great eastern convention to parallel the Cincinnati Convention was planned for September, and Birney's expenses there would be paid. At that time the eastern friends would seriously discuss his removal from Michigan.[11] His accident early in August, however, precluded any possibility of changing his mind.

While William Birney was vacationing at his father's home in Saginaw in the summer of 1845, the two spent much time out of doors hunting and fishing. Riding out through the fields one day, Birney's horse was startled by a prairie chicken which rose from the grass in front of him.

[9] Leavitt to Birney, Dec. 18, 1844, Birney Papers.

[10] William Birney, *James G. Birney and His Times*, pp. 364–365; Theodore C. Smith, *The Liberty and Free Soil Parties in the Northwest*, pp. 88–89.

[11] Henry B. Stanton to Birney, Aug. 11, 1845, Birney Papers.

The horse stumbled and fell, throwing his rider. Though severely jolted, Birney was able to remount and ride home; but a few hours later he suffered a severe paralytic stroke.

Then followed weeks in bed when Birney had to be waited on and could communicate only by sign language. His throat was completely paralyzed. He feared that he would never be able to speak again or, worse yet, that his mind was impaired. The world of his thoughts was one of despair that he would never again be of any value to the antislavery cause and that he would have to lie helpless while his family lived in poverty on the frontier without social or cultural advantages. Slowly, however, his bodily strength returned, and with continued effort he found himself able to utter sounds which gradually became understandable. He was never again able to make a public address.

Most important of all, Birney's mind was as alert as ever, and even while lying in bed he thought out articles he could write and advice he could give on matters of policy to men who would carry on the antislavery effort. When he was able to make himself understood, Elizabeth or one of the children wrote letters at his dictation, and after several weeks he regained enough control of his hands so that his own writing was decipherable. His confinement was productive of a good many articles and letters expressing his views on current developments.

Although Birney feared to overtax his brain with reading that required too much thinking, it was impossible for a man of his literary habits to forego such pleasure. Even when he read Shakespeare for relaxation, he could not refrain from jotting down criticisms and analyses in his diary. Reading was one of the few joys he had to fall back on. He read, as they came out, Prescott's histories of the conquests of Mexico and Peru, Irving's works, Channing's memoirs, and, of course, *Uncle Tom's Cabin*. He and Elizabeth began to read Mrs. Stowe's novel together, but soon discovered, although "not more than others, given to the *'melting mood'*—that it was a book which no one, having a heart, could read aloud to others. Thus we had to read it separately, and for the most part alone." [12] Birney's *The American Churches the Bulwarks of American Slavery* was one of the sources on which Mrs. Stowe relied for her *Key to Uncle Tom's Cabin* which followed.[13]

When Birney thought that he would never recover from his attack,

[12] Birney to Harriet Beecher Stowe, Jan. 12, 1853, Birney Papers.
[13] Leonard Bacon to Birney, Dec. 28, 1852, Birney Papers.

he hastened to put the finishing touches to an essay he had begun on the Bible argument of the sinfulness of slavery. It was published first in the *Signal of Liberty* and later as a pamphlet. It was a rebuttal of the Southern argument that slavery is defended in the Bible, and it closely paralleled his oft-repeated rebuttal of those who defended slavery on constitutional grounds. In the latter case, Birney had insisted that the Preamble's "secure the blessings of liberty" must be considered as a basis for interpreting any other portion; moreover, the Declaration of Independence was just as much a part of the fundamental law as the Constitution. Slavery could not be legislated into being because it violated man's inalienable rights. Similarly, he maintained that slavery could not be defended from the Bible because it violated the whole spirit of Christianity. Justification for a system of hate could not be wrested from the book of God's love. If the Bible taught slavery, he argued, why shouldn't slaveholders be glad to teach their slaves to read it? The Bible commanded men to search the Scriptures; slaveholders were forbidding this to their slaves by law. This was at variance with Divine law. One of the arguments of the South was that slaveholding existed in New Testament times. It may have existed, agreed Birney, but that did not mean that Christians supported it. By defending slavery in the Roman Empire, moreover, Southerners were defending *white* slavery. The standard Biblical illustration used as a basis for returning fugitive slaves—St. Paul advising that Onesimus, the servant of Philemon, be returned—was an entirely different case. Paul had asked Philemon to receive him back *as a brother*. The Southern argument that enslaving African Negroes gave them an opportunity to come to a civilized land and receive the blessings of Christianity were based on wholly false reasoning. The end did not justify the crime. To deprive a person of his natural rights was always wrong even though it might temporarily appear to be beneficial.[14]

Birney had discovered in 1844 that it was impossible to be a candidate without expressing opinions on all of the various issues of current interest, and he foresaw then that the Liberty party would have to broaden its platform, while being careful always to subordinate the

[14] *Signal of Liberty*, Oct. 6, 1845; James G. Birney, *The Sinfulness of Slaveholding in All Circumstances; Tested by Reason and Scripture* (Detroit, 1846). The last point is elaborated in an unpublished manuscript headed, "Is Slaveholding Sinful under All Circumstances?" in private possession.

other questions to that of abolition. "We must be prepared to take on ourselves *all* the administration of the government or *none* of it," he wrote to Lewis Tappan. "A party that does not take the *whole* of it—but seeks a particular object—will soon, in the strife of the other parties, become a lost party." [15] Foster and Beckley agreed with Birney, and Michigan took the lead in advocating a departure from the "one idea" policy. At every county and state convention from then on, they introduced the plan as the one means of saving the party from being swallowed up by the Whigs. Foster wrote enthusiastically that it would

give the antislavery ship a new and most important tack, making her head directly *against* manufacturing, protective, conservative, aristocratic Whiggery, and bringing it directly *alongside* of radical, reformatory young Democracy. The change, however, is a good one, if we are determined to be a permanent party. We must appeal *to the masses*. We shall not succeed well in trading with Seward and Co.[16]

Signs were already pointing to a break-up of the old parties on North-South lines. Foster was of the opinion that the Michigan Whigs would bring their party over to antislavery principles any time if it were not for the Detroit clique headed by the *Advertiser*. The important task was to restrain antislavery men who in their eagerness for success might be too willing to make concessions. Gerrit Smith had already expressed his willingness to unite with the Whigs as soon as they took antislavery ground; Chase and Bailey had sometimes seemed willing to compromise even principle. Birney was unwilling to give up his party. If only patience were exercised, the concessions would be made by the other side. A new name, Foster conceded, would make the process less painful.

Before the anniversary meeting of the Michigan State Anti-Slavery Society in February, 1845, Birney and Foster had agreed on a platform to be submitted to the delegates. Birney was unable to attend, but his ideas were embodied in a letter addressed to the president of the society.[17] Besides abolition and equality of rights, it proposed: (1) that the powers, patronage, and salary of the President be reduced; (2) the

---

[15] Birney to Lewis Tappan, Sept. 12, 1845, Tappan Collection.

[16] Theodore Foster to Birney, Sept. 12, Sept. 29, and Oct. 16, 1845, Birney Papers.

[17] Birney to the president, Michigan Anti-Slavery Society, Jan. 1, 1846, in *Signal of Liberty*, Feb. 23, 1846; Birney to Jewett, Hill, and Garland, Sept. 18, 1845, in *Signal of Liberty*, Sept. 29, 1845.

army and navy should both be decreased and gradually abolished, so that the nation could learn how to subsist without fighting and revise its notion that its honor depended on force; (3) the tariff should be lowered, with free trade the ultimate goal; and (4) travel allowances for Congressmen should be less. Foster suggested several additions: (1) the election of more national and state officers, including postmasters; (2) a thorough judicial reform (which Birney had previously suggested on a state scale); (3) no financial or commercial corporations without full individual responsibility of members; and (4) the single district system of electing legislators.[18]

Most of the delegates at the Marshall convention found the new ideas too radical, and no favorable action was taken. The trouble, as Foster analyzed it, was that most of the antislavery leaders were ministers who were reluctant to take up other than moral issues. The seed had been sown, however, and gradually more and more came over as they gave it more thought. Charles Stewart, the Michigan Liberty chairman, was among the dissenters at the convention; but when he sat down to answer Birney's letter, in studying it, he found himself agreeing on all but two points, the tariff and the navy.[19] Foster and Beckley printed one hundred Extras setting forth their views, which they sent to Liberty men and to other Liberty papers for reprinting. The result was a general commotion. The *Spirit of Liberty* in Pittsburgh immediately came out favorably, but the influential *Emancipator* was decidedly against the proposed change, as was Bailey's *Herald and Philanthropist*. Gerrit Smith replied with an address to the Liberty party advising adherence to the "one idea" policy. He was seconded by Alvan Stewart, national Liberty chairman. Lewis Tappan felt that to add other issues would weaken rather than strengthen the party; still, if the majority of the abolitionists wanted to do so, he was willing to say, "So be it." Beriah Green was one of the few eastern leaders who wholeheartedly supported the Michigan plan.[20]

Foster appealed to Birney to use his influence with the eastern friends; and Beckley was delegated to go to the northwestern Liberty conven-

[18] Foster to Birney, Dec. 7, 1845, Birney Papers.

[19] Guy Beckley and Foster to Birney, Feb. 9, 1846; Foster to Birney, Feb. 13, 1846; and Stewart to Birney, Feb. 19, 1846, Birney Papers.

[20] Gerrit Smith to the Liberty party, May 7, 1846, quoted in Dumond, ed., *op. cit.*, II, 1019n; Beriah Green to Birney, Sept. 23, 1846; and Lewis Tappan to Birney, March 10, 1846, Birney Papers.

tion in Chicago in June to speak on the subject. Birney was also urgently pressed to attend. "It is in your power more than in any other man's to enhance the numbers, the spirit and the strength of the convention," the committee wrote him; but Birney's lack of health and voice disqualified him. "I know not—so frail is my tenure on life," he responded, "at what moment I may be called hence." [21] The results at Chicago were disheartening. Again a large number of ministers objected to venturing out too far politically. Another fear which was heightened by the report Beckley brought home was that the Liberty party in Ohio seemed on the verge of falling in with the Whigs. The Whigs there were already saying they would bolt the party and form a new one rather than support another slaveholder as their candidate. This was exactly what Giddings was working for, with the hope of absorbing the Liberty party in the process.[22]

It was perhaps fear of this which prompted another letter from Birney to the Liberty party written on September 1. He reiterated that he was not able to be their candidate again, but he urged the nomination of someone firm and sensible, conversant with public affairs, not inclined to overlegislation, and one who would truly represent Liberty principles with a Christian spirit. Whoever was chosen should be given their complete confidence. Birney's idea was, obviously, that if an early nomination were made there would be less chance of the party's being swallowed up by the Whigs. Birney also responded publicly to Smith's address with the argument that new additions to the antislavery platform need not diminish zeal for the main cause any more than finding new truths in the Bible diminishes the truth of those previously found. The new ideas were not hostile, but compatible.[23]

Birney did not expect that the proposal of a general reform party would be immediately accepted. Every party must have leaders in advance of the masses, but their new ideas could not always be grafted on to the old principles; often they had to be content to watch them sprout slowly from seedlings. Beckley and Foster, however, were impatient with the negative response, and as the early months of 1847

[21] John V. Smith to Birney, April 4, 1846; and Birney to John V. Smith, April 20, 1846, Birney Papers.

[22] Foster to Birney, Aug. 1, 1846, Birney Papers.

[23] Birney to the Liberty party, Sept. 1, 1846, in *Signal of Liberty*, Sept. 12, 1846; Birney to Gerrit Smith, June 1, 1846, in *Signal of Liberty*, June 27, 1846.

passed it became evident that, either from despair over ever attaining their aim or, possibly, in an effort to exert pressure on the Liberty leaders, their editorial position was veering toward that of Bailey and Chase. Birney addressed a letter to Foster in March which indicated his awareness of such a trend: "For the last few months, the Signal, it seems to me, has not been so *decided* as I wished, as I expected—it would be." [24] Shortly thereafter Birney received his issue of March 20, in which Beckley stated his new position openly. Despairing of budging the Liberty party from its "one idea" policy, they were ready to support the candidates of any party who were sound on antislavery.

Birney's answer was a frank letter of rebuke: "You exhort us to throw aside our strong weapon," he wrote, "and pick up a straw compared with it, to attack a sleepless and well entrenched enemy. . . ." He saw in their action, as in that of the Ohio group, the subordination of the moral question to that of the political, the substitution of the ideal of success for that of principle. It was evident in most of the antislavery newspapers and had been reflected in almost all of the speeches given in the last session of Congress. The failure of the Wilmot Proviso had been "one of the first fruits" of such "distraction." "I cannot look upon it as any other thing than a fresh occasion for diluting our principles," he wrote, "so that we may have a strong party in Church and State to lean on. How very few, Mr. Beckley, are prepared to stand, alone, for what is right, and just and true!" [25]

In protest to the current trend, Birney took the step of opposing the establishment of the *National Era,* an antislavery paper in Washington, D.C. under the editorship of Bailey. If such a paper were to be started at all, and many of the western abolitionists feared it would withdraw support from the Liberty papers already in existence, Birney thought Leavitt should be the man entrusted with it. Disregard for Birney's

[24] Birney to Foster, March 27, 1846, Birney Papers.

[25] Birney to Beckley, April 6, 1847, Birney Papers. Foster's comments on Birney in his notebook on the Liberty party, are interesting in this connection: "He despised that trait of character so common in political men, which renders them incapable of advancing a truth, or attacking an error, unless they have a religious sect or political party to lean upon for support. He rather prided himself upon his independence of the opinions of others; and he was accustomed to say, 'My principles are deduced from the best data in my power to command: I think them to be right: while I think so, I shall certainly adhere to them, although I shall ever be ready to forsake them when convinced that they are wrong.' "

advice in this matter resulted in an unfortunate coolness between Birney and his old friend Lewis Tappan.[26] Birney agreed with Beriah Green that although Bailey's course might be "discreet," what was more needed in the conflict was "a little bravery." [27]

The refusal of the main body of the Liberty party to depart from its one-ideaism and the defection of others to a course that savored of compromise with the old parties left Birney as one of a minority within the ranks of antislavery men organized for political action. It was this minority, centered largely in western New York, which decided the time had come for an affirmation of its principles and the nomination of candidates on that basis alone. William Goodell wrote the call for the convention to be held early in June, 1847, at Macedon Lock, New York. It was accompanied by a declaration of their reasons for action which stated their position clearly:

We do say distinctly, and with great confidence, that without a consistent, well defined, and distinctly enumerated declaration of its position on *all* the great practical questions before the country, and in which the rights of the citizens, the security of our liberties, as well as the liberation of the Slaves, are, *together* involved, the Liberty party cannot, in the very nature of the case, escape ultimate absorption in one of the other political parties, to the shipwreck of all the objects for which it was originally organized, including, signally, the defeat, for the present generation, of the anti-slavery enterprise, so far as political action is concerned.[28]

Birney could not attend the convention, of course, but he did allow his name to be affixed to the Declaration. By doing so, he acquiesced in the platform, which included Goodell's interpretation of the Con-

[26] *Signal of Liberty,* Jan. 23, 1847; Birney to Tappan, May 10, 1847, Birney Papers. Foster adds this to the contrast between Leavitt and Bailey: "Leavitt was strongly attached to the Liberty party, and had strong hopes that it would attain to national supremacy; Bailey cared nothing for the organization, regarding it as an instrument for disseminating antislavery principles." Foster preferred Bailey to Leavitt, terming Leavitt, "secretive, wily and sometimes disingenuous," while "Bailey was frank and manly, and scorned a mean evasion." Notebook on the Liberty party.

[27] Beriah Green to Birney, Aug. 2, 1847, Birney Papers.

[28] *Call for a National Nominating Convention, Declaration, and Reasons for Action,* inclosures in William Goodell to Birney, April 1, 1847, Birney Papers. See also William Goodell, *Address of the Macedon Convention . . . ; and Letters of Gerrit Smith.*

stitution as an antislavery document. Accepting this thesis, that slavery anywhere in the United States was "illegal, unconstitutional and anti-republican," it was but a step more to the position that Congress had the authority to abolish slavery even in the states in which it was legal at the time the Constitution was adopted. The platform denounced monopoly, even that of the federal government in mail delivery; approved an ultimate disbanding of the army and navy; was strongly for free trade; opposed secret societies; and advocated direct per capita taxation, including slaves, as a means of forcing emancipation. Perhaps most noteworthy of all the planks was the one favoring the distribution of the public lands "in small parcels, to landless men, for the mere cost of distributing," a direct forerunner of the Republican party's Homestead Act in 1862. Birney was wholeheartedly behind this last issue. In an article he wrote for the Albany *Patriot* of April 28, he had pointed out that the Irish famine was a direct result of the monopoly of land and a consequent exploitation of the working man.

The main backers of the Macedon convention, besides Goodell, were Gerrit Smith, who had been converted from one-ideaism, James C. Jackson, Abram Pennell, and Elihu Burritt. Goodell had hoped that Birney would accept the nomination. Although his name was entered, there was no possibility of his running, and Gerrit Smith was nominated for president, Elihu Burritt for vice-president. As they were, in fact, seceders from the regular Liberty party, they became known as a distinct group, the "Liberty League." [29]

Birney's support of the Macedon convention resulted in further disagreement with Bailey. In the *National Era* of July 1, Bailey opposed the convention because it was engineered by a few members of the party who had not even consulted the national committee. Birney answered him with an article in the Albany *Patriot* on August 11. The national committee, he charged, had previously agreed not to postpone the nominations beyond the autumn of 1847; but they had done and were doing nothing about it, postponing action to see what the other parties would do. If the decision of the Macedon convention were against the wishes of the plurality of the party, let a convention be called for the spring.

Four articles by Birney on Congressional power over slavery in the

[29] Albany *Patriot*, June 16, 1847.

states further confounded the disagreement.[30] The *National Era* had denied such power.[31] Birney's argument was based on his contention that the Union was formed with the intention that the "establishment" of slavery was only temporary and with the expectation that those states still having slavery would keep faith by getting rid of it. By not doing so, they had broken the compact; therefore, the North no longer need consider binding those parts of the Constitution which were proslavery. He rested his case upon the character of the fathers of the Constitution as well as on the purpose of the Constitution as stated in the Preamble. Slavery was never, could never be, consistent with such objectives as justice, domestic tranquillity, and the blessings of liberty. To Congress was delegated the *duty* of maintaining equal protection of the laws. It followed that Congress must abolish slavery. God alone being the source of right with which government is invested, no people, no nation, could take from an individual his natural rights. There is no obligation to obey a government which attempts to destroy such rights. How could a constitution guarantee that which there was no obligation to obey? The same Constitution extended over the states as over the territories. If Congress could protect citizens in the latter, why not in the former? Also, he asked, how could Congress admit a state to the Union with a constitution establishing slavery, when it had no such right itself? Could Congress confer a power it did not itself possess? Slavery, he concluded, had no legal existence. It continued simply because slaveholders had usurped the government and misinterpreted the Constitution. It was not only the power but the duty of Congress to abolish it.

Birney had done a complete about-face from his position of 1838. Then he had been willing to admit the power of the states over slavery within their own borders. Being a conservative, he had feared that taking too radical ground on the Constitution would alienate rather than gain adherents for the cause, and so he accepted a legalistic interpretation. But the admission had only emboldened the slave power in denying human rights. He was now convinced that higher ground must be taken. Strict legal interpretations of constitutional phrases must give way to interpretations based on, and in accord with, the great prin-

[30] *Ibid.*, May 12, 19, 26, and June 2, 1847. A briefer but similar article was sent to William Cullen Bryant for publication in the New York *Post*, Birney to Bryant, Oct. 18, 1847, Birney Papers.

[31] *National Era*, Feb. 18, 1847.

ciples and purposes expressed in the Preamble to the Constitution and in the Declaration of Independence.

Despite opposition from the "expedients," who feared the commitment of early nominations, the Liberty National Committee called a convention for October 20, 1847. Liberty Leaguers joined the other delegates at Buffalo, but the efforts of Gerrit Smith and William Goodell to secure the adoption of their constitutional interpretation were voted down. Chase's attempt to achieve a postponement of the nominations failed, but the "expedients" did win out on getting their men nominated: John P. Hale, Senator from New Hampshire, and Leicester King of Ohio. As was to be expected, Birney opposed the nomination of Hale, who had not even been a member of the Liberty party previously. His view was expressed in a letter to Lewis Tappan in which he declined the office of vice-president of the American and Foreign Anti-Slavery Society:

Believing the Society in approving of the nomination of Mr. Hale descended from the high and true principles which actuated it for many years, to meet Mr. Hale on the low and false grounds he has assumed, and that he is, by no means, a fair representative of the opinions on slavery which I hold, I respectfully beg to decline holding any office that seems to give a sanction to the measure alluded to.[32]

The Buffalo convention of 1847 marked the end of Birney's influence in antislavery politics. Refusing to be swept away by the current of expediency, he remained aloof from the great 1848 movement for fusion of the Liberty party with the antislavery elements of the Whig and Democratic parties who could not conscientiously vote for Taylor or Cass. Birney's vote was cast for Gerrit Smith. The Liberty League held out in name for several years, but the voting strength of the Liberty party was carried along under the leadership of Chase, Leavitt, and Stanton into the new Free Soil party.

Birney felt that his earliest fears of political organization had materialized. The new leaders were men from the old Whig and Democratic parties, some of whom might be sincere, but some of whom were simply jumping on the band wagon of a party which looked as if it had a promising future. Old leaders, old principles, would be by-passed. Birney's disappointment is revealed in his diary:

[32] Birney to Lewis Tappan, July 10, 1848, Birney Papers.

When they [the Liberty party] became impatient for a quicker success than their principles seemed to promise; they were easily won by any powerful popular fragment who could give them a better prospect of success and who were willing to adopt the least odious of their principles. In this way the Free Soil party was formed. . . . The Free Soil Party now go so far only, in their politeness to me, as they think will conciliate the old Liberty men and bring them to their aid in the election.[33]

Yet, idealist though Birney was, he knew that ideals are seldom achieved in their purity, that one must often be satisfied with a compromise with reality. In subsequent years he voted both the Free Soil and Republican tickets.

[33] Diary of James G. Birney, entry for Feb. 15, 1850.

Chapter XIV

Forgotten Leader

THE years in Saginaw following Birney's accident were trying ones in many ways. He had lost his place of leadership in the anti-slavery movement, and from the side lines it looked as if the cause was making little progress. There were constant financial struggles. It seemed to Birney that his sons brought him trouble and worry more often than help and comfort. His illness, moreover, made all of the other problems appear worse. His physical incapacity affected his spirit and made him irritable and despondent.

On June 20, 1849, Birney suffered his second paralytic stroke and lost his voice again.[1] This was followed by heart attacks in November, 1850, and in February, 1851, and by a third stroke the same month. As a result of these attacks both speech and writing became even more tedious. Birney tried consistently to find some doctor or some cure which would restore his health, but to no avail. The Saginaw doctors, Rogers and Monroe, were still believers in the old-fashioned bleeding, which gave only temporary relief. After the first accident Birney went to Detroit to try J. B. Cross's electrical treatments, the latest discovery in the cure of paralysis. Then, following Beriah Green's advice, he ex-

---

[1] The information on Birney's health is taken from his diary, in private possession.

perimented on his own with the water cure—a daily shower under a bucket of cold water. After his second stroke he made inquiries about water-cure treatments in Cincinnati and Cleveland, but the necessity of leaving home and the cost of boarding out in the city as well as payment for the treatments prevented his going. By 1853, however, his financial condition was much improved, and while on a trip to New York he visited Mrs. Mettler, a famed clairvoyant who had a reputation for curing many people. She went into a trance accompanied by many twitchings and jerkings, and while "under" she told him he could never be completely cured but might be relieved. The prescription was that he leave a lock of his hair and ten dollars. Even such wisdom from the spirit world failed to be effective.

Birney's despondency made him particularly sensitive over what seemed a lack of sympathy from his family. After his second stroke in 1849 he wrote in his diary: "This want of sympathy, brought into more prominent display the harder & at that time, no doubt, the more necessary parts of my character." Later he wrote, "Often the want of kindness and sympathy I feel very sensibly"; and in still another place he noted that the neighbors were all too busy with their own pursuits to be sympathetic and, "in addition to this, hardly any of my children who can *do for themselves* come near me, or give me that consolation which their good conduct & attentions could well minister to my declining years."

As a result of this sensitivity, Birney became very impatient with the boys, perhaps overly harsh in his judgments and condemnations.[2] It seemed to take all of them an unusually long time to get settled in life. Even James, Jr., ordinarily the most precise and calculating of them, could not make up his mind about a career. Neither teaching nor the ministry suited him, and he gave them both up. After considering moving to Saginaw to go into the lumber business or farming, he turned to law, first in Detroit and then in Cincinnati. As a consequence of his frequent changes James was never in a position to be of much help.

In many ways William fulfilled his father's hopes more than any of the sons. He had followed in his father's footsteps in antislavery work and had earned an enviable reputation as a lawyer in Cincinnati work-

---

[2] All the information given on the Birney children, unless otherwise indicated, is taken from their letters to their father, Birney Papers. A last child, Anna, was born in 1844 and died in 1846.

ing with Chase on fugitive slave cases and defending the rights of free colored people. He took both Dion and David under his wing and paid for part of Dion's education. But just when William was in a position where he could help with the cost of educating the younger children, he joined the Masons, and this caused an unpleasant rift with his father. Knowing his father's strong feelings against the organization, he had joined secretly, which made Birney all the more angry when he was informed by James. "I have ever regarded candor as proof of a great mind," Birney wrote to William, "of a mind that was *right,* as far as it was informed;—insincerity, as proof of a mind of entirely opposite structure. Mutual distrust must prevail between us hereafter." Eventually Birney could not deny William's claim to think and decide for himself as his father had taught him, and they were reconciled within the year. This argument, however, and a quarrel resulting from James's jealousy of William's legal success, had sent William off to Europe in a huff.[3]

The third son, Dion, was a big worry. Unable to get along harmoniously at home, unwilling to take his father's correction and advice, he had run off to Cincinnati, where William persuaded him to enroll at St. Xavier's. There he did well in school, married into a good family, took the temperance pledge, and appeared to be settling down. He and David attempted to establish a partnership to take over a match-manufacturing business, but this was a failure, and Dion came home to Saginaw again to try to make a living as a druggist. Even with help from his father-in-law it was a financial struggle, and to make the situation even more trying, his young wife was unhappy with the contrast between life in Saginaw and what she was used to in Cincinnati.

On his fifty-ninth birthday, February 4, 1851, Birney made a retrospective entry in his diary: "My life, I may say has been an unceasing struggle with my own tempers. . . ." After his accident he was impatient with old friends as well as with his sons. There were sharp disagreements with Lewis Tappan, which in the old days would have been accepted as honest difference of opinion without having any effect on their mutual respect and friendship. But in Birney's state of despondency, and without the advantage of being able to talk things over face to face, an unfortunate coolness had resulted between them. First they disagreed over the appointment of Bailey to edit the *National Era*

---

[3] William taught in Paris and while there participated in the Revolution of 1848.

in Washington; then they differed on the acceptance of Hale as the antislavery candidate for the presidency; and then they carried on an argument over the responsibility of Christians to maintain foreign missions. At one point, Birney even refused to act as Tappan's mercantile agent in the Saginaw area, and Tappan responded that he would rather cease correspondence with Birney completely than be addressed formally or coldly.[4] Fortunately, however, such a state of affairs did not last, and Birney and Tappan regained their old cordiality.

Birney's sharpness with his sister was the result of his attempt to make his practical conduct harmonize with his intellectual convictions. Having adopted the principle of nonintercourse with slaveholders, he not only gave up his membership in the Presbyterian church because it refused to exclude them, but also he refused to have anything to do with the Marshalls as long as they held slaves. He even forbade the boys to visit them.

When Judge Marshall died in 1846, one of the Marshall boys wrote to inform Birney and to request that he come to see his sister, who was unwell. On that occasion, Birney did send his sympathy, but was unable to make the trip because of his own health. He wrote:

Were I present, I should be but a poor comforter. All earthly appeals, in such cases, are with me, but of little weight. Comfort, to be abiding must come from above. In all my trials—and I have but lately been called to endure one of no common sort—I have found that the only solid comforter was Jesus Christ; whose religion may be won by all, if sought for with a subdued and humble spirit.[5]

In 1850, when Mrs. Marshall expressed her desire to visit Birney at James's home in Cincinnati, his note was much colder:

It has been my practice for many years to have no intercourse with oppressors of their fellow-beings, except so far as *business* might require. That you are one I entertain no doubt; and that you are becoming an old one certainly makes the case no better. A disease of whatever nature—moral or otherwise,—in my own family—among my natural friends,—is surely not less to be deprecated than when it is a long way off and confined to others.

[4] See especially Birney to Lewis Tappan, April 8, 1847, and Tappan to Birney, April 22, 1847, Birney Papers.

[5] Birney to Charles Edward Marshall, June 13, 1846, Birney Papers. The trial to which Birney refers was his accident and consequent illness.

Under these circumstances, it would be unnecessary for you to come to Cincinnati, on my account.[6]

The Saginaw years were years of religious disillusion, also, and Birney's faith in organized Christianity was seriously shaken. The change in his beliefs, however, was not entirely disillusion; much of it was the result of the intensive thought and study he gave to the subject while confined at home. He had always striven to perfect his own life. On June 23, 1851, he wrote in his diary: "It is very clear to me now that I committed many mistakes but I was always sincere, and nothing made me ever satisfied with myself but purity of life, and nothing made me ever suppose happiness hereafter could be attained by anything but a pure life."

Birney had withdrawn from the Presbyterian church because of its failure to break with slaveholders, and he refused to attend the Methodist preaching in Lower Saginaw on the same grounds. In 1846 he helped to found the first Congregational Church of Lower Saginaw, for which he drew up an article of faith expressing belief in the equality of man: "We believe, that as God has made all men of one blood, they are to be loved, and treated, according to their true worth and character before God, without regard to the factitious distinctions among men." [7] As time went on, however, Birney's studies led him to Unitarianism, particularly after he began to correspond with Theodore Parker. Mrs. Birney, however, remained a Trinitarian, and out of deference for her views he made no definite affiliation with a Unitarian church, nor did he accept the Unitarian tutor for their son Fitzhugh whom Parker had recommended.

He became, in fact, so opposed to sectarianism that even if there had been a denomination with whose views he entirely concurred he would not have joined it. Organized churches, by fostering sectarian pride and prejudice, interposed something between God and man. Their articles of belief were too stereotyped; he needed liberty of investigation no matter where it led him. He even went so far as to criticize as absurd the practice of having only priests or ministers conduct religious services, and he suggested the establishment of lecture halls for the use of all.

[6] Birney to Anna Marshall, June 12, 1850, Birney Papers.
[7] Records of the First Congregational Church of Lower Saginaw, June 21, 1846, in private possession.

As time went on, Birney became more and more unorthodox in his views. He considered the doctrine of predestination "pernicious." [8] Gradually he gave up his belief that the Bible was the revelation of God to be accepted literally. If revelation were all important, he questioned, why did God give man reason? "It is the pure reason of man," he argued, "that has always found objections to the Bible, generally called the revelation of God. Into such absurdities do we fall when we interpret what is called a Revelation of God by other powers than those he has given us!" [9]

Birney came to doubt, and then to deny, the existence of a material devil:

The only Devil or demon that man has to do with, he carries with him— his own *selfishness;* inducing him to prefer for the direction of his conduct the ways of a finite being like himself to the laws of an infinite one, like God, who has made him by those laws for happiness, and who knows what will best promote it, and who regards him with a love too great to be adequately described by a finite being.[10]

To him it seemed absurd that an omnipotent God would create a devil to thwart his own plans, and equally absurd that God would create man and then punish him everlastingly for yielding to influences he was formed to yield to. The problem of free will, however, was one which he could never explain to his own satisfaction.

The stories of miracles, he felt, were especially to be mistrusted. To limit the Supreme Being by an abrogation or suspension of his laws was to take away that very supremeness. The laws of nature, he held, are the highest evidence that can exist and are superior to human evidence. Miracles which affect only a small area and are witnessed to by only unlearned and unscientific men, as was true of Jesus' miracles, are open to much question. Joshua's miracle of the sun standing still should have been noted all over the world, yet report of it came from only one small area. His conclusion was that there was a greater possibility that the witnesses were wrong than that natural law was sus-

[8] William Birney, Extracts from the notebook of James G. Birney, Birney Collection. Most of Birney's religious views are expressed in his diary, 1851–1852.

[9] James G. Birney, "Reason Applied to the Bible, An Answer to Archbishop Whately of Dublin," in private possession.

[10] James G. Birney, "Angels," in private possession.

pended. Yet, withal, Birney saw no real contradiction between faith and reason, because God would not give two such opposing powers. Submission to the will of God was itself reasonable.

His attack on the support of foreign missions [11] revealed his despair and discouragement over the religious situation in our own country. He thought that our country was unprepared to send missionaries abroad because so much was still undone at home. In his own county there was only one preacher because the people were too poor and too scattered to maintain more. Also, he felt that it was absurd for a people who still held others in bondage to send missionaries and that the Gospel should first be carried to the South. Birney could not see anywhere in the Bible that money was connected with the advancement of truth; the disciples had asked for contributions, not to spread the gospel, but to relieve the poor. The present-day businessman, said Birney, was so busy making money that he had no time for either his poor brethren or his own soul; he gave a large sum for foreign missions and considered his deed done. Birney contrasted the honor bestowed on the foreign missionaries with the neglect of those who were giving their lives to teach the colored people in this country. Even the heathen, he maintained, could see the propriety of a course of action by which we would tell them that we had heathen at home and that the neglect here must be attended to before we could send missionaries abroad. The salvation of a soul here, he argued, was as important as the salvation of one in Africa, and as it would be far less expensive, proportionately more could be accomplished here with the same expenditure. He was not optimistic, moreover, about the ultimate success of attempts to Christianize heathen lands.

Birney's illness led him to much consideration of death and the hereafter, about which he never became skeptical. The thought of immortality was a very happy one to him, and he believed that children should be brought up to think of death without any gloom or horror. The possibility of receiving messages from those already dead interested him, but he dismissed the idea on the logic that no wholly spiritual being would be able to communicate with one only partly spiritual. His belief in immortality rested simply on the goodness of God.

[11] James G. Birney, "Foreign Missions," Birney Papers.

Birney's discouragement over the seeming ineffectiveness of the antislavery movement was also reflected in his diary. On February 4, 1851, he wrote:

I have heretofore been very earnest in my wishes and somewhat sanguine in my hopes that the North or free states would so array themselves against slavery, that it would before long be abolished; that the system would never be any stronger, and that whatever changes happened to it, would be to weaken it. I yet think, under the operation of various principles it will ultimately go out—as slavery has in Europe. But when or how it will expire, I must say I see not. It appears to me so far off, that any exertion that I can make by writing or by showing it to be wrong is unnecessary and futile.

He even noted his fear that possibly thirty or forty years hence some modified form of slavery might be found in states already free.

The war with Mexico seemed to Birney to be a definite setback to the abolitionist cause. He disliked war for a so-called just cause; but here, when he felt that the United States should be aiding Mexico rather than wresting territory from her,[12] it was hateful to him. During the debates in Congress on the settlement of the territorial gains, he carried on a correspondence with Kinsley Bingham, Representative from Michigan, making suggestions and lending him moral support in his stand against slavery extension in that area.[13] The speeches of Northern as well as of Southern senators infuriated Birney by their heartlessness. Stephen A. Douglas, for instance, didn't care whether slavery was voted up or down. Vice, declared Birney, could be voted only down, never up. All of them spoke of the Negro as "dead, insensible material," oblivious to him as a brother with a man's desire for freedom.

Southerners continually objected to Northerners who introduced the subject of slavery, on the grounds that they knew nothing about it. If a nonslaveholder could not work against slavery, Birney argued, it was just as logical to say a righteous man was disqualified from preaching against sin. Besides, *some* abolitionists had been slaveholders. Senator Hunter of Virginia, in condescending to discuss the matter at all, had used the threat of disunion. But, Birney pointed out in an article published by Theodore Parker in the *Massachusetts Quarterly*

---

[12] Birney to James B. Hunt, May 20, 1846, Birney Papers.
[13] Birney to Kinsley S. Bingham, Sept. 4, 1848, and Jan. 8, 1849; Bingham to Birney, Sept. 24, 1848, Birney Papers.

Review,[14] the North could get along without the South more easily than vice versa. If they were separated peacefully, slavery would be even more insecure, because fugitives could escape more easily. If separation resulted in strife, the South could not hope to win.

Senator Berrian of Georgia, speaking on the compromise bill, had declared that slavery might exist anywhere that it was not prohibited by law; Birney took the position that slavery could not exist anywhere that it was not protected by law. Senator Clayton of Delaware argued for compromise on the precedent of the Constitutional compromise. On the contrary, said Birney, one must use that as an argument against compromise, for from that one compromise of principle in the Constitution had stemmed the harvest of sectional strife. Clayton urged a Supreme Court decision on the extension of slavery into the territories; Birney declared the Constitution explicitly gave Congress the power to legislate for the territories. He had no faith in the objectivity or impartiality even of Supreme Court judges.

For many years Birney had retained his faith in the use of petitions to Congress to influence action in prohibiting the spread of slavery to the new territories; but now this hope, too, seemed futile. Even a supposedly deliberate body such as the Senate was afraid to discuss topics which they feared were fiery or emotional. Rejections of petitions on slavery had led to a recent petition from the North proposing dissolution of the Union. Birney decided:

If the Union is always to bring on us such slaveholding rule as we have had, almost without intermission, for the last fifty years, if the Union is for confirming, promoting, and extending slavery, at the expense of liberty, we say, so far as we are concerned, let it disappear, it does not deserve to be upheld by any honest and just man, and the sooner it is dissolved and forgotten, the better.[15]

Birney was convinced that the reason nonslaveholders in the South defended the institution was that they hoped to rise into the planter class; but if it ever came to a war in which slavery was sure to be destroyed, the nonslaveholders would immediately desert the slaveholding class.

[14] James G. Birney, "Senatorial Speeches on Slavery," *Massachusetts Quarterly Review,* III (1849–1850), 1–40.

[15] James G. Birney, "Senatorial Opinions on the Right of Petition," *Massachusetts Quarterly Review,* III (1849–1850), 431–459.

The Compromise of 1850, when it was finally passed, was repugnant to Birney and, more than anything else, contributed to his feeling that antislavery efforts had been futile. To Clay it might seem like a settlement; but to Birney a moral question could never be permanently compromised. As for the new fugitive slave law, he said: "They may pass it—they may increase the penalties—they may multiply the number of persons before whom the captured slave may be brought, but it cannot be enforced." [16] He was certain it would but rouse the Northern people to defiance.

The violence of Birney's reaction against the fugitive slave law led him to a detailed study of the decision rendered several years earlier by the Supreme Court in the case of *Prigg* vs. *Pennsylvania*. While visiting in Cincinnati in the winter of 1850, he wrote down his conclusions in the form of an article. He believed it was one of the best pieces he had ever written, but too much time had elapsed since the decision in 1842 to make the article of popular interest, and it was never published.

The Prigg case had involved the escape of a slave woman, Margaret Morgan, from Maryland into Pennsylvania. Some years later Edward Prigg was appointed by Margaret Ashmore, the former owner of Margaret Morgan, as agent to retake and bring back the escaped woman. He secured a warrant from a Pennsylvania justice of the peace, seized Margaret Morgan and her children, and took them back to Maryland. Prigg was indicted under a Pennsylvania law of 1826 on the grounds of kidnapping, but the case was appealed to the Supreme Court to test its constitutionality.

The Supreme Court held that Congress had exclusive power over fugitive slaves and, therefore, that the Pennsylvania law of 1826 was invalid. However, the Court held that authority could be conferred on state magistrates and that state magistrates could exercise the authority given them by the fugitive slave act of 1793 unless prohibited by state legislation. It was this part of the decision which led to the passage of laws throughout the North forbidding state officials to aid in the enforcement of the federal statute. The contest led to the new fugitive slave act of 1850, a part of the Compromise of 1850. It provided that commissioners should be appointed by the circuit courts to enforce the law and to have concurrent jurisdiction with the judges of the

[16] Birney to the Christian Anti-Slavery Convention, April 2, 1850, Birney Papers.

circuit and district courts. This, in turn, resulted in a new storm of protest and an increase of "personal liberty laws," many of them nullifying the provisions of the federal law.[17]

Birney dedicated his essay to the people, in the belief that they were interested in the principle on which the Prigg decision presumed to rest "having *justice* done to everyone." They should not err by thinking that because the decision had to do with Negroes it had nothing to do with them; one cannot look on while injustice is being done to his neighbor, because it may be his turn next. People must be vigilant in thinking for themselves rather than mildly acquiescing in the actions of a government which, like all governments, tended to accumulate power. "Free mind," he declared, "is the strongest and keenest instrument of human elevation—the most unerring proof of human liberty; *fettered* mind is the strongest and keenest instrument of human degradation—enslaved mind the most unerring proof of tyranny and despotism."

Birney denied the statement of the Court that it was historically well known that the object of the Constitutional clause was to "secure to the citizens of the slaveholding states, the complete right and title of ownership in their slaves as property, in every state in the Union into which they might escape from the state in which they were held in servitude." On the contrary, he argued, the makers of the Constitution looked on slavery as only temporary. To deny that they were trying to make effectual the "self-evident" truths of the Declaration of Independence was to charge them with fraud and perfidy. When Pinckney wanted some provision guaranteeing property in slaves, Madison had refused on the ground that it would be wrong to admit in the Constitution that man can hold property in man. One of the first petitions to the new government was headed by Franklin, and it urged Congress to go to the very "verge" of its authority to give the same rights to slaves which *they* enjoyed. The fact that the words "slave" and "slavery" do not appear in the Constitution supported the argument that the founding fathers expected it to be temporary. In addition, the law of 1793 had been an outgrowth of a case of rendition of a man who kidnapped a free Negro, not of a case of a fugitive slave. But the two had been put

[17] Special reference to *Prigg* vs. *Pennsylvania* may be found in Helen T. Catterall, *Judicial Cases concerning American Slavery and the Negro* (Washington, D.C.: Carnegie Institution, 1926–1937), IV, 252–254; Charles Warren, *The Supreme Court in United States History*, II, 83–86; and Charles W. Smith, *Roger B. Taney: Jacksonian Jurist* (Chapel Hill, 1936), pp. 152–153.

into one bill, "An act respecting fugitives from justice and persons escaping from the service of their masters." The latter phrase could refer to indentured servants as well as to slaves. The Court had cited "long acquiescence," "contemporaneous exposition," and "extensive and uniform recognition," as factors in the Prigg decision. Adhering to his strict constructionist viewpoint, Birney held that the Court did not exist to deal out justice on such bases when there was a written Constitution.

The decision had stated that state officers might exercise authority over fugitives if not prohibited by state laws. How, Birney asked, could a state give this power to its officers if the matter belonged exclusively to the federal government? The Court had decided a slaveholder could go into a free state and seize his slaves. All jurisdiction would be in the hands of the federal government. In that case all state laws made for the protection of her citizens were unconstitutional and liable to be invalidated. He denied that recognition of the right of a master to a slave in some states put this right upon the same ground in all states. The states promised only not to pass laws by which an escaping slave would be declared free. They could aid fugitives, as long as they passed no law to aid them, and still keep their promise. Anyway, he continued, states had no power to trade away men's rights. Even if they did not pass laws to impede the course of slaveholders, there were individuals who utterly denied the right of property in man.

In the final analysis, Birney concluded, the Prigg decision failed in its intention to convince and quiet the country. A question of right and wrong could not be changed into one of a nonmoral nature. No valid law could be antagonistic to the Golden Rule. People's emotions were involved in the matter of giving aid to a fugitive, and their individual actions would inevitably be determined by their consciences, not by subservience to a prescribed mode of thinking.[18]

Another fugitive slave case, that of *Strader, Gorman and Armstrong vs. Graham,* stimulated Birney to write another review, which was published in pamphlet form.[19] Christopher Graham was the owner of three slaves who he claimed were received on board a steamboat at

[18] James G. Birney, "The Prigg Decision," in private possession.

[19] James G. Birney, *Examination of the Decision of the Supreme Court of the United States, in the Case of Strader, Gorman and Armstrong vs. Christopher Graham, Delivered at Its December Term, 1850: Concluding with an Address to the Free Colored People, Advising Them to Remove to Liberia* (Cincinnati, 1852).

Louisville, were taken to Cincinnati, and escaped to Canada. He sued Strader and Gorman as owners of the boat and Armstrong as master of the boat. These three claimed that the Negroes were free as they had previously been sent to work in Ohio. They had not, however, been in Ohio for two years prior to their escape. The Louisville chancery court decided they were slaves and that Graham was entitled to three thousand dollars. This decision was confirmed by the Kentucky Court of Appeals before it went to the Supreme Court on a writ of error.

Much of Birney's article was a combination of the ideas he had expressed in the Prigg decision and those he had previously expounded on the subject of slaves escaping into the Northwest Territory from states not included in the original thirteen. A new point which he argued was the Supreme Court's opinion that the Northwest Ordinance no longer applied when states were formed out of that territory. Their opinion was based on the premise that if the Ordinance were still in force, it would place the states of the territory in an inferior position to the other states. Therefore, only those provisions which had been incorporated into the state constitutions remained valid and operative. Consequently, the Supreme Court denied jurisdiction to hear the case.

Birney argued that it had been only in the late decisions that the Supreme Court had declared the Ordinance of 1787 inoperative. The Constitutional Convention carefully observed it, and the legislatures of states carved out of the Northwest Territory considered themselves bound by it. Ohio even gave it precedence over its state constitution, because the constitution was subject to change and the Ordinance was not. All of those states were required to conform to it before Congress would admit them. It was a compact between the original states, on the one hand, and the people and states in the Territory, on the other; and it was to remain forever unalterable except by common consent. It was an engagement entered into as much as was a debt contracted before the Constitution was adopted, and it should be so honored.

Birney's great hope was that the fugitive slave law of 1850 would be declared unconstitutional on the grounds of violating the right of habeas corpus; and his diary reveals the extreme interest with which he followed each case arising under it. He had observed the irony of the necessity for free colored citizens to escape from the United States to a British possession for protection, when we had gone to war with that same empire presumably to secure liberty to our people. There was little hope for a fugitive even when granted a trial by jury, because jurors who did not believe in the constitutionality of the law were disqualified. The only solution, it seemed, was to give jurors the authority to judge not only of the facts, but of the law itself.

Another discouraging development was that meetings were being held to support the enforcement of such a law in several cities of the North. The one in Philadelphia had been presided over by John Sargeant, who at the time of the Missouri Compromise had given one of the best speeches in Congress against slavery and who had previously been the president of the American Convention for Promoting the Abolition of Slavery and Improving the Condition of the Colored Race. Speakers at the same meeting had been George M. Dallas, Birney's college friend and vice-president of the United States under Polk, and Richard Rush and Joseph Ingersoll, sons of Dr. Benjamin Rush and Jared Ingersoll, who had both been known for their antislavery views. A similar meeting in New York had been presided over by another of Birney's old Princeton friends, George Wood. Birney's acquaintance with Wood had been renewed when they lived in Brooklyn during the days of his secretaryship for the American Anti-Slavery Society; and the Woods had been particularly helpful in the last days of Mrs. Birney's illness. Still grateful for their kindness then, Birney did not want to offend them, so he addressed to Wood an anonymous letter urging him to stand for liberty instead of drifting with the current.

The election of a proslavery president in 1848, General Taylor; the recent Supreme Court decisions, and the new fugitive slave law had convinced Birney that it was useless to look to any branch of the federal government for aid in the antislavery cause or even for securing the rights of free colored people in the North, whose seizure as slaves would be easier than ever as far as the legal procedure was concerned. It was resulting in an exodus of free blacks to Canada, which Birney compared to that of the Jews out of Spain in the late fifteenth century. His abandonment of hope resulted in his writing a letter which was received with some astonishment and much misinterpretation in abolitionist circles.

His letter was in answer to the request of some colored people for advice about emigrating to another country. Birney replied that in all honesty he saw little hope that free colored people would ever be accorded equal rights in the United States. Antislavery men, including

Birney himself, had urged them to remain to be leaders for their people and to be of service to those who were still in bondage; but the present outlook seemed to indicate that it had been in vain. He feared that the white man's attitude of superiority would be against them in Canada, also; and he concluded that perhaps, after all, Liberia, though no Elysium, offered the best hope.[20]

Birney had been immediately accused, from the one side, of back-sliding from abolition to support the Colonization Society; and he was once more claimed by the Colonization Society as having arrayed himself again in their defense. Both were wrong. Birney did not believe that colonization was in any way a solution to the problem of slavery, and he was certainly not advocating it as a substitute for abolition nor as an escape from granting equality to the colored people in this country. He was still convinced that the Colonization Society rested on a foundation of racial prejudice, while his own aim was a complete obliteration of class distinction based upon color.

In 1845 he had warned associations who aimed to improve the colored race of the danger in aiding colored people *as a class*, because in so doing they were being set apart in treatment. This, declared Birney, would lead to the same error as the colonization principle. He suggested that if people who wished to help would only "treat the colored people just as Christian gentlemen ought to treat them were they not colored people, they will do more in ten years toward making them virtuous and moral, happy and useful, then by centuries of labor bestowed on them as a separate class." [21]

Between the time he penned that letter in 1845 and the time he wrote his letter advising Negroes to go to Liberia, he had changed his mind on one major point. Then he believed it the duty of the free colored to remain in the United States and become a part of the social structure; now he felt that as individuals they must go wherever they felt they could make the best life for themselves. He was still vehemently opposed to the Colonization Society's advocacy of emigration as a necessary concomitant of emancipation and to their pressure tactics in forcing freed Negroes to emigrate. He had lost none of his mistrust of their motives. In 1847 he had written to Henry Ruffner, president of Washington College in Virginia, who he had heard was interested in the removal of the Negroes, hoping "that the time may soon come" when

[20] *Ibid.*   [21] Birney to William Wright, June 20, 1845, Birney Papers.

he would "think it more important to employ the handsome faculties that God has given you for the extermination of slaveholding, than to remove the slaves from Virginia." [22]

Birney's increasing impatience over the callousness of the country in regard to slavery reached its height in a bitterly satiric piece called "A Christmas Present," written toward the end of 1850.[23] He had read in the *Washington Union* a proposal that a full-blooded Indian, with his native costume and anything else which would illustrate his way of life, should be taken as an exhibit to the industrial convention in London in the spring of 1851. Birney suggested that to really show what our country was, slaves should be taken. An exhibition of full-blooded Negroes, mulattoes, quadroons, octoroons, and so on down the line, would show our " 'industry, genius, and skill' in the bleaching process." The slave exhibit should show them at work with their hoes, dressed in their usual costumes, and accompanied by an overseer "with the ensign of his office." All the operations on the Negroes such as whipping and branding must be shown in the spirit of a sham battle. He was sure the United States could win the prize from any other so-called civilized nation, except, perhaps, Russia.

To make the exhibit effective, continued Birney, who was still vitriolic against the "compromisers," it must be explained by competent men. His nominations for the job were William R. King, president of the Senate, and Henry Clay; with Howell Cobb, speaker of the House, and Henry S. Foote as alternatives. "These gentlemen, I have no doubt, will be acceptable to the South," he wrote, "as they will risk nothing where she is concerned." Attendants should be taken along to care for the Negroes, to perform such tasks as shaking up their beds of straw and removing the offal. For this position he felt Senators Cass [24] and Dickenson particularly qualified, "for up to this time they have not declined any task for the slaveholders—no matter how mean and unworthy it might be considered at the North—when there was a reasonable prospect that it would be crowned with honor."

His next jibe was at the decision that the largest ship in the navy be used to carry our delegates and exhibits in order that other nations

---

[22] Birney to Henry Ruffner, Dec. 20, 1847, Birney Papers.

[23] James G. Birney, "A Christmas Present," in private possession.

[24] On the cover of his copy of *Remarks of Mr. Cass, of Michigan, on the Dissolution of the Union, and the Constitution of California. In the Senate of the United States, February 12 and 20, 1850*, Birney wrote, "A vile and unworthy speech."

might be impressed with our power. Birney suggested that to imple-
ment this impression, Clay should be pitted against any man his age
in Europe to fight for our honor. He would, no doubt, win, especially if
he felt the Union depended on it, continued Birney ironically. "He is
a fast friend of the Union, you know, and he has succeeded in making it
minister much to his elevation." Webster would also be needed at the
convention, as "many of the European representatives who have never
seen a slave, and who, fanatically, to be sure, think that all men are
entitled to Liberty, might make a fuss about it," and Webster must be
on hand to explain its legality.

Toward the end of the display, Webster might regale those present
with a Negro hunt. Birney then put into his mouth the speech with
which Webster would explain it to the English:

Here are no hares—no foxes—those little animals that *you* pursue; no fallow-
deer, almost too tame to run from you, but in our country, the freest on the
globe, we have men and women, as we have now, and sometimes even
children, for our game. . . . The sport is animating, soul-cheering—if very
good to-day we'll end it by shooting the fugitives from the trees in which
they may seek refuge from the fury of the dogs: that you may fully see what
we can do at home—what is constitutional there—what is due to that part
of the country where slaves are found, and what alone can save the charter
of our liberty or preserve the Union.

Birney had intended, he said, to propose that President Fillmore, his
cabinet, and all the members of Congress who voted for the fugitive
slave law of 1850 should go along also; but on second thought, if all
the "great men" left Washington, who would there be to see that the
people did not violate the Constitution and separate the Union?

At least one paper refused to print Birney's article, but it was published in the Boston *Commonwealth* by Elizur Wright.[25]

Birney never recovered his good health completely, but a gradual
improvement in his financial condition restored his optimistic attitude
toward life. A rise in land values finally repaid his investments, and his
experiment of introducing thoroughbred cattle to the Saginaw area
also prospered. In April, 1851, he was able to pay off his last mortgage.
By 1853 he and Elizabeth were able to consider the prospect of leaving

[25] J. N. Sweet to Birney, Jan. 29, 1851, Birney Papers. The manuscript is endorsed
"Published in the Boston Commonwealth."

the wilderness behind and returning to the comforts of the civilized world, where they could once more live among people who practiced the social amenities and experience again the joy of intellectual companionship. Instead of moving to Cincinnati, as James had been urging, or to Philadelphia, where David and William were, he and Elizabeth made up their minds to join his oldest and dearest antislavery colleague, Theodore Weld, in a colony for communal living on the Raritan Bay in New Jersey.

This would be Birney's last move. All the others had been motivated by ambition either for his own career and fortune or for the antislavery cause. Each of them had held out its own peculiar challenge and had required the utmost in expenditure of mental and physical energy. This last move would be different. The rush and turmoil were past, the striving was over. This was to be a simple reaching out for peace. Birney looked forward to spending his last days in the contemplation of things eternal in the gentle and quiet company of those he loved.

Chapter XV

Reconciliation

THERE sat Mrs. Weld and her sister, two elderly gray-headed ladies, the former in extreme bloomer costume, which was what you may call remarkable; Mr. Arnold Buffum, with broad face and great white beard, looking like a pier-head made of the cork-tree with the bark on, as if he could buffet a considerable wave; James G. Birney, formerly candidate for the presidency, with another particularly white head and beard; Edward Palmer, the anti-money man (for whom communities were made), with his ample beard somewhat grayish. Some of them, I suspect are very worthy people.[1]

So wrote Henry Thoreau after a visit to Eagleswood, the community begun by Weld and Marcus Spring, a New York philanthropist, and of which the Birneys were now members. Everyone had gathered on the Sunday morning of Thoreau's visit for one of the morning religious services conducted by Weld himself in a sort of Quaker meeting fashion. Although the Raritan Bay Union had a religious basis, there was no preaching of creed, and unorthodox views on religion, as well as on other topics, were held by most of its members. "Attaching as I long

[1] F. B. Sanborn, ed., *Familiar Letters of Henry David Thoreau* (Boston, 1894), p. 337.

have done such slight importance to mere opinions," Weld had written to Birney in 1848, "creeds have lost all hold upon me, and in the state of mind that exalts them I search in vain for the elements of healthful growth. How speculative notions have usurped the functions of spiritual vitality." [2]

The world to which Birney had come was one of quiet beauty underlying a stimulating intellectual atmosphere. The location of the Union, which they had named Eagleswood, was itself conducive to a sense of peace. Standing on their hill, Birney could view the expanse of Raritan Bay below, and as his eyes followed the line of the bay toward the southeast, they came to rest on the Neversink Hills. Behind him the wooded hillsides shut their little community into a natural amphitheater.[3] It was no wonder everyone was so content to stay there, not venturing even into New York City, only twenty-five miles away, except on compulsion, and then, as Weld laughingly described, "They rush through the streets with their fingers in their ears crying 'Life! Life! Eternal Life!'" [4]

Their settlement contained several buildings. The largest was the Unitary building, in which the Birneys had a suite of rooms next to the Welds on the first floor. Meals could be eaten in a common dining room or prepared privately, as the families preferred. There were several separate houses for those who chose to be somewhat apart, a schoolhouse, workshops, and a wharf where steamboats could land supplies or passengers.[5] All had been built by money invested as stock in the Union. The Birneys had subscribed one thousand dollars.[6]

Few of the inhabitants worked, as most of them, like Birney, had come to retire. Weld, however, kept active as schoolmaster and general director of the community life. His methods and philosophy of teaching were wholly unorthodox, resembling those of Bronson Alcott, who sometimes came himself to visit Eagleswood. There were several children in the community, including Weld's own and Fitzhugh Birney. Other students were admitted from the outside as boarding pupils. But education at Eagleswood was not confined to the children. Teach-

---

[2] Theodore Weld to Birney, Dec. 16, 1848, Birney Papers.

[3] Sarah Grimké to Harriot Hunt, Dec. 20, [1854], Weld-Grimké Papers, William L. Clements Library, University of Michigan.

[4] S. W. Green to Birney, Jan. 29, 1856, Birney Papers.

[5] Weld to Birney, March 20, 1853, Birney Papers.

[6] Sarah Tyndale to Birney, March 7, 1854, Birney Papers.

ing was carried on by means of group activities or projects which included "all on the domain," young and old alike. A band of tragedians
was organized as the most effective method of studying the drama;
oldsters limbered up by joining in the dancing classes held regularly
on Saturday evenings; and a sort of lyceum, in which everyone participated in giving lectures, compositions, dialogues, or declamations,
met on Wednesdays.[7]

Visiting lecturers were in abundance. Henry Thoreau, William Cullen
Bryant, Horace Greeley, Bronson Alcott, William H. Channing,
Octavius B. Frothingham, James Freeman Clarke, Joshua Giddings,
Moncure D. Conway, and Gerrit Smith all came to pay their respects.
Old Nathanial Peabody became a member of the Union, and one of his
famous daughters, Elizabeth, taught for a time in Weld's school.[8] Most
of the people attracted by the Union had been reformers of one sort or
another. Some of them held views bordering on the fanatic, all of them
were unconventional idealists and visionaries of various shades. Now
they sat in their Indian summer, reminiscing about the days that were
gone, yet, with minds still alert, arguing issues of the day or discussing
questions of a philosophical nature. "We advocate the discussion of all
subjects as far as any one chooses to carry it," wrote Birney, "free from
all restraints except what public decency imposes, as being the best,
perhaps the appointed way of approximating to what is right and
true." [9] Such discussions in such an assemblage of minds provided rich
fare for one who had been associating primarily with frontiersmen and
Indians for over ten years.

There was no one for whom Birney had more respect and admiration
than he did for Weld. He wrote of him in his diary before moving to
Eagleswood:

I have a friend who is poor but I presume out of debt. He has supported
himself since he was a small boy. He seems content to be comfortably
situated only and to owe nobody anything. He has a highly cultivated mind
and is a man, I think, of very superior talents. His word is his bond and he
would think he was more injured by violating it than the one to whom it

[7] Weld to Sarah Grimké, Oct. 8, 1855, Weld-Grimké Papers.

[8] Benjamin Thomas, *Theodore Weld, Crusader for Freedom* (New Brunswick, 1950), p. 227.

[9] Christianus [pseud. of James G. Birney], *Concise Examination of Certain Super-naturalisms of the Bible, as Commonly Understood* (New York, 1856), Introd.

was given. He is one of the most punctual men in the performance of all his promises. His wife [Angelina Grimké] I cannot better describe than by saying she is very like him in disposition, etc. She has a sister who appears to be like them both. They are progressive and constantly improving. . . . They never entered the gay world and never, I suppose, wished to do so. They took an humble station as it would be called—accomodating [sic] their wants to their means. They are called fanatics. But I never see them or think of them without its recurring to me how happy they are—for they are virtuous and intelligent and have reasonably good health. It appears to me that they have everything to make them happy. I see my own mistake but it cannot now be corrected, if it ever could. The error was originally in me. I had too dim a view of the right way to follow it and fell into the one generally pursued. It is some satisfaction, however, to *know* my error, if I cannot correct it; to see an error which has affected the whole of my life that is past as well as that part which is to come, even if I cannot undo it. It is some satisfaction to know that we have erred, and cannot change it now—tho' we would act very differently if we had our life to pass over again.[10]

It was Birney's admiration for Weld's way of life and a desire to spend the last years of his life in a similar way that had led to his decision to move to the community. The first winter they were without sufficient heat and suffered from an inadequate water supply; but for Birney the physical discomforts were outweighed by the great pleasure of once more being among his old friends. Here he was more cheerful and relaxed and more at peace with God and man than at any other time or place.

The new atmosphere had a mellowing effect on Birney. Under its influence he recovered completely from any feelings of bitterness over the trials life had dealt him, and he lost much of his sternness; while Mrs. Birney, according to Sarah Grimké, was "quite a sunbeam" to the community.[11] The harshness which had lately characterized Birney's attitude toward his sister was softened, and he once more wrote to her in the affectionate manner of their early days, even inviting her to visit them at Eagleswood.[12] Birney's intolerance toward such "worldly" frivolities as dancing and the theater also yielded to complete approval of Weld's educational system which included them in the curriculum.

[10] Diary of James G. Birney, entry for July 27, 1852.
[11] Sarah Grimké to Harriot Hunt, Dec. 20, [1854], Weld-Grimké Papers.
[12] Anna Marshall Dennis to Birney, March 5, 1855, Birney Papers.

The nearness of David and William with their families in Philadelphia was another source of pleasure for the Birneys. There were visits of children and grandchildren at Eagleswood, and occasionally he and Elizabeth would go up to Philadelphia. Birney was particularly fond of William's wife, Catherine, an intelligent woman with strong antislavery views of her own.[13] The only great sorrow of this period was the death from tuberculosis of George, the youngest of his sons by his first wife.

At Eagleswood Birney had ample time to continue his study and writing, still chiefly on the subject of religion. During 1856 and 1857 he published, at his own expense, four pamphlets containing his essays,[14] but because of the unorthodoxy of the views he expressed, they were not signed with his real name, but with the pseudonym "Christianus." Undoubtedly he recalled his earlier criticism of Garrison for having published extraneous "radical" views which brought odium on the antislavery cause, and he did not wish to incur similar criticism from people who feared the public might ascribe his personal views to the general body of antislavery people.

Most of the Christianus essays were expansions of the ideas he had been in the habit of briefly noting in his diary. His belief in the perfectibility of man as a result of earnest seeking for the truth was dominant. His faith in man's improvement convinced him that public opinion would gradually outgrow beliefs inconsistent with reason, including a literal interpretation of the Bible. Although the questions of creation and of immortality were intensely interesting to Birney, he did not feel the necessity of accepting a particular dogma in regard to them. If the Infinite Wisdom thought immortality best for us, we would have it. Men should be content to rest in God's wisdom.

Birney's contact with the Welds and Sarah Grimké was probably responsible for a modification of his views on supernaturalism, for they had been interested in spiritualism for some time. Previously he had

---

[13] She later wrote a biography of the Grimké sisters, whom she learned to know and admire at Eagleswood.

[14] Christianus [pseud. of James G. Birney], *Concise Examination of Certain Supernaturalisms; Concise Examination of Certain Passages and Events in the Bible Divested of the Miraculous Character* (New York, 1856); *Multum in Parvo: or Short Treatises on Future Life, Immortality, Conscience, Prayer, the Sentence on the Serpent, the Esoteric and Exoteric Doctrines, Truth and Falsehood* (New York, 1856); and *Brief Statements and Arguments* (New York, 1857).

denied the possibility of receiving communications from the spirit world; now he admitted it could happen. But, he maintained, this proved nothing beyond the present moment, for the Infinite may have limited existence of such spirits to that very moment. The idea of communication with God through prayer seemed superfluous to him. Prayer commonly falls into four types: adoration, confession, petition, and thanksgiving. Yet, any adoration we can render, he said, falls far short of what God merits; confession is made to one who already knows; our petitions are unequal to the wisdom of what he bestows; and our thanksgiving but a faint expression of God's daily mercy. If prayer could bring to pass something not already determined, it would mean that the finite could direct or restrain the infinite. Moreover, if God is perfect, why should one seek to change his mind by prayer?

Two of the Christianus pamphlets, *Concise Examinations of Certain Supernaturalisms of the Bible, as Commonly Understood* and *Concise Examinations of Certain Passages and Events in the Bible, Divested of the Miraculous Character,* discussed his reasons for not believing in the divine inspiration of the whole content of the Bible. He believed that the real truths of the Bible, without the miracles, were sufficient to advance man to his highest spiritual elevation, and he particularly criticized the Catholic church for discouraging free inquiry and questioning of creed. Consequently, he charged, the Catholic church did not contribute to the advance of republicanism.

The last of the four pamphlets published under the Christianus pseudonym contained a miscellany of articles on various subjects. The first contrasted early presidents of the United States with those from Jackson on, pairing them in order. Washington and Jackson, said Birney, were both popular when alive, and both left memories much cherished and honored; yet the difference between them was great. Washington strictly adhered to the Constitution and wanted an even stronger one; while Jackson violated it whenever it suited his purpose. Washington was a natural gentleman; Jackson could be one when he chose, but that made him an artificial one. Adams and Van Buren, although different in temperament, each had good qualities, but Adams had more character.

To compare Jefferson to Harrison was like comparing Hyperion with a Satyr. Jefferson, a man of great talent, led his party; Harrison, a man of meager resources, was the tool of his. The contrast between Madison and Tyler was almost as great. He considered Madison one of the ablest and most thoroughly instructed presidents, to be compared with Marcus Aurelius; Tyler, one of the most ignorant. To compare Monroe with Polk was like trying to equate national peace, quietness, and justice with cruelty, violence, injustice, and war.

Despite Birney's severe criticism of John Quincy Adams back in 1843, his final verdict was praise for him as a diligent scholar and a sound republican who never misused his office. Taylor, besides being too imbued with military principles to be republican, was uneducated and uninformed. Fillmore, though a man of respectable talents, was odious for signing the fugitive slave law; while Pierce had, more than any other president, given himself to the slave power by allowing the system to go into all the territories.

Three other essays in this pamphlet dealt with slavery: *The Rationale of Slaveholding; Father, Son and Visitant;* and *England and the United States.* The first attacked slavery for its basic selfishness. Its supporters considered only their own gain, not the greater good of society. The second, written in the form of a Platonic dialogue, discussed the necessity of being true to ideals of freedom rather than compromising them on the excuse of being practical.

In the third essay, however, Birney revealed a change in his opinions. In 1844, while opposing the annexation of Texas, he had denounced all lust for expansion on the part of the United States, even extension to the Pacific coast. By 1857 he had caught the spirit of "manifest destiny." "God seems to have given us," he wrote, "the sublime mission of first controlling the world by our commerce and arts, and then regenerating it by the doctrines of Liberty and Human Brotherhood." As he saw it, only two things retarded us: (1) the demands of the cotton interests and (2) the naval supremacy of England.

He even had a concrete program to end this "maritime despotism" of England. We must: (1) become a great exporting nation; (2) promote social and business intercourse with Canada, Cuba, and Mexico with the aim of finally admitting them peaceably to the Union; (3) exclude all foreign nations from our coasting trade; (4) encourage trade in the Pacific by promoting the whaling and fishing industries, acquiring trade stations on the continent of Asia and island possessions of our own; (5) exclude European powers from the Isthmus of Darien and enforce the Monroe Doctrine for the whole American continent; and (6) secure freedom of the seas.

His essay on women's rights, however, showed little change in his ideas, despite his association with Sarah Grimké and Angelina Weld, who had been among the first women antislavery lecturers and were now expressing their approval of greater freedom for women by adopting the bloomer costume which Thoreau had found "remarkable." Birney thought that instead of striving for equality, women should recognize and emphasize their superiority in their attributes of purity, modesty, and virtue.

Naturally, there was much discussion in the Eagleswood community of the political developments in regard to the slavery issue. Besides the Welds, Sarah Grimké, and Birney, who had been active antislavery workers, there was Arnold Buffum, who had been the first president of the New England Anti-Slavery Society and one of the founders of the American Anti-Slavery Society. Other members who had never been public antislavery lecturers nonetheless had strong antislavery principles. With the passage of the Kansas-Nebraska Act in 1854 and with the Dred Scott decision in 1857, there seemed little hope left to them that the emancipation of the slaves could be accomplished without bloodshed. Birney wrote:

But in the midst of our relapses we have one consolation, and no small one it is too—that when a decided and constantly increasing majority have determined that an abuse, a debilitating abuse, shall go out, it *will* go out. Its extinction is certain, but when it will take place is only a matter of time.[15]

By this time Birney had accepted both the Free Soil and the Republican parties. Although their ideals were perhaps not so pure as those of the Liberty party in his day, they were carrying on the fight and were winning larger numbers all the time. Weld, Buffum, and he had been among the pioneers. Memories of the days when antislavery lecturers had been threatened and mobbed, even in the North, were still vivid; now it seemed that there was scarcely a Northerner to be found, except among the politicians, who was not antislavery. They had seen the movement start as a religious one; they had helped to broaden its

[15] From "Our First and Last Presidents," in *Brief Statements and Arguments,* pp. 31–32.

base by making it political also. Despite setbacks, for which Congressional compromisers would have to take the blame, victory would surely come in the long run. The saddening thought was that it would come by violence. He would be spared that day; other hands, including those of his five sons, would have to take up the burden.[16]

Despite his peace of mind and congenial surroundings, Birney did not regain his health. As the attacks became more severe and more frequent from the spring of 1857 on, he hoped that each one would be his last. Yet through his suffering he maintained a calmness of spirit and his sense of humor. In October, 1857, he wrote to Gerrit Smith, who had just paid him a visit, that he was surprised to be still alive, "But . . . here am I writing you a letter when, according to the view of the *Spiritualists* I should be careering through the 2d sphere, looking out for a habitation." In the same letter he repeated his deep and abiding religious faith: "Judging from what God has done for us heretofore, notwithstanding our peevishness and fretfulness and unfaithfulness shall we at all limit his goodness to us hereafter? Yes, he is God, Gerrit, and there is none like him." [17]

That was Birney's last letter. On November 25, 1857, word quietly went around the little Eagleswood community that Birney had again been stricken. All hearts and hands in the community were given to support Elizabeth, and the children were summoned; but he had already slipped beyond the reach of earthly aid. As the little band of friends wound its way to the cemetery on the hill overlooking the bay,[18]

---

[16] Five of his sons and one grandson were actively engaged in Union service. The first son, James, Jr., as lieutenant governor of Michigan, was active in raising regiments; William rose to the rank of brevet major-general, and in 1863 and 1864 superintended the organization of colored troops; Dion, a physician, became a captain; David became a major-general, commanded the Pennsylvania "Zouaves," and served with Kearney; Fitzhugh left Harvard to enlist, became a first lieutenant under his brother David and rose to the rank of colonel on McClellan's staff. The grandson, James Gillespie Birney, became a captain and served as a staff officer under both Custer and Sheridan. Dion, David, Fitzhugh, and James Gillespie died either during or shortly after the war from wounds or disease contracted in the service.

[17] Birney to Gerrit Smith, Oct. 29, 1857, in Dumond, ed., *The Letters of James Gillespie Birney*, II, 1174–1175.

[18] William Birney, *James G. Birney and His Times*, p. 381; Catherine H. Birney, *The Grimké Sisters, Sarah and Angelina Grimké, the First Women Advocates of Abolition and Woman's Rights* (Boston, 1885), p. 274. His body was later moved to Williamsburg Cemetery at Groveland, in Livingston County, N.Y., the burial place of his second wife's family.

there was little mourning. The soul of James Gillespie Birney had but presented itself to that illimitable goodness of which he had written to his friend.

Far away in Ann Arbor, Michigan, another old friend, Theodore Foster, penned a eulogy:

Posterity will not disregard the memory and services of one of the best and noblest of that band of patriots who freely sacrificed ease and wealth, the applause of their contemporaries, and tempting prospects of political distinction and preferment, for the purpose of redeeming the slave from thraldom, and delivering their native land from its greatest curse.[19]

[19] Theodore Foster, Notebook on the Liberty Party, Foster Papers.

Bibliography

I. MANUSCRIPTS

Official Records

A. *Church Records*

Second Presbyterian and Trinity Churches, Danville, Ky.; Minutes of the Transylvania Presbytery, Danville; Synod of Kentucky Records at the Presbyterian Seminary Library, Louisville; Record of the First Congregational Church of Lower Saginaw, Mich., in private posesssion.

B. *City and County Records*

City of Huntsville, Ala., Minutes, 1828–1834; Madison County, Alabama Circuit Court Minutes, Circuit Court Records, Deed Records, Minutes of Orphan Court, Tract Book, and Will Book; Mercer County, Ky., Deed Books and Marriage Register, No. 1.

C. *Society Records*

American Anti-Slavery Society. Agency Committee Minutes, 1833–1840; Minutes of the Executive Committee, 1837–1840. Boston Public Library.

American Colonization Society Papers. Manuscript Division, Library of Congress.

American Whig Society, Princeton. Annual History, 1802–1816; Constitution; Honorary Orations, 1776–1832; Interhall Treaties; College Honors; Status of Members; Minutes, 1792–1906. Firestone Library, Princeton University.

Princeton Cliosophic Society. History and Annual Reports; Minutes. Firestone Library, Princeton University.

D. State Records

Census of the Alabama Territory, 1818. Department of History and Archives, Montgomery, Alabama.

Governors' Letters. University of Alabama Collections, University of Alabama Library.

E. University and College Records

Centre College. Cash Accounts; Day Book; Early Correspondence of the Trustees. Centre College Library.

Princeton University. Alumni Records; Resolves and Minutes of the Faculty, 1787–1810. Firestone Library, Princeton.

Transylvania University. Records of the Proceedings in the Board of Trustees, 1799–1810. Transylvania University Library.

University of Alabama, Board of Trustees. Expense Accounts; Journal of the Proceedings; Ordinances and Resolutions; Correspondence. University of Alabama Library.

Collections of Personal Papers

James Gillespie Birney Collection. Manuscript Division, Library of Congress.

James Gillespie Birney Manuscripts. Boston Public Library.

James Gillespie Birney Papers. William L. Clements Library, University of Michigan.

William Birney Letters. Filson Club Library, Louisville.

William Birney Papers. Sidney Lanier Room, Johns Hopkins University.

Salmon Portland Chase Papers. Manuscript Division, Library of Congress.

John J. Crittenden Papers. Manuscript Division, Library of Congress.

Theodore Foster Papers. Michigan Historical Collections, University of Michigan.

Lewis Tappan Papers. Manuscript Division, Library of Congress.

Nathan Thomas Papers. Michigan Historical Collections, University of Michigan.

Seymour Treadwell Papers. Michigan Historical Collections, University of Michigan.

Theodore Dwight Weld, Angelina Grimké Weld, and Sarah Grimké Papers. William L. Clements Library, University of Michigan.

Elizur Wright, Jr., Papers. Manuscript Division, Library of Congress.

Other Manuscript Materials

Birney, Arthur A. Memoranda for biographical sketch of James Gillespie Birney. Department of History and Archives, Montgomery.

Birney, James Gillespie. "Angels." In private possession.

Birney, James Gillespie. "A Christmas Present." In private possession.

Birney, James Gillespie. "Is Slaveholding Sinful under All Circumstances?" In private possession.

Birney, James Gillespie. Memoranda of donations, collections, subscriptions, etc., for the American Colonization Society in Tennessee, Alabama, Mississippi, Louisiana and Arkansas.—Commencing Sep. 15, '32. In private possession.

Birney, James Gillespie. Plantation Record Book. In private possession.

Birney, James Gillespie. "The Prigg Decision." In private possession.

Birney, James Gillespie. "Reason Applied to the Bible, An Answer to Archbishop Whately of Dublin." In private possession.

Birney, James Gillespie. "To the Public. Colonization of the Free Colored People, No. 15." In private possession.

Birney, William, to Stuart Weld and Theodore Weld, April 7, 1884. In private possession.

Blue, Matthew P. "History of Counties of Alabama: Madison County." Department of History and Archives, Montgomery.

Green, Ashbel. "History of the American Whig Society." Firestone Library, Princeton.

Jones, Kathleen Paul, and Pauline Jones Gandrud. Alabama Records. Department of History and Archives, Montgomery.

Kooker, Arthur R. "The Antislavery Movement in Michigan, 1796–1840; A Study of Humanitarianism on an American Frontier." Ph.D. dissertation, University of Michigan.

Lynn, Harry R. "Henry Clay and Transylvania University." Master's thesis, University of Kentucky.

Marshall, James W. "The Presbyterian Church in Alabama, 1818–1898." Department of History and Archives, Montgomery.

Memoranda of Marshall, Birney, Green, and Fry Families, made by the late Mrs. McAfee of Kentucky for William Birney. In private possession.

Sellers, James Benson. "History of the University of Alabama." Manuscript in preparation.

Smith, Samuel Stanhope. "Lectures on Moral Philosophy." Firestone Library, Princeton.

Taylor, Thomas Jones. "The History of Madison County, Alabama, with an Autobiographical Sketch." Public Library, Huntsville, Ala.

II. PRINTED MATTER

Source Material

A. *United States Government Publications*

American State Papers, Indian Affairs. 2 vols. Washington, D.C., 1834.

Congressional Globe, 27 Cong., 2 Sess.

House Executive Documents, 26 Cong., 1 Sess.

Royce, Charles C. "The Cherokee Nation of Indians," in *Fifth Annual Report of the Bureau of Ethnology to the Secretary of the Smithsonian Institution 1883–1884* (Bureau of Ethnology Publications, V), 129–378. Washington, D.C., 1887.

Senate Documents, 26 Cong., 2 Sess.; 27 Cong., 2 Sess.

B. *State Government Publications*

Alabama Constitutional Convention. *Constitution of the State of Alabama.* Washington, D.C., 1819.

Alabama Constitutional Convention. *Journal.* Fac-Simile Reprint. Washington, D.C., 1909.

Alabama General Assembly. *Acts [1st, 6th, 8th, 13th Annual Sess., and Extra Sess. of 1832].* Huntsville, 1820; Cahawba, 1825; Tuscaloosa, 1827, 1832.

Alabama House of Representatives. *Journal* [1819]. Cahawba, 1820.

Alabama Senate. *Journal . . . 1829.* Tuscaloosa, 1830.

Hammond, Charles, reporter. *Cases Decided in the Supreme Court of Ohio in Bank at December Terms, 1837, 1838.* Cincinnati, 1872.

Kentucky Constitutional Convention. *Journal of the Convention Begun and Held at the Capitol in the Town of Frankfort* [July 22, 1799]. Frankfort, 1799.

Kentucky General Assembly. *Acts [25th, 26th, 27th General Assemblies, 1816–1819].* Frankfort, 1817–1819.

Kentucky House of Representatives. *Journal [1816–1817].* Frankfort, 1816, 1817.

Kentucky State Bar Association. *Journal of the First Constitutional Convention of Kentucky Held in Danville, Kentucky, April 2 to 19, 1792.* Lexington, 1942.

C. *Newspapers*

Those of particular value for each period in Birney's life:

Alabama: *Alabama Republican, Democrat, Southern Advocate,* and *Southern Mercury,* all published in Huntsville.

Kentucky: Frankfort *Commonwealth,* Lexington *Intelligencer,* Lexington *Observer and Reporter, Western Luminary* (Lexington), and the *Olive Branch and Western Union* (Danville).

Ohio: *Gazette, Philanthropist,* and *Republican,* all in Cincinnati.

New York: *Emancipator* (New York), and *Liberator* (Boston).

Michigan: Detroit *Free Press* and *Signal of Liberty* (Ann Arbor).

Numerous references are made in the footnotes to other papers, including all of the important antislavery papers of the time.

D. Other Periodicals

African Repository and Colonial Journal. 68 vols. Washington, D.C., 1825–1892.

American and Foregn Anti-Slavery Reporter. Vols. 1–IV. New York, 1840–1846.

Centre College Magazine. Danville, Ky., 1859.

Danville Quarterly Review. Danville, Ky., 1861–1864.

Quarterly Anti-Slavery Magazine. Vols. I–II. New York, 1835–1837.

E. Broadsides

Abolitionists Beware [Cincinnati, July, 1836].

Anti-Slavery Nominations, New York State [November, 1839].

A Bill to Amend the Law Concerning the Emancipation of Slaves [Kentucky, 1835].

James G. Birney, To the People of Saginaw County, August 30, 1844.

Call for a National Convention of the Liberty Party, April 29, 1851.

Freeman's Ticket, New York State, 1838.

James Harlan, To the Voters of the 5th Congressional District [Ky.], August 1, 1835.

Liberty Party Nóminations, 1841.

Liberty Party Nominations, 1844.

Saginaw County Democratic Correspondence Committee, Call for Democratic Mass Meeting, October 9, 1844.

The Testimony of Daniel O'Connell, the Liberator of Ireland, against the Infamous System of American Slavery . . . , 1838.

To the Public, Danville, Kentucky [August, 1835].

G. D. Williams, To the People of the County of Saginaw, September 26, 1844.

F. Memoirs, Reminiscences, Biographies

Adams, Charles Francis, ed. *Memoirs of John Quincy Adams, Comprising Portions of His Diary from 1795 to 1848.* Philadelphia, 1876.

Ballantine, W. G., ed. *The Oberlin Jubilee, 1833–1883.* Oberlin, 1883.

Birney, Catherine H. *The Grimké Sisters, Sarah and Angelina Grimké, The First American Women Advocates of Abolition and Woman's Rights.* Boston, 1885.

Birney, William. *James G. Birney and His Times; The Genesis of the Republican Party with Some Account of Abolition in the South before 1828.* New York, 1890.

Birney, William. *Sketch of the Life of James G. Birney.* Chicago, 1884.

Bishop, Robert H. *An Outline of the History of the Church in the State of Kentucky, During a Period of Forty Years: Containing the Memoirs of Rev. David Rice, and Sketches of the Origin and Present State of Particular Churches, and of the Lives and Labours of a Number of Men Who Were Eminent and Useful in Their Day.* Lexington, 1824.

Clay, Cassius Marcellus. *The Life of Cassius Marcellus Clay, Memoirs, Writings, and Speeches, Showing His Conduct in the Overthrow of American Slavery, the Salvation of the Union, and the Restoration of the Autonomy of the States.* 2 vols. Cincinnati, 1886.

Coffin, Levi. *Reminiscences of Levi Coffin, the Reputed President of the Underground Railroad; Being a Brief History of the Labors of a Lifetime in Behalf of the Slave, with the Stories of Numerous Fugitives, Who Gained Their Freedom through His Instrumentality, and Many Other Incidents.* 2d ed. Cincinnati, 1880.

Dallas, George Mifflin. *Life and Writings of Alexander James Dallas.* Philadelphia, 1871.

Dodson, S. H., comp. "Diary and Correspondence of Salmon P. Chase," in American Historical Association, *Annual Report,* 1902, vol. II. Washington, D.C., 1903.

Green, Beriah. *Sketches of the Life and Writings of James Gillespie Birney.* Utica, 1844.

In Memoriam: Lewis Warner Green, D.D. [N.p., n.d.]

Leavy, William. "Memoir of Lexington and Its Vicinity with Some Notice of Many Prominent Citizens and Its Institutions of Education and Religion," in *Register of the Kentucky State Historical Society,* XLI (1943), 44–62.

May, Samuel Joseph. *Some Recollections of Our Antislavery Conflict.* Boston, 1869.

Nevins, Allan, ed. *The Diary of John Quincy Adams, 1794–1845; American Political, Social and Intellectual Life from Washington to Polk.* New York, 1929.

Polk, Jefferson J. *Autobiography of Dr. J. J. Polk: To Which Is Added His Occasional Writings and Biographies of Worthy Men and Women of Boyle County, Ky.* Louisville, 1867.

Robertson, George. *Scrap Book on Law and Politics, Men and Times.* Lexington, 1855.

Stanton, Elizabeth Cady. *Eighty Years and More, 1815–1897; Reminiscences of Elizabeth Cady Stanton.* New York, 1898.

Stanton, Henry Brewster. *Random Recollections.* New York, 1887.

Taylor, Tom, ed. *The Autobiography and Memoirs of Benjamin Robert Haydon (1786–1846).* 2 vols. New York, [1926].

G. *Letters, Pamphlets, Reports, and Other Contemporary Materials.*

Abel, Annie Heloise, and Frank J. Klingberg, eds. *A Side-Light on Anglo-American Relations, 1839–1858, Furnished by the Correspondence of Lewis Tappan and Others with the British and Foreign Anti-Slavery Society.* Lancaster, Pa., 1927.

American and Foreign Anti-Slavery Society. *Annual Report . . . , Presented at the General Meeting, Held in Broadway Tabernacle, May 11, 1847, with the Addresses, Resolutions, and Treasurer's Report.* New York, 1847.

American and Foreign Anti-Slavery Society. *Liberty Almanac.* Syracuse, 1844–1845; New York, 1847–1852.

American Anti-Slavery Society. *Anti-Slavery Almanac.* Boston, 1836–1838; New York, 1839–1844.

American Anti-Slavery Society. *First [to Sixth] Annual Report.* New York, 1834 [–1839].

American Anti-Slavery Society. *Anti-Slavery Examiner, No. 10.* [Theodore Dwight Weld], *American Slavery as It Is: Testimony of a Thousand Witnesses.* New York, 1839.

American Anti-Slavery Society. *A Collection of Valuable Documents, Being Birney's Vindication of Abolitionists—Protest of the American A.S. Society—To the People of the United States, Or, To Such Americans as Value Their Rights—Letter from the Executive Committee of the N.Y. A.S. Society, To the Exec. Com. of the Ohio State A.S.S. at Cincinnati—Outrage upon the Southern Rights.* Boston, 1836.

American Anti-Slavery Society. *The Constitution . . . : With the Declaration of the National Anti-Slavery Convention at Philadelphia, December, 1833, and the Address to the Public, Issued by the Executive Committee of the Society, in September, 1835.* New York, 1838.

American Anti-Slavery Society. *Liberty.* [N.p., 1837.]

American Reform Tract and Book Society. *To All Evangelical Christians. The Suppressed Tract! and the Rejected Tract! Given Word for Word and Submitted to the Publishing Committee of the American Tract Society. Read and Judge. Shall the Society or the Committee Rule?* New York, 1858.

American Unitarian Association. *The Works of William E. Channing, D.D.* 6 vols. Boston, 1866.

Barnes, Gilbert Hobbs, and Dwight Lowell Dumond, eds. *Letters of Theodore Dwight Weld, Angelina Grimké Weld and Sarah Grimké, 1822–1844.* 2 vols. New York, 1934.

Barre, W. L., ed. *Speeches and Writings of Hon. Thomas F. Marshall.* Cincinnati, 1858.

Bingham, Kinsley Scott. *Speech of Hon. Kinsley S. Bingham, of Michigan. Delivered in the House of Representatives of the U. States, August 7, 1848.* Washington, D.C., 1848.

Bingham, Kinsley Scott. *Speech of Mr. Bingham, of Michigan, on the Admission of California. Delivered in the House of Representatives, June 4, 1850.* Washington, D.C., 1850.

[Birney, James Gillespie.] *Address to the Ladies of Ohio.* [Cincinnati, 1835.]

Birney, James Gillespie. *The American Churches the Bulwarks of American Slavery.* 3d Amer. ed. Concord, N.H., 1885.

[Birney, James Gillespie.] "American Slavery vs. Human Liberty," *Quarterly Anti-Slavery Magazine,* II (October, 1836), 22–40.

Birney, James Gillespie. *Correspondence between James G. Birney, of Kentucky, and Several Individuals of the Society of Friends.* Haverhill, 1835.

Birney, James Gillespie. *Correspondence between the Hon. F. H. Elmore, One of the South Carolina Delegation in Congress, and James G. Birney, One of the Secretaries of the American Anti-Slavery Society.* New York, 1838.

Birney, James Gillespie. *Examination of the Decision of the Supreme Court of the United States, in the Case of Strader, Gorman and Armstrong vs. Christopher Graham, Delivered at Its December Term, 1850: Concluding with an Address to the Free Colored People, Advising Them to Remove to Liberia.* Cincinnati, 1852.

[Birney, James Gillespie.] *Headlands in the Life of Henry Clay. No. 1.* Boston, [1844].

Birney, James Gillespie. *Letter on Colonization Addressed to the Rev. Thornton J. Mills, Corresponding Secretary of the Kentucky Colonization Society.* New York, 1834.

Birney, James Gillespie. *A Letter on the Political Obligations of Abolitionists, With a Reply by William Lloyd Garrison.* Boston, 1839.

Birney, James Gillespie. *Mr. Birney's Letter to the Churches: To the Ministers and Elders of the Presbyterian Church in Kentucky.* [N.p., 1834.]

Birney, James Gillespie. "Prospective Gradual Emancipation," *African Repository and Colonial Journal,* X (April, 1834), 43–46.

[Birney, James Gillespie.] "Senatorial Opinions on the Right of Petition," *Massachusetts Quarterly Review,* III (1849–1850), 431–459.

[Birney, James Gillespie.] "Senatorial Speeches on Slavery," *Massachusetts Quarterly Review,* III (1849–1850), 1–40.

Birney, James Gillespie. *The Sinfulness of Slaveholding in All Circumstances; Tested by Reason and Scripture.* Detroit, 1846.

[Birney, James Gillespie], Christianus, *pseud. Brief Statements and Arguments on: I. Our First and Last Presidents; II. Forgiveness; III. How Dreams Were Thought of in Old Times, and How Now Among Rude Tribes and Nations; IV. Rationale of Slaveholding; V. Father, Son and Visitant; VI. Historical Morceaux about Play-Actors; VII. Women's Rights; VIII. England and America; IX. How Shall We Judge of Others? X. A Standard.* New York, 1857.

[Birney, James Gillespie], Christianus, *pseud. Concise Examination of Certain Passages and Events in the Bible, Divested of the Miraculous Character.* New York, 1856.

[Birney, James Gillespie], Christianus, *pseud. Concise Examination of Certain Supernaturalisms of the Bible, as Commonly Understood.* New York, 1856.

[Birney, James Gillespie], Christianus, *pseud. Multum in Parvo; or Short Treatises on Future Life, Immortality, Conscience, Prayer, the Sentence of the Serpent, the Esoteric and Exoteric Doctrines, Truth and Falsehood.* New York, 1856.

[Birney, William.] *A Tribute to James G. Birney.* Detroit, [n.d.].

Breckinridge, Robert J. *An Address Delivered before the Colonization Society of Kentucky, at Frankfort, on the 6th Day of January, 1831.* Frankfort, 1831.

British and Foreign Anti-Slavery Society. *Proceedings of the General Anti-Slavery Convention, Called by the Committee of the British and Foreign Anti-Slavery Society, and Held in London, from Friday, June 12th, to Tuesday, June 23rd, 1840.* London, 1841.

Cass, Lewis. *The Power of Congress over the Territories. Speech of Hon. Lewis Cass, of Michigan, in the Senate of the United States, March 13 and 14, 1850, on the Compromise Resolutions of Mr. Bell, of Tennessee, and the Proposition to Refer Them to a Select Committee.* Washington, D.C., 1850.

Cass, Lewis. *Remarks of Mr. Cass, of Michigan, on the Dissolution of the Union, and the Constitution of California. In the Senate of the United States, February 12 and 20, 1850.* Washington, D.C., 1850.

Channing, William Ellery. *Letter of William E. Channing to James G. Birney.* Boston, 1837.

Channing, William Ellery. *A Letter to the Hon. Henry Clay, on the Annexation of Texas to the United States.* Boston, 1847.

Chase, Salmon Portland. *Speech of Salmon P. Chase, in the Case of the Colored Woman, Matilda, Who Was Brought before the Court of Common Pleas of Hamilton County, Ohio, by Writ of Habeas Corpus; March 11, 1837.* Cincinnati, 1837.

Chase, Salmon Portland. *Union and Freedom, without Compromise. Speech of Mr. Chase, of Ohio, on Mr. Clay's Compromise Resolutions.* [Washington, D.C., 1850.]

Clark, George W. *The Liberty Minstrel.* 5th ed. New York, 1846.

Clay, Cassius Marcellus. *Appeal of Cassius M. Clay to Kentucky and the World.* Boston, 1845.

Cleveland, Charles Dexter, and Salmon Portland Chase. *Anti-Slavery Addresses of 1844 and 1845.* Philadelphia, 1867.

Congregational Union of Scotland. *Address of the Congregational Union in Scotland to Their Fellow Christians in the United States, on the Subject of American Slavery.* New York, [1840].

Dumond, Dwight Lowell, ed. *Letters of James Gillespie Birney, 1831–1857.* 2 vols. New York, 1938.

Dyer, Oliver. *Oliver Dyer's Phonographic Report of the Proceedings of the National Free Soil Convention at Buffalo, N.Y. August 9th and 10th, 1848.* Buffalo, [1848].

Edinburgh Emancipation Society. *A Voice to the United States of America, from the Metropolis of Scotland; Being an Account of Various Meetings Held at Edinburgh on the Subject of American Slavery, upon the Return of Mr. George Thompson, from His Mission to That Country.* Edinburgh, 1836.

Goodell, William. *Address of the Macedon Convention . . . ; and Letters of Gerrit Smith.* Albany, 1847.

Goodell, William. *Call for a National Nominating Convention, Declaration, and Reasons for Action.* [N.p., 1847.]

Goodell, William. *Slavery and Anti-Slavery; A History of the Great Struggle in Both Hemispheres; With a View of the Slavery Question in the United States.* 3d ed. New York, 1855.

Goodell, William. *Views of American Constitutional Law, in Its Bearing upon American Slavery.* Utica, 1844.

Halsey, LeRoy Jones. *The Works of Philip Lindsley, D.D., Formerly Vice-President and President Elect of the College of New Jersey, Princeton;*

and Late President of the University of Nashville, Tennessee. 3 vols. Philadelphia, 1866.

[Jay, William.] The Creole Case, and Mr. Webster's Despatch; With the Comments of the N.Y. American. New York, 1842.

Jay, William. A View of the Action of the Federal Government in Behalf of Slavery. New York, 1839.

Junkin, George. The Integrity of Our National Union, vs. Abolitionism: An Argument from the Bible, in Proof of the Position That Believing Masters Ought to Be Honored and Obeyed by Their Own Servants, and Tolerated in, Not Excommunicated from, the Church of God: Being Part of a Speech Delivered Before the Synod of Cincinnati, on the Subject of Slavery, September 19th and 20th, 1843. Cincinnati, 1843.

Kentucky Anti-Slavery Society. Proceedings . . . : Auxiliary to the American Anti-Slavery Society, at Its First Meeting in Danville, Ky., March 19th, 1835. [N.p., 1835.]

Kentucky Colonization Society. First [to Fifth] Annual Reports. Frankfort, 1830[-1834].

Liberty Party: Thomas Earle. [N.p., n.d.]

Lindsley, Philip. A Sermon Delivered in the Chapel of the College of New Jersey, August 15, 1824. Princeton, 1824.

Marsh, Luther Rawson, ed. Writings and Speeches of Alvan Stewart, on Slavery. New York, 1860.

Massachusetts Abolition Society. The Second Annual Report . . . : Together with the Proceedings of the Second Annual Meeting, Held at Tremont Chapel, May 25, 1841. Boston, 1841.

Massachusetts Anti-Slavery Society. Fourth [to Ninth] Annual Report. Boston, 1836[-1841].

National Liberty Convention. Proceedings . . . Held at Buffalo, N.Y., June 14th and 15th, 1848; Including the Resolutions and Addresses Adopted by That Body and Speeches of Beriah Green and Gerrit Smith on That Occasion. Utica, 1848.

New England Anti-Slavery Society. Proceedings of the Fourth New England Anti-Slavery Convention, Held in Boston, May 30, 31 and June 1 and 2, 1837. Boston, 1837.

New England Anti-Slavery Society. Sixth Annual Report of the Board of Managers . . . , Presented January 24, 1838. Boston, 1838.

New York State Anti-Slavery Society. Address of the Peterboro State Convention to the Slaves and Its Vindication. Cazenovia, 1842.

Ohio Anti-Slavery Society. Debate on "Modern Abolitionism," in the Gen-

eral Conference of the Methodist Episcopal Church, Held in Cincinnati, May, 1836. Cincinnati, 1836.

Ohio Anti-Slavery Society. *Narrative of the Late Riotous Proceedings against the Liberty of the Press, in Cincinnati. With Remarks and Historical Notices, Relating to Emancipation.* Cincinnati, 1836.

Ohio Anti-Slavery Society. *Proceedings of the Ohio Anti-Slavery Convention Held at Putnam* [April 22, 23, and 24, 1835]. [Cincinnati], 1835.

[Plumer, William], Cincinnatus, *pseud. Freedom's Defence; or, A Candid Examination of Mr. Calhoun's Report on the Freedom of the Press, Made to the Senate of the United States Feb. 4, 1836.* Worcester, 1836.

Presbyter, *pseud. An Address to the Presbyterian Church, Enforcing the Duty of Excluding All Slaveholders from the "Communion of Saints."* New York, 1833.

Presbyterian Church, Synod of Kentucky. *An Address to the Presbyterians of Kentucky, Proposing a Plan for the Instruction and Emancipation of Their Slaves.* Newburyport, 1836.

[Rice, David], Philanthropos, *pseud. Slavery Inconsistent with Justice and Good Policy.* Lexington, 1792.

Rice, David. *Slavery Inconsistent with Justice and Good Policy Proved by a Speech, Delivered in the Convention, Held at Danville, Kentucky.* New York, 1812.

Ross, John. *Letter from John Ross, Principal Chief of the Cherokee Nation of Indians, in Answer to Inquiries from a Friend Regarding the Cherokee Affairs with the United States. Followed by a Copy of the Protest of the Cherokee Delegation, Laid before the Senate and House of Representatives at the City of Washington, on the Twenty-First Day of June, Eighteen Hundred and Thirty-Six.* [N.p., n.d.]

Sanborn, Franklin Benjamin, ed. *Familiar Letters of Henry David Thoreau.* Boston, 1894.

Smith, Samuel Stanhope. *An Essay on the Causes of the Variety of Complexion and Figure in the Human Species. To Which Are Added, Animadversions on Certain Remarks Made on the First Edition of This Essay, by Mr. Charles White, in a Series of Discourses Delivered before the Literary and Philosophical Society of Manchester in England. Also, Strictures on Lord Kaim's Discourse on the Original Diversity of Mankind. And an Appendix.* 2d ed. New Brunswick, N.J., 1810.

Smith, Samuel Stanhope. *Sermons by Samuel Stanhope Smith, D.D. President of the College of New Jersey.* Newark, 1799.

Southern and Western Liberty Convention. *The Address of the Convention, Held at Cincinnati, June 11 & 12, 1845, To the People of the United*

States. *With Notes by a Citizen of Pennsylvania* (C. D. Cleveland). [New York, 1845.]

Spooner, Lysander. *The Unconstitutionality of Slavery.* Boston, 1845.

Stanton, Henry Brewster. *Remarks of Henry B. Stanton, in the Representatives' Hall, on the 23rd and 24th of February, before the Committee of the House of Representatives, of Massachusetts, to Whom Was Referred Sundry Memorials on the Subject of Slavery.* Boston, 1837.

Stowe, Harriet Beecher. *Facts for the People. A Key to Uncle Tom's Cabin Presenting the Original Facts and Documents upon Which the Story Is Founded. Together with Corroborative Statements Verifying the Truth of the Work.* Boston, 1853.

Sturge, Joseph. *A Visit to the United States in 1841.* London, 1842.

[Thomas, Thomas E.] *A Review of The Rev. Dr. Junkin's Synodical Speech, in Defense of American Slavery; Delivered September 19th and 20th, and Published December 1843; With an Outline of the Bible Argument against Slavery.* Cincinnati, 1844.

Thompson, George, and Robert J. Breckinridge. *Discussion on American Slavery, between George Thompson, Esq., Agent of the British and Foreign Society for the Abolition of Slavery throughout the World, and Rev. Robert J. Breckinridge, Delegate from the General Assembly of the Presbyterian Church in the United States, to the Congregational Union of England and Wales: Holden in the Rev. Dr. Wardlaw's Chapel, Glasgow, Scotland; on the Evenings of the 13th, 14th, 15th, 16th, 17th of June, 1836, with an Appendix.* Boston, 1836.

Underwood, Joseph R. *Address Delivered before the Colonization Society of Bowlinggreen [sic], on the 4th July, 1832.* [N.p., 1832.]

Underwood, Joseph R. *An Address Delivered to the Colonization Society of Kentucky, at Frankfort, Jan. 15, 1835.* Frankfort, 1835.

[Weld, Theodore Dwight.] *The Power of Congress over the District of Columbia.* New York, 1838.

Woods, Alva. *Baccalaureate Address Delivered December 17, 1836, at the Fifth Annual Commencement of the University of the State of Alabama.* [N.p.], 1836.

Secondary Works

Adams, Alice Dana. *The Neglected Period of Anti-Slavery in America, 1808–1831.* Boston, 1908.

Alabama Historical Society. *Publications.* Vol. I. Montgomery, 1901.

Bancroft, Frederic. *The Life of William H. Seward.* 2 vols. New York, 1900.

Barnes, Gilbert Hobbs. *The Anti-Slavery Impulse, 1830–1844.* New York, 1933.

Barrow, Asa C. "David Barrow and His Lulbegrud School, 1801," *Filson Club History Quarterly,* VII (1933), 88–93.

Beale, Howard K. *A History of Freedom of Teaching in American Schools.* (*Report of the Commission on the Social Studies,* part XVI.) New York, 1941.

Beam, Jacob N. *The American Whig Society of Princeton University.* Princeton, 1933.

Benedict, David. *A General History of the Baptist Denomination in America, and Other Parts of the World.* 2 vols. Boston, 1813.

Betts, Edward Chambers. *Early History of Huntsville, Alabama, 1804–1870.* Montgomery, 1916.

Billington, Ray, ed. *The Journal of Charlotte L. Forten.* New York, 1953.

[Bingham, Stephen D., comp.] *Early History of Michigan with Biographies of State Officers, Members of Congress, Judges and Legislators.* Lansing, 1888.

Biographical Encyclopaedia of Kentucky of the Dead and Living Men of the Nineteenth Century. Cincinnati, 1878.

Bonham, Milledge L., Jr. "A Rare Abolitionist Document," *Mississippi Valley Historical Review,* VIII (1921–1922), 266–273.

Brantley, William H. *Three Capitals. A Book about the First Three Capitals of Alabama, St. Stephens, Huntsville, and Cahawba, including Information about the Politics, Laws, and Men of the Territory and State of Alabama, 1818 to 1826. Also Significant Historical Documents and Remarks.* [N.p.], privately printed, 1947.

Bretz, Julian P. "The Economic Background of the Liberty Party," *American Historical Review,* XXXIV (1929), 250–264.

Brief Memoir of George Mifflin Dallas, of Philadelphia. Philadelphia, 1853.

Brown, John P. *Old Frontiers: The Story of the Cherokee Indians from Earliest Times to the Date of Their Removal to the West, 1838.* Kingsport, Tenn., 1938.

Burroughs, Wilbur Greeley. "Oberlin's Part in the Slavery Conflict," *Ohio Archaeological and Historical Publications,* XX (1911), 269–334.

Catterall, Mrs. Helen Tunnicliff, ed. *Judicial Cases Concerning American Slavery and the Negro.* 5 vols. Washington, D.C., 1926–1937.

Centre College. *The Twelfth Triennial and Thirty-Sixth Annual Catalogue of the Officers and Students of Centre College, at Danville, Kentucky, 1860.* Danville, 1860.

Chaddock, Robert Emmet. *Ohio before 1850; A Study of the Early In-*

fluence of Pennsylvania and Southern Populations in Ohio. New York, 1908.

Clark, Thomas Dionysius. *A History of Kentucky.* New York, 1937.

Clarke, James Freeman. *Anti-Slavery Days. A Sketch of the Struggle Which Ended in the Abolition of Slavery in the United States.* New York, 1884.

Clay, Thomas Hart. *Henry Clay.* Philadelphia, 1910.

Cleveland, Catherine Caroline. *The Great Revival in the West, 1797–1805.* Chicago, 1916.

Coleman, Mrs. Chapman, ed. *The Life of John J. Crittenden, With Selections from His Correspondence and Speeches.* 2 vols. Philadelphia, 1871.

Coleman, John Winston. *Slavery Times in Kentucky.* Chapel Hill, 1940.

Collins, Lewis. *Historical Sketches of Kentucky: Embracing Its History, Antiquities, and Natural Curiosities, Geographical, Statistical, and Geological Descriptions, with Anecdotes of Pioneer Life, and More than One Hundred Biographical Sketches of Distinguished Pioneers, Soldiers, Statesmen, Jurists, Lawyers, Divines, etc. Illustrated by Forty Engravings.* Cincinnati, 1847.

Collins, Varnum Lansing. *Princeton.* New York, 1914.

Commager, Henry Steele. *Theodore Parker.* Boston, 1936.

Corwin, Edward S. "The 'Higher Law' Background of American Constitutional Law," *Harvard Law Review,* XLII (1928–1929), 149–185, 365–409.

[Cutler, Elbridge Jefferson.] *Fitzhugh Birney, A Memoir.* Cambridge, 1866.

Danville Literary and Social Club, "Anaconda." *History and Semi-Centennial Celebration, December 27, 1889. 1839–1889.* Danville, 1889.

Davidson, Robert. *History of the Presbyterian Church in the State of Kentucky; with a Preliminary Sketch of the Churches in the Valley of Virginia.* New York, 1847.

[Davis, Oliver Wilson.] *Life of David Bell Birney, Major-General, United States Volunteers.* New York, 1867.

Dawson, John Charles. *A French Regicide in Alabama, 1824–1837.* Tuscaloosa, 1939.

Dumond, Dwight Lowell. *Antislavery Origins of the Civil War in the United States.* Ann Arbor, 1939.

Dumond, Dwight Lowell. "Race Prejudice and Abolition, New Views on the Antislavery Movement," *Michigan Alumnus Quarterly Review,* XLI, (April, 1935), 377–385.

Dumond, Dwight Lowell. "The Mississippi: Valley of Decision," *Mississippi Valley Historical Review,* XXXVI (1949–1950), 3–26.

Eaton, Clement. "The Freedom of the Press in the Upper South," *Mississippi Valley Historical Review*, XVIII (1931–1932), 479–499.

Eaton, Clement. *Freedom of Thought in the Old South*. Durham, 1940.

Eaton, Clement. *A History of the Old South*. New York, 1949.

Fackler, Calvin Morgan. *A Chronicle of the Old First Presbyterian Church Danville, Kentucky, 1784–1944*. Louisville, 1946.

Fackler, Calvin Morgan. *Early Days in Danville*. Louisville, 1941.

Fleming, Walter L. "Deportation and Colonization, an Attempted Solution of the Race Problem," in *Studies in Southern History and Politics*. New York, 1914.

Foote, Henry S. *The Bench and Bar of the South and Southwest*. St. Louis, 1876.

Fox, Early Lee. *The American Colonization Society, 1817–1840*. Baltimore, 1919.

Franklin Lodge. *By-Laws, Rules of Order, Historical Sketch, 1815–1937, and Past Masters of Franklin Lodge No. 28, F.&A.M., Danville, Kentucky*. [N.p., n.d.]

Frothingham, Octavius Brooks. *Gerrit Smith, A Biography*. New York, 1878.

Garrett, William. *Reminiscences of Public Men in Alabama*. Atlanta, 1872.

Garrison, Wendell Phillips, and Francis Jackson Garrison. *William Lloyd Garrison, 1805–1879; The Story of His Life Told by His Children*. 4 vols. New York, 1885.

Goss, Charles Frederic. *Cincinnati the Queen City, 1788–1912*. 4 vols. Cincinnati, 1912.

Greeley, Horace, and John F. Cleveland, comps. *A Political Textbook for 1860: Comprising a Brief View of Presidential Nominations and Elections: Including All the National Platforms Ever Yet Adopted: Also, a History of the Struggle Respecting Slavery in the Territories, and of the Action of Congress As to the Freedom of the Public Lands, with the Most Notable Speeches and Letters of Messrs. Lincoln, Douglas, Bell, Cass, Seward, Everett, Breckinridge, H. V. Johnson, etc., etc., Touching the Questions of the Day; and Returns of All Presidential Elections Since 1836*. New York, 1860.

Green, Thomas Marshall. *Historic Families of Kentucky. With Special Reference to Stocks Immediately Derived from the Valley of Virginia; Tracing in Detail Their Various Genealogical Connexions and Illustrating from Historic Sources Their Influence upon the Political and Social Development of Kentucky and the States of the South and West*. Cincinnati, 1889.

Grimké, Archibald Henry. *William Lloyd Garrison, the Abolitionist.* New York, 1891.

Harlow, Alvin Fay. *The Serene Cincinnatians.* New York, 1950.

Harlow, Ralph Volney. *Gerrit Smith, Philanthropist and Reformer.* New York, 1939.

Hart, Albert Bushnell. *Salmon Portland Chase.* Boston, 1899.

Hart, Albert Bushnell. *Slavery and Abolition. (The American Nation: A History,* vol. XVI.) New York, 1907.

Hicks, John D. "The Third Party Tradition in American Politics," *Mississippi Valley Historical Review,* XX (1933–1934), 3–28.

Johnson, Allen, and Dumas Malone. *Dictionary of American Biography.* 21 vols. New York, 1937–1944.

Julian, George Washington. *The Life of Joshua R. Giddings.* Chicago, 1892.

Kerr, Charles, ed. *History of Kentucky by William Elsey Connelly and E. M. Coulter.* 5 vols. Chicago, 1922.

Kinkead, Elizabeth Shelby. *A History of Kentucky.* New York, 1896.

Klingberg, Frank J. *The Anti-Slavery Movement in England: A Study in English Humanitarianism.* New Haven, 1926.

Lee, Francis Bazley. *New Jersey as a Colony and as a State, One of the Original Thirteen.* 4 vols. New York, 1902.

Livingston County [New York] Historical Society. *Sixth Annual Meeting . . . Held at Geneseo, Tuesday, January 10, 1882.* Dannsville, N.Y., 1882.

Locke, Mary Stroughton. *Anti-Slavery in America from the Introduction of African Slaves to the Prohibition of the Slave Trade, 1619–1808.* Boston, 1910.

Long, Byron R. "Joshua Reed Giddings Champion of Political Freedom," *Ohio Archaeological and Historical Publications,* XXVIII (1919), 1–47.

Ludlum, David M. *Social Ferment in Vermont, 1791–1850.* New York, 1939.

Luthin, Reinhard H. "Salmon P. Chase's Political Career before the Civil War," *Mississippi Valley Historical Review,* XXIX (1942–1943), 517–540.

Lynch, William O. "Anti-Slavery Tendencies of the Democratic Party in the Northwest, 1848–50," *Mississippi Valley Historical Review,* XI (1924–1925), 319–331.

McCorvey, Thomas Chalmers. "Henry Tutwiler, and the Influence of the University of Virginia on Education in Alabama," in Alabama Historical Society *Transactions,* V (1906), 83–106.

McDougle, Ivan E. "Slavery in Kentucky," *Journal of Negro History,* III (July, 1918), 211–328.

MacLean, John. *History of the College of New Jersey, from Its Origin in 1746 to the Commencement of 1854.* 2 vols. Philadelphia, 1877.

McMaster, John Bach. *A History of the People of the United States, from the Revolution to the Civil War.* 8 vols. New York, 1923.

Macy, Jesse. *The Anti-Slavery Crusade: A Chronicle of the Gathering Storm.* (*The Chronicles of America Series,* vol. XXVIII.) New Haven, 1919.

Marshall, Humphrey. *The History of Kentucky Exhibiting an Account of the Modern Discovery; Settlement; Progressive Improvement; Civil and Military Transactions, and the Present State of the Country.* 2 vols. Frankfort, 1824.

Martin, Asa Earl. *The Anti-Slavery Movement in Kentucky Prior to 1850.* Ithaca, 1918.

Martin, Asa Earl. "Pioneer Anti-Slavery Press," *Mississippi Valley Historical Review,* II (1915–1916), 509–528.

Martin, Thomas P. "The Upper Mississippi Valley in Anglo-American Anti-Slavery and Free Trade Relations: 1837–1842," *Mississippi Valley Historical Review,* XV (1928–1929), 204–220.

Martineau, Harriet. *Society in America.* 3 vols. London, 1837.

Mathieson, William Law. *British Slavery and Its Abolition, 1823–1838.* London, 1926.

Matlack, Lucius C. *The History of American Slavery and Methodism from 1780 to 1849: and History of the Wesleyan Methodist Connection of America; in Two Parts, with an Appendix.* New York, 1849.

Moore, Albert Burton. *History of Alabama and Her People.* 3 vols. New York, 1927.

Morris, Benjamin Franklin. *The Life of Thomas Morris: Pioneer and Long a Legislator of Ohio. and U.S. Senator from 1833 to 1839.* Cincinnati, 1856.

Owen, Thomas McAdory. "An Alabama Protest against Abolitionism," *Gulf States Historical Magazine,* II (1903), 26–34.

Owen, Thomas McAdory. *History of Alabama and Dictionary of Alabama Biography.* 4 vols. Chicago, 1921.

Palmer, Thomas Waverly, comp. *A Register of the Officers and Students of the University of Alabama, 1831–1901.* Tuscaloosa, 1901.

Paxton, W. M. *The Marshall Family; or, A Genealogical Chart of the Descendants of John Marshall and Elizabeth Markham, His Wife, Sketches of Individuals and Notices of Families Connected with Them.* Cincinnati, 1885.

Peter, Robert. *Transylvania University, Its Origin, Rise, Decline and Fall.* (Filson Club, *Publications,* no. 11.) Louisville, 1896.

Peters, Richard. *The Case of the Cherokee Nation against the State of Georgia; Argued and Determined at the Supreme Court of the United States, January Term 1831. With an Appendix, Containing the Opinion of Chancellor Kent on the Case; the Treaties between the United States and the Cherokee Indians; the Act of Congress of 1802, Entitled 'An Act to Regulate Intercourse with the Indian Tribes, etc.'; and the Laws of Georgia Relative to the Country Occupied by the Cherokee Indians, within the Boundary of That State.* Philadelphia, 1831.

Phillips, Ulrich Bonnell. *American Negro Slavery. A Survey of the Supply, Employment and Control of Negro Labor as Determined by the Plantation Regime.* New York, 1929.

Phillips, Ulrich Bonnell. *The Course of the South to Secession.* New York, 1939.

Phillips, Ulrich Bonnell. "Georgia and States Rights. A Study of the Political History of Georgia from the Revolution to the Civil War, with Particular Regard to Federal Relations," in American Historical Association, *Annual Report,* 1901, vol. II. Washington, D.C., 1902.

Pickett, Albert James. *History of Alabama, and Incidentally of Georgia and Mississippi, from the Earliest Period.* 2d ed.; 2 vols. Charleston, 1851.

Poage, George Rawlings. *Henry Clay and the Whig Party.* Chapel Hill, 1936.

Price, Robert. "The Ohio Anti-Slavery Convention of 1836," *Ohio State Archaeological and Historical Quarterly,* XLV (1936), 173–188.

Princeton University. *General Catalogue . . . 1746–1906.* Princeton, 1908.

Quarles, Benjamin. "Sources of Abolitionist Income," *Mississippi Valley Historical Review,* XXXII (1945–1946), 63–76.

Raum, John O. *The History of New Jersey, from Its Earliest Settlement to the Present Time. Including a Brief Historical Account of the First Discoveries and Settlement of the Country.* 2 vols. Philadelphia, 1877.

Reports of Cases Argued and Determined in Ohio Courts of Record as Published in the Western Law Journal. 10 vols. Norwalk, O., 1896.

Rezneck, Samuel. "The Depression of 1817–1822, A Social History," *American Historical Review,* XXXIX (1933–1934), 28–47.

Riddle, Albert Gallatin. *The Life of Benjamin F. Wade.* Cleveland, 1886.

Riley, Franklin L. "A Contribution to the History of the Colonization Movement in Mississippi," *Mississippi Historical Society Publications,* IX (1906), 329–414.

Rodabaugh, James H. *Robert Hamilton Bishop.* Columbus, 1935.

Schuckers, Jacob William. *The Life and Public Services of Salmon Port-*

land Chase, United States Senator and Governor of Ohio; Secretary of the Treasury, and Chief Justice of the United States. To Which Is Added the Eulogy on Mr. Chase, Delivered by William M. Evarts, before the Alumni of Dartmouth College, June 24, 1874. New York, 1874.

Schurz, Carl. *Henry Clay. (American Statesmen, XX.)* 2 vols. Boston, 1899.

Scott, James Brown. *Cases on International Law Selected from Decisions of English and American Courts.* St. Paul, 1906.

Sellers, James Benson. *Slavery in Alabama.* University, Ala., 1950.

Siebert, Wilbur H. *The Underground Railroad from Slavery to Freedom.* New York, 1898.

Simms, Henry H. "A Critical Analysis of Abolition Literature 1830–1840," *Journal of Southern History,* VI (1940), 368–382.

Smith, Charles W. *Roger B. Taney: Jacksonian Jurist.* Chapel Hill, 1936.

Smith, Theodore Clarke. *The Liberty and Free Soil Parties in the Northwest.* New York, 1897.

Smith, Theodore Clarke. *Parties and Slavery, 1850–1859.* New York, 1906.

Sonne, Niels Henry. *Liberal Kentucky, 1780–1828. (Columbia Studies in American Culture,* vol. III.) New York, 1939.

Southall, Eugene Portlette. "Arthur Tappan and the Anti-Slavery Movement," *Journal of Negro History,* XV (1930), 162–197.

Southern Historical Publication Society. *The South in the Building of the Nation.* 12 vols. Richmond, 1909.

Spencer, John H. *A History of Kentucky Baptists from 1769 to 1885, Including More than 800 Biographical Sketches.* 2 vols. Cincinnati, 1886.

Stanton, Robert Livingston. *The Church and the Rebellion: A Consideration of the Rebellion against the Government of the United States; and the Agency of the Church, North and South, in Relation Thereto.* New York, 1864.

Sweet, William Warren. *Religion on the American Frontier, II: The Presbyterians, 1783–1840. A Collection of Source Materials.* New York, 1936.

Tappan, Lewis. *The Life of Arthur Tappan.* New York, 1871.

Taylor, Thomas Jones. "Early History of Madison County and Incidentally of North Alabama," printed in part in *Alabama Historical Quarterly,* I (Winter, 1930).

tenBroek, Jacobus. *The Antislavery Origins of the Fourteenth Amendment.* Berkeley, 1951.

Thomas, Alfred A., ed. *Correspondence of Thomas Ebenezer Thomas.*

Mainly Relating to the Anti-Slavery Conflict in Ohio, Especially in the Presbyterian Church. [Dayton], 1909.

Thomas, Benjamin Platt. *Theodore Weld, Crusader for Freedom.* New Brunswick, N.J., 1950.

Transylvania University. *A Catalogue of the Officers and Students of Transylvania University, Lexington, Kentucky, February, 1821.* Lexington, 1821.

Tyler, Alice Felt. *Freedom's Ferment; Phases of American Social History to 1860.* Minneapolis, 1944.

University of Alabama. *Historical Catalogue of the Officers and Alumni of the University of Alabama, 1821 to 1870.* Selma, Ala., 1870.

Walters, Raymond. *Alexander James Dallas, Lawyer—Politician—Financier, 1759–1817.* Philadelphia, 1943.

Warden, Robert B. *An Account of the Private Life and Public Services of Salmon Portland Chase.* Cincinnati, 1874.

Warren, Charles Austin. *The Supreme Court in United States History.* 2 vols. Boston, 1932.

Weeks, Stephen B. "Anti-Slavery Sentiment in the South; with Unpublished Letters from John Stuart Mill and Mrs. Stowe," in Southern History Association *Publications,* II (1898) no. 2, 87–130.

Weeks, Stephen B. *Southern Quakers and Slavery, A Study in Institutional History.* (*Johns Hopkins University Studies in Historical and Political Science,* extra volume XV.) Baltimore, 1896.

Weisenburger, Francis P. *The Passing of the Frontier, 1825–1850.* (*The History of the State of Ohio,* III.) Columbus, 1941.

Wertenbaker, Thomas Jefferson. *Princeton, 1746–1896.* Princeton, 1946.

Wesley, Charles H. "The Participation of Negroes in Anti-Slavery Political Parties," *Journal of Negro History,* XXIX (January, 1944), 32–74.

Wilson, Henry. *History of the Rise and Fall of the Slave Power in America.* 4th ed.; 3 vols. Boston, 1875.

Wiltse, Charles Maurice. *John C. Calhoun, Nullifier, 1829–1839.* New York, 1949.

Woodson, Carter G. "The Negroes of Cincinnati Prior to the Civil War," *Journal of Negro History,* I (1916), 1–22.

Wright, Philip Green, and Elizabeth Q. Wright. *Elizur Wright, the Father of Life Insurance.* Chicago, 1937.

Index

317